W9-ARB-747

2-7-63   62-51693

THE THREE JAMESES

BOOKS BY C. HARTLEY GRATTAN

Bitter Bierce
Australian Literature
The Peerless Leader: William Jennings Bryan
(with Paxton Hibben)
Why We Fought

Edited

A Bookman's Daybook by Burton Rascoe
The Critique of Humanism
Recollections of the Last Ten Years by Timothy Flint

Contributed to

Behold America!
American Writers on American Literature
Beyond Normality

929.2
6

THE THREE JAMESES

A FAMILY OF MINDS

HENRY JAMES, Sr.

WILLIAM JAMES HENRY JAMES

BY

C. HARTLEY GRATTAN

WITH AN INTRODUCTION BY OSCAR CARGILL

Biography is the concrete form in which all that is is immediately given; the perpetual flux is the authentic stuff of each of our biographies, and yields a perfect effervescence of novelty all the time.

—*William James*

NEW YORK UNIVERSITY PRESS · 1962

WINGATE COLLEGE LIBRARY
WINGATE, N. C.

FIRST EDITION COPYRIGHT 1932
BY LONGMANS, GREEN AND CO.

ALL RIGHTS RESERVED BY THE AUTHOR, INCLUDING
THE RIGHT TO REPRODUCE THIS BOOK, OR ANY
PORTION THEREOF, IN ANY FORM .

PRINTED IN THE UNITED STATES OF AMERICA

＊＊＊

THIS BOOK IS DEDICATED
TO MY GRANDFATHER

GEORGE CAMPBELL
1843–1925

NOVA SCOTIA LABORER AND
FARMER WHOSE REMEMBERED
SAYINGS ARE HUMOROUS AND
LUMINOUS TRUTHS

20396

◆◆

A RETROSPECTIVE INTRODUCTION

ALTHOUGH I majored in literature as an undergraduate forty
years ago in one of the better New England colleges, I encountered there no enthusiast for Henry James, save for
Carey Conley, a teacher without status because he taught
composition, who pronounced *The Turn of the Screw* a
superb example of the storyteller's art. Since he gave us a
heavy load of reading, however, that masterpiece was one of
his assignments that I skipped. After a brief experience reporting for the Worcester *Telegram-Gazette* I renounced
journalism forever and sought the snug comfort of teaching.
My academic paradise was Michigan Agricultural College in
East Lansing, where I taught five classes in English composition and one in public speaking and where I encountered my
second Jamesian enthusiast in the wife of Professor Ben
Roseboom, a Dutch biologist and a bowling companion on
our faculty team. A little remote and critical (as who would
not be toward a callow youth who snatched away her husband of evenings), Mrs. Roseboom must have been a remarkable woman, for she possessed (in 1922!) the New York
edition of Henry James. She warmly bespoke her enthusiasm for the Master and tried to prevail upon me to read him.
I promised, but made no effort to redeem my pledge for several years, when I unhappily chanced upon a first edition of
The Sacred Fount. I tried two or three times on widely
separated occasions to read it and on each occasion threw it
aside in despair. It reads easily enough *after* one has been
properly initiated in Henry James.

Meanwhile I had begun to teach American literature, omitting Henry James as a naturalized Englishman—a person of dubious loyalties. Our literature was then a despised subject and very little concern was felt in the academies as to the preparation of those who taught it. We learned our subject along with our students, which perhaps is not the poorest way to learn or to teach, though a trifle rigorous. The course fattened with the passing years as we added figure after figure to it—Melville, Emily Dickinson, Dreiser, not there at the first, crept in. Even William James (whose *Psychology, Briefer Course* I had dipped into in college) got into my presentation before Henry. The summer came, however, when, considering candidates for fall inclusion, I rashly settled on Henry James, resolved, with a little prodding from Bruce McCullough, my third infatuee, to know something about him, and in the process to initiate others. I read *The American* and *The Ambassadors* with illumination and delight and looked about for a general study to supply me with glib facts to piece out a beginning, passable lecture. I read Joseph Warren Beach's *The Method of Henry James* and Pelham Edgar's *Man and Author* to my improvement I am sure, but they did not satisfy my quest, for they relied upon an acquaintance with James that few, save Beach and Edgar and possibly Mrs. Roseboom (as symbol of the passionate, nonscribbling, widely scattered Jamesian) then possessed. Certainly at the moment these superb critical studies were much beyond me and even my most avid students, who, from ahead, were always beckoning me on.

A new card, meaning a new book, in the library catalogue caught my eye—*The Three Jameses,* by C. Hartley Grattan, a writer whom I had admired for his liberal views in the old *Scribner's* magazine and in *The Nation* and *The New Republic* and for a recent anthology, *The Critique of Humanism* (1930), a subject then very much the vogue. I knew him also for a capital biography, *Bitter Bierce* (1929), of a writer of slight, if any, value, whom, with a small sense of relative worth, I had already included in my course. I secured the book and began taking notes. Before I was through I had filled three blue books. Here were all the biographical facts I needed (or anyone needs, unless he is to specialize), not only about Henry James, but about William, the distinguished psychologist-philosopher, and about the Swedenborgian father. Further, there was a competent intellectual history of each, with an account of their writings, patently done by one who had read everything then available—had read and understood, so that every evaluation appeared soundly based. There was no hard-ridden theory in the book; no plaster-of-Paris mask of Freudian interpretation had been forced down over the fine individual features of this family of minds. Each was treated with respect, but none with reverence or awe. Their relationship to each other seemed properly drawn and they made a joint impact, such as, living, they must have made on Boston, America, and the world. I had all I needed and more, for, with other concerns, it took me a decade to catch up with Mr. Grattan and read the two Henrys and William down.

The Three Jameses appeared in 1932—two years before the "James Revival," which was set in motion, it is generally believed, by the "Henry James" number of *Hound & Horn* for April-June, 1934. Like Miss Stein's Melanctha, Mr. Grattan had fallen in love too soon, and despite the fact that Professor Lyon N. Richardson in his invaluable bibliography of Henry James had marked *The Three Jameses* as "indispensable," the volume has never received the attention which it deserves and has been long out of print.

Invited two years ago to a picnic at Katonah, an islet of civilization and green trees in the vast desert of Greater New York, by a younger colleague who had heard me often express my admiration for Mr. Grattan and who could count him a neighbor, I met my author for the first time and found him the urbane, quiet, deeply informed man I had supposed. When he expressed without bitterness his rueful precipitancy in writing on the Jameses before the vogue, I made a secret resolve: to reprint if possible *The Three Jameses* so that other young men might make the acquaintance, as I did long ago, in the most agreeable way, of these three extraordinary minds. There has been much writing on all three Jameses in the interim since I first opened Mr. Grattan's book, but this volume, for what it does, has not been replaced for any one of its subjects and should be found generally useful, if not "indispensable" for the happy combination of them.

OSCAR CARGILL

CONTENTS

BOOK I
PROLOGUE

BOOK II
HENRY JAMES, SENIOR

BOOK III
WILLIAM JAMES

BOOK IV
HENRY JAMES

BOOK V

NOTE

To THOSE publishers and authors from whose books I have borrowed brief citations I offer my best thanks.

The works of Henry James, Senior, are all out of print and most of them, if I mistake not, are out of copyright as well. However I have the permission of his grandson, Henry James, to quote from them freely. I also have the permission of the authorities of the New York Public Library to make three short excerpts from the James-Parke Godwin correspondence.

Most of the works of William James are published by the publishers of this book. I have the permission of Henry Holt and Company to make citations from *The Principles of Psychology* and *Talks to Teachers* of which they are the publishers. And from Little, Brown and Company to cite passages from *The Letters of William James,* edited by Henry James.

As to the works of Henry James, Jr., I have the permission of Henry James, his nephew, and Charles Scribner's Sons to cite from *The Letters of Henry James,* edited by Percy Lubbock, *The Wings of the Dove, The Golden Bowl, The Princess Casamassima, A Small Boy and Others* and *Notes of a Son and Brother;* of Mr. James and Houghton, Mifflin Company to quote from *Portrait of a Lady* and *The Tragic Muse;* and of Mr. James and Harper and Brothers to quote from *The Awkward Age* and *The Ambassadors.* I have uniformly followed the text of the New York Edition for all the novels and stories included in it. While it is published as a collective work by Charles Scribner's Sons, for permission to quote one must go to the original publishers and Mr. James. The graciousness of all concerned in this tedious business has been most gratifying.

C. H. G.

THE THREE JAMESES

BOOK I

PROLOGUE

I. A FAMILY OF MINDS

THE MASCULINE roots of the James family do not run deep into American history. William James the psychologist and Henry James the novelist, both of whom have been celebrated as typical Americans in their different ways, were grandsons of an immigrant. On the female side, however, the line runs back to the Revolution and beyond, with occasional low hills of eminence to vary the genealogical flatlands. But in our patriarchal society, the female line is of but incidental importance, so it seems, and certain it is in this case that it was the male blood in a new environment that lifted the family from mediocrity to distinction. This fortunate happening makes it unnecessary for us to begin this study of a family of distinguished minds with a catalogue of begats resembling a passage from the Bible. The family story is of one generation of concentrated money making, one generation of diligent application to intellectual concerns with no rewarding fame, and then the flowering of the family genius in two figures, who in widely separated fields, achieved international renown.

The economic foundations of the family were laid by William James, an Irishman born, who arrived in America in 1789 and died in 1832. In a business career covering thirty-six years he amassed a large fortune. His sturdy in-

1

dividuality shows plainly through the obscurity that has necessarily enshrowded the history of a man who was only incidentally a public figure in the very early years of the last century. Everything known about him can be summed up under three headings: he was acquisitive, pious and sternly moral. This combination of virtues made him a man of mark in his community and brought him positions of trust and distinction. It does not, however, tell us why the distinguished among his descendants, in violent contrast to those of early men of wealth of similar characteristics, should have chosen to function exclusively in the intellectual sphere. Curiously enough, there was no gradual shift from business to the intellectual life, nor was the change the product of intermarriage with a family of different background. It was abrupt and in the immediate line. William James's son Henry made the change. Thus it comes about that to a later generation William James is more interesting as the founder of a remarkable intellectual dynasty, as the man who provided the monetary basis for several extraordinary American careers, than he is in himself.

Henry James, Senior, as we have come to call him, wrote almost exclusively about religion. With his father, religion had been a matter of formally adhering to the conventional Presbyterian dogmas. From the barrenness of this position the son revolted, permanently and violently. His writings are distinguished as much by the vigor with which he attacked the prevailing orthodoxy as by the skill he showed in constructing a new outlook. Since he came of age intellectually at a time when the American mind was in a state of flux — during the eighteen thirties and forties — many ways of development were open to him, some of them to our later sense of proportion quite ridiculous. He was saved from being one of the many "freaks" of the time by his sturdy and realistic common sense. He found mental peace in a variety of absolutely supernatural religion that has never engaged many minds, but which has nourished, either in whole or in part, some very distinguished ones — Swedenborgianism. To the embracement of this outlook he was led by his own natural mental development and when he finally came upon it in a moment of extreme crisis, it was as much a confirmation of what he had vaguely felt but had been unable to formulate in terms acceptable to his exacting mentality, as a revelation. This allowed him to accept Swedenborg as a source of wisdom and a stimulation to thinking. He formulated his own conclusions and in such a fashion as to be disowned by the orthodox Swedenborgian church. Consequently he was forced to stand before the public as a religious prophet in his own right and in spite of his persuasive eloquence the sect he founded never had more than one member — himself!

He led a happy life. Intellectually he was allied to the great figures of the New England Renaissance. Emerson was his friend and fellow seeker. But he grew to maturity outside of New England. It was in the bustling commercial city of New York that he lived most intensely. His earliest intellectual friends were not, like himself, men of independent means, disinterestedly seeking the truth. They were journalists and practical reformers. Almost alone among them he was concerned with ultimate problems. As long as he associated with them he formulated opinions on all the burning questions of the day, but when the time came he retired from journalism and concentrated upon larger themes. He was not, then, a typical New York intellectual, nor was he a typical New Englander who was born elsewhere. He was a citizen of the world. If Emerson was his friend, so was Carlyle, and his firmest loyalty was to a Swedish thinker, Swedenborg. His cosmopolitanism was more than merely intellectual. If his home was New York City, he lived in England, France and Switzerland before he lived in Newport, Boston and Cambridge. With calculated deliberation he similarly deracinated his sons and made them acquainted with the world as well as northeastern America.

The immediacy of Europe to this typical American family is
very remarkable and none of them has ever been able to
say, as John Adams was able to say in his youth, that his
native country "was all the country I knew, or which had
been known by my father, grandfather or great grandfather. . ." Beginning with John the Adamses sufficiently
repaired this ignorance. The Jameses had never at any
time lost connection with Europe and if the first William
James never went "home" himself, his son Henry did and
one of his grandsons returned to the Old World for permanent residence.

The grandsons of William James, William and Henry,
were, respectively, a psychologist-philosopher and a novelist.
Their connection with their grandfather, who died before
they were born, is difficult to discover. The younger William has many times been accused of giving philosophical
sanction to the allegedly loose principles of the American
business man. Whether this is true or false we shall later
consider. Certain it is that he was sufficiently disconnected
from the American business influence as a small boy and
youth, however much his opinions may later have been colored by his environment. Henry James the younger, on
the other hand, was as we shall see, utterly and completely
shut off from any understanding of the most powerful class
in American society, a fact which has much to do with an
adequate understanding of his evolution as a novelist.

If the grandfather of these men had little detectable influence on them, the father's influence was immediate and
powerful. As will emerge clearly enough, the continuity of
mind is most obvious between Henry, Senior, and his son
William. Both of them dealt with ultimate problems and
both of them underwent a similar psychological experience
in young manhood which had a determining influence on
how they solved the problems with which they were concerned. William tried to conserve the values his father had
contended for, while restating the entire matter on a different

plane and in the light of different information. Henry, however, was different from his brother and his father in his psychological development and his interests. Like them he was concerned with "problems" and he treated them psychologically. And since nothing in his life led him to a concern with ultimates, he was able to concentrate and narrow his interests in a strikingly unique fashion. He descended from the heavens to the earth and to that small part of the earth inhabited by people of wealth and fashion. He became the supreme analyst of the leisure class under the capitalistic regime.

The story of this family is transacted against the background of American social and intellectual development between the Revolutionary and the World Wars, between the presidencies of George Washington and Woodrow Wilson, a matter, roughly, of one hundred and twenty-five years. When the first William James arrived *The Federalist* had just ceased to appear as a newspaper feature. When the second Henry James died the representative American writers of the contemporary middle generation had all published characteristic books.

2. THE FOUNDER OF THE DYNASTY

THE FOUNDER of the James dynasty in America landed in this country in 1789. What his motive was in coming is impossible now to discover, but legend has it that he did so to avoid becoming a clergyman as his father wished. At any rate he landed with nothing more than a Latin grammar and a small supply of money. The money he expended on a sightseeing tour of certain of the Revolutionary battlefields, but what became of the grammar is not in the records. At any rate he absorbed the information it contained, for one of his sons later was impressed by his command of the subject. He had arrived in America just as the United States was being born. Six years before, when the British at last withdrew from New

York and Washington bade farewell to the army, there had been a definite upturn in economic conditions, but the security necessary for complete success had not been found under the Articles of Confederation. In 1788, just one year before, the required nine states had ratified the Constitution which promised to order American political and economic life in a better manner. The country committed itself to the purposes of the "financial, creditor, commercial and speculating classes" and under the efficient prompting of Alexander Hamilton the government was strengthening the hands of these gentlemen in every possible way. Against the machinations of Hamilton and his cohorts, Thomas Jefferson was marshalling his forces, the agrarian democrats, in the hope of preserving the country for liberty and the farmers. The two great American "interests" were already maneuvering for position.

William James the First was born in Corkish, Country Cavan, Ireland, on December 29, 1771. His father was also named William James (1736–1822) and his mother was Susan McCartney (1746–1824). It was a tradition in the family that the Jameses had immigrated to Ireland from Wales early in the eighteenth century. The family was Protestant — Presbyterian — whose general intellectual disposition was probably that described by Thomas Cummings Hall: "These Presbyterians were actual Calvinists . . . in theological opinion, which they held more intelligently than the dissenting tradition is likely to hold its theology, for it forms a more important part of the religious complex. . ." At any rate it is known that William James was stiff and unrelenting in his religious ideas, a stern moralist and a close friend and patron of the clergymen all his life long. He even tried to have his ideas prevail in his family after his death.

What happened to him between 1789 and 1793 is not known, but in the latter year he appeared in Albany, New York, where for thirty-nine years he labored and prospered exceedingly. He arrived in the city at the age of twenty-two with no resources other than a willing pair of hands and a naturally astute intelligence. His first employment was as clerk in the store of one John Robinson who in those days and for some years thereafter was the principal merchant of the place. Within two years James was ready to embark in business for himself. On the 25th of May, 1795, William James and David Horner "opened a store in Mark Lane (Bloodgood's Slip) opposite the Glass Warehouse." They dealt in tobacco and segars. In December of 1797 James opened another store, this time for the reception of country produce and to deal in dry-goods and groceries. The very next year he still further expanded his business by erecting a tobacco factory. In 1804 he extended his business to New York City, having as agent one James McBride, and opening a store first at 61 John Street and subsequently at 2 Dey Street. By April, 1818 he was, after but twenty-three years of commercial life, ready to retire to the management of his real estate, money lending and other interests, and he announced that his "commercial concerns" would henceforth be managed by his son who would do business under the name of Robert James & Company. The firm consisted of William, Robert and an unidentifiable person named Thomas James. This arrangement lasted but a short time, for in 1821 Robert James died. It sufficed however to take William James out of the storekeeping field into the business of being a leading citizen.

When James arrived at Albany it had a population of less than five thousand. Forty years later it had 26,000 inhabitants. It was described in 1796 in these striking words:

In the old part of the town the streets are very narrow and the houses are frightful; they are all built in the old Dutch taste, with the gable end towards the street, and ornamented on the top with large iron weathercocks; but in that part which has lately been erected, the streets are commodious, and many of the houses are handsome. Great pains have been taken to have the streets well paved and lighted. Here are four places for public worship, and an hospital. Albany is in summer time a very disagreeable place;

it stands in a low situation, just on the margin of the river, which runs very slow here, and towards evening often exhales clouds of vapors; immediately behind the town, likewise, is a large sand-bank, that prevents a free circulation of air, while at the same time it powerfully reflects the rays of the sun, which shines in full force upon it the whole day. Notwithstanding all this, however, the climate is deemed very salubrious. The inhabitants of this place, a few years ago, were almost entirely of Dutch extraction; but now strangers are flocking to it from all quarters, as there are few places in America more advantageously situated for commerce.

It was, indeed, in a strategic point to benefit by the west-ward expansion that followed the Revolutionary War. It stood at the head of river navigation and on the road from New England to the west. The leading citizens were still, theoretically, the Dutch Patroons whose wealth was in land and whose power was by nature agrarian in basis. Before the Revolution they had extended their land-holdings from the Hudson River shores westward along the Mohawk River, but they had been driven from these developments during the conflict. Now the country was being reclaimed and the development extended. Such activities as those of Judge William Cooper, father of James Fenimore Cooper, who was developing Cooperstown on the shores of Otsego Lake were typical of the times. The rage for expansion carried popula-tion far outside the boundaries of the original thirteen states, however, and into Ohio, Kentucky, Tennessee and farther. Within ten years of William James's arrival at Albany, Presi-dent Jefferson added the whole Mississippi Valley to the United States by purchase from Napoleon. The reaction of this rapid expansion on Albany was tremendous and in the commercial prosperity of the time and place James shared to the full. It was further stimulated by the coming of steam-boat transportation in 1807.

In James's day the Dutch Patroons were rapidly losing power and when he died they were a sorry remnant of what they had been. Some of the Dutch families were able to throw off representatives capable of engaging in the new commerce. The principal Dutch merchants at Albany in the early years of the last century were drawn from the Bleecker, Lansing, Douw, Van Shaick, Ten Eyck, Ten Broeck, Pruyn, Hockstrasser, Van Loon and Staatse families. Overshadowing them all as a sort of universal figurehead, touching the life of the community at every point, the sort of man inevitably chosen to be president of almost any public enterprise, business, educational, or philanthropical, was Stephen Van Rensselaer. He lived to become the "last of the Patroons" and on his death in 1839 the old Dutch system was regarded as dead. He stood in William James's light time and again in the achievement of final honors.

But if the Dutch showed some energy, the real life of the community must be attributed to the new-comers, chiefly from New England, but occasionally like William James, from Europe. In this lively group we find such names as Walsh, Townshend, Steward, Gould, Mather, Marvin, Boyd, Spencer, Stafford, Hutton and Webb. The truth is that Albany and indeed all the state — the shift was even more noticeable in New York City — was in a period of transition from the Patroon system to the new capitalism. William James shared in both systems and illustrated a sort of divided allegiance that must have been typical of his time. He bought land freely and he also engaged in commercial undertakings and money-lending.

William James would seem to have prospered particularly by the boom in manufacturing and trading that accompanied and followed the War of 1812. It was in 1818, as already noted, that he was ready to retire from business in the store-keeping sense. During the war he had served as deputy commissioner of purchases for the United States Army in the Albany district. (He had been naturalized in 1802.) It was in the years immediately after the war that he began to accumulate honors. In 1815 he was made a trustee of Albany Academy, then but two years old, and from 1826 on he was Chairman of the Board. In 1815, also, he was a director of the New York State Bank at Albany, which had been chartered in 1803. Five years later, on its founding, he became Vice President of the Albany Savings Bank, the first institution of its kind in the state. The President was Stephen Van Rensselaer. When the Chamber of Commerce was organized, he was made Vice President of that, the President, again, being Van Rensselaer. In 1820 he was elected a trustee of the First Presbyterian Church. Just before his death, in 1832, he became a trustee of Union College in Schenectady.

His association with the latter institution is unique and it gives an excellent insight into the astonishing cash resources of the man. Union College was founded in 1795, the second college in New York State, and the farthest west of any institution of learning of that grade in America. It started with a staff consisting of the President and a tutor. The first year there were nine students. But it prospered exceedingly and at one time counted as a rival of Harvard and Yale. In 1804 the Reverend Eliphalet Nott assumed the Presidency. Dr. Nott had been, for six years previous, pastor of the First Presbyterian Church in Albany and a trustee of the college. In Albany he naturally made the acquaintance of his parishioner William James. Nott was a man of extraordinary ambition, reputedly benignant and not too orthodox in his religious teachings. A contemporary wrote that "His wish was to make men wiser and better, rather than to promote the sectarian interest and speculative tenets of the church." At any rate he took Union under his wing and for sixty years treated it like his own property.

The chief need was money for operation and expansion. In 1805 Nott got permission from the legislature to operate a lottery for the profit of the College and once that fateful step was taken there was no hope of retreat. He inextricably mixed his private means with those of the College until the only way out was for him to turn over all his resources to the College. This he unhesitatingly did, though not until

after some exceedingly involved law suits. In 1821 he began
to borrow money from William James, for the interest of the
College. In that year James advanced fifty-six thousand dollars to Nott, and got as security for it seventy-five thousand
dollars worth of bank stock. During the next five years,
President Nott and James carried through a variety of complicated financial transactions. James became involved in
the guaranteeing of the payment of the lottery prizes, among
other matters. In 1823 the loan totalled seventy-one thousand dollars and in addition to other security James obtained
a mortgage on all the real property of the College ! Three
years later, when the available records cease, the loan had
reached the figure of one hundred thousand dollars, secured
by property of one sort or another valued at double the
amount. James was evidently, then, willing and able to advance that sum of money to one small group of persons, Dr.
Nott being the principal figure, but only on heavy security.
This would seem to testify at once to the possession of unusual liquid resources and canny business sense. It is highly
unlikely, moreover, that James put all his cash he had for
lending into one basket.

Like his Dutch "betters" he expanded his interests into
Mohawk Valley and in other ways than lending money to
Union College. In company with a brother-in-law he leased
and operated the salt works at Syracuse and acquired real
property in that city which remained in the family until the
generation of his grandsons at least. He became a sufficiently important man in Syracuse to have a street named
after him which in later years became the principal residential street. The town of Jamesville in Onondaga County
(in which Syracuse is located) was also a seat for his operations,
since it was named for him. And there are indications that
he sent money northward, investing in Canadian bank stocks.
Furthermore, he did more than establish a store in New York
City. In 1827 he bought lands lying between what were
then Bethune and Troy Streets (the latter now West 12th

Street) in the city.   This land was below tide level and he
proceeded to reclaim it, thus adding a city block to the area
of Greenwich Village section.   It would be a tedious task to
determine just what property he held in the city of Albany,
but during the year 1829 he regularly advertised buildings,
commercial and residential, for rent and for day after day
he selected a different building each time to bring to public
notice.   He was solicitous of his property, too, and willing
to work as hard as a fireman to preserve it.   On November
10, 1827, when he was fifty-six years old, "a fire on the pier
destroyed a block of four stores belonging to William James,
and occupied by Matthews Brown, Joseph H. Green, Slacks
and Roggen and F. Van Horne.   Mr. James was present and
bailed water with great perseverance, but the buildings being of wood were completely destroyed."

In truth, it seems that he was willing to turn his hand to
any sort of transaction that was pretty sure to bring him a
profit.   He was a man of iron will and firm purpose and it
was well known that when "old Billy James" as he was called,
appeared on the scene things went as he wanted them to go.
The upshot of the matter was that when he died in 1832 a
local newspaper estimated his fortune as totaling three million dollars.   Cannily observing that most of it was in real
estate and apt to bring less rather than more in the open
market, the writer nevertheless asserted that it was a personal fortune only exceeded by that of John Jacob Astor.
Unlike Astor, however, James was not an empire builder.
His interests were local, being concentrated in New York
State and particularly in the city of Albany.   He was a solid
citizen with no actual or potential romance about him and
no Washington Irving ever celebrated his achievement.

II

WILLIAM JAMES'S personal life was equally expansive and
successful.   He married three times (within seven years!)

and had, in all, thirteen children. His first wife he took in August, 1796, and in June of the next year she died after giving birth to twins, both of whom lived to maturity. This wife was named Elizabeth Tillman and was of German stock. His next venture into matrimony, also short lived, came in December, 1798. The new wife's name was Mary Ann Connolly. She died in October, 1800, leaving a daughter, born the previous April, who lived to be twenty-three years old. The third and most successful marriage came in December, 1803. By this wife, Catherine Barber, who outlived him several years, he had seven sons and three daughters, born between the years 1805 and 1828. With the exception of two male children who died in infancy, all of this family lived to maturity, married, and many of them had children.

The fourth child of the marriage was Henry James who became the father of William the psychologist and Henry the novelist.

Now an interesting point about the James family is that it was for three generations — all those of interest to us as yet — a Hudson River Valley family. Every James during those generations was born on the shores of the River, usually in Albany or New York City. All of them chose their wives and husbands locally and in that line that leads from the first William James to the two most famous representatives of the family there is no New England blood, which rather disturbs various generalizations about their habits of mind. The line is Welsh (?) and Irish exclusively and does not embody an English strain as Henry James, Jr., falsely believed for his own delight.

William James was not a man who lived in the bosom of his family. He was too preoccupied with his business affairs for that. His contact with his children was confined to family prayers and to having them read to him in the evenings. He was not inquisitive about their lives, rarely taking any active interest in their standing at school and certainly not interfering with their trivial quarrels amongst

WINGATE COLLEGE LIBRARY
WINGATE, N. C.

themselves. On the larger issues he was very strict however, and in spite of a superficial air of freedom about his household, it was yet one carefully controlled by a stern religious and moral outlook, tempered by charity for the unfortunate who might apply to so wealthy a man for alms. The charity, for which he generously provided, was distributed by his wife, not by himself. She was a very womanly woman and a loving mother, both to her own and her predecessors' children.

Indeed it is perfectly clear that other than money making, religious discipline was William James's one consuming passion. It is easy enough to believe that he was one of the signers of the pledge drawn up by the members of the First Presbyterian Church in 1829 in which those who put their names to it promised to "use their best endeavors to dissuade the owners of steamboats, canal boats, stages and hacks, from travelling on the sabbath, and to encourage and patronize such of them as should cease running on that day." And it is notable and indicative of his frame of mind that the two sons with whom he had serious quarrels, one of whom was Henry, disagreed with him on religious matters. Henry carried his rebellion to the point of running away to Boston, no mean journey in those days and though he was subsequently partially reconciled, he reasoned himself completely out of his father's religious fold.

THE EXCELLENCE of James's position in the community is illustrated in the newspaper accounts of his death by the fact that he was intimate with De Witt Clinton, many times Governor of New York State and once a strong contender for the Presidency and Thomas Addis Emmet, son of Robert Emmet and scion of that great family of Irish patriots who was in his last years the most spectacular orator among American lawyers. Just how intimate he was is impossible to know now, but he was a person of sufficient importance so that he could marry one of his daughters to a son of Martin

Van Buren, then a rising politician but later to combine his faction with that of the Clintons and ascend to the national sphere to become the successor of Andrew Jackson in the Presidency. Another of James's daughters married Robert Emmet Temple, obviously a relative of T. A. Emmet. Yet James never became purse-proud nor pretentious in his manners.

More concrete testimony to his position is his connection with the Erie Canal. This great project of internal improvement, first envisioned by that amazing character Elkanah Watson, was the product of De Witt Clinton's energy and as much as anything it distinguishes him from the run-of-the-mill politician. It marks him off from Van Buren, for instance, whose record is a total blank as far as constructive measures go. William James was profoundly interested in the Canal, believing that it was to be the basis of the future prosperity of Albany. He was chosen Chairman of the Citizens' Committee for Albany at both the preliminary celebration in 1823 and at the ceremonies attending the final completion of the Canal in 1825. On both occasions he delivered an oration, on the latter occasion in reply to Mayor Philip Hone of New York, whose diary is now a part of the American historical record.

His speeches reveal the temper of his mind very plainly. At the 1823 celebration he called the Canal:

. . . a work which in grandeur of conception, and benefits resulting to the human family, surpasses every national improvement that has been attempted in any country; a work which sheds additional lustre on the United States, bearing the stamp of the enterprising spirit and resolution which declared our independence and wisdom that cemented the union of different republics by the adoption of the federal constitution . . . by what bounds can we circumscribe the blessings and benefits which may be expected to flow from the great canal ? . . .

And then, a characteristic note indeed:

. . . nothing but the torpid stupidity of atheism can prevent the reflecting mind from perceiving the special intervention of providence in protecting and advancing our national honor and greatness.

Two years later he struck the same notes, but was somewhat more specific in his definition of the probable effect of the Canal than was usual with "orators of the day." After pointing to the recent rapid growth of Utica, Geneva, Canandaigua, Buffalo, Syracuse, Auburn and Rochester, he went on to say that:

Whoever has observed the progress of improvement in our country, the peculiar character of our fellow citizens, and who have noticed the operations and witnessed the benefits flowing already from the canals, need no other inspiration than what God has given in common to men (that of tracing or following cause to effect), to anticipate with certainty many of the obvious benefits that will result from this great state enterprise.

From which point he launched into a flamboyant Fourth-of-July review of the history of the nation from its beginning to the completion of the Erie Canal. In a very decided way his confidence was justified, but he did not foresee the railroads which would make many of the canals, though not the Erie to so great an extent, obsolete.

He was willing, too, to bear his share of the expenses of celebrating so notable an event. On the subscription list he appears second with fifty dollars after his name, preceded only by the inevitable Stephen Van Rensselaer with one hundred. The nearest competitor to these two men of money contributed ten dollars and the rest trailed off gradually until one dollar was reached.

III

WILLIAM JAMES'S career started when the country was getting its first real taste of post-Revolutionary prosperity. If his fortune was greatly augmented during the boom caused by the War of 1812, the final social impetus to his accumulations was given by the opening of the Erie Canal. He was supremely fortunate in his choice of a setting for an American career, though his native sagacity must enter into any explanation of why he prospered beyond his fellows. His last years were devoted cannily to extending his interests and conserving those he already had and to various philanthropies. He was steadily employing several hundred "laborers and mechanics" and was looked upon as one of the very first citizens. So impressive did he bulk that thirty years after his death he was cited as an example of a great Albany merchant.

In the summer of 1832 cholera descended on the city and from early July until the coming of cold weather, the people were in a desperate condition. In August "the city . . . wore a most gloomy appearance. Many stores were closed, and thousands of people had gone away, so that the business portion of the streets had the aspect of a Sunday. Scarcely any one from abroad visited the place, the steamboats ran empty, and the hotels were deserted. The usual supplies of provisions were cut off, farmers not daring to trust themselves in the city and prices were excessively high. . ." In the midst of this dreadful calamity which would turn the thoughts of the hardiest man to death, William James prepared a will which is highly revelatory of his character. The document is dated July 24, 1832. It proved unworkable in its original form and his heirs, instead of being hedged about with extraordinary requirements as he wished, became independently wealthy as they came of age. In all, twelve of them shared the three million he left.

The money did not save them from disaster. The family was stricken with some obscure blight and Henry James, Jr., the novelist has made it vividly plain to us that his father's family appeared to him as made up of "handsome dead cousins, lurid uncles, beautiful aunts, persons all busts and curls. . ." Two of William James's children died in infancy, four failed to attain thirty, three more died short of forty, two achieved the age of fifty-nine and two seventy-one, one of whom was Henry James. The latter was the only one chosen out of the whole family to make a mark of interest to posterity.   In this concentration of the family importance on one figure in a large family, the Jameses exactly parallel the Coopers.   Both of these families accumulated wealth and the later generations were enabled to have the leisure necessary for intellectual pursuits.   For two generations William James's descendants were not guilty of a single stroke of business.   On the other hand we have in contrast the case of Allan Melville who died in Albany the same year as William James, but penniless, leaving a son Herman, one of eight in the family, to be "damned by dollars" even though the author of *Moby Dick.*

The more striking and interesting passages from William James's will read:

In order to preserve my estate from being wasted, and to insure its more judicious management, so that out of the rents and profits thereof ample means may be afforded for [certain annuities] and for the support and education of my numerous offspring, and with the exclusive view to the true interest of all for whom it is my duty to provide, I have determined to confide the care and management of my estate temporarily, to trustees.   In pursuance of these designs and in view also of the lamentable consequences which so frequently result to young persons brought up in affluence from coming at once into the possession of property, I have also determined that this trust shall continue, and that the final division of my estate shall not take place until the youngest of my children and grand-children living at the date of this my will and attaining the age of twenty-one years shall have attained that age.   And in order moreover to provide against accidental inequalities and diversities of condition which at the expiration of the trust may exist among the *cestuy que* trusts, *but more especially with a view to discourage prodigality and vice and furnish an incentive to economy and usefulness* [my italics], I have further determined to invest my trustees with extensive discretionary powers in regard to the disposition of my property to be exercised by them with a just regard to circumstances and especially to the respective merits of the several *cestuy que* trusts hereinafter mentioned. . .

The trustees under the document were Augustus James, a son, James King, a son-in-law and Gideon Hawley, an outsider.   Hawley was willed five hundred dollars a year for the life of the trust for his services. The others were sufficiently rewarded by the provisions of the will itself. It is perfectly apparent from the document that Augustus James was the favorite son. When the final division was made the estate was to be portioned into twelve parts according to a specified method and each heir was to receive a part of a half-part as provided. The share, however, could be lost if at the time of the division the trustees were convinced that the person to benefit "leads a grossly immoral, idle or dishonorable life. . ." Yet no one was to be wholly left out of James's munificence, for he wrote:

In order to provide for the decent maintenance of those, if unhappily there should be any such, whose portions shall be wholly withheld, I order and direct that to every such individual an annuity for life shall be given of such amount as shall be sufficient to supply the probable actual wants of such individuals.

He was conscious that he was writing a will difficult to administer, for he observed that:

. . . although the extensive and extraordinary power herein conferred *of punishing idleness and vice and rewarding virtue,* must from its nature be in considerable degree discretionary, and although its faithful exercise may prove to be a task at once responsible and painful, yet it is my full intention and earnest wish that it shall be carried into execution with rigid impartiality, sternness and inflexibility. [My italics.]

The task, as remarked, proved too difficult for execution, chiefly one suspects because of the impossibility of defining such concepts as "idleness" and "vice" and "virtue."

On Saturday December 15, 1832, William James suffered an apoplectic stroke and on Monday it was reported in the local newspapers that he was not expected to live. He died at three o'clock in the morning, Wednesday the 19th, without losing control of his faculties, self-collected to the last, conscious no doubt, that he had lived a good life for sixty-one adventurous years, and had as far as he could, provided for the triumph of virtue among his descendants.

The mourning at his passing was city-wide. The various

institutions in which he served as an officer or director passed commemorative resolutions, directed his associates to wear the "usual badge of mourning" for thirty days and attend his funeral.   His mortal remains were deposited in the Albany Rural Cemetery.   His career was evaluated in the local papers in superlatives.   The *Albany Evening Journal,* edited by Thurlow Weed, one of the many editors sued by Fenimore Cooper for libel, concluded its account with these words:

Mr. James's death is a severe loss to the city of Albany.   He had done more to build up the city than any other individual.

The *Daily Albany Argus* was more comprehensive in its tribute:

Great as this deprivation is to his afflicted family, and to his numerous relatives and friends, it is equally so in a public sense. He was identified with the growth and prosperity of our city. Everywhere we see his footsteps.   Turn where we may, and there are the results of his informing mind — his energy — and his vast wealth.   His plans of improvement embraced the entire city; and there is scarcely a street or square which does not exhibit some mark of his improving hand, or some proof of his opulence.   In this respect he leaves an example for the emulation of those to whom the means to be useful have been given, if not to the same extent, at least with a liberal hand.

BOOK II

HENRY JAMES, SENIOR

"My religious conscience . . . was from infancy an intensely *living* one. . .."

"The common ore of existence perpetually converted itself into the gold of life in the glowing fire of my animal spirits."

— Henry James, of himself

I. STORM AND STRESS

I WILL NOT attempt to state the year in which I was born, because it is not a fact embraced in my own knowledge, but content myself with saying instead, that the earliest event of my biographic consciousness is that of my having been carried out into the streets one night, in the arms of my negro nurse, to witness a grand illumination in honor of the treaty of peace then just signed with Great Britain. From this circumstance I infer of course that I was born before the year 1815, but it gives me no warrant to say just how long before. The net fact is that my historic consciousness, or my earliest self-recognition, dates from this municipal illumination in honor of peace. So far, however, as my share in that spectacle is concerned, I am free to say it was a failure. That is, the only impression left by the illumination upon my imagination was the contrast of the awful dark of the sky with the feeble glitter of the streets; as if the animus of the display had been, not to eclipse the darkness, but to make it visible. You, of course, may put what interpretation you choose upon the incident, but it seems to me rather emblematic of the intellect, that its earliest sensible foundations should thus be laid in 'a horror of great darkness.' "

As a matter of exact fact, Henry James was born on June 3, 1811 at Albany, New York, the fourth child of his father's third marriage. He was born to ease and affluence and throwing over entirely any concern for the business life which had so thoroughly engrossed his father, he spent his days and nights in trying to make an illumination that would in truth dissipate the great darkness in which all mankind was wandering.

Unusually precocious in his sensitivity to religious thought, he early became morbidly conscious of his relations to his Maker and from an early age tried to resolve his conflict with some formula more humane than that taught in the Presbyterian church of the day — or in any other church that then flourished in America. On the other hand, however, he was full of lusty animal spirits which served as a life-preserver in times of most acute distress. Even though his great concern was to settle the case of man with God, he never felt it necessary to become other-worldly. His sense of humor assisted him greatly in saving himself from any destructive mortification of the flesh, which is the frequent upshot of a combination of religious sensitivity and animal spirits. He was a man as well as a religionist and his vigor was as much a part of him as his sensitivity.

The atmosphere in which he was brought up would have permanently ruined a spirit less virile. In his father's house he was made acutely aware that his duty was to a hostile God who looked with disdain upon the human personality in its normal form. God looked with disdain too, upon human pleasures and condemned most of them as temptations of the Devil. His normal disposition toward man was enmity. To placate Him it was necessary to pay assiduous court to Him according to the prescribed forms of churchly ritual. Any attempt to escape was utter folly; any attempt to vary the approach to Him was loathsome heresy. Religion in those

days was a "remorseless formal dogmatism." It was Henry
James's task to evolve a philosophy which would place man
in a more rational relation to his creator. His struggles to
achieve peace were the chief efforts of his first thirty-three
years of his life, and the remaining thirty-eight were given
over to announcing his solution to an utterly indifferent
world.

As a boy he delighted in angling, gunning, swimming and
all the active games then played. He took his part with infinite gusto and the excessively severe Sunday regimen which
forbade them weighed upon him with exceeding harshness:

The dawn always found me on my feet; and I can still vividly
recall the divine rapture which filled my blood as I pursued under
the magical light of morning the sports of the river, the wood, or
the field. . . Just conceive the horror of leading the tender mind
of childhood to believe that the Divine being could under any
circumstance grudge it its natural delights; could care, for example, for the holiness of any stupid day of the seven in comparison with the holiness of the innocent mind and body ! Herod's
politic slaughter of the innocents were mercy itself beside this
wanton outrage to nature.

It is illustrative of the permanent dichotomy of his temperament that even while supposedly listening to the word of
God orthodoxly expounded, he found a way to divert himself with more worldly pleasures. The family pew in the
First Presbyterian Church was on the side of the church next
to a window which gave one a view of the street. Henry
James tells us that he would try to get to church early so
that he could get seated in that part of the pew which gave
one the best view. He was thus able to spend his time watching the passers-by and he took especial pleasure in the actions
of the house-maid of the family across the way who took advantage of her employer's absence to do her work leisurely
and with frequent appearances on the front porch to glance
"with critical appreciation at the well dressed people who
passed by."

James was, naturally enough in so lively a youngster, beset

by many of the temptations that get in the way of all boys
of spirit. But his occasional reminiscences of them differ
from those usually given in that they are not bedaubed with
conventional moralizings about the inherent wickedness of
the young. He was, as a grown man, healthily aware of the
essential innocence of his derelictions, even though they be
thieving from his father's change-box to pay his bill to the
candy vendor on the corner. As a boy it had been otherwise, and an incident like "throwing snow balls, and that
effectually too, at a younger brother in order to prevent his
following me at play, had power, I recollect, to keep me
awake all night, bedewing my pillow with tears, and beseech-
ing God to grant me forgiveness."

It was inevitable that he should seek to escape the somewhat exacting regime of his home life into a freer world.
He found entertainment and enlightenment as to the ways
of secular life by talking to the cook and coachman and by
spending hours at the shoemaker's listening to criticisms of
the theatre and reading declamatory orations to the work-
men. Yet barring the severely dogmatic religious attitude
of his father it must be admitted that he was the child of
extraordinarily benign parents. They indulged their children and made freedom within the circumscribed bounds, the
law of the house. However, it was freedom and indulgence
within an iron cage and confinement none the less to an essentially free spirit.

Henry James was first sent to school at Albany Academy,
where his father was a trustee. In the latter part of his
course he was under the particular care of Joseph Henry who
became Professor of Mathematics at the Academy in September of 1826. In the years immediately following Henry
James's attendance on his classes he had Herman Melville as
a pupil. Joseph Henry was the most distinguished member
of the faculty. In March, 1828, he announced before a
group of cultivated people at Albany his solution of the problem of sending electric current over a long stretch of wire,

thus laying the basis for the electric telegraph. He did not profit materially by his invention, however, and spent the bulk of his career as director of the Smithsonian Institution. When Alexander Agassiz first came to America he cited Henry as one of a small group of scientists in whom Americans could take legitimate pride. Henry James remembered him with affection all his life long, and it was undoubtedly under his tutelage that he laid the foundation of his persistent interest in science which was characteristic of him to the end of his days.

It was while under Joseph Henry's care that James experienced a painful accident which had a very definite effect upon his subsequent way of life. It made him, even more than his temperament would have normally, a sedentary city dweller. The boys had met in an open space in front of the Academy to fly balloons which were kept aloft by hot air supplied by "a tow ball saturated with spirits of turpentine." Henry James saw one of the balls go flying into a barn. He rushed in to stamp out the fire and in so doing burned his legs very severely. The accident kept him in bed for two years and required that one of them be amputated twice at the thigh before the crude surgery of the day was satisfied that a proper healing could be made. The young fellow — he was no more than fifteen — endured the pain of these operations, undertaken without anaesthetics of course, with admirable fortitude. When the healing was affected, he was permanently barred from the active life he had so much enjoyed and forced to accommodate himself to a sedentary urban life for the rest of his days.

These years in bed were probably devoted to study, under the direction of Professor Henry, in preparation for college. And we may reasonably assume that the long hours of idleness which must necessarily have been part of his regimen, gave him ample opportunity for reflections on religious themes. The total effect of his upbringing had been to give him a "thorough and pervading . . . belief in God's existence as

an outside and contrarious force to humanity. . ." Yet
while he was thus caught in the prevailing outlook, his religion was never an external affair as it usually becomes with
the ordinary person, for whom conformance to ritual prescriptions quite takes care of all religious necessities, whether
personal or social in genesis.   On the contrary, the effect on
Henry James was to drive him into himself and to develop
to an unusual extent his interior life.   This tendency was
encouraged and accentuated by his unfortunate accident.

. . . my religious conscience in its early beginnings practically
disowned a moral or outward genesis, and took on a free, inward,
or spiritual evolution.   Not any literal thing I did, so much as
the temper of mind with which it was done, had power to humble
me before God or degrade me in my own conceit.   What filled
my breast with acute contrition, amounting at times to anguish,
was never any technical offence which I had committed against
established decorum, but always some wanton ungenerous words
or deed by which I had wounded the vital self-respect of another,
or imposed upon him gratuitous personal suffering.   Things of
this sort arrayed me to my own consciousness in flagrant hostility
to God, and I never could contemplate them without feeling the
deepest sense of sin.   I sometimes wantonly mocked the sister
who was nearest me in age, and now and then violently repelled
the overtures of a younger brother who aspired to associate himself with me in my sports and pastimes.   But when I remembered
these things upon my bed, the terrors of hell encompassed me,
and I was fairly heartbroken with a dread of being estranged from
God and all good men.

He was, then, a boy marked out from the average thought-
less youths of his age when he went up to Union College in
1828 to take his place in the Junior Class.

His father had become financially interested in Union two
years before, but quite apart from that connection the College was a logical place for him to go for it was famous and
flourishing under the presidency of Eliphalet Nott.   The
student body was drawn from all over the country, number-
ing a particularly large group of students from the South.
The general spirit was one of liberality according to the conceptions of the day and while the scholastic requirements

were not high to modern eyes, they compared favorably with similar institutions in the country. John Howard Payne, later to write "Home Sweet Home" and to make love to Mary Shelley, had flourished at Union a few years earlier, though he did not graduate, and a decade later Lewis Morgan, author of the classic anthropological work, *Ancient Society,* found the institution to his taste. Among James's classmates were two who became college presidents, G. W. Eaton of Colgate and Silas Totten of Trinity. In truth the institution was decidedly flourishing, though the tendency was to enter the upper classes rather than to take all of one's work there.

Socially the College was rather different from the others in the same general region. To be sure the expense of attending was not markedly different, the sum of $115 covering board, tuition, rent, stove and the use of books, and the usual requirement of "a most scrupulous attendance upon Church, Prayers, Recitations and all Collegiate exercises," was strictly enforced. The distinguishing mark was rather the fact that President Nott allowed, and mayhap encouraged, the formation of fraternities. At that time secret societies were looked upon with violent and militant suspicion by the rank and file of the citizens. An informed commentator remarks that the ordinary person had been taught that "secrecy was inherently evil, and only evil; that the sole reason for existence of any institution which veiled itself, however slightly, from the gaze of the world, must of necessity be for selfish, immoral and if the truth were known, for revolutionary ends." It was precisely at this time that the anti-Masonic party flourished in New York State and the bulk of its support came from the very region in which Union was located. It was in the midst of this atmosphere of suspicion and hostility that the fraternity system developed at Union and as times became quieter it spread from there throughout the country. Sigma Phi was established on March 4, 1827, most of the founders being Southern students and Henry James was taken into the society on October 21, 1828, a month after his arrival on the campus. What his relations with his fraternity "brothers" were we have no means of knowing, but he would seem to have been highly respected and to have joined in their doings with enthusiasm. A freshman was appointed each term to help him get about what must have been an exceedingly rough campus and when it was decided that badges were necessary to distinguish the fraternity men from the "barbarians," James made a special trip to Albany and return simply to be the first to sport the new insignia. It is highly likely that he was the first man in America actually to wear a fraternity "pin!"

As a student James was equally successful, though he stood far from the top of his class. He was graduated in June of 1830, being granted "the first degree in Arts." His father was present to see the first James achieve a degree which was then still a mark of distinction. In later life Henry James became so thoroughly indifferent to college education as to be very tepid about having his sons attempt it at all.

College certainly did not bring him to any realization of his true purpose in life. To be sure he was but nineteen years old when he graduated and entirely incapacitated for an active career. But in those serious days, lack of a career was something about which to worry in severely moral terms. He would seem to have played with the idea of becoming a lawyer, for he studied Blackstone as a senior and it is the legend that he attempted to apply himself to law more seriously after graduation. It is also very possible that he spent the year immediately following his graduation in travel, for in the memoirs of Henry James, Jr., reference is made to a trip to the old home in Ireland which would seem to come at this time, a speculation vaguely confirmed by a passage from one of Henry Senior's letters quoted in that record. If that is the case he travelled in high style, accompanied by a negro servant, to appear among his Irish relatives in the

role of an American swell. But absolutely confirming data
for this trip has not yet come to light. It is possible, too,
that he had difficulties with his father and that he asserted
his independence by running away to Boston. For this sup-
position we have no more substantial proof than certain
passages from the reminiscences of his son Henry. We do
not come upon precise evidence until the year 1832, when
from his father's will it appears that he was to be cut off with
an annuity of $2500 a year instead of sharing the estate *pro
rata* with the other heirs. This would seem to indicate that
he was laboring under his father's disapproval, but his crime
could not have been very serious, for in the end he seems to
have been granted his portion of the estate along with the
rest.

If a little light shines upon him in 1832, it is not until
1835 that we know precisely where his thoughts were carrying him. In that year he entered Princeton Theological
Seminary and remained through two academic years. He
took that long to discover that he was irreconcilably opposed
to Presbyterian orthodoxy: I ". . . never knew a misgiving
as to the perfect truth of its dogmas, until I had begun to
prepare myself for its professional ministry. Then I could
no longer evade the enormous difficulties which inhered in
its philosophy. . . I was sure that while orthodoxy had
somehow succeeded to a celestial inheritance, it was yet a
most unrighteous steward of that inheritance; but how to
dispossess it God alone knew." In a report from the faculty
to the Board of Directors made at the beginning of the
academic year 1838, his name heads a list of those ". . . who
. . . did not return to the Seminary during the present session." He would seem to have definitely embarked upon
his independent search for a suitable philosophy during the
preceding summer.

Clearly he was involved in a particularly excruciating dilemma for one of his intellectual disposition. Later on

(*cira* 1852) when he had found the philosophy that was finally to satisfy him he cogently set forth the development of his mind during this period:

"DOUBTLESS the main reason of my discontent with popular Christian theology, the theology of the pulpit, and the main reason therefore of my betaking myself to the gospels only for light, was the extreme mental suffering induced in me by that theology, or what is the same thing, the extreme violence done by it to my instincts of the Divine perfection. From my infancy I had been religious as to the bent and purpose of my mind, and although remarkable for nothing in character or conduct, I felt a peculiar activity of conscience ever scourging me into more and more timorous *personal* relation with Deity. I was not conscious of any heinous offences. I was full of health and spirits, convivial and prone to pleasure, and occasionally no doubt, like every one else, capable of excesses, but with no consciousness of an injurious relation to any human being that I can remember. Indeed, the morbid susceptibility of my conscience — my extreme sensibility to public opinion — secured my general inoffensiveness, while it left me a prey to the most poignant sorrows for mistakes and accidents so trivial that I am ashamed to mention them.

"To soothe this conscience, and fulfill moreover what I deemed a sacred obligation on every man, I joined the church. I believed the theology of the church quite as fully before this event as afterwards; but I felt insecure of the right to appropriate the Christian hope until I had made a formal profession of faith. My consciousness of sin was now perfectly pacified. I had found a refuge against every muttering of vindicative wrath. So far good. But after all I felt uneasy. The church had delivered me from a consciousness of sin, but had given me no consciousness of righteousness in its place. The house of my soul had been swept of its evils, but it still remained desolate of goods. I could accuse myself of no lukewarmness in the exercises of piety, and yet was miserably unhappy a large portion of my time. Rather let me say unblessed, for what I wanted was an indefinable inward or upward repose, whose absence did not actually destroy my happiness in outlying things, but whose presence seemed somehow necessary to authenticate it.

"The entire influence of the pulpit went to the intensifying of this condition. Every sermon I heard aggravated my inward remoteness from God, my sense of utter disproportion between Him and me. Neither my clergyman nor my devout acquaintance appeared to understand my trouble. My bosom harbored no secret guilt, nor did my actions betray any overt iniquity. It was not a conscience of sin in any respect which burdened me, but a simple unconsciousness of righteousness. I had found perfect repose from a guilty conscience in the doctrine of Christ. But I had found no assurance of God's personal love or complacency in me. I was studiously, even superstitiously pure in thought and act. I cherished no emotions but those of complete benignity towards my kind. I spoke no evil of any man, much less devised any. I gave freely of my goods to the poor; contributed profusely to missionary and similar enterprises; read every famous book, and diligently observed every precept of mystical and ordinary piety. I vowed my life to the service of the gospel, and placed myself in the chief seminary of my sect with a view to the ministry. I abounded in prayer, day and night. I sought the aid of eminent Christians in both hemispheres, and obeyed their counsels. In short, touching the righteousness which was in the law of my sect and nation, I was utterly blameless. And yet for all this my soul was destitute of peace, and while my lips were familiar with the traditional formulas of Christian praise and jubilee, I yet in all my practice cherished the spirit and exhibited the manners of an abject slave.

"It would be tedious to report the gradual dawn of the truth upon my understanding. Reading one day the Epistle to the Romans, my attention became arrested by words, read before a thousand times without notice — *Faith cometh by hearing.* I said to myself, Faith then means belief of the truth, and not any magical operation in the bosom. Do I not believe the truth ? I have taken it for granted that I do all long; but perhaps I am unacquainted with some of its profounder features. So I betook myself to a new reading of the Gospels, and of the older Scriptures, as bearing upon the advent of a Christ, and I soon perceived that I had not been just to the truth. I had divorced the Christ from that historical position which gives him all his meaning, and tacitly attributed to him a purely arbitrary supremacy. Looking at him now as related to a certain exclusive hope on the part of the Jew towards God, his character began to assume an unparalleled majesty, and to reveal a depth of humanitary perfection in God who sent him, such as I had never conceived until then. Before this I had been wont to regard the Christ as an *absolute* person, so to speak, or as one whose extraordinary virtue was a matter of course, flowing from some special liberality of Divinity to him, and dispensing us therefore from any rational homage. In short, I practically esteemed his dominion as reflecting some passive relation he was under to Deity, rather than as wrought out and won by simple obedience to the spirit of universal love, the spirit of humanity, the spirit of God. Now my view was completely changed. I saw clearly now why it behooved the Christ to die — why the Divine glory absolutely forbade him to live. For the living or personal Christ belonged to the Jew alone. To the Jew all the promises belonged in the letter. And if, therefore, the Christ intended to erect a fleshly kingdom to God upon the earth, the Jew alone was entitled to its admission. But to the mind of Jesus God was spiritual — was the Father of the Gentile as well as the Jew — and hence it would be flat treason in him to recognize the Jewish pretension. In short, unless he impeached out and out the letter of their Scripture, in which case, of course, he would vacate his own claim to the Messiahship, he was bound either rigidly to fulfill it, or else manfully die in testimony of its having a larger or spiritual and universal import. Thus his very death became the irrefutable evidence of his truth, and the Divine glory, as identified with the welfare of universal man, gathered its best lustre even from the extremity of his sufferings.

"Looking at my past history as illumined by this new and glorious revelation of the Divine character, I began to perceive that I had been wrong hitherto in craving a *personal* righteousness, or in desiring to be distinguished by God's personal favor to me. I perceived that this was only a Christian form of the Jewish error, and that the only righteousness, the only experience of inward amity with God, which I could ever attain to, must lie simply in my participation of the spirit of God, the spirit of humanitary or universal love which had animated all the actions of Christ. What I had all along been groaning for was a righteousness in myself, was an assured conviction that God had some esteem for me, Henry James, that he knew my features, recognized me when I knelt down to pray, and said to himself in effect, 'There is a person whose interests I shall certainly look after, while that unscrupulous John Smith, and that prayerless Tom Jones may go to purgatory, or further.' I now perceived that God could not possibly sustain any such personal relation to me as this. Being a spirit of universal love, He of course could become related to me only in so far as I imbibed this spirit, only in so far as I dropped all personal pretension or hope — such hope or pretension as stood in my moral differences from other men — and consented to identify myself with the great interests of humanity. God had no *passive* relation to man. Being a purely active or living force, being a spirit of living love, of course no one could come into anything but *active* relation with Him, a relation which utterly ignored the natural personality of the subject, and pertained wholly to the spirit of his mind. Hence I perceived that all

my solicitude for a personal or passive nearness to God, a
nearness superior to that of the publican and sinner, had in
fact involved a complete insensibility to the Divine perfection — had argued a complete oversight of his spiritual character, or of his essential love to all mankind; and that to urge
it any longer would be the most flagrant affront I could possibly offer to the gospel.

"And I now discerned very clearly how utterly fatal the
sensuous idea of God, which regards Him not as a spirit, but
as an external person, finited in space and time, must ever
be to that inward repose, to that conscience of perfect unity
with Him, which I had so long and so vainly solicited. For
in measure as this external person grew and towered in all
perfection to my imagination, must I myself decline to all
imperfections. Should I throughout eternity, therefore, feel
a growing adoration of the Divine fullness, it was clear that
this adoration must be dogged step by step by a growing
sense of my own emptiness, of my own destitution. This result was totally undesirable to reason. According to the
sensuous theory of the Divine existence, the very perfection
of the Creator became demonstrable only through the imperfection of his creature, and that relation which in all
rational estimation should have secured the happiness of the
latter, became the bond of his endless and unspeakable misery. Could it then really be a divine end in creation to
ordain such a relation between Himself and his creature ?
Could the great God take satisfaction in seeing Himself perpetually aggrandized at the expense of his own offspring ?
Did the splendor of creation attest no higher disposition in
the Creator than this, namely, to display his own endless perfection by means of the endless imperfection of another, and
that other his own absolute progeny ? Which were the
worthier thought of God, to conceive of Him displaying his
essential perfection through the *elevation* of his creature, or
through his *debasement?* It seemed to me that the latter
conception, which logically inheres in the sensuous theory

of creation, was incredible and diabolic, turning creation upside down, and making God infinitely less estimable than man. Thus I learned, through this doctrine of a crucified Christ, and a consequent spiritual kingdom of God, to discard the sensuous notion of Deity, the notion of his being an external, and therefore finite person. For I saw plainly that if such were the real relation between man and God, it must prove, in the exact ratio of the former's sincere adoration and homage, one of incessant and immitigable torture to him."

HENRY JAMES embarked upon his quest at a critical period in the history of the American mind. With the decay of the orthodox system, a remarkable variety of proposals were put forth for redeeming the world and raising the status of man. The movement went forward on the highest plane of American intellectual life as well as in the slums of the mind, and never was it more necessary for one to have a balance wheel perfectly functioning if one chose to thread one's way along the difficult path to freedom. It was much easier to go hopelessly wrong than to find one's solution of the plaguing dilemmas in intellectually respectable quarters. The rage for cults was descending upon the country and the year 1830 is a milestone marking the point where many minds left what had hitherto been the main highway to go wandering off in search of a new route to Elysium.

Almost every man capable of thought, or the motions of thinking, believed in some variety of reform, and belief in one seemed to be a warrant for belief in an unlimited variety of others. The more thoroughgoing were not satisfied until they had figured out an entirely new scheme of society and they were far from being reluctant to put their plans into execution. According to Ralph Waldo Emerson the New England mind began to wake up about 1820 with the activity of Channing, Webster and Everett. Webster and Everett were quickly left behind by the advancing tide of moral reform, but Channing definitely forecast the direction in which the American mind was to move. In two remarkable addresses, both delivered outside of New England, in 1819 and 1826, he laid down the principles of Unitarianism summarized by a competent historian as "God is love, man is potentially noble, religion is an excellent life." Even though somewhat hampered by a naturally timid disposition, Channing also ventured into the field of political radicalism, further emphasizing the fact that he was a forerunner of the new times. He was forecasting, to be precise, Transcendentalism. Henry James was quite obviously a single, searching figure in the vast army of minds to which Channing's radical religious and political doctrines were a summons, though he rapidly passed beyond this Lockean rational supernaturalism.

Such a man as Channing was in the upper brackets of the American intellectual hierarchy. It was just as possible for James to be taken in by prophets of a much inferior sort. He embarked upon his search but a few years after the celebrated George Humphrey Noyes had announced his conversion to perfectionism and begun his career which came to flower in the direction of the Oneida Community, where he combined religious heresy with economic and sexual communism. This sort of life appealed to James as merely "disorderly," the product of a "deplorable fanaticism" backed by "great sincerity" but not "amenable to the tribunal of common sense." In 1830 Adin Ballou, a man inferior to Noyes both in intellectual adventurousness and practical sagacity, began his career in radicalism which resulted in the establishment of the Hopedale Community in Massachusetts. It was also during the thirties that the revivalist, Charles Grandison Finney, started on his spectacular career. James could not be reached by the appeals of the revivalists for he judged them to be directed toward "men for the most part of a fierce carnality, of ungovernable appetite and passion, susceptible at best only of the most selfish fears, towards God."

But when Finney proposed to leave western New York and invade New England and encountered the vigorous opposition of Lyman Beecher, the leading conservative of the day in a clash vivid and historic but inconclusive, James could join forces with him. He too was against orthodoxy and one of his earliest polemics was directed against Beecher, though on quite different grounds from those assumed by Finney. The thirties were also marked by the establishment of numerous special reform movements. During the period the abolition movement, woman suffrage, temperance, labor and a large miscellany of other agitations were launched. James made his peculiar contribution to many of them but largely indirectly. For instance he assisted woman suffrage by assigning woman a high place in his explanation of the spiritual evolution of mankind and he helped the labor movement by his interest in a new social scheme that would provide a more adequate basis for the redeemed form of society he envisaged. But toward one of the most powerful and, once the original barriers were broken down, most respectable of reforms he remained singularly cold. No enthusiast could have penned these critical words about abolition:

Though I have a great respect for the 'Abolitionists' personally, based upon their thorough truth and manliness as contrasted with the sordid and skulking crew who have always formed the bulk of their assailants, I yet have never been able to justify philosophically their attitude towards slavery. They attack slavery as an institution rather than as a principle; that is, on moral grounds rather than spiritual; making it primarily a wrong done the slave rather than one done the master; and hence wound the self-love of the latter and exasperate his cupidity, in place of conciliating his good will, and enlightening his understanding. The practical working of the institution has been on the whole, I doubt not, favorable to the slave in a moral point of view; it is only the master who from recent developments seems to have been degraded by it, spiritually, out of every lineament of manhood.

All of these reforms have been vigorously cultivated in the course of the hundred years since that day and we have wit-

nessed the triumph of many of them.   In the beginning they
were all decidedly *outre* and to declare for them was frequently to court the disapproval of the self-consciously conservative.   To be radical and at the same time to steer one's
course through this sea of "causes" without foundering, required a skill not common to many of the intellectual adventurers of the time.   It is frequently put down to Emerson's credit that he maintained his balance in the midst of
the whirlwind.   Henry James was almost equally successful,
though the solution to which he eventually came was radically different from that of Emerson and he did not go as
directly to his position.   He wandered in the wilderness for
seven years before he found a resting place that satisfied his
agitated mind.

His first move was to go to England where he found and
brought home a 'doctrine which was the first of the substitutes for orthodoxy that engaged his attention.   Curiously
enough the chief proponent of the cult lived the last years of
his life in America and died there, but there is no way of
knowing whether James was conscious of the fact before his
discovery of the doctrine in England.   In any case he was
away from America about a year, returning to New York
sometime in 1838 and preparing an edition of Robert Sandeman's *Letters on Theron and Aspasio*.   This book was the
chief literary document of the Sandemanians or Glasites, a
sect which originated in Scotland as a reaction against the
reigning Presbyterian Church.   It may have been this fact
that brought it to James's attention for he had just abandoned the American Presbyterian Church himself.

The Sandemanians held a variety of primitive Christian
beliefs, derived from a literal interpretation of the Scriptures, particularly Matthew XVIII and John XVIII, 36 and
37 which deal directly with Jesus's teachings.   The passage
from John on which they placed emphasis reads:

Jesus answered, My kingdom is not of this world: if my kingdom
were of this world, then would my servants fight, that I should

not be delivered to the Jews: but now is my kingdom not from hence.

Pilate therefore said unto him, Art thou a king then? Jesus answered, Though sayest that I am a king. To this end was I born, and for this cause came I into the world, that I should bear witness unto the truth. Every one that is of the truth heareth my voice.

Starting from this authority the Sandemanians evolved a whole theology based upon Scriptural example. They abstained from eating blood and 'things strangled'. They held a weekly love feast, on Sunday, and made a point of the 'kiss of brotherhood.' Members were required to take communion every week. And they practiced a kind of communism. While property was ostensibly held individually, it was at all times subject to the call of the Church. Which of these doctrines appealed to Henry James, if any of them, we do not know. In the preface to his edition of Sandeman's *Letters* he placed the emphasis elsewhere. Nevertheless he made this comprehensive observation:

The sole reason of its republication here, lies in the deliberate conviction which the editor entertains, of its being a far more faithful exhibition of Gospel truth than any other work which has ever come to his knowledge.

But from a knowledge of his final beliefs, one would speculate that the following passage from the text of the work indicates the true focus of his interest:

In fine, the whole New Testament speaks aloud, that as to the matter of acceptance with God, there is no difference betwixt one man and another; — no difference betwixt the best accomplished gentleman, and the most infamous scoundrel; — no difference betwixt the most virtuous lady and the vilest prostitute; — no difference betwixt the most revered judge, and the most odious criminal standing convicted before him, and receiving the just sentence of death from his mouth; — in a word, no difference betwixt the most fervent devotee, and the greatest ringleader in profaneness and excess.

Something like this became a favorite doctrine with Henry James and he found support for it in the system he finally

embraced, that of Swedenborg.   Many times in his writings
he returned to it and illustrated it and insisted upon it.   It
was of supreme importance to him because it offered light
upon the relation of Creator and Creature, a subject which
had originally agitated his mind, and to which his best thinking was addressed.   There would seem to be little question,
however, that James was but tentative in his acceptance of
Sandemanianism.   He had come to it as a result of his
studies in the Scriptures and no doubt it seemed to him a
valuable contribution to the matter he had most deeply at
heart: it offered an escape from dogmatic Calvinism.   In his
"Preface" he places special emphasis on the fact that Sandeman's theology is destructive of Presbyterianism.

There is no available evidence to show that he ever did
more for Sandemanianism than the publishing of its principal literary document.   The act was but an incident in his
prolonged study of the Scriptures in the hope of finding
light.   His studies continued with unabated vigor.   In 1840
he printed a pamphlet, *Remarks on the Apostolic Gospel* *
in which "he affirmed the divinity of Christ, though denying
the doctrine of the Trinity."   What else he was getting from
the Bible at this time has been told earlier in his own words.
But he was, in truth, stumbling about.   His heart and mind
were at comparative peace but the system that would finally
appease them was yet to be discovered.   His only consolation in a dark world was, in fact, the Scriptures.

2. A TRUTH DISCOVERED

THE EIGHTEEN-FORTIES were crucial in Henry James's history.
He married and became a father.   He touched absolute bottom psychologically and was providentially rescued from

* One of three publications, all early pamphlets, that I have not seen.
My information is derived from a secondary source, *The National Cyclopedia
of American Biography*, Volume XIII. The other unseen publications are
What Constitutes the State (1846) and *Tracts for the New Times* (1847), the
first number in a proposed series. In 1951 F. H. Young (see Bibliog.) said
scholarly consensus was that *Remarks* is "non-extant."

chronic mental invalidism by the discovery of a system in which he could believe. At the same time he associated himself with some of the most brilliant minds of the day, preoccupied like himself with the future. In association with them he cultivated an interest in the contemporary radical economic doctrines and took a part in the propaganda for them. He wrote a good deal for the press on one topic or another and he began to lecture and write books. By a process of restatement and refinement he began to reduce his beliefs to those few which were to satisfy him during the later years of his life and to the propagation of which he brought his extraordinary literary resources. Though he had companions on the road, he found no disciples to accept his final message. He was, at the last, an unregarded sage. But while so many of his fellow travellers fell by the wayside, he remained loyal to his inspiration to the end. He sloughed off his passing and incidental interests and stood before the world as a religious prophet exclusively.

On the 28th of July, 1840, he took as wife Mary Robertson Walsh, daughter of James and Elizabeth Walsh and sister of one of his fellow seminarians at Princeton. They were married at the bride's home, 19 Washington Square, by Mayor Isaac Leggett Varian of New York City and went to live, after the fashion of the day, at the Astor House. It was there, in 1842, that Henry's first son, William was born. Apparently finding an hotel ill-adapted to family life, he spent a few months in Albany and then established a home at 21 Washington Place. In this home, in 1843, his second son was born and named Henry. Unfortunately these happy events did not free him from religious anxiety and he began to plan a trip to Europe, partly in search of health, and partly in the hope that he would there find a resolution for his troubles.

His mind had begun to move toward Swedenborgianism. In 1841 he had read some articles on the subject in the *Monthly Magazine* of London. They were written by J. J. Garth Wilkinson and James wrote to him about the matter.

The correspondence thus initiated was never entirely re-
mitted during James's life time and Wilkinson became one
of his most valued friends.   J. J. Garth Wilkinson was one
of the most extraordinary men of the time.   He was a doctor
by profession and the translator and editor of Swedenborg
by avocation.   As is so frequently the case, he was not satisfied with one deviation from the usual and in addition to
Swedenborgianism, seriously investigated the claims, as they
came along, of mesmerism, hypnotism, spiritualism, healing
as an immediate divine gift, Fourierism and T. L. Harrissism.
All of these he in some way supported since they all confirmed the supernaturalism which was the most characteristic
expression of his mind.   In the end, though, he placed them
all in a definitely subordinate position to Swedenborgianism.
Only one other doctrine engaged his fervent allegiance.
About 1850 he became a homeopathic doctor and ardently
defended the ideas of Hahnemann.   His success as a home-
opathist was so great that for many years Swedenborgianism
was forced to take second place in his life.   Furthermore, he
became deeply interested in Eddic literature of Scandinavia,
learned the various languages and translated some of the
more famous documents.   But he always came back to
Swedenborg and at the time his work came under Henry
James's notice, he was still some years from his other interests.   According to Emerson, who met him through Henry
James, "Wilkinson, the editor of Swedenborg, the annotator
of Fourier, and the champion of Hahnemann, has brought
to metaphysics and to psychology a native vigor, with a
catholic perception of relations, equal to the highest attempts, and a rhetoric like the armoury of the invincible
knights of old.   There is in the action of his mind a long
Atlantic roll not known except in deepest waters, and only
lacking what ought to accompany any such powers, a manifest centrality.   If his mind does not rest in immovable
biases, perhaps the orbit is larger, and the return is not yet;
but a master should inspire a confidence that he will adhere

to his convictions, and give his present studies always the same high place." Swedenborg was in the American and British air in the thirties and forties. Carlyle and Emerson and many others of a similar disposition * read him and he was one of the many authors who contributed to the formation of the romantic mind. Practically all of the transcendentalists of Massachusetts were acquainted with his work and the probability is that James would have come around to him in the long run anyhow. The interest stimulated by Wilkinson was not immediately fruitful however. It did not lead James to acquaintance with Swedenborg's writings. The seed was dropped, but the plant did not grow.

In February (?) of 1842 James met Emerson and tried to get from him something that would satisfy his questing mind. At the time of the meeting Emerson was thirty-nine and James thirty-one. Emerson had then published but two major works, *Nature* (1836) and *Essays: First Series* (1841), while James was still buried in the Bible. Though he never got anything very valuable from Emerson, James remained his life-long friend. His final judgment on Emerson was at once laudatory and full of disappointment. The first meeting was excruciating and momentous. Emerson had come to New York to deliver a course of lectures and James attended them and also entertained Emerson at the Astor House.

"I often found myself thinking: if this man were only a woman, I should be sure to fall in love with him," James recalled years later. "Good heavens ! how soothed and comforted I was by the innocent lovely look of my new acquaintance, by his tender courtesy, his generous laudatory appreciation of my crude literary ventures ! and how I used to lock myself up with him in his bedroom, swearing that before the door was opened I would arrive at the secret of his immense superiority to the common herd of

* So far as I know, there has been no attempt to trace out the influence of Swedenborg on literature and philosophy except Lewis F. Hite's *Swedenborg's Historical Position* (Boston, 1928), which is concerned with testimonials. Certain obvious literary cases come to mind: William Blake, Coleridge, and W. B. Yeats. Garth Wilkinson, by the way, published the first *printed* edition of Blake's *Songs of Innocence and Experience* (1839).

literary men ! I might just as well have locked myself up with a
handful of diamonds, so far as any capacity of self-cognizance existed in him . . . the immense superiority I ascribed to him was
altogether personal or practical — by no means intellectual; that
it came to him by birth or genius like a woman's beauty or charm
of manners; that no other account was to be given of it in truth
than that Emerson himself was an unsexed woman, a veritable
fruit of almighty power in our *nature*. . . On the whole I may
say that at first I was greatly disappointed in him, because his intellect never kept the promise which his lovely face and manners
held out to me. . . It turned out that any average old dame in a
horse-car would have satisfied my intellectual rapacity just as well
as Emerson.

At this time James had already begun to lecture, but the
response to his efforts was discouraging. He had rejected
the idea that anything worthwhile could come of the *literal*
interpretation of the Scriptures after the fashion of the
Sandemanians, and had adopted the alternative of inter-
preting them mystically and symbolically. It was to announce the meaning of Genesis according to this system that
he turned to lecturing. What he lacked was a comprehensive system of interpretation and apparently he didn't know
enough about Swedenborgianism to turn, without prompting, to a study of it. He appealed to Emerson to help him
in spite of his original and often confirmed impression that
it was impossible for Emerson to help anyone except indirectly. What discouraged James was the fact that he was
interested in getting a hold of some "central facts which may
make all other facts properly circumferential and orderly . . ." and could find no guide to them. Emerson
was not interested in such facts and he could do nothing
for Henry James when he exclaimed: "Here I am these
thirty-one years in life, ignorant in all outward science, but
having patient habits of meditation which never know dis-
gust or weariness, and feeling a force of impulsive love
toward all humanity which will not let me rest wholly mute,
a force which grows against all resistance that I can muster
against it. What shall I do ?"

His own solution was a quiet home in the country, a solution of his difficulties often thought of and never carried out. Instead he resolved on a trip to England where he could settle down to concentrated study in a climate that pleased him very much. Emerson gave him an introduction to Carlyle. From a distance, and before his Swedenborgian revelation, James thought Carlyle quite the most important writer of the day. He even told Emerson that Carlyle was made important by the fact that Calvinism was so real to him. Any sense of the reality of it was absent from Emerson, to his detriment one infers. One of James's most characteristic notions was that without a profound idea of the reality of evil, one could not become a religious thinker. His own definition of the meaning and source of evil came to be radically different from that of the Calvinists, but he retained his belief in that fundamental constituent of human nature to the end. Unfortunately, Carlyle remained permanently stuck in Calvinism. Nevertheless he was always to remain one of James's permanent interests along with Emerson. Of all the thinkers of the day who had something to say to James, none so permanently engaged his attention as these two. In his books he almost invariably made reference to both and illustrated points by their personalities or writings or scored points off them in the interest of his own position. And at the end of his life, when both were dead, he reviewed them at length as we shall see.

Carlyle's immediate impression of Henry James was highly favorable. "James is a very good fellow, better and better as we see him more," he wrote to Emerson on November 17, 1843. "Something shy and skittish in the man; but a brave heart intrinsically, with sound, earnest sense, with plenty of insight, and even humor. He confirms an observation of mine, which indeed I find is hundreds of years old, that a stammering man is never a worthless one. Physiology can tell you why. It is an excess of delicacy, excess of sensibility to the presence of his fellow-creature, that makes him

stammer. . ."   Carlyle had just published *Past and Present*.
What James's first impression of him was, can only be
guessed.   Years later he confessed that he went to see him
as he went to the theatre: to be entertained by this "harle-
quin in the guise of Jeremiah."   He was attracted by the
moral interest in reform that Carlyle showed in *Past and
Present* and other works of that period, but was alienated
when he fell into his later wailing mood.   About fourteen
years after, when Henry James's own thoughts were pretty
well straightened out, he still spoke of "my admired friend
Carlyle."   Yet he wrote: "Carlyle has apparently not the
slightest conception of the new and perfect manhood which
is dawning, and cherishes every vestige of the old forceful
and fanatic type in that sort, as *Old Mortality* cherished the
fading *hic jacets* upon the tombstones of the martyrs."
Furthermore, his "infatuation consists not in the desire rev-
erently to bury the past, but to revive it in conditions which
would be obviously and utterly fatal to its continued existence for a moment."   That is accurate and destructive hit-
ting at Carlyle's intellectual foible and the following is just
as telling: Carlyle has "the essentially Barnum conception of
manhood, never unconscious youthful grace and symmetry,
but everywhere gigantic overgrowth contrasted by dwarfish
undergrowth . . . Carlyle's Caesars, Mohamets, Cromwells,
Napoleons, were above all things men of a defective spiritual
fibre. . ."   But the sharpest censure was to come later when
the two men were further apart than they were in the fifties.
   The experience that was to separate Henry James, intellectually, in the end, from Carlyle, Emerson and most of his
other friends occurred at precisely this time and in its catastrophic effect makes all his other experiences but a prelude
and an aftermath of it.   Fortunately he left a brilliant auto-
biographic account of it which he embedded in one of his
theological books, written thirty-five years later.   He discovered Swedenborg at a time of crisis and found confirmation for what his *heart* had long affirmed and which his *head*

with so little of satisfactory results had struggled to support.

"In the spring of 1844 I was living with my family in the neighborhood of Windsor, England, much absorbed in the study of the Scriptures. Two or three years before this period I had made an important discovery, as I fancied, namely: that the book of Genesis was not intended to throw a direct light upon our natural or race history, but was an altogether mystical or symbolic record of the laws of God's *spiritual* creation and providence. I wrote a course of lectures in exposition of this idea, and delivered them to good audiences in New York. The preparation of these lectures, while it did much to confirm me in the impression that I had made an interesting discovery, one which would extensively modify theology, convinced me, however, that a much more close and studious application of my idea than I had yet given to the illustration of the details of the sacred letter was imperatively needed. During my residence abroad, accordingly, I never tired in my devotion to this aim, and my success seemed so flattering at length that I hoped to be finally qualified to contribute a not insignificant mite to the sum of man's highest knowledge. I remember I felt especially hopeful in the prosecution of my task all the time I was at Windsor; my health was good, my spirit cheerful, and the pleasant scenery of the Great Park and its neighborhood furnished us a constant temptation to long walks and drives.

"One day, however, towards the close of May, having eaten a comfortable dinner, I remained sitting at the table after the family had dispersed, idly gazing at the embers in the grate, thinking of nothing, and feeling only the exhilaration incident to a good digestion, when suddenly — in a lightning flash as it were—'fear came upon me, and trembling, which made all my bones shake.' To all appearance it was a perfectly insane and abject terror, without ostensible cause, and only to be accounted for, to my perplexed imagination, by some damned shape squatting invisible to me within the pre-

cincts of the room, and raying out from his fetid personality
influences fatal to life. The thing had not lasted ten seconds
before I felt myself a wreck, that is, reduced from a state of
firm, vigorous, joyful manhood to one of almost helpless infancy. The only self-control I was capable of exerting was
to keep my seat. I felt the greatest desire to run inconti-
nently to the foot of the stairs and shout for help to my wife,
— to run to the roadside even, and appeal to the public to
protect me; but by an immense effort I controlled these
frenzied impulses, and determined not to budge from my
chair till I had recovered my lost self-possession. This purpose I held to for a good long hour, as I reckoned time, beat
upon meanwhile by an ever-growing tempest of doubt,
anxiety, and despair, with absolutely no relief from any
truth I had ever encountered save a most pale and distant
glimmer of the Divine existence,— when I resolved to
abandon the vain struggle, and communicate without more
ado what seemed my sudden burden of inmost, implacable
unrest to my wife.*

"Now, to make a long story short, this ghastly condition
of mind continued with me, with gradually lengthening intervals of relief, for two years, and even longer. I consulted
eminent physicians, who told me that I had doubtless over-
worked my brain, an evil for which no remedy existed in
medicine, but only in time, and patience, and growth into
improved physical conditions. They all recommended by
way of hygiene a resort to the water-cure treatment, a life in
the open air, cheerful company, and so forth, and thus
quietly and skilfully dismissed me to my own spiritual meditation. At first, when I began to feel a half-hour's respite
from acute mental anguish, the bottomless mystery of my
disease completely fascinated me. The more, however, I
worried myself with speculations about the cause of it, the
more the mystery deepened, and the deeper also grew my in-

* For a similar experience in the life of his son William see below pages 122–
123.

stinct of resentment at what seemed so needless an interference with my personal liberty. I went to a famous water-cure, which did nothing towards curing my malady but enrich my memory with a few morbid specimens of English insularity and prejudice, but it did much to alleviate it by familiarizing my senses with the exquisite and endless charm of English landscape, and giving me my first full rational relish of what may be called England's pastoral beauty. To be sure I had spent a few days in Devonshire when I was young, but my delight then was simple enthusiasm, was helpless aesthetic intoxication in fact. The 'cure' was situated in a much less lovely but still beautiful country, on the borders of a famous park, of both of which, moreover, it gave you unlimited right of possession and enjoyment. At least this was the way it always struck my imagination. The thoroughly disinterested way the English have of looking at their own hills and vales, — the indifferent, contemptuous, and as it were *disowning* mood they habitually put on towards the most ravishing pastoral loveliness man's sun anywhere shines upon, — gave me always the sense of being a discoverer of these things, and of a consequent right to enter upon their undisputed possession. At all events the rich light and shade of English landscape, the gorgeous cloud-pictures that forever dimple and diversify her fragrant and palpitating bosom, have awakened a tenderer chord in me than I have ever felt at home almost; and time and again while living at this dismal water-cure, and listening to its endless 'strife of tongues' about diet, and regimen, and disease, and politics, and parties, and persons, I have said to myself: *The curse of mankind, that which keeps our manhood so little and so depraved, is its sense of selfhood, and the absurd abominable opinionativeness it engenders. How sweet it would be to find oneself no longer man, but one of those innocent and ignorant sheep pasturing upon that placid hillside, and drinking in eternal dew and freshness from nature's lavish bosom!*

"But let me hasten to the proper upshot of this incident. My stay at the water-cure, unpromising as it was in point of physical results, made me conscious ere long of a most important change operating in the sphere of my will and understanding. It struck me as very odd, soon after my breakdown, that I should feel no longing to resume the work which had been interrupted by it; and from that day to this — nearly thirty-five years — I have never once cast a retrospective glance, even of curiosity, at the immense piles of manuscript, which had erewhile so absorbed me. I suppose if any one had designated me previous to that event as an earnest seeker after truth, I should myself have seen nothing unbecoming in the appellation. But now — within two or three months of my catastrophe — I felt sure I had never caught a glimpse of truth. My present consciousness was exactly that of an utter and plenary destitution of truth. Indeed an ugly suspicion had more than once forced itself upon me, that I had never really wished the truth, but only to ventilate my own ability in discovering it. I was getting sick to death in fact with a sense of my downright intellectual poverty and dishonesty. My studious mental activity had served manifestly to base a mere 'castle in the air,' and the castle had vanished in a brief bitter moment of time, leaving not a wrack behind. I never felt again the most passing impulse, even, to look where it stood, having done with it forever. Truth indeed! How should a beggar like me be expected to discover it? How should any man of woman born pretend to such ability? Truth must *reveal itself* if it would be known, and then how imperfectly known at best! For truth is God, the omniscient and omnipotent God, and who shall pretend to comprehend that great and adorable perfection? And yet who that aspires to the name of man, would not cheerfully barter all he knows of life for a bare glimpse of the hem of its garment?

"I was calling one day upon a friend (since deceased) (a Mrs. Chichester) who lived in the vicinity of the water-cure

— a lady of rare qualities of heart and mind, and of singular
personal loveliness as well — who desired to know what had
brought me to the water-cure. After I had done telling her
in substance . . . she replied: 'It is, then, very much as I
ventured from two or three previous things you have said,
to suspect; you are undergoing what Swedenborg calls a
vastation; and though, naturally enough, you yourself are de-
spondent or even despairing about the issue, I cannot help
taking an altogether hopeful view of your prospects.' In
expressing my thanks for her encouraging words, I remarked
that I was not at all familiar with the Swedenborgian tech-
nics, and that I should be extremely happy if she would follow up her flattering judgment of my condition by turning
into plain English the contents of the very handsome Latin
word she had used. To this she again modestly replied that
she only read Swedenborg as an *amateur,* and was ill-
qualified to expound his philosophy, but there could be no
doubt about its fundamental postulate, which was, that a
new birth for man, both in the individual and the universal
realm, is the secret of the Divine creation and providence:
that the other world, according to Swedenborg, furnishes the
true sphere of man's spiritual or individual being, the real
and immortal being he has in God; and he represents *this*
world, consequently, as furnishing only a preliminary
theatre of his natural formation or existence in subordina-
tion thereto; so making the question of human regeneration,
both in grand and in little, the capital problem of philosophy: that, without pretending to dogmatize, she had been
struck with the philosophic interest of my narrative in this
point of view, and had used the word *vastation* to characterize one of the stages of the regenerative process, as she had
found it described by Swedenborg. And then, finally, my
excellent friend went on to outline for me, in a very interesting manner, her conception of Swedenborg's entire doctrine
on the subject.

"Her account of it, as I found on a subsequent study of

Swedenborg, was neither quite as exact nor quite as comprehensive as the facts required; but at all events I was glad to
discover that any human being had so much even as proposed
to shed the light of positive knowledge upon the soul's history, or bring into rational relief the alternate dark and
bright — or infernal and celestial — phases of its finite constitution. For I had an immediate hope, amounting to an
almost prophetic instinct, of finding in the attempt, however
rash, some diversion to my cares, and I determined instantly
to run up to London and procure a couple of Swedenborg's
volumes, of which, if I should not be allowed on sanitary
grounds absolutely to read them, I might at any rate turn
over the leaves, and so catch a satisfying savor, or at least an
appetizing flavor, of the possible relief they might in some
better day afford to my poignant need. From the huge mass
of tomes placed by the bookseller on the counter before me,
I selected two of the least in bulk — the treatise on the
Divine Love and Wisdom, and that on the *Divine Providence.* I gave them, after I brought them home, many a
random but eager glance, but at last my interest in them
grew so frantic under this tantalizing process of reading that
I resolved, in spite of the doctors, that, instead of standing
any longer shivering on the brink I would boldly plunge into
the stream, and ascertain, once for all, to what undiscovered
sea its waters might bear me.

"I read from the first with palpitating interest. My heart
divined, even before my intelligence was prepared to do justice to the books, the unequalled amount of truth to be
found in them. Imagine a fever patient, sufficiently restored of his malady to be able to think of something beside
himself, suddenly transported where the free airs of heaven
blow upon him, and the sound of running waters refreshes
his jaded senses, and you have a feeble imagine of my delight
in reading. Or, better still, imagine a subject of some petty
despotism condemned to die, and with — what is more and
worse — a sentiment of death pervading all his conscious-

ness, lifted by a sudden miracle into felt harmony with universal man, and filled to the brim with the sentiment of indestructible life instead, and you will have a true picture of my emancipated condition. For while these remarkable books familiarized me with the angelic conception of the Divine being and providence, they gave me at the same time the amplest *rationale* I could have desired of my own particular suffering, as inherent in the profound unconscious death I bore about in my *proprium* or selfhood.

"At the moment I am speaking of — the moment of my first encounter with Swedenborg's writings — my intellect had been so completely vastated of every semblance of truth inherited from the past, and my soul consequently was in a state of such sheer and abject famine with respect to Divine things, that I doubt not I should have welcomed 'the father of lies' to my embrace, nor ever have cared to scrutinize his credentials, had he presented himself bearing the priceless testimony which these books bear to the loveliness and grandeur of the Divine name. Nor should I counsel any one, who is not similarly dilapidated in his intellectual foundations — any one who is still at rest in his hereditary bed of doctrine, orthodox or heterodox — pay the least attention to them. For on the surface they repel delight. They would seem to have been mercifully constructed on the plan of barring out idle acquaintance, and disgusting a voluptuous literary curiosity. But to the aching heart and the void mind — the heart and mind which, being sensibly famished upon those gross husks of religious doctrine whether Orthodox or Unitarian, upon which nevertheless our veriest swine are contentedly fed, are secretly pining for their Father's house where there is bread enough and to spare — they will be sure, I think, to bring infinite balm and contentment."

Henry James had found his truth. Henceforth he never travelled without carrying Swedenborg's works along with him. He found them "insipid with veracity."

After a brief visit to Paris, James returned to America. Early in 1845 he was busy lecturing in New York City, presumably to announce his new discovery though he was living at his mother's house in Albany and did not come down to the city to live until 1847. Unfortunately his thoughts did not immediately clarify themselves and although he produced several books and pamphlets and a good deal of journalism in the next few years it was not until the sixties and seventies that he really managed to deliver his message. That he ever said himself out seems doubtful and no one was more conscious of the inadequacy of his printed words than he was himself. Immediately after they were published, he was disgusted with his books and in spite of the fact that he came to concentrate on a very small handful of basic ideas, a fundamental clarity was not one of his virtues. He was incorrigibly discursive and was given to prophetically announcing his truths rather than logically arguing for them. "I am sure it is not in *your* way," wrote Garth Wilkinson apropos a book of his own, "being altogether critical, literary, biographical, controversial, British Museumish; and not universal, spiritual, organic."

During the late forties and early fifties he continued in ferment, attaching himself to the ex-Brook Farmers and the Fourierites and attempting to reconcile economic reform with Swedenborgianism. He also engaged in controversies over marriage and lectured miscellaneously on democracy, art and so on. It is easy enough to see where he was going intellectually, for no matter how interested he was in the current reforms, or how brilliantly he generalized on incidental topics, he was first and foremost a religious prophet. The vigorous stretchings and strainings of American society did not engage his attention. He had nothing to say about gold-rushes and the settlement of the West. He was an adventurer and an explorer, but his adventures were of the mind and his explorations were of the spirit. Herman Melville is the only other American of the generation who went so far into the mental world of final things, but he carried his body to distant places of the earth as well, while James did not stray beyond the great cities of Europe and America. James's concern for reform was only secondarily related to the terribly depressed condition of the hands in the growing factories. His eyes were turned toward a brighter society to which this one was a mere prelude. Thoroughly to understand him it is necessary to look into the details of his intellectual history during this rather disjointed period.

Fourierism swept over the American intellectual world in the late thirties and early forties. François Charles Marie Fourier (1772–1837) was born in good circumstances and was well educated. He travelled extensively in Europe as a young man, lost his private fortune, joined the army for a short term of service, became a clerk and finally a broker. He began to publish his theoretical treatises on man and society in 1808, at first anonymously. The bulk of his publications came between 1822 and 1831. He made a deep impression and gathered loyal adherents about him who assisted him in his propaganda and established several magazines to advance his cause. His theories developed under two headings, the psychological and the economic. Psychologically his argument was that human happiness is only possible when human nature can develop fully, freely and without restraint imposed by society upon the gratification of desire. His economic system was designed as a complement to his psychological dogmas. Society was to be divided into "phalanges" consisting of sixteen hundred persons each, each "phalange" to live in a common building. The basic industry of each group was to be agriculture. While not demanding that property be held on a communistic basis, Fourier did insist on absolute democracy as to tasks. Each member was to draw his subsistence from the common stock and profits were to be distributed according to a fixed scheme, $\frac{5}{12}$ to labor, $\frac{4}{12}$ to capital and $\frac{3}{12}$ to talent. Marriage was to be abolished and sex relations were to be regulated by an exceedingly complicated scheme of organized license.   Minor variations in this scheme were introduced into the American Fourieristic experiments, but the basic outlines were carefully followed.

The principal propagandist for Fourierism in this country was Albert Brisbane (1809–1890).   He met Fourier abroad, accepted his doctrines, and returned to America to spread the good word.   His book, *The Social Destiny of Man* (1840) converted Horace Greeley to the cause and he gave Brisbane space in *The Tribune* for his propaganda.   In addition Brisbane edited and contributed to a variety of other publications.   He was convinced that America was ripe for the new economic system because of the suffering during the great panic of 1837.   When he visited his home in Western New York after his trip to Europe in the late thirties he found that but six men in the whole district had escaped bankruptcy. His first move was to agitate for currency reform, but that failing he turned to a more drastic renovation of the social system and blossomed forth as a complete Fourierite.   As a result of his efforts and those of his convinced followers, there were three notable Fourieristic establishments founded, the Wisconsin Phalanx (as they were called in America) (1844– 1850), the North American Phalanx, near Red Bank, New Jersey (1843–1856) and Brook Farm.

Of them all, the Brook Farm experiment was the most notable in its effect upon the intellectual life of America.   It was not originally a Fourieristic experiment at all, but an off shoot of Transcendentalism.   First discussed in the Transcendental Club in 1836, it was received with dubiety by Emerson and the more individualistic members of the group, but was supported with enthusiasm by George Ripley.   In 1841 the plan was carried into execution at Roxbury, Massachusetts, with a sizable group of members including Ripley, Charles A. Dana, (who in later years more thoroughly repudiated his youthful ideas than any of the others — in his brilliant and erratic editing of the New York *Sun*), and

Nathaniel Hawthorne, whose *Blithedale Romance* is the literary monument of the experiment.   It was visited by other sympathetic souls, including Margaret Fuller, the younger Channings, Emerson and Alcott.   Starting with fifteen active members it numbered one hundred and twenty at the height of its prosperity.   It showed every sign of being a success, so far as such a project of setting up a small society within a large and hostile society could be a success.   But the fly in the ointment was the manifest impossibility of carrying on both physical and intellectual labor.   Under Albert Brisbane's influence it was remodelled on a Fourieristic basis in 1845 and thereafter rapidly declined.   Brisbane was unquestionably the "evil genius" of Brook Farm.   The settlement broke up in 1847 and the members scattered.   A group of them settled in New York and continued the Brook Farm propaganda organ, *The Harbinger,* for two years as the official publication of *The American Union of Associationists.*   The editor was Parke Godwin, who later became William Cullen Bryant's son-in-law and an editor of the New York *Evening Post,* and the more important contributors were George Ripley, C. A. Dana, John Sullivan Dwight the only critic of music among the Transcendentalists, W. H. Channing and Henry James.   It was the last gasp of the Fourierites and it is interesting to see how James regarded the whole affair.

According to Emerson, Fourier "had skipped no fact but one, namely Life."   It seems anomalous, therefore, that James should have taken any interest in the doctrine at all, for if there was one thing he demanded it was life, and life abundantly.   The enigma is solved when we discover that he considered it a mere adjunct to Swedenborgianism and one that could be lopped off when the time came that social reform ceased to interest him.   It suggested a possible way to assist mankind to that *social* redemption which was its high and inevitable destiny.   In his view man was "under a threefold subjection, first to nature, then to society, and finally to

God. His appetites and his sensuous understanding relate him to society or his fellow man; and his ideas related him to God. . . He who obeys his appetites merely finds himself speedily betrayed by the inflexible laws of nature to disease and death. He who obeys his passions merely finds himself by the inflexible laws of society to shame and seclusion. But he who obeys his ideas, he who gives himself up to the guidance of infinite goodness, truth, and beauty, encounters no limitation at the hands either of nature or society, and, instead of disease and shame, plucks only the fruits of health and immortal honor." Unfortunately, however, as society is constituted it is impossible for man to follow God's guidance. He cannot free himself from the burdensome conditions imposed by a false social system the drive of which is toward "gross materiality." In order to usher in a society of men relying exclusively on God it is necessary that society be rearranged to bring about economic and social freedom. It is at this point that Fourier comes into the picture.

James did not consider Fourier's doctrines the last word in economic and social wisdom, but merely as the most suggestive body of thought available. He was acutely aware of the injustice of a social system that allowed him economic ease and leisure to cultivate his highest powers while others were denied bread and shelter. In addition to his friendship with such men as Parke Godwin and his acquaintance with Horace Greeley as a reason for his concern with Fourierism, there was the fact that many other Swedenborgians were trying to fit Fourier into their system. Garth Wilkinson in London wrestled manfully with the problem, but at last gave it up as insoluable. In 1849 a book was published in New York entitled, *The True Organization of the New Church* (the name taken by the ecclesiastical Swedenborgians) *as indicated by Emanuel Swedenborg and scientifically demonstrated by Charles Fourier.* The author announced as his purpose "to prove from Swedenborg himself the theory of Association as taught by Fourier." James was, then, merely following a general trend in Swedenborgian circles. Characteristically, he was concerned with generalities and not with particulars, a habit of mind which brought him considerable criticism from the more exacting reformers. In his view:

The idea or truth which animates human society, and which incessantly stimulates political revolutions and reforms with a view to its own fuller and eventually perfect embodiment, is the idea or truth of the exact fellowship or equality of man with man. This is an eternal truth, because it grows out of the superior truth, that there is one God and Father of the whole family of man. Human history is simply a slow, but increasing approximation to the realization of this idea, or its embodiment in institutions. And this embodiment becomes perfect, becomes worthy of the spiritual truth, as the family of man increases in material wealth, or what is the same thing, in so far as the equilibrium of plenty and want becomes extended over the race.

Consonant with this is James's declaration in a lecture before the Town and Country Club of Boston (subsequently printed in *Moralism and Christianity* (1850) delivered November 1, 1849:

By Socialism, I mean not any special system of social organization, like that of Fourier, Owen or St. Simon, but what is common to all these systems, namely, the idea of a perfect fellowship or society among men. And by Civilization, of course, I mean the present political constitution of the nations. Between the fundamental idea of Socialism, which affirms the possibility of a perfect life on earth, or the insubjection of man both to nature and his fellow-man, and the fundamental idea of Civilization which affirms the perpetual imperfection of human life, or the permanent subjection of man to nature and society, a great discrepancy exists. . . Socialism promises to make God's great life in man possible, promises to make all our relations just, so beautiful and helpful, that we shall be no longer conscious of finiteness of imperfection, but only of life and power utterly infinite.

Obviously James's only interest in Socialism, of which Fourierism seemed to him the most commendable formulation, was based on the fact that it forecasted a preliminary necessity to the reign of God on earth. This view is underlined in his fundamental distinction between Moralism and Christianity: "Two doctrines exist in the world, that of Moralism, which affirms man's rightful subjection to nature and society;

and that of the Christ, or Divine Man, which affirms man's
rightful subjection only to God. . ." Under the heading of
Moralism James bundled all ecclesiasticisms and material-
isms whatsoever, together with conventional social practices
of all sorts.   His free use of his more or less private distinction gave a piquancy to his talk and writing and forever
disabused his sons of the idea that respect must be paid to
conventional social values.   They were free to discover for
themselves what was worth paying attention to.   As for himself, his greatest concern was to make it clear how man was
related to God.

He was constantly lecturing.   One of the most vivid pictures of him at this time, summoned up years later by his
son Henry, was of him departing for the lecture hall just as
the children were being hustled off to bed.   But if he could
summon an audience, he was far from satisfied with what he
was saying.   He wrote Emerson that on reading over a new
series he was about to deliver he was horrified "with their
loud-mouthed imbecility !" What disturbed him was the apparent incommunicability of truth.   There was without
doubt a grain of very valuable truth shining through what
he was saying and a grain that seemed to him of the very
first importance, but he could not make it shine brightly
enough.   It was, after all, impossible to communicate life
to his hearers and if they were not alive any intellectual
formulae they might get from his talks were just so much
learned lumber.   They could take in the idea, but they could
not translate it into action.   For ". . . life is simply the
passage of idea into action; and our crazy theologies forbid
ideas to come into action any further than our existing institutions warrant." The only thing to do apparently was
to resolve to be as effective as possible himself in breaking
down the resistance.   "I shall try to convert *myself* at least
into an army of Goths and Huns, to overcome and destroy
our existing sanctities, that the supernal splendours may at
length become credible and even visible."

He held most of his fellow New York writing men, other than the reformers, in profound disesteem. Nothing met with quite so much of his honest scorn as a "mere" literary man and no type of writer was more common in New York of the fifties than just that type. It was the era of Poe's "literati." There flourished Halleck, Washington Irving retired to eulogize John Jacob Astor, Mrs. Elizabeth Oakes Smith, N. P. Willis, Ike Marvell, the Reverend Rufus Wilmot Griswold (with whom James was acquainted), all the minor fry bilked by Poe in his reviews and the gang at Pfaff's where Walt Whitman * hung out and Fitz James O'Brien corruscated. James could find little in such minds, except possibly Whitman's, for they lacked the prophetic bias. They were not lifted by any very divine afflatus and were quite content to operate within the limits of the "sensuous" imagination. James demanded that the artist aim higher. "Nature *rules* only in the young and immature, only where the sensuous imagination still predominates. . . Art does not lie in copying nature. Nature only furnishes the Artist with the material by means of which to express a beauty still unexpressed in nature. . . The Artist works to produce or bring forth in tangible form some conception of use or beauty with which not his memory but his inmost soul is aglow." Furthermore, in defining critical procedure, James anticipated a very modern principle: "Thus in estimating a work of Art, you would seek to ascertain how far its genetic idea or mental

* The first edition of *Leaves of Grass* came out in 1855 about the time that James left America. He returned for a few months in 1859, but was otherwise in Europe from 1855 to 1860. Yet in the spring of the latter year he wrote a correspondent: "You ask me 'why I do not brandish my tomahawk and, like Walt Whitman, raise my barbaric yawp over the roofs of all the houses.' It is because I am not yet a 'cosmos' as that gentleman avowedly is, but only a very dim nebula, doing its modest best, no doubt, to solidify into cosmical dimensions, but still requiring an 'awful sight' of time and pains and patience on the part of its friends." This would seem to bespeak an aliveness to literature, even though it tells us nothing about his opinion of Whitman. In 1881 when Whitman was in Boston preparing the ill-fated Ticknor & Fields edition of the *Leaves* he met Henry James. He mentions him in a letter to a friend as "old Henry James" as though he were sufficiently identified in that fashion; as though, perhaps, he knew of him from the early New York days.

conception had been fulfilled, how far in other words the sentiment of the piece impressed you." *   There would seem to be little doubt but that had circumstances bent his thoughts toward literature, James would have developed into a distinguished critic.   So far as contemporary American literature, went, James's sympathies were with the New England type of author of whom Emerson was the finest representative.   He could even be friendly with A. Bronson Alcott, though he regarded him as a bit of a fool, because he looked beyond the "sensuous."   But he had no patience with writers who were concerned exclusively with "mere" writing; they were "poor things, vain, conceited nobodies."

It is a little difficult to see, then, what he found in Thackeray.   He dismissed Dickens: "The purblind piddling mercenaries of literature, like Dickens. . . " Yet, in a peculiar fashion, he admired Thackeray and on the occasion of his visit to America took pains to cultivate his friendship.   When *Vanity Fair* appeared in 1849 he wrote and published an article on Becky Sharpe and when Thackeray approached our shores in 1852 he inserted the following paragraph in *The Tribune*:

He comes on the invitation of the Mercantile Library Association.   The Merchant's Clerks of New York aspire to the culture of scholars and gentlemen, and import from abroad — not the latest teacher of double entry, but the most thoughtful critic of manners and society the subtlest humorist, and the most effective, because the most genial, satirist the age has known.

He entertained Thackeray in his home and in return for many services rendered, both personal and through defences in the press, Thackeray had his secretary-companion, Eyre Crowe the painter, do a portrait of James.   Furthermore the friendship continued when James went abroad again in 1855 and Thackeray was an intimate of the James household in Paris.   Nevertheless when Emerson saw Henry James in New York sometime in 1853, he got a rather critical view of the great novelist: "In New York, Henry James quoted

* Compare with the position of Henry James, Jr., page 232 and elsewhere.

Thackeray's speeches in society, 'He liked to go to West-minster Abbey to say his prayers,' etc. 'It gave him the comfort,—best feeling. . .' He thought Thackeray could not see beyond his eyes, and has no ideas, and merely is a sounding board against which his experiences thump and resound: he is the merest boy." Yet in printed references he remains "my manly friend Thackeray." And he is treated at length in this fashion:

This masterly writer, who sounds at will all the depths of human nature, is no stronger nor wiser at bottom than the rest of us: he too feels life insecure, he too lifts a pallid face in prayer to God lest some hideous calamity engulf his fairest hopes. Few persons have maintained their natural naivete and candour so unbronzed by contact with the world, as this great and hearty Thackeray, this huge, yet childlike man; but if the secret bosom of men were canvassed, there would be none found who does not profoundly sympathize with him.

James must have been somewhat overwhelmed with Thackeray's personality, for if there ever was a victim of "moralism" it was Thackeray, and he nowhere more clearly exhibited his limitations in that respect than in precisely those lectures he was delivering in America: those on the English humorists. It was one of James's most human traits that he could like men of whom he intellectually most heartily disapproved. His animal spirits prevented him from becoming a prig, just as before his illumination they had prevented him from becoming a fanatic.

Entertaining Thackeray was, after all, but an episode in James's history. His true interest was not in a social life among the literary men of the day, though if it had been he would have had no difficulty in making his way, but in advancing the truth. Almost at the moment that Thackeray arrived in America, he was embroiled in a controversy over marriage with Stephen Pearl Andrews. Andrews was a typical example of the universal reformer who flourished during the period. His particular panacea was the universal application of the anarchistic principle of the "sovereignty of

the individual." The upshot was to be a "natural scientific
social order without government, law, marriage, the family or
punishment." As a gateway to this utopia, he was willing to
accept Fourierism, but only as a gateway. Along with his
other foibles he was a passionate abolitionist, the chief exponent of Pitman shorthand in America and the inventor
of a universal language.

Andrews really "horned into" a controversy which was
none of his concern. James had reviewed a book in *The
Tribune* and in the course of his remarks had set down a
few dicta which had been picked up, distorted and excoriated
by the editor of an orthodox Presbyterian paper called *The
Observer*. The tone of these remarks must have been decidedly offensive, for when James returned to the battle he
wrote: "Doubtless, Mr. Editor, you address an easy, goodnatured audience, who do not care to scan too nicely the
stagnant slipslop which your weekly ladle deals out to them."
It was in an effort to combat this "stagnant slipslop" that
James set forth his notions more at length, in *The Tribune*.
It was at this point that Andrews entered the lists to condemn James as too conservative and to advocate the "sovereignty of the Individual." His importance to us is that he
provoked James to a more elaborate exposition of his views
than would otherwise have followed. With his own we have
no particular concern.

James's fundamental objection to the institution of marriage as conceived in the eighteen-fifties was that "It is not
administered livingly, or with reference to the present need
of society, but only traditionally, or with reference to some
wholly past state of society." He was far from wishing to see
it destroyed, which was Andrews's idea of how to renovate
it, but wished to liberalize it by freer divorce. It is not
"essential to the honor of marriage that two persons should
be compelled to live together when they held the reciprocal
relation of dog and cat, and that in that state of things divorce might profitably intervene, provided the parties guaran-

teed the state against the charge of their offspring. . . I had no idea I was . . . weakening the respect of marriage in advocating this position. I seemed to myself to be plainly strengthening it, by removing purely arbitrary and damaging obstructions. The existing difficulty of divorce is one of those obstructions." Furthermore he saw plenty of evidence to support him in the position that narrow divorce laws were undermining the institution. "No doubt there is a very enormous clandestine violation of the marriage bond at the present time; careful observers do not hesitate to say, an almost unequalled violation of it; but that is an end which no positive legislation can prevent, because it is *manifestly based upon a popular contempt for the present indolent and vicious administration of the law.*" Nevertheless, it was folly to argue from these patent present difficulties to the total abolition of marriage which, after all, has values of supreme importance. He was not interested in breaking "bottles." He is interested in setting forth "how I conceive our good old *family* bottle, *conjugal* bottle, and *social* bottle generally — might be *destroyed?* No! Might be saved from destruction, *renewed, regenerated,* and *reformed,* by wise and timely legislation." He was interested in breaking down restrictions; he was not an anarchist; he was a libertarian.

The same attitude runs through all of his writings on social matters. His concern is always with the liberating and never in the restrictive. Viewing the business classes through his private microscope he found them conspiring to advance his ends:

. . . in a transition stage of society like ours, the commercial class exercises the most universal function, because now the problem of humanity is to destroy existing nationalities, or those things which divide the brotherhood of man, and fuse mankind into one grand unitary family. And commerce is effectually promoting this end. Hence the commercial class is now chiefly in honor. No matter how soulless a clod the individual merchant may be, and however impracticable a subject he may prove to be your mere pedantic and diletante uses, still his function is superb, and both church and state accordingly, by infallible instinct, lavish upon him their tenderest caresses.   They give the merchant the best house of any man in the community, and celebrate his births, marriages and deaths with a gusto that somewhat affronts the uninstructed understanding.

In truth the "uninstructed understanding" can be pardoned for not seeing that the business class of the eighteen-fifties, the "respectable blockheads" as Nathaniel Hawthorne called them, was working to such an ideal end.   This class is still entirely unconscious that that is their purpose eighty years later.   But if James was willing to grant the business class a divine purpose, he was not willing to grant property a very high standing.

"Property," he told his readers, "symbolizes the perfect sovereignty which man is destined to exercise over nature." However, "The institution of private Property . . . must never be allowed to dominate, but only to serve, the interests of universal man."   In fact:

. . . in proportion to its magnitude, it tends to belittle the possessor by overlaying his true sovereignty, his true humanitary attributes. . . Men are *ashamed* of the respect they pay it.   Property cannot be a final fact of history, cannot be a good in itself, cannot be a divine end in humanity, because every man in proportion to his genius, is ashamed of the deference he pays it.

That nothing on which contemporary eyes gazed was a "final fact of history" was the burden of Henry James's remarks on all social institutions.   They were, on the one hand, obstacles in the way of progress toward the reign of God on earth, or indications of the loosening of the hold of evil over man.   He attacked restrictive institutions and he applauded all those that seemed to him to be making for a larger liberty for mankind.

He regarded Protestantism, not as the final upshot of religious life, but as an important step along the path away from all ecclesiasticisms.   It moved in the direction of freedom by destroying the universal sway of the Catholic Church which he pungently disliked. He spoke of its "inveterate imbecility." But he disliked it chiefly because it was the most ecclesiastical of ecclesiasticisms. He applauded Democracy on the same grounds as Protestantism:

The function of Democracy . . . is to prepare the way, by a disorganization of the political life of men, for their perfect society or fellowship. . . Its doctrine is one essentially of repentance or preparation, denouncing old abuses, revealing the iniquity of past legislation, exalting every valley of inequality, abasing every mountain of privilege, making straight whatsoever is crooked and smooth whatsoever is rough, so that all flesh from the smallest to the greatest shall experience the salvation of God.

As the fifties advanced his interest became more and more concentrated upon "the salvation of God." All else, while it had never been other than subordinate to his great concern, was slowly sloughed off and he began to settle down mentally to his great task of exposing the reigning ecclesiasticism and announcing the true revelation. Always sensitive to the pull of Europe, even though when there he was sensitive to the pull of America, he began definitely to plan to leave New York. As early as 1849, when he was but four years resident there, he had hinted to Garth Wilkinson that he would soon come to England and at the same time he wrote Emerson that since the city was bad for his boys, he was thinking of taking them to Europe for education, both bookish and "sensuous." In 1855 he abandoned the city, never to return, after ten years of implication in its intellectual life. In 1855, 1856, and 1857 he published three small books that were designed to settle his case with ecclesiasticism and the old theology and to state his own position. The case proved to be one not so easily disposed of, but the effort was exhilarating both to himself and his readers. From the positions he now took up he never retreated and his later books — longer if not clearer than these — are simply restatements of his fundamental insights.

While his sons applied themselves to getting educated in

London (where the family lived as neighbors to Garth Wilkinson), Paris and Boulogne-sur-Mer, James applied himself to writing. He shut himself up every morning in his study as though his living depended upon the products of his pen. For books, he relied only on the works of Swedenborg, from which he derived the amplest inspiration. By unceasing toil, he produced in three years *The Nature of Evil* (1855), *The Church of Christ Not an Ecclesiasticism* (1856) and *Christianity, the Logic of Creation* (1857). Like all of James's books these are discursive and repetitive and they overlap. He was eternally finding a new and frequently more brilliant way of saying something that he had said before. It is more profitable to treat the group as a unit and separate the themes for treatment, rather than to treat each book as a tight entity. By borrowing back and forth and rearranging the topics in a logical order, it is possible to make it somewhat clear what Henry James tried so desperately to say.

His attack on orthodoxy was made in a peculiarly exhilarating and forthright way and it is as enjoyable to heretics who have no interest in the religious doctrines with which he designed to replace it as to those who are chiefly interested in them. The fundamental objection he had to orthodox ecclesiasticism, and to all ecclesiasticisms whatever for that matter, was that they stood in the way of man's direct commerce with God. He did not seek to reform them. He was not interested in them *as ecclesiasticisms*. If, for a moment, he regarded them in the light of their efficiency in serving their ostensible purpose, he logically supported the Catholic Church as the best. According to James he was but following Swedenborg in his view of the essential worthlessness of all ecclesiastical organizations:

He (Swedenborg) waged no war whatever with the church as an ecclesiasticism, though I doubt not he had his just Protestantism predilections, but only as a corrupt spiritual economy. He complained of it only in that respect wherein the Lord complains of it, namely, as being destitute of the life of charity, and being therefore to all heavenly intents and purposes dead or inactive. Accordingly you never find him proposing so cheap and superficial a remedy for so grave a disease, as the creation of a new ecclesiastical organization. How should a new ecclesiastical hierarchy mend matters? The complaint was not against a particular set of persons, as contrasted with another set. The complaint was not that certain persons called God's church were worse men spiritually than certain other persons, which other persons must therefore be formed into a new ecclesiastical body, and made to supersede the old one. By no means. The complaint was that the entire mind of man, as ecclesiastically exhibited, was in spiritual ignorance or darkness, and hence the remedy befitting this condition could not be a change in the personal administration of the church, or a change in the persons composing it, but an entire renewal of its spirit. What the church wanted was not a new body, or a new literal constitution, but exclusively a new spirit, the spirit of unfeigned love.

The gravamen of this argument is against the so-called New Church which set itself up as the official expression of Swedenborgianism, but it applies in equal measure to all ecclesiastical organizations. James believed that whereas the final value of Protestantism was that it contributed to the breaking up of Catholicism, so the next step was to abandon ecclesiastical organizations altogether.

Against the God of the orthodox churches he felt a genuine hatred if his words are taken at their most obvious value. How that God poisoned his youth was something he never forgot or forgave. He referred to Him as the "obscene and skulking god of the nations." "Against this lurid power — half-pedagogue, half-policeman, but wholly imbecile in both aspects — I . . . raise my gleeful fist, I lift my scornful foot, I invoke the self-respect of my children, I arouse their nascent philanthropy. . ." It is in the service of this despicable God that the orthodox theologians bend their efforts. The total effect of their ministrations is "to aggrandize and intensify the *moral* life of man, to inflame that sentiment of personal difference and distinction among men, which litters all our existing contrasts of good and evil, rich and poor, wise and simple, proud and grovelling, and so immortalizes the reign of hell on earth." James's reasons for considering the intensification of the moral life a base service will sufficiently appear later. In the meantime, let us see what he found to be the effect upon the communicants of such a regimen as that offered by orthodoxy: "Priest-ridden and police-ridden, amidst all God's overwhelming bounties they nourish only the furtive courage of mice, and under the kindling sunshine of truth contentedly maintain the darkened intelligence of owls and bats." The cause of all this suffering is that theology has become exclusively naturalistic with the upshot that:

. . . we now have Unitarianism as the only vital theologic doctrine extant, and Atheism or Pantheism as the only vital philosophical doctrine. We live under the Iscariot apostolate. The star of the forlorn Judas culminates at length in our ecclesiastical horizon, and we have little left to do but to burst asunder in the midst, or resolve our once soaring Divine hopes into the mere poetry and sentimentality of nature.

Henry James, of course, aimed to "burst asunder in the midst." Nothing less than that would satisfy him. In the meantime he had to turn the eyes of his readers away from the obscene sight of the orthodox theologians, "wrangling regiments of spiritual old-clothesmen diligently dividing the empty garments of Truth among themselves, and hawking the dislocated fragments about as if they were the immortal substance itself." They exhaust themselves debating such things at "the momentous question, whether or not God was identical with the contents of a certain sanctified breadbasket." And so James advises his readers that:

if any nasty spiritual person should contrive to come to us through the reeking chinks of our still unscientific mental sewage, saying that he has been divinely relegated to a certain charge over our servile and constitutional interests, over our natural affections and intelligence, let us tell him in return that he is a very precious ass to affect a mission of that nature, since all the good we do each other in such connection is strictly contingent upon our being utterly unconscious of it. And if he go on, on the other hand, to allege that he bears even the faintest conceivable relation to our real and immortal parts, or to that life which is alone worth our thought because it alone comes from God, let us greet him with a cachination so hearty and derisive, as shall bid him instantly disperse, nor ever show his foolish face again. . .

The sort of theology with which Henry James wished to replace orthodoxy was supernaturalistic through and through as distinguished from the decadent naturalistic religious thought. He started from the beginning of things and re-defined the meaning of creation. In his view, the old theory of creation as a physical act performed in time and space was the merest tosh and nonsense. The old theology:

. . . looks upon Time and Space, which are the universal ele-ments of Nature, as absolute, or as furnishing the elements of the Divine existence also; and hence of necessity it regards creation as primarily natural, or as a phenomenon of space and time. . . Thus the cosmological method unspiritualizes the Divine ex-istence and operation, by reducing God to the dimensions of nature, or making creation a physical phenomenon. It assumes . . . the essential incarnation of Deity, and hence by anticipation utterly vacates the truth of his alleged historical incarnation in Christ Jesus. . . (The orthodox) suppose that some six thou-sand years ago, more or less, man was effectively created, and that his entire subsequent history consequently has been little better than a vigorous and unaccountable kicking up of his heels in his Creator's face. . . The abject childishness of this concep-tion fails to strike them, only because the application of reason to sacred subjects has been so effectually discouraged by the clergy, that our popular intellectual stomach has grown indu-rated and ostrich-like — stowing away all manner of unnutritious corkscrews, jack-knives, and rusty nails, which may be presented to it by its lawful purveyors, as if they were so much reasonable and delectable Christian diet.

In James's view creation was "a purely spiritual process, fall-ing wholly within the realm of affection and thought. . ." This denaturalizing of creation was an indispensable pre-liminary to his other views. The origin of all his thinking was his perturbation over the problem of evil. He wanted to know how the existence of evil could be reconciled with

the Creator's perfection.   The solution of the problem he
found in Swedenborg and it was his version of Swedenborg's
position that we are now examining.   The reason it was
necessary to spiritualize or supernaturalize creation was that
it cast a blazing beam of light on the problem of evil.   For
if creation is the result of an arbitrary physical act of God,
then He alone must be held responsible for the existence of
evil.   This is an intolerable position, though a logical one,
and to escape it was James's desire.

To do so he had not only to make creation a supernatural
and not a natural act, but he also had to deny the omnipo-
tence of natural laws and the final reality of the natural
world.   He contended, therefore, for the familiar view that
the natural world was not the world of reality but the world
of appearances.   The world of reality was the spiritual world.
Unlike other thinkers of this disposition, however, James
did not argue from the facts of the natural world to those of
the spiritual world by the technique of analogy.   He held
that by the very fact that it was supernatural, it must be
therefore entirely different from the natural.   Unlike Emerson's heaven, James's bore *no proportion to earth*.   The best
that could be said for the natural world was that it was a
"seminary or nursery for the spiritual world."   And as a
consequence of this science could not be held to be final
truth.   It was knowledge of nature and was therefore inferior
to knowledge of the truths of the supernatural sphere.   By
thus escaping what he thought was the tyranny of the senses,
he was enabled to erect a theory of God's relation to man
which could be neither denied nor ratified by nature or by
man's considered knowledge of nature.   He became, therefore, a dogmatic supernaturalist.   His saving knowledge of
the superior supernatural world was derived from Christian
revelation — proved by Jesus Christ.

Now the problem was how to relate, and intimately relate,
God and man.   By denaturalizing God the problem was considerably simplified, for if He was not to be measured in

terms of time and space the manipulation of his power could not be so confined either. Still and all, there remained the undoubted fact that God was *not* in absolute control of man, for if he were the beneficent utopia toward which James saw man moving would not be in the future. It would be present reality. The reasoning here was that while God was present in every man, his efforts were opposed by a contradictory element in human nature, and that element was selfhood. Glancing back to the account of his great illumination in 1844, the reader will discover him italicizing these words: *"The curse of mankind, is its sense of selfhood, and the absurd abominable opinionativeness it engenders."* In seeking to account for the rise of this dissident and destructive principle, James re-examined the story of Adam's fall and presented a new version of it.

Adam, alone in the Garden of Eden, was a mere clod involved in all the lower forms of life. Adam alone

is still a mere natural form sprung from the dust, vivified by no Diviner breath than that of the nostrils, mere unfermented dough, insipid and unpracticable: and the Lord makes haste accordingly to add the spiritual leaven which shall ensure his endless rise into human and ultimately Divine proportions.

But how is this to be done?

He brings him Eve, or *spiritually quickens him;* for Eve, according to Swedenborg, symbolizes the Divinely vivified selfhood of man. The Adamic dough, heavy and disheartening before, becomes lively enough now in all conscience, becomes instinct and leaping with vitality, although that vitality has no more positive form than a protest against death, a struggle against mortality. Thus had we had Adam, "male and female," alone for progenitor, we should never have emerged from our Edenic or infantine gristle: we should have remained for ever in a state of Paradisiac childishness and imbecility: in a word, we should have been destitute of our most human characteristic, which is history or progress. . . Human history dates from Eve. Existence dates from Adam, but life, or progress towards God, begins with Eve: hence she is named Eve, mother of all living.

Such a scheme of things would seem to put Adam, companioned by Eve, well on the way to heavenly bliss, but we have not yet come to the fall. On that occasion things went radically awry:

The Fall . . . signalized . . . the gradual access of self-love, and the consequent cessation of love to God and the neighbor . . . eat of the tree of knowledge of good and evil, whose fruit is death. That is, we cease to live by God, and begin to live by ourselves . . . the pride of moralism, or the conceit of one's moral endowments, those endowments which make a man feel that he has an absolute or independent selfhood, and lead him therefore to make much of difference between himself and other men. This is original sin, the great parental fount and origin of all the evils that desolate humanity. Here lies the great mother-fallacy at whose exuberant paps cling and feed all the minor fallacies of the universe. The sentiment of independent selfhood: the conviction of being the source of one's own good and evil: such is the sole ground of every evil known to the spiritual universe, and here accordingly we must take our stand if we wish to gain a philosophic mastery of the problems which agitate humanity.

But if with Adam's Fall selfhood took its rise, it would seem that with the years that have elapsed since that alleged event the power of selfhood would have considerably augmented. Some striking example of the benefits to be derived from destroying it would seem to be necessary to convince men of the inutility of the principle. Such an example is to be had in the person of Jesus Christ:

What a mere obscenity every great name in history confesses itself beside this spotless Judean youth, who in the thickest night of time, — unhelped by priest or ruler, by friend or neighbor, by father or mother, by brother or sister, helped, in fact, if we may so consider it, only by the dim expectant sympathy of that hungry rabble of harlots and outcasts who furnished His inglorious retinue, and still further drew upon Him the ferocious scorn of all that was devout, and honorable and powerful in His nation — yet let in eternal daylight upon the soul, by steadfastly expanding in his private spirit to the dimensions of universal humanity, so bringing, for the first time in history, the finite human bosom into perfect experimental accord with the infinite Divine Love.

Such then, was the mission of Jesus. His example was to show men how to break the bondage of selfhood and reunite themselves with God.

The spiritual life or freedom which men had forfeited in Adam, or by lapse into selfhood, became restored in the second Adam, or the Lord from heaven, and the eternal consequence was not merely that the well-disposed man might henceforth follow his heavenward inclinations without gratuitous embarrassment, but also that the ill-disposed man might pursue his infernal inclinations without coercion, or simply at the beck of such delight as they freely afforded.

The upshot is that man is in a peculiar and unique relation to God and Nature. He is lifted out of the subjection to Nature's laws which control the beasts and bugs and birds and vegetables by his indestructible connection with God. He alone among all the living things of the world is imbued with a spiritual principle. And in him alone is there a struggle between hell and heaven. The principle of hell is selfhood and the principle of heaven is brotherly love. The former is external and natural while the latter is internal and supernatural. Man's psychological life, then, is the struggle that goes on between these two principles. The moral life becomes, then, a conflict between the inflowing of God's Divine Love and Wisdom on the one hand and the inflowing of the infernal influence of selfhood on the other. But it must be *emphatically* underlined that in speaking in this fashion, James was speaking supernaturalistically. In naturalistic terms all this is the most palpable nonsense. Consequently:

. . . Let us remember always that the spiritual world is not lodged *spacially* within our bosoms. That is to say, it is not lodged there as a pound of figs is lodged in a box, or as one's foot is lodged in his boot, but correspondentially, that is, as sensation and volition are lodged in a muscle, or as affection and intelligence are lodged in an action.

Since the idea that we are responsible for our acts, good and evil, is one of the delusions of selfhood, it follows that,

we are properly conceived, but passive theatres of the struggle
between heaven and hell, God and the Devil, and in no way
to be either reprobated or applauded for our conduct. It
follows too, that we cannot hope to gain true righteousness
by conformance to social and ecclesiastic codes. To follow
that course is to boggle oneself in "moralism."

(God) would have me abstain from evil, not for the purpose of
winning any puerile rewards from him in the shape of sensuous
celestial joys, but purely because by such abstinence I repel the
inflow of infernal dispositions from my interiors, and by such
repulsion invite and attract those sweeter and angelic dispositions which alone constitute the heart's delight to eternity.

But if, through the triumph of the principle of selfhood man
repels God's Divine Love and Wisdom and so commits a
sort of spiritual suicide, God is not angered, nor does he
immediately abandon his Creature to summary punishment
according to the traditional prescriptions of the reigning
ecclesiasticism.

. . . it is really most untrue that God has ever felt, or can ever
feel, an emotion of personal approbation or personal disappro-
bation towards any human being. All this is the mere abject
gossip of the kitchen, the mere idle bavardise of cooks and scul-
lions theorizing in their dim subterranean way upon the great
solar mystery of life.

Good and Evil conduct should be evaluated in quite different terms. It should be ascribed:

. . . exclusively to the hereditary influx of good and evil spirits,
and hence (man should feel) no more responsibility for it, no
more sense of merit or demerit in regard to it, than we should
feel in regard to a fair or muddy complexion, to a sunny or som-
bre natural disposition.

This discourse applies to *spiritual* evil only. The other
kinds of evil are physical evil, like hunger, and moral evil,
like stealing and slander. They are the products respectively
of our animal and our "rational" organization of selfhood.

One suffers from physical evil, one commits moral evil, but one IS spiritual evil. The first two kinds are cultivated by our evil institutions and can be mitigated and perhaps entirely eliminated by reforming those institutions, but the last can only be eliminated by opening oneself to the inflow of the Divine Love and Wisdom. By social reform and the resolute destruction of selfhood the way is made open for such a consummation and when it is achieved God will once more reign in glorious sovereignty upon the earth — in a society which will be the redeemed form of man.

After a siege of Henry James's theological discourse it is easy to sympathize with Julia Ward Howe's friend who, when coming away from a James lecture, said that she "would give anything at this moment for a look at a good fat idiot."

Indeed, it must have exhausted him too, for after publishing *Christianity, the Logic of Creation* (1857) he remained silent for six years, so far as religion was concerned, and published but one small pamphlet on any other topic. His mind was not quiescent however, but he was merely laying up strength for a new attack upon the defeating difficulties of expression. Henry James mended his helmet more times than Don Quixote ever did and never relied on a green ribbon finally to assert the solidity and completeness of his message to the world.

He continued his exploration of Swedenborg's ever fascinating books and he ventured into secular writings also. Among other things, he discovered George Eliot's work and enthusiastically recommended it to friends. He looked in on Carlyle once more and found him "the same old sausage, fizzing and sputtering in his own grease, only infinitely *more* unreconciled to the blest Providence which guides human affairs. He names God frequently and alludes to the highest things as if they were realities, but all only as for a picturesque effect, so completely does he seem to regard them as habitually circumvented and set at naught by the politicians." Carlyle was, indeed, one of James's great disappointments in life, and he would seem never to have gotten over being drawn to what he thought would be an exciting fire only to discover that he had answered a false alarm.

A good deal of his energy was expended in correspondence, for he was as great a writer of letters as either of his famous sons. He cast many of his books in the epistolary form and much of his later magazine work was in that form also. Anything from a social note to a learned theological discourse was sure to be elevated and distinguished by his peculiarly living style. His correspondents were family and personal friends on the one hand, and persons entirely unknown to him who wrote for advice and counsel on their personal problems. Among the latter one was the mother of James Gibbons Huneker. Perhaps she was the one he described to E. L. Godkin as "a devil of a woman."

The qualities of vigor and surprise which characterized his writing * will hardly have escaped the reader, nor will his penchant for the grotesque. Indeed, his delight in the downright, in which he is to be compared to Whitman and Emerson, or what have come to be called the Anglo-Saxon elements in our English, occasionally ran away with him and he was forced to draw back. He had communicated something to *The Evening Post,* and wrote to ask Parke Godwin to substitute a milder word for one he had originally selected. His note illustrates his attitude in the matter:

Please run your eye, or rather your nose, along my Ms. till it comes to the word 'stink' and substitute for it the less honest and pictorial word 'scourge' . . . It is a good Anglo Saxon word much disliked by those to whom the thing signified by it is dear; but I presume it is better to conciliate the weaklings when nothing is to be got by affronting them. . .

Evidently he had designated some orthodoxy as a 'stink.'

The last words of his letter illustrate one of his peculiarities: he delighted in the controversial manner, even to the

---

* May one say that the style of Henry James, Jr., was an elaboration of his father's and that of William a simplification?

point of arrogance and effrontery. He rationalized it many
times and the gist of what he had to say might serve as a
model for constitutionally timid writers. He felt that if one
were too mild and did not emphasize and underline the differences between oneself and one's enemies, the indolent and
unobserving readers would never become conscious of the
true import of what one was saying. In his own effort to
keep his opposition to orthodoxy to the fore in anything he
wrote, he hesitated not a moment to use any device that came
to hand. He resorted to 'stink' and similarly outlawed
words and he deliberately cultivated the amusing but disconcerting habit of overstatement.

Examples of his grotesque humors abound. Writing to
a friend he spoke of God as a duck:

If the Deity were an immense Duck capable only of emitting an
eternal quack we of course should all have been born webfooted,
each as infallible in his way as the Pope, nor ever have been at
the expense and bother of swimming-schools.

Again, in writing of Ritualism and Revivalism as the two
ugly heads of the professional religion which was devastating
the world, he went on to say:

I must say, we are not greatly devastated here in Boston —
though occasionally vexed — by either head of the beast; on the
contrary, it is amusing enough to observe how afraid the great
beast himself is of being pecked to pieces on our streets by a little
indigenous bantam-cock which calls itself Radicalism, and which
struts, and crows, and scratches gravel in a manner so bumptious
and peremptory, that I defy any ordinary barnyard chanticleer to
imitate it.

But by far the most famous of his grotesqueries was that in
which he insisted that to any reasonable man a crowded
horse-car was the nearest possible approach to heaven on
earth:

I can hardly flatter myself that the frankly chaotic or a-cosmical
aspect of our ordinary street-car has altogether escaped your en-

lightened notice in your visits to the city; and it will perhaps surprise you therefore, to learn that I nevertheless continually witness so much mutual forbearance on the part of its *habitués;* so much spotless acquiescence under the rudest personal jostlings and inconvenience; such a cheerful renunciation of one's strict right; such an amused deference, oftentimes, to one's invasive neighbors; in short, and as a general thing, such a heavenly self-shrinkage in order that "the neighbor" handsome or unhandsome, wholesome or unwholesome, may sit or stand at ease; that I not seldom find myself inwardly exclaiming with the patriarch: *How dreadful is this place ! It is none other than the house of God, and the gate of heaven.* Undeniably on its material or sensuous side the vehicle has no claim to designation as a Bethel; but at such times on its spiritual or supersensuous side it seems to my devout sense far more alert with the holy Ghost, far more radiant and palpitating with the infinite comity and loveliness, than any of the most gorgeous and brutal ecclesiastical fane that ever gloomed and stained the light of heaven.

On the other hand, he could write with charming quietness of humor as is excellently shown in the following letter to Parke Godwin who had asked him for a photograph:

I obey your request . . . with high gratification, and send you no less than three photographs, reflecting my various styles of beauty. The standing one will shew you the gay and elegant manner, the air of perfect gentlemanliness, which has given me such distinction before the world. The sitting one will reveal to you the tender and pensive melancholy which comes over my soul in solitude, when thinking of the saddening things I have left behind me in' the world. Some partial friends imagine themselves recalled by this aspect to the days of saints and martyrs. The reclining figure presents me in my domestic aspect, in the bosom of that home of which I am &c, and surrounded by those happy faces of which I am &c &c. You cannot fail to be touched by this fidelity of art to nature and truth; the first portraying my secular graces; the second my profoundly religious nature (undimmed by the very bad companionship I underwent in New York); the third my inexhaustible household worth. I suppose there are few women (unmarried) who could look at such a series of faces without an instinctive hope that their lot might be prefigured there. And I presume there are few married ones (poor things) who could help under the same circumstances saying — Ah ! Why *was* my lot so different !

In 1858 James made a year's visit to America, stopping at Newport, returned to Europe for the winter of 1859–60 in Geneva, and then once more settled at Newport to stay for four years.   His boys were growing up.   William was placed under William Morris Hunt to study painting, Henry was sent to William Leverett's school, and the younger boys were placed in Frank Sanborn's experimental school in Concord. William and Henry made many friends in Newport, some of them life-long.   It was there that they came to know Thomas Perry, Steele Mackaye and John La Farge, the latter a bit older than the rest.   James found the society congenial, especially since it included a favorite relative, his brother-in-law, Edmund Tweedy.

Newport, in the days just before the Civil War, was an oasis for the tiny American leisure class in the great politico-economic American desert.   Here, if anywhere in the country, could those few recalcitrant souls who refused to be gobbled up in business or the professions, gather with some hope of finding sympathetic companionship.   Most of them had lived in Europe and were possessed of some part of that very general thing called culture.   It was but natural that Henry James should gravitate to such a place for residence, now that he had permanently resigned all active participation in the intellectual life of his time as it expressed itself in journalism.   Other than the books over which he continued to labor, and occasional lectures in private houses for the benefit of friends, he was content to leave to others the toil and moil of life on the firing line.   He gently chaffed Parke Godwin for becoming involved in daily journalism and attributed his fine qualities to his association with him in the old *Harbinger* days.

Though he was never again to go to Europe, he constantly kept himself in an unsettled state by planning such a venture.   The question vexed him, for he had no intellectual doubts about the superiority of America.   When he was

asked to deliver the Fourth of July oration in 1861, he tried
to state his conclusions. While they were not spread-
eaglish, they were in effect intensely patriotic. What he
missed in Europe was the feeling that man as man was held
in honor. Europeans had been trained for centuries to give
their regard to persons, whose distinction was derived from
adventitious circumstances like birth. In Europe the most
advanced radicalism was Protestantism in religion and constitutional liberty in politics. America had inherited both
of these boons in the fullest measure, but whereas in Europe
they were the "topmost waves of . . . progress, the bound
beyond which European thought cannot legitimately
go . . ." in America they are mere points of departure.
From them the Americans are destined to take the next steps
of making religion solely an affair of individual conscience
and in politics of asserting the "inalienable sanctity and freedom of the subject as against the state. . ." His bias was for
democracy of the body and spirit and for liberty.

. . . I venture to say that no average American resides a year in
England without getting a sense so acute and stifling of its hideous class-distinctions, and of consequent awkwardness and *brus-
querie* of its upper classes, and the consequent abject snobbery or
inbred servility of its lower classes, as makes the manners of
Choctaws and Potawatamies sweet and christian, and gives to a
log-cabin in Oregon the charm of comparative dignity and peace.

But the pull of Europe was constantly at work upon him!
And the unrest he felt was transmitted to his distinguished
sons, so that in one Europe triumphed and in the other
America!

He was continually running up to Boston. In conversation with Emerson he was as pessimistic as his constitutional
and philosophic optimism would let him be. He thought
that the heavenly powers had lost interest in talent and that
the terrible emphasis on material activities was proof of it.
Louis Napoleon seemed to him to be ruling all of Europe

by fear. He could let loose the dogs of revolution in any
country if the rulers were so unfortunate as to offend him !
But in his opinion, in the spiritual world governing was the
very lowest function, and it was a pretty mean task in the
natural. Much more important was the enunciation of religious truths, one may suppose ! It was at Emerson's that
he had his epic encounter with Aunt Mary Moody Emerson,
upset Alcott and aroused the disapproval of Thoreau. It
must have been a memorable evening !

James had known both Thoreau and Alcott since the New
York times. Emerson had sent them both to him. Thoreau was, in 1843, when he made James's acquaintance, tutor-
ing in William Emerson's household on Staten Island and
Alcott was bustling about giving "conversations." James
found Alcott a tolerable irritation. He said that in Alcott
"the moral sense was wholly dead and the aesthetic sense had
never yet been born." On one occasion when he was entertaining him in New York, he found that he could not
accompany his guest to Brooklyn to hear him talk. Alcott
therefore proposed to review his principal points with his
host before leaving. They fell into an argument about the
premises on which Alcott based his discourse. Alcott said
something about his Divine paternity as it related to himself.
"My dear sir," exclaimed James, "you have not found your
maternity yet. You are an egg half hatched. The shells are
yet sticking about your head." To which Alcott indignantly
returned, "Mr. James, you are *damaged goods* and will come
up *damaged goods in eternity.*"

On the momentous night when Mary Moody Emerson got
after Henry James, Alcott was discoursing at random about
something or other, when James completely boggled him
with a question. Whereupon James launched into a long
and exceedingly paradoxical monologue on the pernicious-
ness of moralism. This was too much for Aunt Mary who
arose from her chair, took James by the shoulders and gave

him a good shaking, and rebuked him in no uncertain terms !
Thoreau got at the practical import of all this excitement
in his note on the occasion:

I met Henry James the other night at Emersons's, at an Alcottian
conversation, at which, however, Alcott did not talk much, being
disturbed by James's opposition. The latter is a hearty man
enough, with whom you can differ very satisfactorily, both on
account of his doctrines and his good temper. He utters *quasi*-
philanthropic dogmas in a metaphysic dress; but they are, for all
practical purposes, very crude. He charges society with all the
crime committed, and praises the criminal for committing it.
But I think that all the remedies he suggests out of his head —
for he goes no farther, hearty as he is — would leave us about
where we are now. For, of course, it is not by a gift of turkeys
on Thanksgiving Day that he proposes to convert the criminal,
but by a true sympathy with each one, — with him, among the
rest, who lyingly tells the world from the gallows that he has
never been treated kindly by a single mortal since he was born.
But it is not so easy a thing to sympathize with another, though
you may have the best disposition to do it. There is Dobson
over the hill. Have not you and I and all the world been trying
to sympathize with him since he was born (as doubtless he with
us), and yet we have got no further than to send him to the
House of Correction once at least; and he, on the other hand,
has sent us to another place several times. This is the real state
of things as I understand it, at least so far as James's remedies.
We are now, alas ! exercising what charity we actually have, and
new laws would not give us any more. But perchance, we might
make some improvements in the House of Correction. You and
I are Dobson; what will James do for us ?

Thoreau here put his finger on the weakness all James's contemporaries, who troubled themselves to think of him at all,
emphasized. He might be, as Emerson said, a "sub-soil
plower," but he was not good at reorganizing the police
force !

Anyhow he set the company by the ears and that delighted
him. He made a practice of stirring up arguments at the
dinner table in his own home. With his habit of exaggeration and salty humor, he was usually able to get a "rise" out
of his boys and his guests. He would talk with his boys as

an equal on morals (both of his sons became moralists like himself) and taste and literature, and the argument frequently became so heated that they would leave the table and vociferate from the floor. They would freely oppose their father and solemnly pray that for maintaining such an absurd point of view he might always have lumps in his mashed potatoes.

At this time, too, he began to attend the dinners of the Saturday Club. His first experience was on January 26, 1861, when he was an invited guest along with Ellery Channing. Emerson was there and so were Hawthorne and Longfellow. James inspected his dinner-companions with close attention and reported his findings to Emerson:

Hawthorne isn't a handsome man, nor an engaging one personally. He has the look all the time, to one who doesn't know him, of a rogue who suddenly finds himself in a company of detectives. But in spite of his rusticity, I felt a sympathy for him amounting to anguish, and couldn't take my eyes off him all the dinner, nor my rapt attention.

And the good inoffensive, comforting *Longfellow*, he seemed much nearer the human being than any one at that end of the table — much nearer.

Ellery Channing . . . seemed so humane and good — sweet as sunshine, and fragrant as pine woods. He is more sophisticated than the others, of course, but still he was kin. . .

On the whole, the Club would seem to have provided fairly good company. In 1863 he was elected a member of it, the only one taken in that year.

The Civil War exhilarated him as an upburst of spiritual energy. He entertained a deep confidence in Lincoln and resented Charles Sumner's disparaging criticisms to which he listened in disapproving silence one evening in Longfellow's study. "Before the rebellion broke out," he wrote,

almost every name of honor in our politics, our literature, and even our science, cringed meekly to the slaveholder's lash, and

kissed the feet of his insolent and vulgar rapacity.   There was
to be sure a Fremont, who was a candidate for popular favor;
there were a Sumner and Seward in the Senate; a Wilson, a
Giddings, and others in the House; none of whom had bowed
the knee to Baal.   But these men were never in office, because
absolutely no man had any chance of political distinction who
did not abjectly truckle to Slavery.   Literature boasted the generous warmth of Lowell and Whittier, and lent the noble Emerson and well-beloved Curtis to the sacred cause.   Greeley and
Bryant in the secular press won immortal laurels by their fervid
constancy to truth, while Bacon and Leavitt and Thompson performed the same thankless service in the religious press.   But as
a general thing, politics, literature, and the press were utterly
subsidized, and no sign of a better day, but only of an everlasting
night, met the eye until the assault upon Fort Sumter.   What an
enormous — what a Divine change — has flashed upon the country since that auspicious hour !   What a stifling air had we
breathed before !   What a bellying volume our lungs now unreef
themselves to catch every breath of God's awakening gale !   And
as yet two years have barely passed !

His two younger sons went to the war as soldiers and he must
have suffered considerable personal anxiety.   Garth Wilkinson and Robertson were both wounded, but recovered,
though they would seem to have been adversely affected by
their experiences.   At least it is a curious thing that the
two sons who did *not* go to the war (because of poor health)
were the very ones who became distinguished.

In the midst of the war Henry James put out a new book,
Substance and Shadow (1863) another attempt to say exactly
what he meant.   According to Charles Peirce the book contained sublime insight.   But in the family James's difficulties had become a gentle private joke.   William made a little
picture to be printed on the title page of the new book.   It
represented a man flogging a dead horse.

3. THE UNREGARDED SAGE

IN 1864 Henry James moved to Boston to be near his boys
who were studying at Harvard.   William had entered the
Lawrence Scientific School in 1861, after finding art not to

be his *forte,* while Henry was making an abortive experiment with law.   James intended to stay in Boston but a year and then go once more to Europe, but he lived in Boston — and Cambridge — for the rest of his life.

The Boston in which he found himself was a Boston rapidly drifting out of a Golden Age into a Silver Age. With the Golden Age he had much in common, but with the Silver, very little indeed.   Yet he was sufficiently the outsider intellectually and socially to look at the whole Massachusetts situation with rather dispassionate eyes.   His acceptances and rejections were definitely idiosyncratic and so far as he pronounced judgment upon the leading figures, they were critical and unsuperstitious.   Flattery was no part of his stock-in-trade.   William Dean Howells tells of meeting him on the street and hearing him describe ". . . a group of Bostonians from whom he had just parted and whose reciprocal pleasure of themselves he presented in the image of 'simmering in their own fat and putting a nice brown on each other.' "

The ideals of the Golden Age of New England were sufficiently those of Henry James for him to have a fellow-feeling for the finer figures of the time: "To humanize (the) emerging society, to awaken it to a nobler faith in human destiny, to further the cause of social justice, to create a democracy of the spirit — this was the deeper romantic purpose, however vaguely comprehended, that was fermenting in the New England renaissance. . ."   Certainly these three major ideals have been amply illustrated from James's early writings and if, in his later life, he tended to concentrate upon the *religious* portion of his message, he never repudiated any of the rest.   He was, indeed, to continue loyal to the great inspirations of the thirties and forties long after the other voices were either silenced by death, fatigue or indifference.   Margaret Fuller (with whom James had a casual acquaintance) had been drowned off Fire Island in 1850. (James got the news of the catastrophe from Washington

Irving, whom he met the morning after on a Hudson River steamboat.) Theodore Parker died in Europe, whither he had gone in search of health, in 1860. Thoreau died in 1862 and Hawthorne in 1864. Emerson was far from being the man after the Civil War he had been before that event and Walt Whitman was broken by the War also.

These great figures were not being replaced by others of equivalent importance. Lowell retreated from reform to browsings among old books and the composition of learned but disjointed essays about them and then emerged once more to enter diplomacy and become a *bon viveur*. His logical successor turned out to be the egregious Thomas Wentworth Higginson. Poor old Alcott was succeeded by his daughter Louisa, the "Conversations" and "Orphic Sayings" by *Little Women*! William Dean Howells appeared from Ohio to take on a protective coloration of New Englandism and Thomas Bailey Aldrich got himself Boston-plated. Sarah Orne Jewett gave the world her charming and delicate, but exceedingly feminine, pictures of the Yankee in decay. Mark Twain came roaring out of the West, a man writing, and getting little encouragement for his manhood. Bret Harte rode high on the sky-rocket of his sketches of California life. It was definitely a decline from the prophetic age, especially if one takes the prophetic as the essential essence of literature as James did. He had survived his own times and lived to see his companions drop away and the very social forces he had optimistically hoped could be brought under restraint by idealistic socialism, more definitely in control of America's destiny than ever. He made the best of it. He entered the circle of Charles Eliot Norton, who was to serve as mortician to so many men of James's generation — and who was to be obstetrician to the talent of his son Henry!

Nor did he ever despair. He wrote the fullest expositions of his ideas, and the clearest, during the late sixties and the seventies, and even in the early eighties when his

strength was all but gone he was at work upon a new version
of the old story. Emily Dickinson was *privately* recording
her notes on her commerce with God during these blowsy
years. Henry James was diligently placing *his* notes before
an unregarding public. He engaged, as he said with his
remarkable humorous detachment, in "preternatural activity, lest the world fail of salvation. . ."

He was a fine old man. That liveliness which was characteristic of him from earliest youth never deserted him.
He actively participated in the lives of his sons. He made
friends with William's friends — with Chauncey Wright and
Charles Peirce — and he read the books of the men Henry
was seeing in Europe. He took pleasure in Turgenev's
novels. William Dean Howells who got to know him early
in the final period, described him thus: "his whitebearded
face, with a kindly intensity which at first glance seemed
fierce, the mouth humorously shaping the mustache, the
eyes vague behind the glasses; his sensitive hand gripping
the stick on which he rested his weight to ease it from the
artificial limb he wore." His vivid, humorous talk made
him a delightful companion to all those who could bear the
surprise of his striking and somewhat devastating critical
adjectives and adverbs, which he brought out deliberately
and plumped down before his startled audience. He exploited paradox and exaggeration to the confusion of the
conventional. Analysis was his second nature. He never
seemed to exhaust his anecdotes and his mercurial temperament gave them a vigor and point that made them striking
works of art. Yet he did not care for formal society; and
liked best to talk to his friends when they assembled by
chance. In spite of his sociability and his vigorous humor,
his natural drive was toward contemplation. Even had he
not been hampered by his wooden leg, he would not have
been a man of action. "The bent of my nature," he wrote,
"is towards affection and thought rather than action. I love
the fireside rather than the forum. I can give ecstatic hours

to worship or meditation but moments spent in original deed, such as putting a button upon my coat or cleansing my garden-walk of weeds, weigh very heavily upon my shoulders."

We are doing no violence to the tenor of his experience then, when we concentrate our attention on his books.* Where his treasure was there was his heart also.

Swedenborg remained the great inspiration. If Swedenborg was not, as Emerson said of Alcott and the Platonic world, a native of Heaven and Hell, to Henry James he was the Marco Polo at any rate. In 1869 he brought out a book entitled *The Secret of Swedenborg*, but as Howells remarked, "he kept it." Nevertheless he did succeed, in that book and elsewhere, in making it clear enough how he regarded Swedenborg and that is of the very first interest.

Swedenborg, he wrote, "is no blear-eyed Rip Van Winkle dug up out of the drowsy past to affront the lively present, but a man of the freshest sympathies, and principles that contemplate only the broadest or most impersonal human issues. In a word, he is an unaffectedly genial, wise, and good man, all the higher parts of whose mind are bathed in the peace and light of heaven, and who aspires to no manner of leadership among men, because the access of an interior life has weaned him from that restless bondage." To James, he was not a reasoner or an original thinker, but a reporter and observer of facts of the spiritual realm. He attributed no more dogmatic authority to him than he would to Socrates

* James's books of this period were: *Substance and Shadow* (1863), *The Secret Swedenborg* (1869), *Society the Redeemed Form of Man* (1879). The posthumous volume, *The Literary Remains of Henry James* (1885) gathers up most of the manuscript he left behind him. Now these volumes are in themselves repetitive, like all of James's books. Moreover they are elaborations and restatements of what he had already said in his earlier works. In this sketch, therefore, I have not rehearsed at this point what has already been set out before. The reader is warned, however, that what is now about to be summarized is merely the new matter this group of books contains and that *to be understood it must imaginatively be embedded* in the general setting provided by the earlier discussion of James's position. I have also followed the same plan here as earlier of treating the group of books as a unit and freely borrowing back and forth in an effort to appropriate the best statements of his meaning as I understand it.

or John Stuart Mill. "Swedenborg," he said, "gives me a great deal of information about spiritual things which I am very glad to get; and I accordingly feel the same qualified esteem, in kind if not degree, for him, that I do for Humboldt, or Fourier, or any other veracious man of science, whose labors, in any sphere of the mind, go to promote the race's progress." Above all, he should not be taken authoritatively, but if properly read he transvaluates all one's values. Here, unquestionably, we are at the center of the secret of how it came about that Henry James of all the men of his generation most thoroughly transvaluated the reigning values.

He described Swedenborg's world in these terms:

It is a world whose deepest night is our present intellectual day, whose remotest west is our kindling east, whose frostiest winter is our most blooming summer, the obvious solution of the enigma being, that our current intellectual life proceeds upon the acknowledgment of nature as a fixed achievement of the divine power, while these books represent it as an altogether fluid and obedient *medium* of such power. Our infallible doctors make nature a divine terminus, whereas Swedenborg makes it at most a starting-point of the creative energy. Our old intellect is fashioned upon a conception of nature, which reports her organizing a real or essential discrepancy between creator and creature. The new intellect beholds in nature on the contrary a real or essential marriage of the divine and human, and admits only a contingent or logical divorce. In short, while the old world regards nature as the realm exclusively of finite or created existence, and hence at best of fossilized or inactive divinity, the world to come, of which we catch in Swedenborg's books the tenderest vernal breath as it were, is built upon the recognition of the spiritual only in the natural, of the divine only in the human; and hence exhibits the creature instinct and alive with creative personality.

Now in spite of the fact that this tremendous revolution is accomplished in Swedenborg's books, James felt that he was decidedly deficient in literary appeal and indeed rather resented the fact. ". . . Swedenborg's books, utterly priceless as they are to me considered as vehicles of refined celestial and spiritual information, yet practically lack *atmos-*

phere to my appreciation; are destitute of that exquisitely divine and exhilarating *natural* aroma which all discourse relating to these high themes ought in this day to leave behind it.   Thus it is, that whether I read of heaven and its orderly peaceful vicissitudes, or of hell and its insane delights, and feel the whilst my moral sense amply satisfied, I must say that to my aesthetic sense, which is the organ of the spontaneous or divine-natural life in me, the result is very much the same in either case, being always very dull and prosaic, with the poetic element very nearly eliminated." But if Swedenborg's writings cannot be compared to "the enamelled offspring of Mr. Tennyson's muse, or the ground-and-lofty-tumbling of an accomplished literary acrobat like Macaulay" they have higher merits and properly viewed his books have transcendent merits:

Such sincere books it seems to me were never before written.   He [Swedenborg] grasped with clear intellectual vision the seminal principles of things, and hence is never tempted to that dreary Socratic ratiocination about their shifting superficial appearance, which give great talkers a repute for knowledge.   Full however as his books are on this account of the profoundest philosophic interest, they naturally contribute almost nothing to one's scientific advantage.   You need never go to them for any *direct* help upon existing social and scientific problems.   You might as well go to a waving wheat-field to demand a loaf of bread.   Just as in the latter case before getting one's loaf, one would be obliged to harvest his wheat and convert it into flour, and then convert the flour itself into dough, and afterwards allow the dough to ferment before putting it in the oven and baking his bread; so in the former case before getting the slightest scientific air from Swendenborg, he will be obliged first of all intellectually to harvest his spiritual principles, and then gradually bring them down through the hopper of his imperious daily needs, and under the guidance of the great truth of human equality and fellowship, into social and personal applications wholly unforseen I doubt not and perhaps undreamt of by the author himself.

Whether or not this is the orthodox way to treat Swedenborg's writings it certainly seems to be a complete description of how Henry James treated them.

Furthermore, it must be kept in mind that James had an

active intellectual life before he came to Swedenborg and that Swedenborg, as we have seen, ratified and confirmed certain ideas that he had already evolved in his heart without being able to confirm them with his head. Above all else, Swedenborg confirmed his intuition that the source of all evil was in the selfhood — in self-righteousness. When he came to reckon up Swedenborg's contributions, he put down the identification of the evil principle with selfhood as the main philosophic obligation owed to him. Furthermore, what James put into his briefest summary of Swedenborg's meaning is in essence the gist of what he himself had to say in his many books: Swedenborg's "ontologic doctrine is summed up in the literal veracity of CREATION, meaning by that term the truth of God's NATURAL HUMANITY, of the most living and actual unition of the divine and human natures, avouching itself within the compass of man's historic consciousness, and generating there the stupendous harmonies of a spontaneous human society, fellowship, or brotherhood."

IN HIS description of Swedenborg's world we found James writing that "our current intellectual life proceeds upon the acknowledgment of nature as a fixed achievement of divine power, while these books represent it as an altogether fluid and obedient *medium* of such power." This statement leads us directly to the heart of the most interesting part of James's later writings and a part which should be kept firmly in mind in reading the account of the intellectual life of his son William. As the power and force of speculative romanticism declined and science began once more to assert itself, it put James on the defensive. His ideas, like those of Emerson, were non-scientific without being especially anti-scientific. His problem was to define the place of science in his intellectual scheme and to appropriate all that was of utility in it without giving an inch in his maintenance of his own position.

James preserved his equanimity in the face of advancing knowledge. The basis of his intellectual method was the mystical interpretation of the Scriptures whereby he arrived at the true meaning of the Christian revelation and of the significance of the great exemplar of Divine-Natural humanity, Jesus Christ. When the Biblical critics began to make a definite impression upon the religious world, he found himself unable to take them seriously, because (and this was his avenue of escape) they were concerned only with the letter of the Scriptures and not with its spirit.

I confess for my part I should as soon think of spitting upon my mother's grave, or offering any other offence to her stainless memory, as of questioning any of the Gospel facts. And this, not because I regard them as literally and absolutely true — for the whole realm of fact is as far beneath that of truth, as earth is beneath heaven — but simply because they furnish the indispensable WORD, or master-key, to our interpretation of God's majestic revelation of Himself in human nature . . . which conviction keeps me blessedly indifferent to, and utterly unvexed by, the cheap and frivolous scepticism with which so many of our learned modern pundits assail them. I have not the least reverence nor even respect for the facts in question, save as basing or ultimating this grand creative or spiritual truth; and while the truth stands to my apprehension, I shall be serenely obdurate to the learned reasonings of any of my contemporaries in regard to the facts, whether *pro* or *con*.

It is perfectly plain from this statement, and the fact has been emphasized again and again before, that James's religion was entirely and completely a supernatural religion. It was implicated in the natural only in man, and in man only in his psychology. It was therefore, untouchable by the conclusions of scientists whose studies were exclusively concerned with Nature. What they arrived at was the testimony of the senses with regard to the external world which was, to James, but a mere illusion with only correspondential relation to the supernatural world of reality.

He was concerned to combat, however, the pretentions of the scientists to *finality* of knowledge. Their finalities were the merest gossip to him. They had, nevertheless, to be taught their place. To that task he addressed himself.

He divided intellectual life into three categories: Religion, Science and Philosophy and entered himself under the rubric Philosophy. As we have seen he regarded what was called Religion by his contemporaries as a rather stinking mess of pottage, in which spiritual values had been brought low and extinguished by the naturalistic tendencies of the orthodox theologians. Furthermore, he condemned it for cultivating the sense of selfhood in man and thus exasperating his hellish, or moralistic, tendencies. By identifying "moralism" with the Godly life the orthodox were guilty of a heinous crime against the spiritual welfare of mankind, for "moralism" was not the true spiritual welfare of mankind but only the basis of it, and the recognition of its adventitious relation to true Godliness was the beginning of wisdom. From it one proceeded upward to Godliness by cultivating the constant influx of the Divine Love and Wisdom. Anything that contributed to the wrecking of the preposterous Religion of the orthodox was sure of James's applause.

Looking at its activities from this angle he applauded Science:

(The) whole business (of science) on earth, or in the evolution of the human mind, may be thus formulated: the gradual exhaustion or draining off of religion as a doctrine of Nature, in order to its permanent resuscitation by Philosophy as a life of Man. In other words the church as it has hitherto existed in purely typical or isolated institutional form, will disappear in the progress of our scientific culture, only to reappear as a perfect human society or fellowship, animated and held together by no doctrinal *consensus* of any sort on the part of its members, but by their cordial unforced and filial acknowledgement of the Divine Name as alone adequate to explain the stupendous marvel and mystery of Life.

By wrecking naturalistic religion it was, then, contributing to the triumph of supernaturalistic religion, or the religion of Henry James. "Accordingly in so far as our recent bellicose science goes to discredit an historical or literal creation, I have no quarrel with it. For I see in it only the augury of a new faith, based upon a profounder acknowledgment of creation, as being no preposterous physical exploit of God accomplished in the realms of space and time, but a wholly spiritual operation of His power in the realms of human affection and thought."

On the other hand, his indictment of science is extremely severe. He wrote:

When science, disdaining the humble but honorable office of ministering to a new intellectual faith and a new spiritual life in man, assumes itself to constitute or even forecast such faith and life, she is no longer amiable nor respectable, and invites as it seems to me a just disclaimer on the part of the outraged common sense of mankind.

Why ?

Science admits no conclusion within her own sphere which is not *verifiable* by sense. And (Philosophy) in her sphere disowns and distrusts every conclusion not distinctly and persistently *falsified* by sense.

My intellect accordingly, if it should succumb to the limitations of science, or deliberately submit itself to the arbitrament of sense, would virtually renounce the whole of its characteristic life, which lies in a heartfelt surrender to infinite goodness and truth, and is compatible with no other or lesser instinct.

. . . if . . . science constitute the perfected form of the mind the full measure of its expansibility: I, for one at least, have no hesitation in saying that it would have been better for the race to have remained to this day in its cradle, hearkening to the inspiration of naiad and dryad, of sea-nymph and of faun, than to have come out of it only to find its endless spiritual capacities, its capacities of spontaneous action, hopelessly stranded upon these barren rocks of science, ruthlessly imprisoned in her lifeless laws or generalizations.

These passages need but the lightest underlining to bring to the reader's memory that this attitude toward science and religion is in essence romantic. The aspiration of the eighteenth century Deists was to assimilate supernatural truth to naturalistic truth. From the rational supernaturalism of John Locke to the materialistic atheism of Holbach, the religious evolution of the period was away from supernaturalism and toward naturalism. The true Deists came about in the middle of this contrast, between Locke and Holbach, adhering to the truths of what they called Natural Religion — or strictly speaking the moral principles which seemed to correlate with the scientific notions embodied in the Newtonian World Machine, plus a bow to God as embodying to the highest knowable degree of perfection of moral excellence to which all rational men aspired. Henry James, when he got a perspective on it, regarded his childhood religion as little better than Deism for it too was impregnated with the naturalistic bias and led logically to atheism. This is the identical indictment that John Henry, Cardinal Newman, drew against Protestantism and to escape it he retreated into Catholicism. James retreated into absolute, individualistic supernaturalism, sustained by Swedenborgianism. Both men were, however, but individuals in the larger romantic movement which, beginning with Kant, reacted against the eighteenth century rationalistic aspiration and tried to re-establish religion on the basis of emotion, or feeling. They relied upon those aspirations of man to sustain religion, which, however grounded, seemed avenues to truths that transcended sense. In this fashion they hoped to save religion from being gobbled up by naturalistic thought, or science and its philosophic rebound. They, too, were forced to "put science in its place." In this they were joined by another branch of the romantic reaction, the dogmatic supernaturalistic authoritarians of the Roman Catholic Church, like Joseph de Maistre. De Maistre wrote: "Science undoubtedly has its value, but it is necessary that it should be kept within bounds. . . It has been very aptly said that science resembles fire: confined to the hearths which are destined to receive it, it is man's most useful and powerful servant; left to the hazard of chance, it is a terrible scourge." This general attitude has been taken up by all sorts of romantics and traditionalists from that day to this, even unto the present moment and the American Humanists. Science, naturalism, for the two terms are equated, are the enemy. James was merely typical of his century in his attitude. Unfortunately by his example he fed the worst side of his son William's mind as we shall see.

In the meantime it is necessary to back-trail a bit and pick up Henry James's thoughts on Philosophy, which, it was remarked, he identified with his private religious opinions. "The realm of Philosophy," he wrote, "is invariably soul, or inward consciousness. . ." It was, indeed, precisely that realm wherein man, according to James, differentiated himself from Nature and identified himself with God. It was there that the Divine Love and Wisdom got its entry into the human personality and lifted it above the realm of sense. It was because all men alike, thieves, murderers, and adulterers as well as saints and martyrs, possessed this identification with God in common, that redemption would be *social* and not individual. With the suppression of selfhood, or the diabolical principle, the inflow of Divine Love and Wisdom would be unimpeded and the beneficent society, of which Fourieristic socialism was a forecast, would inevitably follow. And, to reverse the approach, such a society would reduce the necessity for the cultivation of those characteristics of selfhood which are encouraged by the materialistic emphasis of the society of the day. "Philosophy accordingly," he concluded:

stands ready when science has finished her critical and negative function, to assume the positive office to which the latter has proved herself plainly incompetent, that, namely of reconstructing religion or putting it on a permanent because living basis. Philosophy denies the absoluteness which science under the guidance of reason ascribes to personal existence, by resolving the personally good and personally evil man quite equally into a higher aesthetic unity, consummate fruit of the Divine operation in human nature: so vacating the only imaginable ground of a scientific religion.

With these notions in mind it is highly instructive to glance at James's evaluations of, or comments on, some of the leading men of science of his time. Ever since his contact with Joseph Henry as a schoolboy in Albany he would seem to have taken an interest in the science of the day. Occasionally in his books one will run across a reference to some work of science, either in English, French or German, that he had read and from which he drew a metaphor to illustrate his meaning. There is nothing extraordinary in the fact that he kept up with the writings of such men as Comte, Darwin, Spencer, Huxley, and Haeckle. To be sure he never undertook any direct criticism of these men, for while they stayed within their sphere as he defined it, he applauded their efforts. But when they attempted to intrude upon the preserves of Philosophy, he came down on them like a thousand of brick.

Typical of his reflections are those on Auguste Comte, *fondateur de la religion de l'humanité:*

M. Comte . . . whatever may have been his merits as a scientific observer, upon which I am utterly unskilled to pronounce, was ludicrously devoid of philosophic insight. He so persistently rubbed the nose of his intelligence in the mud of mere Existence, so wilfully restricted its complacent feet to paddling in the shallowest waters of Fact, that he became obdurately blind to all the higher problems of Life and Truth, and ended by running the stupendous edifice of human destiny into a thing of such abjectly culinary dimensions as would revolt even the imagination of a cook. It was the case of a serious-minded conceited hodman fancying himself an architect, and aspiring to construct a new Alhambra or St. Peter's.

It is distressingly obvious that James was philosophically incapable of ingesting the most distinctive doctrine of nineteenth century biology: evolution. Had he accepted the implications of it he would have had immediately to give up his belief in the reality of a connection between God and man, a reality upon which his whole philosophical structure hinged.   For if man's evolution is a purely and exclusively physical process, the idea of a supernatural intrusion into his constitution to distinguish him from the rest of the animal kingdom as well as from the minerals and the vegetables, is difficult to entertain.   Naturally James did not surrender his fort to the oncoming naturalists.   He reasserted in the face of their dogmas, *his* dogmas:

It is evident . . . that — *pace* Messrs. Darwin and Spencer — man's natural genesis is not at all physical, but on the contrary strictly metaphysical, involving as it does his transformation or development out of a selfish being into a social one.   For humanity is not a material fact discernible to the outward eye; it is a spiritual truth, discernible solely to the inward eye, an eye rendered clear by love.   It is a SOCIETY not a *herd* of men, and claims a distinctly qualitative not a quantitative unity.   On his animal side man is doubtless physical enough, his origin connecting him not only with the animal tribes, but with the vegetable and mineral kingdoms as well.   But when we speak of human *nature,* we speak of what logically belongs to man alone, and therefore disconnects him with all lower existence.

His reply to Huxley is along similar lines:

Professor Huxley is consciously no doubt a very independent man, and an uncommonly able writer; but it seems to me very odd, to say the least, that any one interested not in the pursuit of scientific knowledge primarily, but of philosophic truth, should be at all moved, and especially disconcerted, by his facts: for whether they be scientifically valid or not, they are properly irrelevant to philosophy.   Like Mr. Spencer, M. Taine, and all the other men who desire not only to make science the king, but also to invest it with the priesthood of the mind, Professor Huxley restricts his researches to the principle of *identity* in existence — that point in which all existence becomes essentially chaotic or substantially indistinguishable.   The philosopher, on the other hand, who sees science to be not the end but the means of the mind's ultimate enfranchisement, enlarges *his* researches to the principle of individuality in existence, or that comprehensive spiritual unity in which all existence becomes essentially cosmical, or formally differentiated *inter se.* Far be it from me to question Mr. Huxley's statistics, for I know nothing about them; I only question, nay I am heartily amused by, the extravagant intellectual conclusions he deduces from them. I have no doubt, on his own showing, that the initial fact in all organization is protoplasm. But at the same time I avow myself unable to conceive a fact of less vital significance to philosophy. *Philosophy cheerfully takes that and every similar fact of science for granted.* The initial fact in the edifice of St. Peter's at Rome was a quantity of stone and lime. This fact was assumed by the architect as necessarily included in the *form* of his edifice, about which form alone he was concerned. The identity of his edifice, or what it possessed of common substance with all other buildings, interested him very little; only its individuality, or what it should possess of differential form from all other buildings, was what exercised his imagination. To conceive of Michael Angelo concerning himself mainly with the rude protoplasm, or mere flesh and bones, of his building, is at once to reduce him from an architect to a mason. And, in like manner, to conceive the philosopher intent upon running man's immortal destiny, or spiritual form, into the abject slime out of which his body germinates, is to reduce him from a philosopher to a noddle.

That is superb and resounding rhetoric, but it is hardly very convincing argumentation, for all it amounts to is saying to Huxley that he fails to admit *as a fact,* James's supernaturalistic explanation of the constitution of the human personality.

Interesting as all this is, and illustrative as it is of the fact that James's fundamental ideas were few and firmly held, it is not so illuminating of his position as his criticisms of his contemporaries like Carlyle and Emerson. They, after all, were products of the same general intellectual atmosphere as he, and their intellectual methods were comparable to his. Friend of both, he differed from both. Through the years of his intellectual pilgrimage he retained his respect for Emerson, but he came to have a profound disrespect for Carlyle. He differed from both in spite of the fact that they all lived in the same intellectual climate. For while James fits into the broad general tradition of romanticism, and has pronounced relations to the German philosophers who contributed to the development of Carlyle's thought as well as to that of Emerson and the Transcendentalists, he differed from them sufficiently so that he could criticise not only the adventitious weaknesses of Carlyle and Emerson but also their fundamental principles. This is particularly obvious in his treatment of Carlyle. Moreover, Henry James was one of the very few intellectual associates of Emerson who was not an Emersonian. It gave him a singular independence of judgment.

Carlyle plagued him. James delivered private lectures about Carlyle at odd intervals during his Boston period. Longfellow records in his journal going with Howells to hear one of them in 1874. When Carlyle died in 1881, James poured the concentrated essence of his thoughts on him into an essay for *The Atlantic Monthly*. This essay is a striking example of James's independence and of his vigor of expression. The very opening paragraph is a bugle-blast calling the multitude to an execution. The man was dead, but nothing is sacred, least of all a pernicious moralist like Carlyle !

Thomas Carlyle is incontestably dead at last, by the acknowledgment of all newspapers. I had, however, the pleasure of an intimate intercourse with him when he was an infinitely deader man than he is now, or ever will be again, I am persuaded, in the remotest *saeculum saeculorum*. I undoubtedly felt myself at the time every whit as dead (spiritually) as he was; and, to tell the truth, I never found him averse to admit my right of insight in regard to myself. But I could never bring him, much as he continually inspired me so to do, to face the philosophic possibility of this proposition in regard to himself. On the contrary, he invariably snorted at the bare presentation of the theme, and fled away from it, with his free, resentful heels high in air, like a spirited horse alarmed at the apparition of a wheelbarrow.

Now the great weakness of Henry James as a critic is that he assaulted men for not *agreeing* with him. His criticism then, quickly resolves itself down to a statement of wherein he differed from his opponent on the one hand, and a state-

ment of what he conceives to be the truth on the other.
The worth of his criticism, as in this striking essay on Carlyle,
is the vigor with which he goes after a man who displeased
him deeply. He went after Carlyle, indeed, hammer and
tongs. Carlyle's admirers,

. . . at least his distant admirers, generally mistook the claim he
made upon attention. They were apt to regard him as eminently a man of thought; whereas his intellect, as it seemed to
me, except where his prejudices were involved, had not got beyond the stage of instinct. They insisted upon finding him a
philosopher; but he was only and consummately a man of genius.
They had the fatuity to deem him a great teacher; but he never
avouched himself to be anything else than a great critic.

. . . he was without that breadth of humanitary sympathy which
one likes to find in distinguished men; . . . he was deficient in
spiritual as opposed to moral force.

His own intellectual life consisted so much in bemoaning the
vices of his race, or drew such inspiration from despair, that he
could not help regarding a man with contempt the instant he
found him reconciled to the course of history. Pity was the
highest style of intercourse he allowed himself with his kind. He
compassioned all his friends in the measure of his affection for
them. "Poor John Sterling," he used always to say; "Poor John
Mill, poor Frederic Maurice, poor Neuberg, poor Arthur Helps,
poor little Browning, poor little Lewes," and so on; as if the
temple of his friendship were a hospital and all its intimates
scrofulous or paralytic.

Especially did Carlyle conceive that no one could be actively interested in the progress of the species without being intellectually off his balance. . .

A moral reformer like Louis Blanc or Robert Dale Owen, a political reformer like Mr. Cobden or Mr. Bright, or a dietetic
reformer like the late Mr. Greaves or our own Mr. Alcott, was
sure to provoke his most acrid intellectual antipathy.

Moral force was the deity of Carlyle's unscrupulous worship —
the force of unprinciples, irresponsible will; and he was ready to
glorify every historic vagabond, such as Danton or Mirabeau in
whom that quality reigned supreme.

It always appeared to me that Carlyle valued truth and good as a painter does his pigments, — not for what they are in themselves, but for the effects they lend themselves to in the sphere of productions. Indeed, he always exhibited a contempt, so characteristic as to be comical, for every one whose zeal for truth or good led him to question existing institutions with a view to any practical reform. He himself was wont to question established institutions and dogmas with the utmost license of scepticism, but he obviously meant nothing beyond the production of a certain literary surprise, or the enjoyment of his own aesthetic power. Nothing maddened him so much as to be mistaken for a reformer, really intent upon the interests of God's righteousness upon the earth, which are the interests of universal justice.

He was indeed, as James wrote elsewhere, "mother Eve's own darling cantankerous Thomas, in short, the child of her dreariest, most melancholy old age; and he used to bury his worn dejected face in her penurious lap, in a way so determined as to shut out all sight of God's new and better creation." But after all, he had "a perfect right to be what he was, and no one had a keener appreciation of him in that real light than I have." Nevertheless . . "the remorseless bagpipes" . . . "puerile gabble. . ."

"It is profaning Emerson's chaste and reverent muse to associate it, even in thought, with the *ignis fatuus,* or imp of the bogs, that inspires Carlyle's grim and labored *facetiae,*" wrote James. Yet an accident of circumstance always seemed to bring them together in his mind. They were the two great intellectual friends of his career. To them he constantly returned in his writings when he sought to illustrate something from contemporary literature. His final judgment on Emerson was, like that on Carlyle, the distilled essence of all his thinking on the subject. It was also refined from a lecture he delivered off and on during his Boston years.

My recently deceased friend Mr. Emerson, for example, was all his days an arch traitor to our existing civilized regimen, inasmuch as he unconsciously managed to set aside its fundamental principle in doing without conscience, which was the entire secret of his very exceptional interest to men's speculation. He betrayed it to be sure without being at all aware of what he was doing; but this was really all that he distinctively did to my observation. His nature had always been so innocent, so unaffectedly innocent, that when in later life he began to cultivate a. club consciousness, and to sip a glass of wine or smoke a cigar, I felt very much outraged by it. I felt very much as if some renowned Boston belle had suddenly collapsed and undertaken to sell newspapers at a street corner. "Why Emerson, is this *you* doing such things?" I exclaimed. "What profanation! Do throw the unclean things behind your back!" But no; he was actually proud of his accomplishment! This came from his never knowing (intellectually) what he stood for in the evolution of New England life. He was lineally descended to begin with, from a half-score of comatose New England clergymen, in whose behalf probably the religious instinct had been used up. Of, what to their experience had been religion, became in that of their descendant *life*. The actual truth, at any rate, was that he never felt a movement of the life of conscience from the day of his birth till that of his death. I could never see any signs of such life in him. . . In short he was . . . fundamentally treacherous to civilization without being at all aware himself of the fact.

He was full of living inspiration to me whenever I saw him; and yet I could find in him no trivial sign of selfhood which I found in other men. He was like a vestal virgin, indeed, always in ministry upon the altar; but the vestal virgin had doubtless a prosaic side also, which related her to commonplace people. Now Emerson was so far *unlike* the virgin; he had no prosaic side relating him to ordinary people!

In his talk or private capacity he was one of the least remunerative men I ever encountered.

. . . his genius (was) strictly mystical or living, consisting altogether in his own vivid personal lustre or significance. Not what he (thought) has ever interpreted Mr. Emerson's genius to me, although his thought (was) always grand, majestic, manly; nor yet what he (said), although his speech (was) color and melody and fragrance itself to my senses; nor even in what he (did), although his action (was) always free, spontaneous, fearless: but all simply what he personally (stood) for or represent (ed) — what his peculiar genius symboliz (ed) — in the divine drama of the Incarnation.

I . . . diligently cultivated Mr. Emerson's acquaintance, as I . . . diligently cultivated Mr. Carlyle's. But Mr. Carlyle (was) an egregiously secular person, and you (went) to Chelsea, as you go to the theatre, for entertainment or diversion. Mr. Emerson, on the other hand, (was) an eminently sacred person, and you frequent (ed) Concord as you frequent (ed) the Cathedral — for self-recoil, self-examination, and reproof.

He (had) not the least vital apprehension of that fierce warfare of good and evil which has desolated so many profounder bosoms, which has maddened so many stouter brains.

Incontestably the main thing about him . . . was that he unconsciously brought you face to face with the infinite in humanity.

On the 29th of January, 1882, Mrs. James died. Her death seemed to kill the will to live in Henry James. He was working on a new book which he thought would at last make crystal clear what he had been trying to say for thirty-eight years, but even that could not keep his mind from dwelling upon his terrible loss. The life of routine and habit proved inadequate as a prop against his trouble. He sank rapidly into a state of indolence that alarmed his daughter. His sons gathered about him. Fortunately Henry, Jr., was home from England on a visit. But the end was not yet. He recovered sufficiently for Henry to return to England in May and go on his "little tour of France."

A few months in the country seemed to brace up the weary and sad old man considerably. In the fall William departed for the continent also on one of his periodical excursions. On October 1, 1882, James reported on his condition to his old friend Parke Godwin: "The making of the book has been my only refuge against the suffering involved in the loss of my wife. That was such an unexpected calamity that I was fairly prostrate under it. For four or five months I didn't see how I was going to live without her. I had actually run down to death's door when we moved to the country and I have been slowly pulling up ever since. But even now I am miserably feeble, and look forward to nothing with so much desire as to a reunion beyond the skies with my adorable wife." His writing then, kept him up —

but deceptively. He was seventy-one years old, and tired.

He labored over the new dress for his truth and reconsidered the strange case of his friend Emerson who had died in April. But his heart was not in his work and in the early winter he suffered a relapse. His sons were notified and hurried to gather about him. William was kept a bit in the dark about his father's exact condition, for it was thought unwise to break up his much needed vacation. He took leave of his father in one of the most beautiful of letters.* Henry arrived from England too late. His father died the day his boat docked in New York, December 18, 1882.

As James lay serenely dying, full of hope that he would be reunited with his beloved wife in Heaven, his daughter Alice asked him what he would prefer to have said at his funeral. He reflected for a while, and then said: "Tell him to say only this: 'Here lies a man, who has thought all his life that the ceremonies attending birth, marriage and death were all damned non-sense!'"

* Printed in *The Letters of William James*, Vol. I, pages 218–220.

BOOK III

WILLIAM JAMES

Philosophers are very severe towards other philosophers because they expect too much. Even under the most favourable circumstances no mortal can be asked to seize the truth in its wholeness or at its center. As the senses open to us only partial perspectives, taken from one point of view, and report the facts in symbols which, far from being adequate to the full nature of what surrounds us, resemble the coloured signals of danger or of free way which a railway engine-driver peers at in the night, so our speculation, which is a sort of panoramic sense, approaches things peripherally and expresses them humanly. But how doubly dyed in this subjectivity must our thoughts be when an orthodoxy dominant for ages has twisted the universe into the service of moral interests, and when even the heretics are entangled in a scepticism so partial and arbitrary that it substitutes psychology, the most derivative and dubious of sciences, for the direct intelligent reading of experience! But this strain of subjectivity is not in all respects an evil; it is a warm purple dye. When a way of thinking is deeply rooted in the soil, and embodies the instincts or even the characteristic errors of a people, it has a value quite independent of its truth; it constitutes a phase of human life and can powerfully affect the intellectual drama in which it figures.

— *George Santayana*

1. EDUCATION

ONE DAY early in the year 1842 Ralph Waldo Emerson encountered Henry James in the Astor House, New York City, and was immediately invited upstairs to his friend's room to view his first-born son. The boy had arrived on January 9th and was named William after his grandfather, then ten years dead. It was entirely fitting that this prophet-to-be of the open universe, this partisan of the unfixed, should have come into the world in such a traditionless place as an American hotel. Place of temporary rest for the freely circulating American population, it required a certain marked ability to find in the improvised satisfactions it offered what more settled people could only discover in the long established and the hallowed by time. Furthermore it was an urban hotel. Only as a mature man — the same was true of his brother Henry — did William James get into the country and then as a summer visitor. He knew nothing of the toil and trouble of the farmer's life, the alternation of the seasons to which the farmer adapts his very being, plowing, planting, harvesting, the immemorial round. William James's history for the first thirty years of his life was, indeed, a record of temporary abodes, of fleeting identifications with places of residence and study, all of them urban. From this he was translated into an academic environment. In 1872 he was to settle down to a life time of residence in the vicinity of Harvard College, there to develop a philosophy which one given to strained interpretations might see as a reflection of the impermanence of his early life.

As a boy William James exhibited all those traits of character which marked him as a man. To his brother Henry, one year younger, he figured as one marvelously gifted with the ability to make friendships, to extract the finest essence from the various situations into which they were thrown; he could even in his New York days tread without fear countries from which he kept his brother by warning him that "*I* play with boys who curse and swear!" It was the basis of a life-long devotion.

The distinctive mark of William's personality was activity, just as that of his brother's was passivity. Quick, nervous, athletic qualities of mind marked him all his life. Yet with all these qualities, he looked back upon his years of schooling with scorn, finding nothing in them which seemed to justify the labor expended. Such a summary judgment hardly does justice to the fact that in his schooling in various countries and cities — London, Paris, Boulogne-sur-Mer, Geneva, Bonn — he acquired a facility with languages that made it possible for him to devour psychological and philosophical literature with no pausing at linguistic boundaries. His progress to his life career was not as direct as that of his brother. His greater facility did not make it so obvious in what field he could best function. Though he was educated for nothing in particular, in harmony with his father's desire not to "make" his boys anything definite, he showed rather early certain tendencies which if encouraged might have given his life a greater directness than it actually did show. From his earliest days he was interested in drawing and one of Henry's earliest memories of him was of him "drawing and drawing, always drawing, especially under the lamplight of the Fourteenth Street back parlour. . ." This talent might very well have been cultivated into a career in art and, as we shall see, even without cultivation by his parents, it nearly carried him in that direction after all.

The fact that he assiduously recorded his observations of the world about him * is an early indication of the fact that there was nothing vague or indefinite about his contact with the external world. The characteristic note of his early and late life is swift, impressionistic observation. If in Paris he was given better instruction in drawing than had hitherto been his lot, a new turn was given to his imagination when, on his fifteenth birthday, his father presented him with a microscope. This is the earliest "scientific" note in his history, but in Geneva a year or two later he betrayed the drift of his mind by borrowing a copy of Sappey's *Anatomie* and puzzling over that subject by himself. He even gained permission to visit the Museum that he might examine an actual skeleton. Yet he was never so absorbed in himself and his own private interests that his social genius was al-

---

* Not only have we the evidence of his drawing to show him "observing" but this passage from *The Principles of Psychology* is also illustrative: "As a child, I slept in a nursery with a very loud-ticking clock, and remember my astonishment more than once, in listening for its tick, to find myself unable to catch it for what seemed a long space of time; then suddenly it would break into my consciousness with an almost startling loudness."

lowed to lapse. He joined the Swiss students' club *Société de Zoffingue,* and actively cultivated both its sociability and its beer from April to July, 1860.

Later in the same year he turned to art once more and determined, not without some parental opposition, a rare article in the family, to study in a professional way. With characteristic originality his father decided not to put him into a Parisian studio but to satisfy William's demand by placing him under William Morris Hunt in Newport. Hunt was then on the threshold of an impressive career. Lately a student of Couture in Paris, he was imbued with "classical" ideals of art. As a man he was unusually impressive and his legend pictures him as working, working, always hard at work until in middle life he was an old man and went to an early grave. It was under his tutelage that William explored the possibilities of a career in art, acutely aware fortunately that there is nothing quite so pitiful as a bad artist. He must shortly have decided that that fate was reserved for him. At any rate, in 1861 he threw up his work in the studio * and betook himself to the Lawrence Scientific School at Cambridge. The conflict between art and science was at last resolved. He was always to remain an artist by temperament, as such things are loosely denominated, a fact which numerous critics of his later work were to comment on with no apparent understanding of the deep-seated nature of the trend.

Even in the midst of his momentary absorption with art he did not lose touch with larger interests and found time to discover Schopenhauer and to discuss Renan with his brother and their friend Thomas Sergeant Perry. William's problem, very apparently, was to reconcile his versatility with the

* The reason, it seems obvious, is in this passage, written many years later as a footnote in *The Principles of Psychology:* "I am myself a good draughtsman, and have a very lively interest in pictures, statues, architecture and decoration, and a keen sensibility to artistic effect. But I am an extremely poor visualizer, and find myself often unable to reproduce in my mind's eye pictures which I have most carefully examined." His curious defect in visualization must certainly be related to his abandonment of painting.

necessity of learning some one thing thoroughly. All his life long he professed a horror of the specialist, ill-concealing his own incapacity for following a narrow and unbranching path. Though he was now dedicated to science he can hardly be said ever to have become a "scientist" as we today understand the term. The smell of the laboratory never got into his mind nor the mustiness of great learning into his talk.

In a letter written to his family late in the year 1861 he sketched out his plans for a career: "One year study chemistry, then spend one term at home, then one year with Wyman, then a medical education, then five or six years with Agassiz, then probably death, death, death with inflation and plethora of knowledge." This programme was never carried out, though an excellent start toward its realization was made. His one year of chemistry, taken under Charles W. Eliot, went off according to schedule. James was not greatly impressed by Eliot's scientific knowledge, though he did perceive his strength of character and tenacity of purpose. Under Eliot's instruction he ventured into chemical analysis, testing out on himself the effect of yeast upon the urine. Simultaneously he studied comparative anatomy with Professor Jeffries Wyman, finding his lectures "prosy perhaps a little and monotonous, but plain and packed full and well arranged (nourris)." The influence of this teacher was considerable. A man of wide and extraordinary learning, he was characterized, according to President Eliot, by "scientific zeal, disinterestedness and candor." His modesty was rather too well developed and it prevented him from making a mark in the world commensurate with his talents. But it did not prevent him from communicating to his pupils just those qualities in which he personally excelled. Nor could a man of such unique excellence fail to appeal to William James. He entertained, indeed, a "filial feeling" toward him. In 1863 James transferred himself from the Department of Chemistry after two years of labor and became a student in the Department of Comparative Anatomy and Physiology. He worked in the museum "at a table all alone surrounded by skeletons, crocodiles and the like, with the walls hung about with monsters and horrors enough to freeze the blood."

The following year he once more shifted the base of his operations and entered the Medical School, continuing with momentous interruptions until he took his degree. Once more he studied under Wyman and under Oliver Wendell Holmes and Charles Ed. Brown-Séquard. His own zeal and carefulness came out in the fact that he was the only member of his class to make drawings to record his microscopic work. His family was now located in Boston and his brother Henry's life was beginning to take firm direction, but his own was as yet without perceptible outlines. Although he did intend taking a medical degree, he had no plans for practising. The inspiring influence of Louis Agassiz had touched him early in his Harvard career (he had attended Agassiz's public lectures in Boston during 1861) and now when Agassiz began to plan his expedition to Brazil, William James immediately applied for a berth. Ever since he had read Captain Mayne Reid as a boy of ten he had admired field naturalists.

There had been no question of William's enlisting in the Federal Army for service in the Civil War. His precarious health (a constant factor throughout his career) made any such course impossible and indeed his Brazilian trip almost ended in summary disaster on just that ground. He was severely ill in Rio and considered returning home without further ado. As his spirits rose during convalescence he changed his mind and remained on. The expedition left New York on the 1st of April, 1865. As the vessel sailed past the Virginia coast the booming of the guns could be heard. But their mission was quite other than the bringing of death to their fellow citizens. Agassiz was bent on studying the distribution and classification of the fishes of the Amazon.

He had been dominated by a passionate interest in ichthyology from early manhood.

When he went to Brazil Agassiz was in the midst of his American career and at the height of his powers. Twenty-three years after his death, in 1873, William James could say: "He left a sort of popular myth — the Agassiz legend as one might say — behind him in the air about us. . . Since Benjamin Franklin, we had never had among us a person of more popularly impressive type."

Jean Louis Rodolphe Agassiz was born on May 28, 1807, at Mortier on the lake of Morat in what is now Switzerland, but which was then under the control of the King of Prussia. His father was an indigent clergyman and his mother came from a family of doctors and merchants. Agassiz was given the best schooling available at the cost of sacrifices on the part of his family. He pursued a swift and brilliant course through the College of Lausanne where he first obtained instruction in zoology (according to Cuvier's system), at Zurich where he chiefly studied medicine and at the Universities of Heidelberg and Munich, obtaining both his Ph.D. and M.D. from the last.

While an undergraduate he was introduced to a field which remained his special interest to the end of his life. One of his professors was Martius, who together with his associate Spix, had made a journey to Brazil in the year 1819. Spix died before he was able to complete his reports and Martius engaged Agassiz to do the necessary work on fishes. Ichthyology became thereafter Agassiz's dominant interest. It far outranked in importance any of his other preoccupations, significant though they were. Before he was twenty-one he issued his work on the Brazilian fishes and became a man of European reputation. After completing his work at Munich he went to Paris to study under Cuvier, specializing on fossil fishes. His skill was so great that Cuvier turned all of his material on the subject over to Agassiz, who thus became one of his direct heirs. Always short of money (he once said he had no time to make money), Agassiz soon ran himself deeply in debt and was on the point of giving up his work when he was rescued by Alexander von Humboldt, who became his life-long friend.

In 1832 Agassiz began his career as a teacher, but did not give up his research work. With highly inadequate resources at his command, he yet managed to bring his work on fossil fishes to completion and so solidified the reputation he had won as a student. He was always, moreover, looking for new worlds to conquer and beyond all else he desired to engage in collecting expeditions in unexplored territory. When a chance offered to go to America, he seized upon it with avidity.

When Agassiz landed in Boston in 1846 he was in possession of all of the major ideas to which he ever gave allegiance. He found himself in an intellectual environment quite different from that of Europe but one which allowed him unlimited freedom. He was able to bring his ideas and information to the attention of a vast popular audience which was thirsty for knowledge, but woefully ignorant of modern science.

He early perceived the nature of the difficulties under which the American scientists labored and put his finger on the major scientific superstition. He wrote of the ". . . new world, where the institutions tend to keep all on one level as part of the general mass . . . the strength of America lies in the prodigious number of individuals who think and work at the same time. It is a severe test of pretentious mediocrity, but I fear it may also efface originality." Again, he noted that "This deference toward England (unhappily to them Europe means almost exclusively England) is a curious fact in the life of the American people. They know us (i. e., the Continental scientists) but little, even after having made a tour in France, or Italy, or Germany. From England they receive their literature, and the scientific work of central Europe reaches them through English channels. . . Notwithstanding their kind of dependence upon England . . . I have formed a high opinion of their acquirements, since I have learned to know them better, and I think we should render a real service to them and to science, by freeing them from this tutelage, raising them in their own eyes, and drawing them also a little more toward ourselves." The scientists whose work so impressed him were such men as Professor Silliman of Yale, Professor Henry, later head of the Smithsonian Institution (and an early teacher of William James's father) and Asa Gray, the self-trained botanist, later a colleague at Harvard and chief proponent of Darwinism in America when it became an issue.

For it was to Harvard that Agassiz gravitated, the first of a long line of influential scientists Harvard brought to this country. Agassiz was fascinated with American problems in natural history and a fortunate conjunction of circumstances made his permanent residence here feasible. In February, 1848, the canton of Neuchâtel broke away from Prussia and joined the general confederation of Switzerland. This acted as a confirming factor in Agassiz's determination (already taken) to remain in America and take the chair of Natural History at the newly founded Lawrence Scientific School. He therefore discharged his obligations to the King of Prussia and started his lectures at Cambridge in April, 1848. He was guaranteed a minimum salary of fifteen hundred dollars and that was all he had. There was no equipment, no laboratory, no museum. It was his labors in this vineyard that made him the idol of the American people.

His scientific ideas were overlaid by religious presuppositions. It is indeed curious that Agassiz who insisted that "a physical fact is as sacred as a moral principle. Our own nature demands from us this double allegiance" and who wrote to a friend during the Darwinian controversy that "this sensational zeal reminds me of what I experienced as a young man in Germany, when the physio-philosophy of Oken had invaded every center of scientific activity; and yet what is there left of it? I trust to outlive this mania also . . ." should have failed to recognize wherein he departed from the facts and believed without evidence; believed so firmly in fact that no facts could shake his certainty. As a matter of fact Oken's "manias" did not entirely leave Agassiz's mind. He got a fundamental notion from him (and from Schelling). That was that the facts of natural history and the resulting system developed for their classification were the "translation into human language of the thoughts of the Creator." This idea is essentially Platonic in origin but had been early adopted by the Christian apologists as a justification for science and was frequently held by the Romantic philosophers. In America it received a statement at the hands of Emerson who taught that the laws of nature were discovered by the sudden establishment of a connection between the mind of man operating on nature with the mind of God which was behind nature. The position, at any rate, allowed Agassiz a wide theological latitude and indeed he had no interest in theology. Nor was he a Bibliolater. And finally the time element meant nothing to him, for otherwise his glacial theory would never have been propounded. What he was concerned with retaining was God as the intellectual director of the Cosmos, intimately concerned with the minutest details of its operation. The whole system of nature exhibited His wonderful wisdom and foresight and nothing was that God did not make — nothing could be discovered which did not cast further light upon the mental power of God. Agassiz's God, then, was a very clever fellow, but unlike Aristotle's prime mover, who, by the operation of a syllogism was reduced to thinking eternally about himself, Agassiz's God was allowed no time to think about anything other than the operation of an exceedingly complex Cosmos. Indeed most of his time was taken up with the earth, for Agassiz was remarkably geocentric in his thinking, taking no perceptible interest in astronomy.

It is easy to see why Agassiz opposed Darwin's theories.

Even though he went far along the path in his emphasis on homologies and analogies, a study which he pursued diligently into the field of embryology, doing much original work and proclaiming Von Baer one of the greatest of scientists, he could not hold to the immutability of species and their independence of physical forces, and make the necessary steps and become a Darwinian. Such a move would have meant, to an emotional mind like Agassiz's, banishing an ever present God to the remotest corner of Heaven and the repudiation of the teachings of his master, Cuvier. He was not equal to the strain. So he fought back, rationalizing his position by insisting that Darwinism was a mania that he would outlive.

Such was the man with whom William James was closely associated for upwards of a year. His response to the inspirational side of Agassiz was complete but he did not find himself drawn to Agassiz's specific scientific interest. "If there is anything I hate, it is collecting," he wrote home from Brazil. This did not prevent him from being deeply influenced by Agassiz in other ways. It seems altogether likely that it was Agassiz's example that confirmed him in the resolution to make his career in America. Here was a man of European training who was finding it possible to do fine work, the importance of which was instantly ratified by European critics, in the American environment, and who, moreover, deprecated any exaggerated deference to European opinion. On the other hand, it seems likely that Agassiz's reconciliation of science and religion and morals must have made an appeal to James. It confirmed, in a way, the importance of his father's preoccupations. Conscious as he was that "never did a man utter a greater amount of humbug," he did not take Agassiz's ideas *too* seriously. Therefore, he did not become entangled in the particular formulation that satisfied Agassiz. Agassiz's example must have had a part, however, in inspiring James to make a new reconciliation for himself. And, finally, James himself confessed that he drew from the contact one major habit of mind which stayed with him all of his life: *Respect for concrete Facts.*

When he returned from Brazil in March 1866 James served for a summer as an interne at Massachusetts General Hospital and in the fall returned to the Medical School. His parents were by then established in Cambridge where they were to remain for the rest of their lives. Everything seemed arranged for a happy issue of William's already sufficiently protracted preparation for life. It was, however, to last six more very difficult years.

Though ostensibly studying medicine he was obviously extending his range of interests. He reported himself as attending a philosophical lecture by Charles S. Peirce "which I could not understand a word of." He wrangled over philosophical problems with Oliver Wendell Holmes, Jr., and took it upon himself to recommend Marcus Aurelius to a depressed friend as something he had found helpful himself. It was to Holmes that he confessed that he was "blest if I'm at Materialist" who spends his time "in the laudable pursuit of degrading every (sensibly) higher thing into a (sensibly) lower." He was slowly moving toward philosophy. Nothing is more impressive about William James's thirty years of preparation for life than the fact that he betrayed so many of his original intellectual interests at an early date — all of which, excepting painting, he carried to fruition.

The struggle for direction continued through the year and half, from April 1867 to November 1868, that he spent in Europe in search of health. His collapse had been complete in spite of the fact that he had returned full of health from Brazil. The whole situation threw him back upon his own internal resources and for the next four or five years he strove manfully to recover some grip on life which the mental depression that accompanied his illness seemed to have made impossible. It was at this period that he was constantly preoccupied with the idea of suicide and later in life he maintained that a man was not psychologically complete unless he had meditated on self-destruction. The protracted interruption of his medical studies was not entirely without profit for he studied physiology in Germany and caught a glimpse of a direction in which he could go with interest. He came briefly into contact with powerful personalities like Helmholtz, Virchow and Bernard. Although his opportunities for rewarding study were pitifully limited he did imbide the idea that "the time has come for psychology to begin to be a science" and he "blocked out some reading in physiology and psychology" which he hoped to carry through that winter. It is curious to observe this indication of the movement of his mind in the midst of a time when he was constantly preoccupied with the question of whether or not to live at all !

More extraordinary still is that in the midst of this depression he managed to extract considerable pleasure, not to say gaiety from life. He visited about when he was able, catching a revealing glimpse of the German learned man who never for a moment felt it necessary to appear in any other character, in contrast with the American: "A learned man at home is in a measure isolated; his study is carried on in private, at reserved hours. To the public he appears as citizen and neighbor etc., and they know at most *about* him that he is addicted to this or that study; his intellectual occupation always has something of a put-on character, and remains external at least to some part of his being." But such considered observation was frequently replaced with chaff like writing lovenotes in crude Bohemian to his landlady's daughter, or discussing matters humorously with T. S. Perry who roomed with him in Berlin. He found time, too, seriously to reflect upon the peculiarities of American psychology, and lamented to Perry, *apropos* the impeachment of President Johnson, the "way all our political questions resolved themselves into haggling over legal points with no reference to higher principles." And, by way of contrast, he was willing so far to depart from conventional paths as to dine *en famille* with a hotel keeper's family on a soup that tasted like nothing so much, so he said, as the perspiration of pigs !

He found it impossible either to recover his health or to get any satisfactory amount of work done in Europe, so he returned to Cambridge. In 1869 he took his M.D., finding himself somewhat less ready in answering questions than he had hoped, but passing well enough. He had no intention of practicing even had be been able. He settled down instead to three years of invalidish life made profitable only by indefatigable reading during the few hours a day allowed him by his eyes which now chose to bother him most desperately. It was during these difficult years that he touched a lower point of depression than any he had reached in Germany.

The reading he got over was unusual in its range and not all purposeless. He acquired the habit of making critical notations on the margins of the books he looked through, a habit which continued throughout life, of copying out quotations and of making summaries of what he had read in indexed notebooks. Gifted with a capacity for rapid reading, he early learned to get the meat out of a book in short order, invariably assessing the merit of a work by a rapid glance through the pages. On occasion he would try to get ideas of his own into words, even attempting an ambitious essay on the inadequacies of contemporary psychology and actually composing a few book reviews for *The Nation, The Atlantic Monthly* and *The North American Review.* There is no way of knowing how many books he turned over in these explorations, but from one notebook a list of reading (or so it is thought), has been rescued and it includes the writings of Browning, Littré, Comte, Mill, Spencer, Lecky, Froude, Turgenev, Lewes, Sand, Mérimée, Grote, Muller, Fichte, St. Beuve and Schopenhauer.

Furthermore, he was talking philosophy with Charles

Peirce at the latter's Metaphysical Club — Peirce whose thinking struck James as "exceedingly bold, subtle and incomprehensible" — and Chauncey Wright. Whatever influence Wright had on James was immediate, just as that of Peirce was to come to expression in the far future. Wright, as James wrote on his death a few years later, was motivated entirely by a desire for "consistency or unity in thought" and was entirely disregardful of "solid outward warrant for our emotional ends." He was satisfied with "the mere principle of parsimony as a criterion of universal truth." "Behind the bare phenomenal facts," he used to say with a force which certainly deeply impressed James negatively, "there is *nothing.*" But exactly what influence Wright had, no one can now say. Certainly it was not a positively determining influence, but George Herbert Palmer felt that Wright offered James a corrective of his father's mystical idealism. In any case Wright's way was not to be James's, for he wanted just precisely that "solid outward warrant for our emotional ends." One day James summed up Wright to Palmer in a way sharply critical: "Chauncey is the damndest rationalist that ever I saw."

Yet in spite of all this activity, remarkable in a man ill in body and confined to but a few hours a day for using his eyes, he suffered from a sense of purposelessness. It was in the midst of this period, in all probability, that he had his most shaking psychological experience, and lived perilously on the "ragged edge of his consciousness" for several months. His own account of what happened to him is exceedingly vivid:

Whilst in this state of philosophic pessimism and general depression of spirits about my prospects, I went one evening into a dressing-room in the twilight to procure some article that was there; when suddenly there fell upon me without any warning, just as if it came out of the darkness, a horrible fear of my own existence. Simultaneously there arose in my mind the image of an epileptic patient whom I had seen in the asylum, a black-haired youth with greenish skin, entirely idiotic, who used to sit all day on one of the benches, or rather shelves against the wall, with his knees drawn up against his chin, and the coarse gray undershirt, which was his only garment, drawn over them inclosing his entire figure.   He sat there like a sort of sculptured Egyptian cat or Peruvian mummy, moving nothing but his black eyes and looking absolutely non-human.   This image and my fear entered into a species of combination with each other. *That shape am I,* I felt, potentially.   Nothing that I possess can defend me against that fate, if the hour for it should strike for me as it struck for him.   There was such a horror of him, and such a perception of my own merely momentary discrepancy from him, that it was as if something hitherto solid within my breast gave way entirely and I became a mass of quivering fear. After this the universe was changed for me altogether.   I awoke morning after morning with a horrible dread at the pit of my stomach, and with the sense of the insecurity of life that I never knew before, and that I have never felt since.   It was like a revelation; and although the immediate feelings passed away, the experience has made me sympathetic with the morbid feelings of others ever since.   It gradually faded, but for months I was unable to go out into the dark alone.

In general I dreaded to be left alone.   I remember wondering how other people could live, how I myself had ever lived, so unconscious of the pit of insecurity beneath the surface of life.   My mother in particular, a very cheerful person, seemed to me a perfect paradox in her unconsciousness of danger, which you may well believe I was very careful not to disturb by revelations of my own state of mind.   I have always thought that this experience of melancholia of mine had a religious bearing. . . I mean that the fear was so invasive and powerful that if I had not clung to scripture-texts like "The eternal God is my refuge," etc. "Come unto me, all ye that labor and are heavy-laden," etc. "I am the resurrection and the life," etc., I think I should have grown really insane.

This was undoubtedly the low-water mark of the period, but there was soon an answering voice to his cry of "Help ! Help !"

The answer had come by the 30th of April, 1870 for on that day he made an entry in one of his notebooks which tells us that he had recovered his balance:

I think that yesterday was a crisis in my life.   I finished the first part of Renouvier's second "Essais" and see no reason why his definition of Free Will — "the sustaining of a thought *because I*

choose to when I might have other thoughts" — need be the definition of an illusion.   At any rate I will assume for the present
— until next year — that it is no illusion.   My first act of free
will shall be to believe in free will.   For the remainder of the
year, I will abstain from the mere speculation and contemplative
Grublei (Grubbing among subtleties) in which my nature takes
most delight, and voluntarily cultivate the feeling of moral freedom, by reading books favorable to it, as well as by acting.   After
the first of January, my callow skin being somewhat fledged, I
may perhaps return to metaphysical study and skepticism without danger to my powers of action.   For the present then remember: care little for speculation; much for the *form* of my action;
recollect that only when habits of order are formed can we advance to really interesting fields of action — and consequently accumulate grain on grain of wilful choice like a very miser; never
forgetting how one link dropped undoes an indefinite number.
Principiis obsta — Today has furnished the exceptionally passionate initiative which Bain posits as needful for the acquisition
of habits.   I will see to the sequel.   Not in maxims, not in
Anschauungen. (Regardings or contemplate views) but in accumulated *acts* of thought lies salvation.*   *Passer outre.*   Hitherto,
when I have felt like taking a free initiative, like daring to act
originally, without carefully waiting for contemplation of the
external world to determine all for me, suicide seemed the most
manly form to put my daring into; now, I will go a step further
with my will, not only act with it, but believe as well; believe in
my individual reality and creative power.   My belief to be sure,
can't be optimistic — but I will posit life (*the real, the good*) in
the self-governing *resistance* of the ego to the world.   Life shall
(be built in) doing and suffering and creating.

The resolve was carried out.   Like John Stuart Mill in a
similar crisis Wordsworth also contributed to his regeneration by his emphasis on the presence of an eternal moral order behind the reality of appearances.   Through a combination of influences, then, James had come, on *moral grounds,*
to a belief in the freedom of the will and the necessity of
action.   In writing to his brother Henry (the devotion of the
brothers was boundless and their confidences the freest) in

* See *Principles of Psychology,* I, 215: "No matter how full a reservoir of
maxims one may possess, and no matter how good one's *sentiments* may be,
if one have not taken advantage of every concrete opportunity to *act,* one's
character may remain entirely unaffected for the better. With mere good
intentions, hell is proverbially paved."

the next month he made another significant declaration: "I can't bring myself, as so many men seem able to, to blink the evil out of sight, and gloss it over. It's as real as the good, and if it is denied, good must be denied too. It must be accepted and hated, and resisted while there's breath in our bodies . . ." We have in this profession of a profound conviction of the reality of evil the root from which two of James's most fundamental philosophical doctrines grew — meliorism and pluralism.

These ideas, even in their very primitive state, allowed him to regain his balance and face life once more with interest if not enthusiasm. As a thinker he was never to progress far beyond a rationalization of the principles he found necessary to his own mental health. His thinking was always to remain strikingly and obviously personal and subjective. He made his private problems those of mankind. His feeling of indebtedness to Renouvier, then, continued throughout his life and he directed that the last book on which he worked — *Some Problems of Philosophy,* published posthumously — be dedicated to him. With free will and a concern for meliorative activities it was but a step to his definition of larger issues. His first task was to develop a psychology fitted to these fundamentals. In 1872 he was appointed Instructor in Physiology at Harvard College, a long-delayed fruit of his study under Charles Eliot in 1861, for it was then that Eliot had been impressed by his capabilities. He had begun his life of "studying, experimenting, observing, reading, reflecting, investigating, instructing, talking and writing." In the spring of 1873 he told his father that the difference between his frame of mind at that moment and his condition of the year before was "the difference between death and life."

2. VOICING A ROMANTIC PROTEST

WHEN William James began to teach at Harvard the country was well into the most profound transformation in its history.

Already the Civil War was taking its place as an episode in the larger movement rather than a decisive event in itself. The triumph of Northern industrialism was complete and it but remained to extend its victory indefinitely. Under the stimulus of the normal American optimism there was a concerted rush to make money, with the inevitable development of an exploiting plutocracy. It was during these years that such men as the Rockefellers, Carnegie, Gould, Drew, Cook, Harriman and J. P. Morgan the elder flourished. At the same time, and as a necessary complement, immigrants flooded the country in swarms, providing the manpower for the new industries and for the development of the West. Between 1870 and 1900 the United States, at one and the same time, eliminated the frontier and built up an unparalleled industrial organization.

Intellectually the country reflected similar expansive trends. It was the era of vast new educational enterprises. In 1876 Johns Hopkins was established under Gilman; in 1889 Clark under G. Stanley Hall was started with a flourish, but never succeeded in breaking the shackles of personal disagreements between the intellectual founder and the economic master; and Chicago was transformed under Harper. Charles W. Eliot was installed at Harvard in 1869, on the very edge of the exciting period, and became the great educational leader of the time, the Puritan Rousseau, the five foot sage, philistine apostle of culture! The Darwinian conflict was over and men like Louis Agassiz who opposed Darwin were, by 1873, considered stumbling blocks in the way of advancing knowledge. John Fiske, the apostle of Herbert Spencer in America, was appointed to a position at Harvard in 1869. For a while all Americans who troubled themselves about being advanced thinkers at all, followed Spencer and Haeckel. The opponents of Darwinism retired to the hinterland where they moulded and rusted until suddenly reborn over fifty years later. Shortly a movement was underway to release the mind from the "tyranny" of the terribly convincing, but carelessly put together monistic materialism of the evolutionists. A new science, psychology, showed its head, and it was from a man who made his first fame as a psychologist that the criticism came. That man was William James who sought to escape the Spencerian cage without giving up science. Like Goethe confronted with Holbach's *Système de la Nature,* James found Spencer's philosophy "so dark, so Cimmerian, so deathlike."

Much can be made of the external progression of his career: his progress from anatomy and physiology to psychology to philosophy, and the Scholastics can heartily sneer at his peculiar way of learning philosophy from the ground up rather than from the sky down. But such a schematic representation of his progress does violence to the actual development of his mind. It is unquestionably true that he looked not up but down from the answers to his problems. He sought guidance not from supernatural revelations, for he considered that way too easy, but from a careful study of the constitution of man and the social situation in which he found himself. He came around to God, however, if in a circuitous fashion. In 1882 he wrote to Thomas Davidson, who objected to a justification for theism James had given: "I can sympathize perfectly with the most rabid hater of him and the idea of him when I think of the use that has been made of him in history and philosophy as a *starting point,* or premise for grounding deductions. But as an Ideal to attain and make probable, I find myself less and less able to do without Him." His principal subject was always himself and in satisfying his own needs, he found himself satisfying those of thousands. Naturally he could not live upon the husks of physiology, nor the schemata of psychology and then suddenly decide that philosophy and religion were the truly important studies. He carried his whole burden along with him all the time, changing the emphasis of his interests in the succeeding years. Just as he was interested in the whispering about psychology in Germany in 1867 while really studying physiology, so he would interrupt his physiological lectures to spend the hour talking philosophy. In 1879–80 he gave a course on "The *Philosophy* of Evolution." Before he had finished his *Principles of Psychology* he was busy justifying God !

Unfortunately the title he bore on the college records gives us no indication of his subject at the moment. Long before he officially ceased to be a physiologist, he was primarily concerned with psychology. In 1875 he offered graduate study in "The Relation between Physiology and Psychology" and in 1877 he extended his teaching to undergraduates. Nevertheless it was not until 1880 that he was really free from physiology. In 1876, moreover, he was pointing out in *The Nation,* in response to Stanley Hall's bugle blast, that philosophy should be studied "as if there were no official answer preoccupying the field . . . its educational essence lies in the quickening of the spirit to its *problems.* What doctrines students take from their teachers are of little consequence provided they catch from them the living, philosophic attitude of mind, the independent, personal look at all the data of life, and the eagerness to harmonize them. . ." Like Emerson, James was not interested in disciples, but time and again quoted the passage from Ezekiel: "Son of Man, stand upon thy feet, and I will speak to thee." We must conceive of him therefore, as a man with a multiplicity of interests at every point of his career and as one who persistently sought to bring to flower in his lifetime, whether consciously or not, all the interests to which he early gave attention.

In James's thought evolution is a foundation doctrine but he felt under no obligation to accept the official deductions from the theory which were the deductions of Spencer. He was, however, at first overwhelmed by Spencer himself and received the earliest criticism he listened to, that advanced by Charles Peirce, with genuine annoyance. But once the spell was broken he gave no quarter. Spencer was the enemy. Occasionally W. K. Clifford, rarely Huxley, but always Spen-

cer. Thus while evolution remained a basic part of his intellectual equipment, the word did not become imbued with
a sort of sympathetic magic as in the case of Stanley Hall.
He started his campaign by making ruinous criticisms of
Spencer's psychology, but he did not ignore the larger interests.

"The craving for Monism at any cost," he wrote in 1879 by
way of explaining Spencer's popularity, "is the parent of the
entire evolutionist movement of our day, so far as it pretends
to be more than history. The Philosophy of Evolution tries
to show how the world at any given time may be conceived
as absolutely identical, except in appearance, with itself at
all past times. What it most abhors is the admission of anything which, appearing at a given point, should be judged
essentially other than what went before. Notwithstanding
the *lacunae* in Mr. Spencer's system; notwithstanding the
vagueness of his terms; in spite of the sort of jugglery by
which his use of the word 'nascent' is made to veil the introduction of new primordial factors like consciousness, as if,
like the girl in *Midshipman Easy,* he could excuse the ille-
gitimacy of an infant, by saying it was a very little one — in
spite of all this, I say, Mr. Spencer is, and is bound to be, the
most popular of all philosophers, because more than any
other he seeks to appease our strongest theoretic craving.
To undiscriminating minds his system will be a sop; to acute
ones a programme full of suggestiveness." He was not at all
fooled, therefore, about the strength of the Spencerians, but
that did not deter him. He felt that he could prove that
many of Spencer's "brilliant and seductive" statements were
lacking in supporting detail and that it was by examining the
details that one could bring him to the ground. Spencer was
a "vague writer;" James wrote of the "scandalous vagueness
with which this sort of 'chromo philosophy' is carried on." It
was above all on the question of details that William James
wrecked, to his own satisfaction, the Spencerian scheme. It
was a primary doctrine with him that one cannot see further

into a generalization than one's knowledge of the details lets one take it in.

Furthermore, he was entirely unimpressed by the contemporary aspiration to be 'scientific.' He considered the aspiration to be an idol of the tribe of his generation "so sucked in with his mother's milk by every one of us, that we find it hard to conceive of a creature who should not feel it, and harder still to treat it freely as the altogether peculiar and one-sided subjective interest which it is." What James was getting at was the fact that in the name of science the Spencerians and their relations were passing off a scheme of the universe as the inescapable truth, which was in reality nothing but a personal and subjective scheme. In it there was no warrant for our "emotional ends." He did not propose, however, to revive in any way the traditional Calvinistic orthodoxy nor was it his purpose merely to continue transcendentalism. What James wanted to do was to break up this cast-iron, monistic evolutionary vision and substitute for it an open universe, giving a place to novelty that would allow for ethical strivings on the basis of free will. To him the ethical approach was of primary importance and he wasn't going to admit defeat at the hands of pseudo-scientific dogmatism. Like his father, he was not overawed by the "official answers." Yet for all his unconventionality William James fitted into the hollow that the departed Calvinistic orthodoxy had left, and which transcendentalism had failed permanently to fill, for he was animated by an intensely religious aspiration even while not possessing a religious personality himself. He was predominantly a moralist and with a religious bent — an ethical theist.

But this is running far ahead of his actual progress. It is necessary to realize that he was activated by such ideals in all his work, however, even though it was to be many years before the general reading public became aware of his efforts. In the early years of his teaching he was a member of a small club of congenial friends who were threshing out philosophic problems from one angle or another, a club of which the membership varied in the course of his Harvard years. At this particular time however, it brought together James, Chauncey Wright, Thomas Davidson, W. T. Harris, Oliver Wendell Holmes, Jr., and Charles Peirce, to name only those who still mean something to the present generation. Most importantly, it was in company with men such as these that James first listened to the exposition of Peirce's pragmatism, and it lay dormant in his mind for twenty-five years before he brought it to light in one of his most original addresses to announce his own philosophic position. Peirce was a fellow student in the Scientific school and a friend during the years of invalidism at home. He was also, it appeared, to provide him with his greatest weapon for attacking philosophic problems.

Nothing came of Peirce's paper summing up his approach even after its publication six years later. Certainly James was too immediately interested in psychology at that time. The learned journals began to publish his papers in the field in 1876.

In the same year he met his wife-to-be, Miss Alice Gibbens, at the time a teacher in a private school of Boston. Her family had been settled in New England for generations. The legend is that Henry James the Elder met her at the Radical Club in Boston and on his coming home told William that he had seen "the woman you are to marry." The actual introduction was brought about by his friend Thomas Davidson. Though it seems to have been a fairly good case of "love at first sight" the marriage was postponed for two years. A friend describes Mrs. James a year or two later: ". . . in figure she was short and thickset. She had great dark luminous eyes, an abundance of soft brown hair, and a girlish wild-rose complexion, which together gave extraordinary beauty to somewhat heavy features. She spoke in a resonant organ-like voice, which made the most ordinary words sound significant. And she had a smile which lit up her face, and seemed to light up the world." In 1878 they married in Boston. It was a supremely, a continuously happy marriage. The same year — almost at the same time indeed — James signed a contract to produce a text book on psychology for Henry Holt's "American Science Series." At one and the same time he put a temporary period to his long siege of ill-health and uncertainty, he discovered new sources of energy, and began his climb to fame. His marriage worked an immediate transformation on his health so marked that he regretted that he had not sought that solution of his difficulties ten years earlier. Not the least of Mrs. James's contributions was to bring some order into William's somewhat fantastic days, to save him from his constitutional "Zerrissenheit" or "torn-to-pieces-hood," to protect him from all petty household worries, to guard him from unnecessary interruptions, and arrange his social contacts so that there would appear to be both the informality his nature demanded and the formality his position required.

Though he started out with the idea that he would produce his text book in two years, it was twelve before it was done. Nevertheless his career progressed steadily, if not at times by leaps and bounds. He found himself stimulated by his explorations of the still virgin field. He told his wife that he took his profoundest pleasure, not in guaranteed victories, but in those ventures where there was an element of active tension. We have here a key to his personality and we shall later find the same attitude reflected in his philosophy. It was the risk, the striving, not the achieved victory that solaced his spirit. Yet his whole effort was to impose some rational pattern upon the chaotic world. If he was unusually impressed with the flux and flow of the universe, with its instability, he fully accepted the implication of science that there was a discoverable system according to which nature functioned.

In forging his way through the jungle of psychology, he also had constantly in mind the ethical implications of his scientific labors. There was a hortatory strain in him that would not down. And his struggles to express himself were occasioned as much by a desire to speak inspiringly as to speak clearly, accurately, scientifically. He was convinced that "not the man of the most delicate sensibility but he who on the whole is the most *helpful* man will be reckoned the best man."

He sought, therefore, to be helpful, and a great step was to depart from Spencer's definition of the mind as correspondence and announce that "The organism of thought . . . is teleological through and through." This was in 1878. He had here formulated his fundamental psychological doctrine and established the necessary nexus between his belief in free will and his belief in the necessity of meliorative activities. Three years later he was telling a group of ministers that the end of every philosophy was action. In the monistic science of the day he saw forces at work to defeat action because no adequate account was taken of our subjective propensities. We needed God in the universe adequately to stimulate us. For a-theistic science he proposed to substitute theistic science which would galvanize man into moral action. Nothing could well be a clearer definition of purpose.

In 1882 he made a tour of the European universities seeking to meet the great workers in his field. William James's feeling for Europe almost exactly duplicated that of his father. It was a matter of attraction and repulsion. In America Europe appeared tremendously attractive. He had hardly set foot in Europe than he longed once more for America. In his caustic commentaries upon the "cramped and inferior England" he never failed to arouse his brother Henry. To the latter contrast was already fixed on the side of Europe and of England in particular. But there can be small doubt that Europe did answer to some deep need in William's nature. His early days were dominated by European ways of thinking. He had recovered his intellectual balance on Renouvier and Wordsworth and not on any American thinker. His psychological work was almost entirely based upon European productions. In this trip of 1882 he was to find himself heartily welcomed by the German psychologists, particularly such men as Stumpf and Mach but he did not get far with Wundt, who represented a method for which he had but little personal aptitude. His extraordinary devotion to laboratory experimentalism irked James. Yet in his writing James drew heavily upon the results reported by the experimentalists. His own forte was introspection and his most brilliant chapters are based upon introspection and the hortatory implications of his findings. His book was developing along synthetic lines, as we shall see in due time, rather than in the groove marked out by any one school. His trip, however, did not rouse in him any envy for the situation of the European workers. "The total lesson of what I have done in the past month is to make me quieter with my home-lot and readier to believe that it is one of the chosen places of the Earth."

His father died while he was in Europe and when he returned home in March of 1883 he found himself acutely conscious of the place his parent had played in his own mental life. He went about wondering what he would have said to this idea and that fact and discovered that as he grew older he found it necessary more and more to take account of those kinds of facts to which his father had given his attention. Though William James never came around to his father's intellectual methods, he did both first and last betray his influence. How and in what manner will sufficiently appear, especially when his notions on religion are discussed. But it must be admitted that William did not borrow his father's ideas directly. He tried to give them a "scientific" psychological twist which in most cases seems to a critical student to have resulted in their debasement. In fact, William James's whole intellectual life might be summed up with perhaps unwonted critical sharpness as composing unconscious parodies on excellent ideas. His father's bent was so decidedly supernaturalistic that it is hardly to be supposed that William could take over any more than certain attitudes; and here we can emphasize that the psychological bias runs through the work of Henry James Sr., William and Henry. Whether there was a reciprocal influence at work is a point no one can finally decide. William unquestionably was fascinated with Swedenborg as he grew older and more interested in religion. George Herbert Palmer once heard him talk of writing a life of the great seer.

Certainly his father's example must have helped him escape the prevailing evolutionary monism. And his desire to upset that, as he felt, suffocating outlook, led him to welcome even the most unorthodox attempts to master the universe. In 1884 he became actively interested in psychical research. The English Society for Psychical Research had been founded two years earlier and he had been so far interested that in 1884 he took part in the organization of an American society of the same name in Boston. With uncomplaining fortitude he took part in all sorts of bizarre investigations of ghosts, second sight, spiritualism, and all sorts of hobgoblins, helping to dissipate what in 1869 he had declared to be the "extraordinary, anomalous and discreditable" attitude of society toward the phenomena. Though he found all this, and particularly materializing mediums, "A strange and in many ways disgusting experience," he continued interested all his life. The final upshot of his investigations was negative. The nearest he came to belief was in the case of Mrs. Piper, "twenty-eight years old, a mass of yellow hair, and big eyes full of mystery." "If I may be allowed a personal expression of opinion . . . ," he wrote in 1898, "I would say that the Piper phenomena are the most absolutely baffling thing I know." And though he was ul-timately completely unconvinced that beings of another world could communicate with us, he accepted Frederic Meyer's concept of the Subliminal Self, "the enveloping mother-consciousness in each of us from which the conscious-ness we wot of is precipitated like a crystal," as a suitable rubic under which to gather all the bizarre phenomena he indubitably observed. He was not going to see the whole question ruled out of respectable society as "fraud," "rot" and "rubbish."

An extension of his interest in the bizarre and socially out-lawed was his serious discussion of the New Thought, when it came along. To later readers there is something shock-ingly ludicrous in his serious discussion of this sort of intel-lectual gymnastics in *The Varieties of Religious Experience*. And one becomes positively wearied of his vagaries when he begins to talk about Yoga and the various prescriptions of the ancient and modern Hindu prophets for breathing exercises and eupeptic regimens. He was not going to see any ques-tion ruled out. To him no question was closed. Neither was any way of looking at things entirely without its utility. It was this positive liking for all sorts of cranks and prophets and warped philosophers and every other variety of "think-ing" creature that carried him into many anomalous situa-tions. He did not care. He was determined to keep watch for a white crow no matter how often he was assured that they were all black.

His personal situation rapidly and markedly improved in the eighties. On his father's death he had handed the management of his inheritance over to Henry Higginson the Boston financier and public benefactor. In 1886 he was given a full professorship with an increase in salary. He moved into a larger house immediately and three years later he built a Cambridge home of his own in which he lived the rest of his life. Furthermore he found and began to develop his summer home at Chocorua, New Hampshire, which became as integral a part of his life as Cambridge, and to which he went each summer with increasing pleasure. He was not, and never became, a country-man. His enjoyment of the life was that of a visitor and a devotee of the pictorial aspects of the scenery. If he had actually purchased as many of the hill-tops he admired or all the fine views he coveted as another man covets *objets d'art*, he would have died of that disease so familiar to farmers, "land poverty." Nor was he, for all his intellectual brightness, the equal of his neighbors in a horse deal. He would let it be known that he wanted an animal and would pay sixty — even seventy-five — dollars for one. Of course he paid seventy-five. But it was good fun to pretend to expert knowledge of horse-flesh, and to go about thinly dressed, to bathe in a deep spot in the brook, and to take long hikes. It was a welcome relief from academic routine. He jokingly invited his brother Henry to retire to Chocorua when he was ready to admit that he was a failure and revel in the fact that he was a resident of the township of Tamworth Iron Works!

At the same time he plowed on through his psychology and each year turned up some new subject to teach. In 1888 he worked his way through ethics with a class. The next year he was in Europe again and attended the International Congress of Physiological Psychology at Paris, being chosen to open the sessions. His fame was spreading and the time was rapidly approaching when every meeting of scholars in his fields solicited his presence.

The writing of *The Principles of Psychology* was a torturous task. James wrote with extreme difficulty. Though the finished product is notable for its easiness and seemingly careless grace, it was really produced with the utmost labor. He was a "fusser" proceeding through a long process of scratching out, rewriting, substituting word for word until he arrived at something that pleased him. A good day's production would be twenty-five hundred words. "Everything comes out wrong with me at first; but when once objectified in a crude shape, I can torture and poke and scrape and pat it till it offends me no more." The result was a rapid, athletic style, comparable in its quality to that of William Dean Howells. But unfortunately, like Howells, the very skill and completeness with which he uttered himself would seem to be indicative of the fact that his thought had no heights and depths toward which he unavailingly strained. His writing is lacking in that density we associate with profundity. He conveyed a sense of excitement and bright, electric, light, but no sense of deep thought or protracted contemplation.

He cared nothing for conventional correctness either in grammar or spelling. "Isn't it abominable," he once said to Professor Palmer, "that everybody is expected to spell in the same way? Let us get a dozen influential persons to agree to spell after his own fashion and so break up this tyranny of the dictionary." His style was carefully considered and its spontaneity the product of deliberate art. His friends liked it in proportion as it seemed like his talk. His sensitivity to the style of others was also acute. American philosophical *writing,* seemed to him worse than the German. He remarked that the style of a junior whose philosophical brilliance was unchallenged "was damnable; in fact it was God damnable."

Naturally it is easy to see why it was that he literally plowed his way through the *Psychology.* He was, in addition to struggling to a normal degree with expression, eternally encountering gaps that had to be filled in, standard generalizations that needed reexamination and restatement and so on. "Every chapter," he wrote, "bristles with obstructions that refer one to the next ten years of work for their mitigation." In 1890, however, it was completed and published. The reception through the civilized world was exceptionally enthusiastic and the sale so remarkable that he soon began to talk of looking down on Mark Twain. He had written a classic. Yet his immediate reaction was:

"Nasty little subject! Nothing in it! All one cares to know lies outside!"

"THE YEAR which shall have witnessed the apparition of your *Hazard of New Fortunes;* of Harry's *Tragic Muse,* and of my *Psychology,* will indeed be a memorable one in American Literature!!" wrote James to William Dean Howells. As the years pass by this light observation is assuming a larger truth, for James's psychology is increasingly considered to be brilliant because of its literariness rather than for any scientific validity it may have had. Indeed those very chapters which made the deepest impression at the time — on habit and the will and so on — were predominantly literary in expression and hortatory in intent. Yet by advancing science into the field of the personality, he unconsciously struck his most destructive blow against tradition.

James's psychology, the historians of the subject tell us, was synthetic and reducible to clearly separate influences: German, French, English and "original." He progressed out of physiology into psychology, moved by his old perception that the time was coming for psychology to be scientific. But while he tried to think in terms of neurological concepts, it is pretty generally agreed that he had too little to go on to make any definitive contributions. In such contributions as he did make his chief reliance was upon the German experimental psychologists whose methods he described as follows:

Within a few years what one may call a microscopic psychology has arisen in Germany, carried on by experimental methods, asking of course, every moment for introspective data, but eliminating their uncertainty by operating on a large scale and taking statistical means. This method taxes patience to the utmost, and could hardly have arisen in a country whose natives could be *bored.* Such Germans as Weber, Fechner, Vierordt, and Wundt obviously cannot; and their success has brought into the field an array of younger experimental psychologists, bent on studying the *elements* of the mental life, dissecting them out from the gross results in which they are embedded, and as far as possible reducing them to quantitative scales. The simple and open method of attack having done what it can, the method of patience, starving out, and harassing to death is tried; the Mind must submit to a regular seige, in which minute advantages gained night and day by the forces that hem her in must sum themselves up at last into her overthrow. There is little of the grand style about these new prism, pendulum, and chronograph-philosophers. They mean business, not chivalry. What generous divination, and that superiority in virtue which was thought by Cicero to give a man the best insight into nature, have failed to do, their spying and scraping, their deadly tenacity and almost diabolic cunning will doubtless some day bring about.

Though he introduced large blocks of the material these men were contributing into his two volumes, he had little fundamental sympathy with their method as the tone of his remarks shows. He respected their industry but he could not imitate it. Indeed his impatience was so great that he could not even bring himself to direct the psychological laboratory at Harvard and at the earliest possible moment he resigned its direction to the hands of Hugo Munsterberg. For the true introduction of the laboratory method into America we must not look to the activities of James, although it seems fairly clear that he did establish the first laboratory, but to the activities of G. Stanley Hall and E. B. Titchener. When James's book appeared, these more patient men took proper revenge upon him, Hall remarking (according to James's paraphrase) that it was "the most complete piece of self-evisceration since Marie Bashkirtseff's diary." *The Principles* utterly ignored, by the way, Hall's great effort to get the genetic point of view into psychology ! Wundt, the father of all the experimentalists, thought it fascinating literature, but hardly psychology.

James's true allegiance was to the British school of introspectionists, though he found occasion to criticize some of their views very severely. It is now generally conceded that no one has ever surpassed the brilliance of his "literary" descriptions of his observations. Just as we shall make mention of the fact that philosophically James was in the British tradition, so the generalization should be made here. Even his so-called original chapters are frequently English in basis, particularly that on habit which the historians say derives from Bain. After the Germans and the British James found most sustenance in the work of the French investigators, particularly Charcot and Janet, who were working on such problems as multiple personalities, hypnotism and related subjects. In this he was a romantic, according to his own description. However, he did not go beyond their own formulations to any great extent and it was reserved to a later psychologist to take their findings as a point of departure for a truly original psychology. This man was Sigmund Freud, whose work James recognized, while it was still in embryo, as likely to revolutionize the subject.

It is as a piece of self-evisceration, or more properly as an indication of his larger views that we are going to take *The Principles*. It is of considerable interest to the general reader that certain of James's contributions, like those to the study of emotions, perception of space and memory have provided points of departure for later workers, but how and why can hardly be demonstrated without a too elaborate consideration of rather irrelevant psychological data. It may be taken as fact, therefore, that the book provided a fertile field for later investigators looking for problems and for critics looking for points to demolish. For our purposes we shall look at the work not as technical psychologists, but as readers interested in James's view of the world.

"The physiological study of mental conditions is thus the most powerful ally of hortatory ethics," he remarks very early in Volume I. He rarely missed an opportunity to make a contribution in the field. Writing on Habit, he characteristically gave free reign to his weakness. After a brilliant literary statement of the significance of Habit, he lapsed into a hortatory passage on the necessity of making "automatic and habitual, as early as possible, as many useful actions as we can." "There is no more miserable human being," he wrote, "than one in whom nothing is habitual but indecision, and for whom the lighting of every cigar, the drinking of every cup, the time of rising and going to bed every day, and the beginning of every bit of work, are subjects of express volitional deliberation. Full half the time of such a man goes to the deciding, or regretting, of matters which ought to be so ingrained in him as practically not to exist for his consciousness at all. If there be such daily duties not yet ingrained in any one of my readers, let him begin this very hour to set the matter right." For, he has just said:

Habit is thus the enormous fly-wheel of society, its most precious conservative agent. It alone is what keeps us all within the bounds of ordinance and saves the children of fortune from the envious uprising of the poor. It alone prevents the hardest and most repulsive walks of life from being deserted by those brought up to tread therein. It keeps the fisherman and the deck-hand at sea through the winter; it holds the miner in his darkness, and nails the countryman to his log-cabin and his lonely farm through all the months of snow; it protects us from invasion by the natives of the desert and the frozen zone. It dooms us all to fight out the battle of life upon the lines of our nurture or our early choice, and to make the best of a pursuit that disagrees, because there is no other for which we are fitted, and it is too late to begin again. It keeps different social strata from mixing. Already at the age of twenty-five you see the professional mannerism settling down on the young commercial traveller, on the young doctor, on the young minister, on the young counsellor-at-law. You see the little lines of cleavage running through the character, the tricks of thought, the prejudices, the ways of the 'shop,' in a word, from which the man can by-and-by no more escape than his coat-sleeve can suddenly fall into a new set of folds. On the whole, it is best he should not escape. It is well for the world that in most of us, by the age of thirty, the character has set like plaster, and will never soften again.

That such a passage should be quoted from a supposedly scientific work is surely anomalous. It clearly proves that

James's bias was permanently deep set in favor of the moralistic.

But instead of studding the pages that follow with further examples of this sort of thing, let us attempt to put in order a few passages illustrating James's conception of the mind as a connecting link between his dogma of free will and his belief in the necessity of meliorative activities. He firmly believed that the mind was a teleological or purposive instrument. The guiding force in this activity was the will. "The essential function of the will," he wrote, "in short, when it is not 'voluntary,' is to attend to a difficult object and hold it fast before the mind. The so-doing is the fiat; and it is a mere physiological incident that when the object is thus attended to, immediate motor consequences should ensue." The will, then, is the indispensable instrument in motor activities, in action. To attend implies selection, and it was James's idea that the mind was a selecting instrument. It has to select that to which it would attend from the stream of consciousness. This latter idea is one of the most famous of all of James's ideas and one which gives him a firm and abiding place in *literature* whatever may be his place in psychology. (Parenthetically, it may be said that the Gestaltists criticize him for playing down the matter of structure of the mind.) For in literature, as the reader will immediately recognize, the idea of the flux and flow of the mind as the primary data upon which to build a true picture of a man's mental life is one which fascinated a whole school of writers whose master is James Joyce, and whose mistress is Dorothy Richardson. "Consciousness . . . ," James wrote, "does not appear to itself chopped up in bits. Such words as 'chain' or 'train' do not describe it fitly as it presents itself in the first instance. It is nothing jointed; it flows. A 'river' or a 'stream' are the metaphors by which it is most naturally described. *In talking* of it hereafter, let us call it the stream of thought, of consciousness, or of subjective life." Again: "Once more take a look at the brain. We believe the brain to be an organ whose internal equilibrium is always in a state of change, — the change affecting every part. The pulses of change are doubtless more violent in one place than in another, their rhythm more rapid at this time than at that. As in a kaleidoscope revolving at a uniform rate, although the figures are always rearranging themselves, there are instants during which the transformation seem minute and interstitial and almost absent, followed by others when it shoots with magical rapidity, relatively stable forms thus alternating with forms we should not distinguish if seen again; so in the brain the perpetual rearrangement must result in some forms of tension lingering relatively long, whilst others simply come and pass." Naturally no man can pretend to be equally interested and impressed by all that turns up as his thought streams along. It is given meaning by the phenomena of selective attention: ". . . the mind is at every stage a theatre of simultaneous possibilities. Consciousness consists in the comparison of these with each other, the selection of some, and the suppression of the rest by the reinforcing and inhibiting agency of attention."

What makes our particular private world, then, is that to which we pay attention, and this is determined by purely *subjective*, emotional influences. To emphasize these was his hobby. It was exactly at this point that his individualism found its origin. The question of "whether attention involve . . . a principle of spiritual activity or not" is crucial, for one's answer to it is the "very hinge on which our picture of the world shall swing from materialism, fatalism, monism, towards spiritualism, freedom, pluralism, — or else the other way." For *ethical* and not scientific reasons William James believed that a spiritual force did determine matters here; it was in that direction that his general philosophy inclined "the beam." His ethical reason was the necessity for defending the freedom of the will. Similarly subjective was the matter of conception. "The whole function of conceiving, of fixing, and holding fast to meanings, has no significance apart from the fact that the conceiver is a creature with partial purposes and private ends." And in fact reality is in this category as well:

In the relative sense, then, the sense in which we contrast reality with simple unreality, and in which one thing is said to have more reality than another, and to be more believed, reality means simply relation to our emotional and active life. This is the only sense which the word ever has in the mouths of practical men. In this sense, whatever excites and stimulates our interest is real; whenever an object so appeals to us that we turn to it, accept it, fill our mind with it, or practically take account of it, so far it is real for us, and we believe it. Whenever, on the contrary, we ignore it, fail to consider it or act upon it, despise it, reject it, forget it, so far it is unreal for us and disbelieved.

The extraordinary subjectivity of James's fundamental points, as shown by the quoted citations, requires a little emphasis. We have already had occasion to note that his objection to Evolutionary monism was occasioned by his conviction that it allowed no place for a "solid outward warrant" for our subjective trends. His psychology, then, is a justification of his position against the monists, just as it is, as previously remarked, a connecting link between the two great doctrines he brought with him out of his period of depression, 1869–1872. With his fundamental psychological ideas in mind, it will be easy to understand the essays in popular morals that followed in the immediately succeeding period and the philosophical essays which culminated his career. That to achieve his position he had to introduce a spiritual principle did not in the least disturb him. He felt that what he was contending for was more important than any fear of dualism. Indeed, he not only accepted dualism, but multiplicity. What he wanted to escape was monism, and any avenue was welcome. His whole intellectual career was a rationalization of personal necessities.

Behind all this elaboration there was the fundamental idea of the freedom of the will. Everything in James's psychology comes back to this point sooner or later so far as it has relation to the problems of belief and action.   "Will and Belief, in short," he wrote, "meaning a certain relation between objects and the Self, are two names for one and the same PSYCHOLOGICAL phenomenon."   "If our wills are indeterminate," he goes on, "so must our beliefs be, etc.   The first act of free will, in short, would naturally be to believe in free will, etc."   This is almost a paraphrase of his notebook entry of 1870.   He followed out his thought as follows:

If belief consists in an emotional reaction of the entire man on an object, how can we believe at will ?   We cannot control our emotions.   Truly enough, a man cannot believe at will abruptly. Nature sometimes, and indeed not very frequently, produces instantaneous conversions for us.   She suddenly puts us in active connection with objects of which she had till then left us cold. "I realize for the first time," we then say, "what that means !" This happens often with moral propositions.   We have often heard them; but now they shoot into our lives; they move us; we feel their living force.   Such instantaneous beliefs are truly enough not to be achieved by will.   But *gradually* our will can lead us to the same results by a very simple method; we need only in cold blood ACT as if the thing in question were real, and keep acting as if it were real, and it will infallibly end by growing into such a connection with our life that it will become real.   It will become so knit with habit and emotion that our interests in it will be those which characterize belief.   Those to whom "God" and "Duty" are now mere names can make them much more than that, if they make a little sacrifice to them every day.

Here again, he is elaborating from the 1870 diary entry. The great and overwhelming necessity is action. If we lack the necessary automatic belief, we can act as if we had the belief and belief will come.   But the thing is: ACT.

Man acting is James's greatest concern.   "If the 'searching of our heart and reins' be the purpose of this human drama, then what is sought seems to be what effort we can make. He who can make none is but a shadow; he who can make much is a hero."   This is certainly clear enough.   And so is the following expression of his tragic sense of life:

When a dreadful object is presented, or when life as a whole turns up its dark abysses to our view, then the worthless ones among us lose their hold on the situation altogether, and either escape from its difficulties by averting their attention, or if they cannot do that, collapse into yielding masses of plaintiveness and fear. The effort required for facing and consenting to such objects is beyond their power to make. But the heroic mind does differently. To it, too, the objects are sinister and dreadful, unwelcome, incompatible with wished-for things. But it can face them if necessary, without for that losing its hold upon the rest of life. The world thus finds in the heroic man its worthy match and mate; and the effort which he is able to put forth to hold himself erect and keep his heart unshaken is the direct measure of his worth and function in the game of human life. He can *stand* this Universe. He can meet it and keep up his faith in it in presence of those same features which lay his weaker brethren low. He can still find a zest in it, not by "ostrich-like forgetfulness," but by pure inward willingness to face the world with those deterrent objects there. And hereby he becomes one of the master and the lords of life. He must be counted with henceforth; he forms a part of human destiny. Neither in the theoretic nor in the practical sphere do we care for, or look for help to, those who have no head for risks, or sense for living on the perilous edge.

But as a rule this mood is not allowed expression in James's writing. He kept it under cover. He averted his eyes from it. Only on analyzing his private psychological history do we realize that he was constantly trying to escape from such a vision of life. Unfortunately he averted his eyes so long and so insistently as to approach the fatuous. By his optimistic emphasis he subtracted from his thought all those strengths which should normally have stemmed from his tragic sense of life. His cult of optimistic action led him to strip his mind and writings of all feeling of reflection, of density, of complexity, of living perilously in the dark, leading to a mental nudity which is quite shocking.

The immediate issue of the completion of *The Principles* was the free application of the implied doctrines to hortatory speeches and essays. It has not been generally recognized that in this interlude between the completion of James's psychological labors and his taking up philosophy in a serious manner, he (to all intents and purposes) turned his

energies to a popularization of his general outlook. It is
not only that he used psychology to bring new ways and
means of pedagogy to the attention of teachers, but that he
very actively tried to propagate a view of the world, in
essence moral.

The occasion was in the fact that he seriously needed
money to educate his family and provide for his old age.
For these reasons he was willing to lecture here and there as
opportunity offered, particularly in the summer vacation
period. It led to an excessively crowded life, one with a
minimum of rest, and perhaps in the end shortened his lifetime measurably. It should not be thought that because
his marriage brought him sudden access of health and made
his spirits more uniformly optimistic, that he completely did
away with the bugaboo of ill health. It was his misfortune
to live a life which is marked off into periods by the recurring attacks of serious illness. By straining himself to
increase his material resources, he was very definitely de-
pleting his physical powers.

It was at this time that he emerged as a popular thinker
and leader. He let his generation know what he had to give
it and that it was highly acceptable. Hitherto his light had
been hidden under the academic bushel but henceforth it
would burn brightly in the market-place as well. People
discovered that he had a consolatory message for them to
which they could freely and admiringly respond because he
could present it understandably. They discovered also that
he was a charming person socially. In William James his
father's animal spirits became good fellowship — he was
easily and happily "one of the boys." With one bound he
became a "typical" representative of his generation and a
very popular man.

James always entertained clearly marked views and at this
time they came to the surface in their simplest and most
obvious form. Reference has been made to four or five
leading ideas which he entertained: to his belief in free will,

in meliorative activities, in the purposive conception of mind, to his concern for a free and open universe, to his individualism. Starting from this latter idea we can profitably concern ourselves with an elaboration of a basic position.

Individualism was a fundamental notion with James as it was with Emerson and he beautifully presented it in an essay entitled "On a Certain Blindness in Human Beings." The blindness he was getting at was "the blindness with which we all are afflicted in regard to the feelings of creatures and people different from ourselves." From his point of view this fact that we are constitutionally incapable of livingly entering into the lives of others was warrant for declaring that no one way of looking at the world could possibly be a sufficient answer. He could even pointedly ask a class of undergraduates, "How do we know whether a man sees less or more truth when he is drunk?" * From this doctrine of tolerance he led directly up to his hospitality to all sorts and conditions of men and thinkers and on the other hand he arrived at his notion that it was impossible to find a view of the world from which the universe will appear as "absolutely single fact." (Philosophically this became pluralism.) If we admit a blindness to the feeling of others we are then in a position to understand that "neither the whole of truth nor the whole of good is revealed to any single observer, although each observer gains a partial superiority of insight from the peculiar position in which he stands."

Granting that every thinking being has his own view of things we may proceed to examine the conditions necessary to a life of action, for action is the necessary end of every philosophy, however crude, in this world. In James's view

* See also *Principles of Psychology*, II, 284: "One of the charms of drunkenness unquestionably lies in the deepening of the sense of reality and truth which is gained therein. In whatever light things may then appear to us, they seem more utterly what they are, more 'utterly utter' than when we are sober." And *The Varieties of Religious Experience*, pg. 387.

society thrives only because of the interaction between it and "individuals whose genius was so adapted to the receptivities of the moment, or whose accidental position of authority was so critical that they became ferments, initiators of movement, setters of precedent or fashion, centers of corruption, or destroyers of other persons, whose gifts, had they had free play, would have led society in another direction." Naturally holding this view it was important that all individuals be freed for action, but the important thing was to guarantee in some fashion the moral quality of the action. James must not be suspected of conspiring to support the corrupters of society. "Perfect conduct is a relation between three terms: The actor, the objects for which he acts, and the recipients of the action." All should conspire to a moral end.

A glance has been stolen at James's belief in the necessity of God as a stimulus to action. He felt that any view of the world which did not allow for God was a defeatist view, a position which led him to call such philosophies 'scientificisms' — of which Spencer's was the outstanding type. He went on immediately to say that they would suffocate our subjective impulses and lead to stagnation and death. Belief in God was necessary then as a subjective preliminary to action. And it was in defence of our subjective impulses that he was contending. It was they that were the basis of all action. Scientificisms were to him "irrational because they are inadequate stimuli to man's practical nature."

A distinction which James made between the scientific, the moral and the aesthetic views of the universe may be elaborated. In his view man acted chiefly from moral impulses and they were subjective and peculiar to each individual. In the moral impulses we find "the essential root of human personality." Believing that the question of free will vs. determinism was not soluable on scientific data, he posited free will as the necessary corrolary of such a conception of personality and as a necessary preliminary to moral action. And "to take life strivingly is indestructible in the race." Naturally he believed in some universe other than reported by scientific investigators. "Science," he wrote in *The Principles,* "must be constantly reminded that her purposes are not the only purposes, and that the order of uniform causation which she has use for, and is therefore right in postulating, may be enveloped in a wider order, on which she has no claims at all." Like all other kinds of thought scientific thought "goes by selection and emphasis exclusively." So also are ethical and aesthetic thought. However, "the peculiarity of those relations among the objects of our thought which are dubbed 'scientific' is this, that although they are no more inward reproductions of the outer order than the ethical and aesthetic relations are, yet they do not conflict with that order, but, once having sprung up by the play of the inward forces, are found . . . to be *congruent* with the time- and space-relations which our impressions affect." On the other, ethical and aesthetic thought are not congruent. They are characterized by being *incongruent,* and their world is "a Utopia, a world which the outer relations persist in contradicting, but which we as stubbornly persist in striving to make actual." The ascending scale of difficulty is scientific, aesthetic, moral. The moral struggle thus becomes the most acute, most difficult, and if we can imagine the resolution of any, the last to bring about a congruency between the ideal and the actual. In this sense both the saints' belief in heaven and the ideals of the socialists, communists and anarchists are social leavens of equal importance.

To act, to strive, one must believe. Since we must frequently act, particularly on moral issues, before the data are absolutely complete, James elaborated his idea of the will to believe. The options presented to us in such situations he defined as "forced, living and momentous." We were obliged to settle them. The decision is living because it is a "real possibility to him to whom it is proposed." And it

is momentous when the issue itself is of some radical significance to the person confronted with it.   In such situations,
then, we must take a risk, and life gains a large part of its
interest from the fact that it is made up of risks.   If we
waited for all the evidence to come in, we would perish on
the spot.   We must hold ourselves in readiness to act and
"faith is the readiness to act in a cause the prosperous issue
of which is not certified to us in advance."   Instead of the
"will" to believe the idea might better have been called the
"necessity" to believe.   We cannot live unless we are constantly ready to risk action on the basis of conceptions and
notions unsupported by final evidence.   It is unlikely that
we ever shall be able to reduce life to a matter of acting in
harmony with ultimately tested ideas, though an immense
amount can still be done to bring our ways into congruence
with scientifically tested conceptions.   Indeed James was
engaged in just such activity when he lectured teachers on
the psychology of pedagogy !

If then "it is only by risking our persons from one hour to
another that we live at all," it follows that it is in taking the
risks for a moral purpose that life becomes worth living.
"The 'scientific proof' that you are right may not be clear
before the day of judgment (or some stage of being which
that expression may serve to symbolize) is reached.   But the
faithful fighters of this hour, or the beings that then and
there will represent them, may turn to the faint-hearted,
who here decline to go on, with words like those with which
Henry IV. greeted the tardy Crillon after a great victory had
been gained: 'Hang yourself, brave Crillon !   We fought at
Arques and you were not there !' "

How personal all this was to James may justly be underlined here.   Glancing back over his own life we find that he
dragged himself out of mental depression by deciding that
his first act of will would be to believe in the freedom of the
will.   We further find that he found it impossible to blink
evil out of existence and that therefore it became necessary

to strive against it.   To act against evil it was necessary to act in situations where all the evidence was not in, hence the "will to believe."   Again we have discovered him writing to his wife that he did not enjoy action without a large element of risk, ergo that principle appears in his public lectures.   And finally we may once more glance back at the most difficult period of his life and discover that he decided that in action only could he discover salvation.   Hence the justification of action became his greatest concern, once the sacredness of individuality had been granted.   William James was a great philosopher of action, of striving in an open universe for moral ends whose triumph was never guaranteed in this world.   He was that from personal necessity.

How completely these views were in harmony with contemporary conceptions is very remarkable and we need only note, without surprise, that James found his moral ideas perfectly illustrated in Kipling's *The Light that Failed.* Certainly no writer of the nineties was more popularly accepted than Kipling.   When his imperialistic views came to the front an appreciable part of his audience left him, including William James.   At this time, however, James was with him.   He preceded Kipling with Stevenson and followed him with H. G. Wells.

He rowed as little against the current as any of the Jameses. Even his "rebellion" came at a time that insured his popularity.   Like Dostoevsky, he grounded his whole case on the necessity of living despite logic, but his solution of the problem led him far from the paths Dostoevsky trod.   His work fitted in neatly with the mood of America.   His teleological bias was in harmony with American practicality just as his insistence on the necessity of action was in harmony with a cardinal dogma of American life.   This latter emphasis led to much misunderstanding of what he was about, for he was far from advocating action for pecuniary ends.   It was moral ends he had in mind.   But the confusion has stuck to him with the insistence of a burr to the detriment of his reputation.

Numerous prestigious critics of his day and later insisted that his philosophy was vulgarly complementary to the outlook of the dominant business class if not an outright rationalization of the point of view of that class. His critics often professed a preference for Royce or Santayana, this by logic placing them against James. James was of course a man-of-his-time, as who is not? and it is easy to establish links and parallels between him and his thinking and currents of action and thought in the great world, not the least interesting of which tie him to developments in politics and journalism (rather than business): reform politics and muckraking journalism. But this is more to point out how he was related to his time than to establish that he was a propaedeutic agent or a rationalizer of these developments. One's final evaluation of James should not depend upon adventitious associations, often pointed out in malice, but upon his own recorded thinking. If the verdict be critical, as it is here, it can be accompanied by high respect for the man and arrived at in full recognition of the fact that, with all his lapses and faults, he was ordinarily on the side of the intellectual "angels." Unless academics should communicate only with their kind, it is to James's credit that he successfully reached his extramural contemporaries.

During these years James's life flowed along on a remarkably even keel. In 1892 he went to Europe for a year, most of which was spent in Switzerland and Italy. He enjoyed himself thoroughly and rested his mind from the labors of writing the *Principles*. One of his neighbors in Italy was Mark Twain — "a fine, soft-fibred little fellow with the perversest twang and drawl, but very human and good. I should think that one might grow very fond of him, and wish he'd come and live in Cambridge." William James's irreverent humor was a solid link between him and Mark Twain as well as the lesser literary comedians of the time,

Bill Nye, Petroleum V. Nasby and the others. They were all preparing for the new American realism.

The University of Padua held its Galileo anniversary in this year and William James was one of the visiting foreigners honored with degrees. The PH.D. and L.H.D. he got from Padua were the first of a long line of honorary degrees from European and American universities.

When he returned to Cambridge to resume his teaching, he found his psychological interests very definitely on the decline. At the same time that he gave popular expression to his moral viewpoint, he was developing an interest in the psychology of religion, a topic which was to find full expression at the beginning of the next period of his life. Though he could cry out against the professor, he was at the height of his powers. "What an awful trade that of professor is — paid to talk, talk, talk. . . It would be an awful universe if *everything* could be converted into words, words, words." But the James family had an unconquerable affection for words !

His classroom manner was one of informality and alert nonchalance. The Harvard requirement that all professors teach undergraduates was not a suffocating restriction to him as it was to more sensitive souls. He moved about, short, handsome, of upright bearing, emphasizing his remarks by illustrative gesticulations and by freehand drawings on the blackboard.* Far from being ponderous even when dealing with traditionally ponderous subjects, he was even reproached for flippancy. His incorrigible raffishness allowed him to say that God was certainly no gentleman ! He did not talk formally, but dropped easily into slang and colloquialisms. His voice was admirably controlled and tempered. His best lecturing was delightful talk. He did not write out his lectures but, mastering his subject, improvised. This

---

* See *Principles of Psychology* II, 305: "Some persons, the present writer among the number, can hardly lecture without a blackboard: the abstract conceptions must be symbolized by letters, squares or circles, and the relations between them by lines."

allowed him large liberty which he further expanded by digressions, suggested by his discourse or by questions. He gave his thoughts, like Emerson, by a process of moral radiation rather than by systematic exposition. Often he was carried away in the digressions and brought himself up, exclaiming, "What *was* I talking about ?" Spontaneous humor was a native endowment and he made large use of it. His protest against what he disliked was as apt to be comical as serious. In assaulting the Hegelians, whom he intensely disliked for their peculiarly involved intellectualism, he said:

One is almost tempted to believe that the pantomime-state of mind and that of the Hegelian dialectics are, emotionally considered, one and the same thing. In the pantomime all common things are represented to happen in impossible ways, people jump down each other's throats, houses turn inside out, old women become young men, everything "passes into its opposite" with inconceivable celerity and skill; and this, so far from producing perplexity, brings rapture to the beholder's mind. And so in the Hegelian logic, relations elsewhere recognized under the insipid name of distinctions (such as that between knower and object, many and one) must first be translated into impossibilities and contradictions, then "transcended" and identified by miracle, ere the proper temper is induced for thoroughly enjoying the spectacle they show.

To emphasize a point he would seize upon an extreme statement, being as much a devotee of exaggeration as his father. "This universe," he once said to a class, "will never be completely good as long as one being is unhappy, as long as one poor cockroach suffers the pangs of unrequited love."

In carrying his message to the people, he travelled more in America than had ever before been his privilege. Not only did he accept every lecture offer in the area freely within reach of Cambridge, but he also went as far afield as Chicago, Colorado and California. In the summer of 1896 he went to the Chautauqua encampment, in New York state, and from the experience drew many amusing and instructive lessons. He was chiefly impressed by the flatness of unmitigated goodness. He emerged from his experience feeling that to relieve the tedium "the flash of a pistol, a dagger, or a devilish eye, anything to break the unlovely level of 10,000 good people — a crime, murder, rape, elopement, anything would do." "Even an Armenian massacre, whether to be killer or killed, would seem an agreeable change from the blamelessness of Chautauqua. . ." Such life lacked significance for him and characteristically he sought until he found the reason — and it was of a piece with his world-outlook. "I soon recognized," he wrote a few years later, "that it was the element that gives to the wicked outer world all its moral style, expressiveness and picturesqueness, — strength and strenuousness, intensity and danger. What excites and interests the looker-on at life, what the romances and the statues celebrate and the grim civic monuments remind us of, is the everlasting battle of the powers of light with those of darkness; with heroism, reduced to its bare chance, yet ever and anon snatching victory from the jaws of death. But in this unspeakable Chautauqua there was no potentiality of death in sight anywhere, and no point of the compass visible from which danger might possibly appear. The idea was so completely victorious already that no sight of any previous battle remained, the place just resting on its oars. But what our human emotions seem to require is the sight of the struggle going on. The moment the fruits are being merely eaten, things become ignoble. Sweat and effort, human nature strained to its uttermost and on the rack, yet getting through alive, and then turning its back on its success to pursue another more and rare and arduous still — this is the sort of thing the presence of which inspires us, and the reality of which it seems to be the function of all the higher forms of literature and fine art to bring home to us and suggest. At Chautauqua there were no racks, even in the place's historical museum; and no sweat, except possibly the gentle moisture on the brow of some lecturer, or on the sides of some player in the ball-field. Such absence of human nature *in extremis* anywhere seemed, then, a suf-

ficient explanation for Chautauqua's flatness and lack of zest."
And does not this criticism tell us under what conditions
life became meaningful and significant to William James?
There is a large element of confession here!

The basic simplicity of his position is further illustrated
by a passage from a letter written to his children in 1898.
He was then in California lecturing at the University and
visiting in the Yosemite Valley. "I saw a moving sight the
other morning before breakfast in a little hotel where I
slept in the dusty fields," he wrote. "The young man of the
house had shot a little wolf called a coyote, in the early morning. The heroic little animal lay on the ground, with his
big furry ears, and his clean white teeth, and his jolly cheerful little body, but his brave little life was gone. It made
me think how brave all these living things are. Here little
coyote was, without any clothes or house or books or anything, with nothing but his own naked self to pay his way
with, and risking his life so cheerfully — and losing it —
just to see if he could pick up a meal near the hotel. He
was doing his coyote-business like a hero, and you must do
your boy-business, and I my man-business bravely too, or
else we won't be worth as much as that little coyote."
Bravery and a willingness to risk all in the game with no
certainty of reward is the most elementary summary of
James's philosophy it is possible to give.

Yet with all this, James was always fascinated by the question of abnormal mental states. At this very time when he
was preaching the gospel of striving and risk, he was preoccupied with that very question. During 1897 he delivered
a series of lectures on the subject in Boston and to his students of psychology he had for years back emphasized that
from the abnormal we could get glimpses, and there only,
of the potentialities of the normal. No small part of his
interest is attributable to the fact that he felt that mentally
as well as physically, we live on the "perilous edge." He
was considerably impressed by the fact that no *sharp* line

could be drawn between President Eliot and the inmates of the Dedham Insane Asylum. The difference was too intangible to be rudely grasped. The zoo, the prison, the hospital, the insane asylum, the seance room of the medium were all dumping down their material for alive psychologists and philosophers to consider. And James was surely one of these.

Indeed in James the explorations assumed particular importance because of the fact that he was not encumbered with any distaste for the revelations that might come from twisted minds. He resolutely cultivated an open-eyed attitude toward all the many varieties of men, "sentimentalists, mystics, spiritualists, wizards, cranks, quacks and impostors . . . ," as well as to all sorts of facts. He loved the cranks and they loved him. So great was his tolerance of aberrant humans that the upshot was, according to Professor Palmer, that "His judgment of men was not good; it was corrupted by kindness."

In 1898 James was invited to give his lectures on pedagogy at the University of California. In addition he undertook to address the Philosophical Union on August 26th on "Philosophical Conceptions and Practical Results." In this address he forecast definitely and unmistakably the whole range of his interests for the next decade, both philosophical and religious. Harking back to the early seventies when he had listened to Charles Peirce talk in the Metaphysical Club, he revived Peirce's principle of pragmatism, giving it his own "twist" or interpretation. He marvelled that no one had happened to see the significance of the term during all the years since its publication in 1878. And then he launched into an exposition of it, illustrating his remarks by bringing up the old conflict between theism and materialism.

"The ultimate test for us of what a truth means is indeed the conduct it dictates or inspires . . ." he said, "and I should prefer for our purposes this evening to express Peirce's principle by saying that the effective meaning of any philosophic proposition can always be brought down to some particular consequence, in our future practical experience, whether active or passive; the point lying rather in the fact that the experience must be particular, than in the fact it must be active." "There can be no difference," he went on, "which doesn't make a difference — no difference of concrete fact, and of conduct consequent upon the fact, imposed on somebody, somehow, somewhere, and somewhen." This was the germ from which much of his later work was to grow.

In illustrating this principle, he remarked that retrospectively the theism-materialism issue was of no importance. Prospectively it was of the utmost importance. The value of theism was that it answered the "need of an eternal moral order. . ." "Materialism means simply the denial that the moral order is eternal, and the cutting off of ultimate hopes; theism means the affirmation of an eternal moral order and the letting loose of hope." From the point of view we have shown James as cultivating, the reason for tipping the scales in favor of theism are perfectly obvious. A world without moral meaning was to him no world at all. Furthermore, a world which denied pertinence to moral strivings was worse than no world because it dried up the springs of action. And to act one must believe in the *ultimate* triumph of good.

Yet if James supported theism, he did not support dogmatic theology, which he regarded as a secondary accretion upon a mass of concrete religious experiences. It was with the more direct experiences that he was concerned. "These direct experiences of a wider spiritual life with which our superficial consciousness is continuous, and with which it keeps up an intense commerce, form the primary mass of direct religious experience on which all hearsay religion rests, and which furnishes that notion of an ever-present God, out of which systematic theology thereupon proceeds to make capital in its own unreal pedantic way . . . they

are certainly the original of the God-idea, and theology is
the translation. . ."

We have here a forecast of the book which was to mark
the opening of the next period in James's life, *The Varieties
of Religious Experience*. It was predicated therefore on a
pragmatic justification and upon, particularly, the necessity of religion as a basis for action in the open universe.

BEFORE going to California James had spent a brief holiday
in the Adirondacks during which he injured his heart in a
way not immediately apparent. He had been sleeping
badly, a recurrent affliction with him, especially when under
any sort of intellectual tension. It eventually came out (for
James tried to make light of the feeling of difficulty he experienced) that the trouble was a "valvular lesion that was
irreparable, although not great enough seriously to curtail
his activities if he had given heed to his general condition
and avoided straining himself again." It was precisely this
that he did not do. The following June, moreover, he lost
his way while once more hiking in the Adirondacks, and
overstrained himself severely. With his usual habit of trying to ignore his physical condition, he passed from this
overexertion to the excitement and strain of preparing for
a trip to Europe, and when he got on the boat he immediately collapsed. A period had been put to another phase
of his life.

3. REDEFINING ULTIMATE PROBLEMS

WILLIAM JAMES'S collapse was not entirely a matter of heart
trouble. He also suffered from a severe nervous debility
and in treating one he at first failed to help the other. His
fight back to health was slow and painful. For the moment
it frequently seemed that he had come to the end of his
career. His reading was reduced to the minimum and his

writing to the quick composition of postcards to intimate
friends.   The effort of writing a letter would frequently put
him to bed for the rest of the day.   Yet he did struggle back
to health and by May 1901 was able to deliver the first series
of lectures in his course on the varieties of religious experience.

These two inactive years gave him greater occasion to
formulate his thoughts on public affairs than was hitherto
the case.   The end of the century was marked by three
events which interested him tremendously: the Dreyfus case
in France, the Boer War and the Spanish-American War.
Upon each of these he passed essentially moral judgments
and it is notable that his conclusions seem wisest in the
Dreyfus case where the moral judgment was quite relevant.
James did not think sociologically or even historically, but
almost exclusively in individualistic or biographical terms.
If his judgment of people was corrupted by kindness, his
judgment of public affairs was corrupted by his individualism.   He was pro-Dreyfus, a Little Englander and an anti-
Imperialist.   For each of these judgments there is the amplest justification, of course, but especially for the first.

James hated war while still believing that war-like instincts were an ineradicable part of man's constitution.   He
proposed to eliminate war by the elaboration of every sort
of conciliatory institution and by the conscious substitution
of peaceful counterparts for those values developed by the
military life.   He wanted to conserve adventure, fortitude,
discipline, but he did not want armies and war.   Each "war
scare" aroused him to feverish action in his search for
methods with which to counteract it.   The Spanish War
aroused his deepest concern, not in its original intention
of rescuing the Cubans from oppression, but in its final issue,
imperialism.

In this position he was one of an appreciable minority
of first citizens.   He joined hands with Andrew Carnegie
and men of similar contemporary respectability.   "Empire,"

he wrote to an English friend whom he was applauding for his Little Englandism, "is half crime by necessity of Nature, and to see a country like the United States, lucky enough to be born outside of it and its fatal traditions and inheritances, perversely rushing to wallow in the mire of it, shows how strong these ancient race instincts are." It was not so much the economic aspect of the matter that offended him, for of that he had very little to say, but it was rather the idea of reforming the Philippines by force that was the "unpardonable crime." He was instinctively anti-imperialist in an American tradition that was to persist very actively into utterly different times.

A similar inadequacy runs through his other judgments. It was the peculiarity of his mind that he was never to lag behind his age or to run far in front of it. It is very easy to overemphasize the connection between James's ideas, major and minor, and those of the Gilded Age or even, as some writers contend, those of the frontier period. While there is no question about his delight in a fluid society and equally no question about the fact that his ideas were roughly ratified by American social experience (though their personal basis is more obvious), it must be pointed out that James never actually adopted the cruder standards of his time. He was always a refining influence. And if, in the succeeding years, this social ratification has been withdrawn by the tightening up of American society which has become "trimmed and closed," science has left behind the cast-iron world machine against which he contended and advanced in his direction — toward the idea of an open universe. In his social opinions, James was, with strange persistence, just abreast with the best contemporary expressions of social optimism. In fact he raised the desire to be up-to-date-on-the-whole to the level of an intellectual principle. Yet by the strictly pragmatic test he was not a rebel in the social sphere. Though he ardently believed in the necessity of a melioristic struggle, or a constant war on evil, he never envisaged a utopia and had no social formulae to propose. This left his social views peculiarly amorphous and since his interests deflected his mind from the fundamentals of social change, peculiarly inadequate. Where he was perhaps rebellious, in the philosophical sphere, he had the good fortune not to offend any of the non-philosophical powers of his day who perchance glimpsed what he was driving at. James was, indeed, essentially conservative in his pronouncements on morals, the family, religion (where his originality was in explanation), politics (where his physiologically based individualism allied him with the current *laissez-faire* attitude) and economics. While he justified experimentation in all of these fields, he contributed nothing himself.

It has already been made clear that his moral preachments were mostly designed to increase efficiency in action. He had nothing in particular to say about codes of conduct and his reflections on the contemporary mores were of the mildest. He could stop on occasion to poke fun at the New Englandish habit of mind that substituted limbs for legs and stomach for belly, but he did not go beyond this. He never played with any scheme for changing sex relations. He never found fault with the institution of marriage. His perception of the future importance of the work of Sigmund Freud was based entirely on his firm belief in the importance of the unconscious, the subliminal, and not at all upon the sexual ideas.

James's economic principles were equally conservative. He was an individualist and of course had no truck with the nascent socialism. He praised his friend Thomas Davidson for ignoring the economic entanglements in which his workingmen students were involved and concentrating upon their mental and 'spiritual' development. While he did think that a more equitable distribution of wealth would eventually have to be arranged, he had no ideas as to how it would be done. He got some stimulation out of H. G. Wells's idea of a society governed by the superior types.

His reaction was chiefly against the aimless accumulation of great wealth and the moral undesirability of the emphasis of contemporary society upon it. "The prevalent fear of poverty among the educated classes is the worst moral disease from which our civilization suffers," he wrote. He thought of poverty in its moral, its disciplinary aspect, and the life of the poor appealed to him because it was heroic! When an economic issue turned up in politics, as in 1896, he instinctively turned to the conservative side, to McKinley and the gold Republicans. His desire not to be blind to the values of other individuals saved him from unfairness to Bryan and his followers, however. Similarly when economic troubles became acute and broke out into strikes, he treated the matter as a mere case of growing pains. He pointed out to his brother Henry (surely here is blindness of a kind!) that all the Chicago anarchists were continental foreigners. Native Americans would not engage in such activities! There is no record of his protesting against the executions that followed on this outburst of social passion. In this respect James was not so advanced as the benign William Dean Howells!

What contemporary trends he did condemn, like imperialism and undisciplined wealth getting, were condemned for moral reasons. He was offended by the American emphasis on mere bigness. He railed against the American worship of the "bitch goddess" success. And he wrote movingly against the PH.D. octopus. Here he was simply trying to guard against the submergence of the individual in organization and the poison of merely external signs of success. Whenever he could he sought to break up the conventional straight-jackets as when he tried to get his friend Thomas Davidson — an incorrigible enemy of convention — an appointment at Harvard. It was the moral example of the good individual that was his chief remedy for all undesirable situations, whether it be in wealth getting, Tammany corruption or whatever. He laid down a sharp contrast be-

tween the institutionalized corruption of European society
with its monarchies, its armies and its churches and the
American system where corruption in social matters was
alleged to be a matter of monetary bribes passed between
individuals. His belief in democracy was strong. It was
not based upon any mere matter of a voting system, but
upon a perception of the necessity of free circulation of individuals in society. Like so many Americans of his time
and earlier he had a firm belief that while the East might
be banal and somewhat corrupted by European example,
the new West would bring the American spirit to fine flower.
He could imagine an outburst of intellectual energy on the
shores of the Pacific as the natural accompaniment of the
expansive force of American society.

It is a notable fact that two out of the three most representative American philosophers, Emerson and James — the
third is Jonathan Edwards — were free will individualists
and social optimists. James's reactions to his colleagues
at Harvard, which came out most clearly in his letters of
this time, were reactions against essentially uncharacteristic
types of American minds. Royce and Santayana have never
been claimed as representative of the American intellect in
its philosophical expression. Santayana in particular has
been classed as an anomalous development in American society and his roots have uniformly been referred to European
soil. James himself was plentifully nourished by European
sustenance, but his position in the British tradition of psychology and philosophy kept him always fairly within the
range of the British tradition in American life. The principles to which he gave firmest allegiance brought him to a
remarkable agreement with Emerson and such trends in
Emerson as he disagreed with he also disagreed with in
Josiah Royce.

The part that Royce played as a foil for James's thinking needs a little emphasis. Though he was in a sense one
of James's proteges (one of James's cranks Royce himself

said) he was not one of James's allies. Royce was chiefly concerned with the elaboration and defence of a monistic philosophy, something which inspired abhorrence in James. Just as his early days were devoted to demolishing Spencer's evolutionary monism, so his later days were devoted to destroying the idealistic monism of such men as T. H. Green ("this apostolic human being but strenuously feeble writer . . ."), F. H. Bradley and Royce — above all Royce as the man of the type closest to him — an intimate and beloved friend, indeed. James spoke feelingly to his classes against "that overweening desire of wallowing in unbridled unity."

In the atmosphere of free criticism cultivated at Harvard there was nothing anomalous in this sort of thing. In writing to Royce, James frankly confessed that he wrote his own books with one eye on what Royce had said. He was inspired to action in a large measure by his desire once and for all to pulverize Royce's absolute. When the latter's most substantial books came out James found himself applying the adjectives "charming" and "pretty" to them. "In spite of the great technical freight he carries," James wrote a fellow philosopher, "and his extraordinary mental vigor, he belongs essentially among the lighter skirmishers of philosophy. A sketcher and popularizer, not a pile-driver, foundation-layer, or wall-builder." His work was "in the line of philosophic fancy-work, perhaps the most important of all except religious fancy-work." Yet he could also call Royce a "perfect little Socrates in wisdom." He recommended his books freely, quoted him largely and when possible approvingly, in every way advanced his audience and enhanced his reputation. He could not avoid taking Royce's arguments for absolute idealism with tremendous seriousness when it came to formulating his own thought. It has already been noted that James laid considerable stress upon the deepseated passion in mankind for monistic philosophies. He therefore recognized that Royce was answering a trend in the human mind and indeed, he later came to the admission that judged by its fruits in consolation, there was considerable pragmatic justification for the absolute. But he could not accept it and his arguments were all directed against it. Royce retorted in kind and wrote a paper in which an imaginary German, centuries hence, convicted James of drunkenness on the basis of passages in his works!

George Santayana dissented from the philosophies of both Royce and James. As a student under the latter he had a tremendous affection for the man which has found excellent expression on many occasions. But his mature conclusions were against those of James and he has decided that, aside from the appeal of James's personality, the principal contributions James made to his development came from *The Principles of Psychology*. Of James's philosophy Santayana developed a very low opinion, only very reluctantly admitting that he was a philosopher at all. Indeed he has advanced the theory that James only made incursions into philosophy; that he was a sort of "raider" of the philosophical garden; and that residence on the premises was not native to his disposition. "What a curse philosophy would be if we couldn't forget all about it!" Santayana quotes James as saying and then sadly he comments: "In other words, philosophy was not to him what it has been to so many, a consolation and sanctuary in a life which would have been unsatisfying without it. It would be incongruous, therefore, to expect of him that he should build a philosophy like an edifice to go and live in for good. Philosophy to him was rather like a maze in which he happened to find himself wandering, and what he was looking for was the way out. In the presence of theories of any sort he was attentive, puzzled, suspicious, with a certain inner prompting to disregard them. He lived all his life among them, as a child lives among grown-up people. . ." If Santayana came to think poorly of James as a philosopher and highly of him as a man, James in his turn thought poorly of Santayana's

philosophy and praised his uncompromising stand on his
intuitions. Santayana's philosophy, James wrote in 1905,
"has no *rational* foundation, being merely one man's way of
viewing things. . ." "What a perfection of rottenness in a
philosophy !" he had exclaimed on an earlier occasion. "I
don't think I ever knew the anti-realistic view to be propounded with. so impudently superior an air. It is refreshing to see a representative of moribund Latinity rise up and
administer such reproof to us barbarians in the hour of
our triumph. . . Nevertheless, how fantastic a philosophy !
— as if the 'world of values' *were* independent of existence.
It is only as *being*, that one thing is better than another.
The idea of darkness is as good as that of light, as ideas.
There is more value in light's *being*. All the exquisite consolation, when you have ascertained the badness of all fact,
in knowing that badness is inferior to goodness, to the end
— it only rubs the pessimism in. . . Dramatic unities; laws
of versification; ecclesiastical systems; scholastic doctrines.
Bah ! Give me Walt Whitman and Browning ten times
over, much as the perverse ugliness of the latter at times
irritates me, and intensely as I have enjoyed Santayana's
attack. The barbarians are in the line of mental growth,
and those who do insist that the ideal and the real are
dynamically continuous are those by whom the world is to
be saved." And yet James was thankful that Harvard had
Santayana; it thickened the atmosphere; and he recommended his books to his own followers and advanced his
reputation whenever he could ! Royce, however, was the
true "enemy."

The Harvard atmosphere fairly crackled with disagreement. It was not an accidental condition, moreover, but one
consciously cultivated and a good deal of the credit for
fostering the situation must go to George Herbert Palmer.
Palmer was the senior member of the department, the oldest
member of the Harvard school of philosophy. "In our
lectures," he has written, "we were accustomed to attack each

other by name, James forever exposing the follies of the idealists, particularly Royce and me, Royce in turn showing how baseless all empiricism is, lacking a metaphysical ground." James was the attraction for all those students who were filled with the spirit of revolt. Royce gathered in the traditionalists, the pious and the lovers of "law and order." It was a healthy atmosphere from which two major figures emerged triumphant, both thinking poorly of the other philosophically: James and Santayana.

When William James was a young man he heard his father read from a Boston paper that Lord Gifford's will had provided for certain lectureships at Edinburgh. The fact meant nothing to him, for at that time he had not determined to be a philosopher. Yet it stuck in his mind and when he delivered his first series of lectures on the foundation in May of 1901, he recalled the fact in his ninth discourse. Furthermore he pointed out that his first philosophical diet was of Scotch origin. Fraser's *Essays in Philosophy* was the first book of philosophy he ever looked into and Sir William Hamilton's works were the "first philosophic writings I ever forced myself to study, and after that I was immersed in Dugald Stewart and Thomas Brown." To complete the identification it was "chief glory of the English and Scottish thinkers to have kept the organic connection in view. The guiding principle of British philosophy has in fact been that every difference must *make* a difference, every theoretical difference somewhere issues in a practical difference, and that the best method of discussing point of theory is to begin by ascertaining what practical difference would result from one alternative or the other being true." This was pragmatism in essence and it was from this point of view that William James proposed to discuss religion, both in the first series of lectures delivered in 1901 and in the second series delivered in April of the following year. In these lectures he had his say on the religious issue more fully than ever before. *The Varieties of Religious Experience* (1902) immediately took its place as one of the classics of modern religious thought, the first great book he had produced since *The Principles of Psychology* of 1890. It was a fitting prelude to the last period of his life.

James posited his religion on an individualistic basis. Religion was, when it was alive, a personal matter based upon experience. He was opposed to all orthodoxies and had small interest in theological subtleties. They were both secondary elaborations of the personal experience and once the vital spark had departed from them they degenerated into bigotries which attempted to impose their "closed-in theoretic system" upon mankind. It was but a step from that stage to persecution. Religion by its very nature needed to change from age to age. It was only by keeping alive the tradition of personal religious experience that growth could come. Furthermore, the 'great man' was always the indispensable trail maker in society. He set the pattern after which the less fortunate members of the community modelled their lives. If we are to understand the true meaning of the religious experience, we must go to these men and not try to discover it in the life stories of the ordinary believers, whose religion was inevitably based upon "suggested feeling and imitated conduct."

In the terminology of the eighteenth century religious controversies, James was a "rational supernaturalist" and hence religiously orthodox. Had he lived then he would have herded along with John Locke, Archbishop Tillotson and Samuel Clarke; he would have opposed the Deists like Tindal and Voltaire; and he would have abhorred the sceptical and destructive Hume and the materialistic atheist Holbach. But he did not live in the eighteenth century and it is only secondarily illuminating to place him there. The thought of that sensible century was foreign to his mind. He rested his case briefly on the last named below of the three great bases for religion advanced in the nineteenth century: feeling, intuition and a special religious sense. To the latter he brought what he thought was psychological support. In his ethical bias, he was, of course, close to Fichte (whom he read *cira* 1870) and Ritschl.*

It was too easy, James thought, to discredit the religious experience by pointing to its pathological origin. Many of the great religious leaders, and a large proportion of the lesser, were undoubtedly pathological types. But to take this tack was to confuse origins with results. In James's opinion this was a fatal confusion. It was his purpose then, not to take account of the explanations pathology had advanced, but to look to the results and evaluate them. In this task "Immediate luminousness . . . philosophical reasonableness and moral helpfulness are the only available criteria." Thus while his detractors frequently referred to his book as *Wild Religions I Have Known,* he felt that he was getting at the root-bases of religion in the only way open to a candid observer.

Of course it was exceedingly difficult to say just what religion really was, and the difficulty points directly at the fact that no single selection of elements can possibly cover the whole case. Only the most generalized statement can possibly be useful. "As there thus seems to be no one elementary religious emotion, but only a common storehouse of emotion upon which religious objects may draw, so there might conceivably also prove to be no one specific and essential kind of religious object, and no one specific and essential kind of religious act." . . . "Religion, therefore, as I now ask you arbitrarily to take it, shall mean for us the feelings, acts, and experiences of individual men in their solitude, so far as they apprehend themselves to stand in relation to whatever they may consider the divine." Yet there was one quality which must be found in an attitude in order that it be called religious. "There must be something solemn, serious, and tender about any attitude which

* Matthew Arnold was in this general tradition also. See *Literature and Dogma.* The whole movement was anti-intellectualistic which made it appealing to William James, for reasons to be elaborated later.

we denominate religious." The *problem* of religion, finally, is to get into contact with "an unseen order" and the "supreme good" of religion is "in harmoniously adjusting ourselves thereto."

The question immediately comes up as to how the contact is to be made. Like his father, William James did not intend to separate God and his creature. To bridge this terrific gap, James had recourse to his idea of the subliminal which he had taken over from Frederic Meyers in the course of his psychical investigations. It is to this factor in the mental life of man that we must look for the resolution of this great riddle. "If there be higher powers able to impress us, they may get access to us only through the subliminal door." Yet if we agree that the contact can be made through this avenue, we have still not solved the problem of what is to be discovered on the other side. The subliminal is, then, like a door which opens in a ghostly fashion and lets *something* through from the other side without allowing us any glimpse of what there may be there. When we begin to talk about *that,* we are in the realm of over-beliefs and one man's pious guess is just as good as another's, always keeping within the bounds of reason. It may be possible that God and Heaven are through that door. It may equally be that there is nothing there but a sort of mother-sea of influence of which we receive periodical draughts. And it may be the residence of a whole collection of gods. William James himself vacillated between the idea of one god and polytheism. John Locke, one of James's admirations, said that "the existence of more than one God (was) contrary to reason." But James was not overly impressed by "reason!"

At any rate, there is in the religious experience a conviction "that the conscious personality is continuous with a wider self through which saving experiences come. . ." In *The Varieties* James tended to look upon this influx through the subliminal in terms of power, as an inflow of energy. This, it will be recalled, is different from his earlier conception of God as a stimulator to action. And if we combine the two notions we have the complete Jamesian God: half the source of personality-power, half stimulator to moral action in the mundane world — wholly imaginary?

These fundamentals in hand, we may examine the more detailed study of religious personalities to which James treats us. The book, it must be pointed out, is in large part a series of case histories illustrating each point he makes. In this respect it is immensely erudite, drawing as it does on the whole range of autobiographical literature in the field. The material includes citations from such standard religious autobiographies as Fox's *Journal,* St. Francis de Sales', *Chemin de la Perfection,* St. Teresa's, *Autobiography,* Marcus Aurelius, Bunyan's *Grace Abounding,* Tolstoi's *My Confession,* Annie Besant's *Autobiography,* St. Augustine's *Confessions,* the writings of Jonathan Edwards, John Woolman's *Journal,* and *The Life of the Blessed Henry Suso,* by himself, besides a large number of obscure American, French, Polish and other documents whose fame has never been celebrated but which kind friends brought to James's attention. In harmony with his inveterate habit of pointing up his work with free quotations he introduced matter from Emerson, Renan, Frederick Locker Lampson, Havelock Ellis, Theodore Parker, Marie Bashkirtseff, Whitman, Stevenson, Alphonse Daudet, Victor Hugo, Sainte Beuve, Thoreau, Edward Carpenter, J. A. Symonds, Richard Jefferies, Amiel, Maeterlinck and Ralph Waldo Trine. Finally, it is freely larded with long citations from the narratives of anonymous religious sufferers collected by Professor Edwin D. Starbuck and Professor Theodore Flournoy, his friends. As an exhibition in odd and sometimes outrageous learning, the book is decidedly impressive.

From this material James teased out generalizations on certain fundamental matters some of which we have taken from their places to preface this account. One of his dis-

tinctions has gained a good deal of popular acceptance that
has kept it in circulation long after his explorations of the
subliminal have been relegated to the realm of the mistaken.
He drew a distinction between the healthy-minded religious
person and the sick soul, and he equated the first with the
once born person and the second with the twice born.
Healthy-mindedness we are told is "the tendency which looks
on all things and sees that they are good. . ." It is based
upon "a constitutional incapacity for prolonged suffering,
and in which the tendency to see things optimistically is
like a water of crystallization in which the individual's character is set." An excellent example of a healthy-minded,
once-born, type is Emerson. Another is Walt Whitman.
"In the Romish Church," James explains, "such characters
find a more congenial soil to grow in than in Protestantism,
whose fashions of feeling have been set by minds of a decidedly pessimistic order. But even in Protestantism they
have been abundant enough; and in its recent 'liberal' developments of Unitarianism and latitudinarianism generally,
minds of this type have played and still are playing leading
and constructive parts." The religion of this type consists
in settling scores "with the more evil aspects of the universe
by systematically declining to lay them to heart or make
much of them, by ignoring them in his reflective calcula-
tions, or even, on occasion, by denying outright that they
exist. Evil is a disease; and worry over disease is itself an
additional form of disease, which only adds to the original
complaint. Even repentance and remorse, affections which
come in the character of ministers of good, may be but sickly
and relaxing impulses. The best repentance is to up and
act for righteousness, and forget that you ever had relations
with sin." On the other hand the sick soul is plagued in
one or more or all of three ways. He feels the vanity of
mortal things; he is plagued with a deep sense of sin; and
he suffers from the fear of the universe. His situation resolves itself into the cry of Help! Help! To the religious

person of this type the "experience of evil" is something absolutely essential. The healthy-minded person appears as astoundingly trivial. "To the healthy-minded way, on the other hand, the way of the sick soul seems unmanly and diseased. With their grubbing in rat-holes instead of living in the light; with their manufacture of fears, and preoccupation with every unwholesome kind of misery, there is something almost obscene about these children of wrath and cravers of a second birth." A second birth. That is the phenomenon of conversion.

Conversion is a process of unification. Those who experience it obviously have been suffering from a divided personality which has allowed them no peace. "To be converted, to be regenerated, to receive grace, to experience religion, to gain an assurance, are so many phrases which denote the process, gradual or sudden, by which a self hitherto divided, and consciously wrong, inferior and unhappy, becomes unified and consciously right, superior and happy, in consequence of its firmer hold upon religious realities." This is a description of conversion in psychological terms, but in the case of religion the change is supposedly very sudden and the intervention of God is taken as the cause. While conversion is normally associated with adolescence it is by no means exclusively confined to that period of life. Most conversions as experienced by the ordinary run of people are plainly influenced by conventional instruction, appeal or example. These take place constantly and no particular attention needs to be given them. What really needs study and explanation are those cases of sudden and radical conversion of mature people who have long since ceased to be influenced by the surrounding environment in any obvious way. This is one of the more extraordinary phases of man's religious life. While no cause can positively be given for it, it seems reasonable to suppose that the crisis is brought about by the conjoint working of deliberate thinking and the "subconscious incubation and maturing of motives deposited by the experiences of life." Once again then, James relies upon the subconscious or subliminal for the explanation of religious experience.

The immediate effects of conversion are to be observed in the transformation of the subject's character. The effect is to release new sources of energy. "The collective name for the ripe fruits of religion in a character is Saintliness. The saintly character is the character for which spiritual emotions are the habitual centre of the personal energy; and there is a certain composite photograph of universal saintliness, the same in all religions, of which the features can easily be traced." Now of course James does not take saintliness to mean anything priggish or 'sanctimonious.' He clearly defines the characteristics of the saintly character as follows:

1. "A feeling of being in a wider life than that of this world's selfish little interests; and a conviction, not merely intellectual, but as it were sensible, of the existence of an Ideal Power."

2. "A sense of the friendly continuity of the ideal power with our own life, and a willing self-surrender to its control.

3. "An immense elation and freedom, as the outlines of the confining selfhood melt down.

4. "A shifting of the emotional centre towards loving and harmonious affections, towards 'yes, yes,' and away from 'no' where the claims of the non-ego are concerned."

It is very clear from this that James regarded the religious personality as one of higher power than the ordinary personality. We have noted all along that he insisted on the importance of God as a stimulator to action and now we have ample evidence of what is meant by saying that he added to it at this time the concept of God as a source of power. But the two ideas are not utterly different, for the influx of the God-power is of importance chiefly in its effect on conduct. The difference is that whereas in his early writings he placed no emphasis at all upon the relation of the subject to God, now it has become all important. Yet the possibility re-

mains that persons who have no sense of this communion
can still find inspiration in the God idea and energize themselves by working to assist in God's alleged purposes.

For the religious experience is in essence mystical and
the great characteristic of mysticism is the difficulty or indeed
the impossibility of communicating a sense of it to those
who have not experienced it.   William James was not of a
mystical nature himself.   He spoke of the subject second-
hand.   Yet he looked upon those who did experience mysticism with great respect.   In the final analysis, however, he
laid down the principle that "non-mystics are under no
obligation to acknowledge in mystical states a superior authority conferred on them by their intrinsic nature."   Like
all other phases of the religious experience, this one must
also be judged by its results.   And the results seemed to
him to be by and large good.   This was a somewhat expected judgment, for he had begun with a firm conviction
that "the best fruits of religious experience are the best
things that history has to show."   It was hardly likely that
he would end by rejecting the most characteristic form of
the personal religious experience.   Indeed he set great store
by the ratification mystics gave to ideas arrived at on naturalistic grounds.   It worried him quite a bit that the mystics
almost universally ratified the doctrine of the Absolute.   It
gave him greater confidence in his own pluralism when it
too received mystical confirmation by the experiences of
Benjamin Paul Blood, whose writings he assiduously followed all of his life and to whom he devoted one of the last
articles he wrote.   Blood's pluralistic mysticism was developed under the influence of anaesthetics, but no matter,
it was at least a ratification, and the conclusions were expressed in peculiarly impressive and elevated language.
The fact brought comfort to James's mind.

The Varieties of Religious Experience was an attempt
at a natural history of the religious experience.   In undertaking it James had deliberately rejected any concern for

theology and when he came to the end of his discussion of the various case histories and had formulated his conclusions, he was faced with the necessity of formulating something like a philosophy of religion. Any philosophy of religion is pointless, he felt, which did not start with the experiences he had examined. If such a philosophy had any function whatsoever it is to explain them in abstract terms. But the conventional religious philosophies make the opposite pretension and "assumes to construct religious objects out of the resources of logical reason alone, or of logical reason drawing rigorous inference from non-subjective facts. It calls its conclusions dogmatic theology, or philosophy of the absolute, as the case may be. . ." Either sort of activity seemed immensely futile to James.

"In the middle of the century just past, Mayne Reid was the great writer of books of out-of-door adventure. He was forever extolling the hunters and field-observers of living animals' habits, and keeping up a fire of invective against the 'closet-naturalists,' as he called them, the collectors and classifiers, and handlers of skeletons and skins. When I was a boy, I used to think that a closet-naturalist must be the vilest type of wretch under the sun. But surely the systematic theologians are the closet-naturalists of the deity, even in Captain Mayne Reid's sense. What is their deduction of metaphysical attributes but a shuffling and matching of pedantic dictionary-adjectives, aloof from morals, aloof from human needs, something that might be worked out from the mere word 'God' by one of those logical machines of wood and brass which recent ingenuity has contrived as well as by a man of flesh and blood? They have the trail of the serpent over them. One feels that in the theologian's hands, they are only a set of titles obtained by a mechanical manipulation of synonyms; verbality has stepped into the place of vision, professionalism into that of life. Instead of bread we have a stone; instead of a fish, a serpent. Did such a conglomeration of abstract terms give really the gist of our knowledge of the deity, schools of theology might indeed continue to flourish, but religion, vital religion, would have taken its flight from this world. What keeps religion going is something else than abstract definitions and systems of concatenated adjectives, and something different from faculties of theology and their professors. All these things are after-effects, secondary accretions upon those phenomena of vital conversation with the unseen divine, of which I have shown you so many instances, renewing themselves *in saecula saeculorum* in the lives of humble private men.

So much for the metaphysical attributes of God! From the point of view of practical religion, the metaphysical monster which they offer to our worship is an absolutely worthless invention of the scholarly mind.

This is, surely, a major flight of James's dislike of abstractionistic thinking! Yet it gets us only a little way toward his own formulation of a philosophical justification for religion. Indeed any justification that he had to offer was more in the nature of a rationalization than anything else, for he started with the conviction too deep set for mere argumentation to confirm or upset it, that religion was necessary and desirable. As we shall see shortly his own personal religious ideas were of the slackest, but the conviction that "there was something in" religion was firm and abiding. It was "absolutely hopeless" he thought "to demonstrate by purely intellectual processes the truth of the deliverances of direct religious experience." This was a resignation of function in a philosopher, surely, for if he fell back upon the position that it *was* truth and stubbornly refused to say more, how did he differ from any man who chose similarly to assert the truth of his religious convictions?

Philosophy he therefore said could serve a sifting function, purging religious revelations of the personal and accidental and removing from the "spontaneous religious constructions . . . doctrines that are known to be scientifically absurd or incongruous." In the end then, philosophy in James's hands abased itself before the religious experience as completely as any Scholastic could demand. For while he firmly refused to *start* from God and an officially sanctioned religious code, he was willing to arrive at God and "religious experience" after long travail and stand awed before his own handiwork! In result, his position was little different from that of the Scholastics. They both resigned their function, one in the beginning, the other in the end. It was all the same after all.

We began this discussion of William James's most extensive canvass of the religious question by taking note of the fact that he intended to view his subject pragmatically. Earlier we had discovered that he had justified theism pragmatically in his important lecture at the University of California in August, 1899. In the end, we find him once more returning to the pragmatic justification of religion as the only philosophic contribution to the subject he cared to make. The important point about any idea, according to pragmatism, was the consequences that flowed from it in conduct. Religion, as presented in *The Varieties,* was chiefly of importance for the direct and unmistakable difference it made in the conduct of those who experienced it. Therefore:

That the God with whom, staring from the hither side of our own extra-marginal self, we come at its remoter margin into commerce should be the absolute world-ruler, is of course a very considerable over-belief. Over-belief as it is, though, it is an article of almost every one's religion. Most of us pretend in some way to prop it upon our philosophy, but the philosophy itself is really propped upon this faith. What is this but to say that religion, in her fullest exercise of function, is not a mere illumination of facts already elsewhere given, not a mere passion, like love, which views things in a rosier light. It is indeed that, as we have seen abundantly. But it is something more, namely, a postulator of new *facts* as well. The world interpreted religiously is not the materialistic world over again, with an altered expression; it must have, over and above the altered expression, a *natural constitution* different at some points from that which a materialistic world would have. It must be such that different events can be expected in it, different conduct must be required.

It was then, in the fact that religion does make a difference in the conduct of its devotees that its pragmatic justification was found. That was the essential philosophic contribution to the discussion of religion made by William James. He also contributed to the development of the idea of recurrent revelation and so made religious thought more flexi-

ble, freeing it from the motion of a once-for-all revelation
authenticated by rigid theology. His other contributions
were purely explanatory and dealt with the nature of the
experience. As the years have passed his explanations have
been discredited. Analysis of the unconscious has not
brought any justification for a belief in the idea that it is a
point of contact with supernatural powers. But if one
holds to the pragmatic conception of truth, then religion
remains as potent a factor in the world as James found it
to be. One would be forced on those terms to agree with
him that the religious experience must play an eternal part
in the drama of human experience.

From the foregoing one might legitimately conclude that
James was himself a profoundly religious person. Such a
conclusion would be untrue, for the strange fact is that while
he expended an enormous amount of energy in justifying
the position of religious people, most of the material he
handled was second-hand to him. He could link it up with
nothing in himself. Naturally enough he did not traffic
with any established ecclesiasticism. The habits formed in
his youth would have barred that possibility short of conversion. He did however attend chapel with considerable
regularity while he taught at Harvard and he took a sympathetic interest in every reasonable religious project. What
he had was a firm conviction of the importance and significance of religion without any very deep personal warrant
for the nature of the religious experience. In answering
a questionnaire on religious belief, circulated by Professor
James B. Pratt of Williams College, he clearly formulated
his own position on the more fundamental problems. "Religion means primarily a universe of spiritual relations surrounding the earthly practical ones, not merely relations
of 'value,' but agencies and their activities. I suppose that
the chief premise for my hospitality towards the religious
testimony of others is my conviction that 'normal' or 'sane'

consciousness is so small a part of actual experience. Whatever be true, it is not true exclusively, as philistine scientific opinion assumes. The other kinds of consciousness bear witness to a much wider universe of experiences, from which our belief selects and emphasizes such parts as best satisfy our needs." Now, as pointed out earlier, that is a sort of parody on his father's religious position. That he tied it up so closely with his interest in psychical research and the mind-cure experiments he investigated, is also worthy of remark, showing that to him religion was simply one more 'romantic' psychological fact needing exploration and explanation. Going on, he confessed that his belief in God was the product of an admiration for the "tradition of religious people, to which something in me makes . . . response." He found no justification for religion in the Bible and he did not pretend to belief in God on the evidence it presented. In fact he did not think that a candid reader of the Bible could continue to believe in its divine authorship ! God to him was an ally of his own ideals, yet he could not pray to Him however without feeling foolish and his "experience" of him was nil. Finally, he had but a weak belief in immortality.

On 1898 he had delivered the Ingersoll Lecture on Immortality at Harvard and there gave expression to a concern about the doctrine at least. His concern was to save it from total destruction at the hands of the 'philistine' scientists. In doing so he resorted to the theory of influx from the divine sphere which he expanded so radically in *The Varieties*. Indeed the Ingersoll Lecture may be taken as the first effort to formulate this idea in public discussion. Before attempting to indicate the line James took on this occasion, it is necessary to present an earlier and more primitive phase of his belief which found expression in *The Principles of Psychology*. "The reason of the belief," he wrote, "is undoubtedly the bodily commotion the exciting idea sets up. . . The surest warrant for immortality is the yearning of our bowels for our dear ones; for God, the sinking sense it gives us to imagine no such Providence or help." This is astonishingly crude and obvious, and the lecture of 1898 has at least the advantage of greater complexity, if not of greater validity.   He argued that one could legitimately take the brain as an organ of transmission.   Positing that the natural world is surrounded by a spiritual world, he went on to argue that the barrier between the two might occasionally be thinned down to the point that contact between the two could be made.   The organ by which the contact was made was the brain.   Consciousness, on this theory, would be transmitted from the spiritual world to the natural world by way of the brain.   "And in transmitting it — to keep to our extremely mechanical metaphor, which confessedly throws no light on the actual *modus operandi* — one's brain would also leave effects upon the part remaining behind the veil; for when a thing is torn, both fragments feel the operation.   And just as (to use a very coarse figure) the stubs remain in a check-book whenever a check is used . . . so these impressions on the transcendent self might constitute so many vouchers of the finite experiences of which the brain had been the mediator; and ultimately they might form that collection within the larger self of memories of our earthly passage, which is all that, since Locke's day, the continuance of our personal identity beyond the grave has by psychology been recognized to mean."   Now this ingenious theory, based on so many *ifs* as to be almost entirely fabulous, is testimony to nothing so much as what G. Stanley Hall sarcastically called James's anxiety "concerning the postmortem future of his soul."   It hardly does honor to the realism for which he is famous.   His only excuse is that he needed Heaven as the place where the moral drama he observed on earth would be resolved. It was a rather desperate effort, inspired by paternal loyalty, to put earth-bound man in touch with the supernatural world.

GEORGE SANTAYANA does not think that William James was a philosopher at all. What, then, is a philosopher? Writing to a friend Henry Adams gave excellent expression to one commonly held conception of the philosophic attitude. A philosopher, he wrote, "delights in studying phenomena, whether of his own mind or of matter, with absolute indifference to the results. His business is to reason about life, thought, the soul, and truth, as though he were reasoning about phosphates and square roots; and to a mind fairly weary of self, there is a marvellous relief and positive delight in getting down to the hardpan of science. He never stops to ask what the result of a theory or demonstration is to be on his own relations to God or to life. His pleasure is to work as though he were a small God and immortal and possible omniscient." Certainly William James was not this sort of philosopher. He was too temperamental to meet the requirements and he carried into his studies too many personal biases.

There is a certain logic in the fact that he, first of all "philosophers," emphasized the personal equation in philosophy. To understand a philosopher, he wrote on several occasions, try to grasp the central point in his vision and then all the rest of what he says will fall into its place. It was altogether wrong to expect to master a man's point of view by trying to relate carefully arranged passages from his work into logical series. Nothing good could come of it, for while one might erect an admirable logical structure, one would certainly miss the man. Certainly this is true of William James. His general vision far outweighs in importance any particular piece of technical exposition he may have published. The latter are all subordinate to his larger purpose. It is his vision that still retains importance long after his technical arguments have been reduced to powder.

In his pursuit of the personal equation in philosophy he laid down certain humorous dicta and he also made a sweeping gesture in a direction since followed by more precise investigators. He told his small son that to be a philosopher one had only to read things in books and copy them down. The hardest part of the job was the writing. And he told Thomas Perry that to be a philosopher it was primarily necessary to hate the other fellow's way of thinking. This latter observation is really serious humor, for certainly few of his books would have been written had he not "hated" the various and sundry types of monism that flourished in his day. Without Royce to joust with, his own thoughts would have remained rather amorphous. On the other hand, his sweeping gesture, a contribution to the discussion of personality types, was really a hurried excursion into a field now being assiduously cultivated. His purpose was to drive home his point about really original philosophies being based in the idiosyncracies of personalities. Personality being basic, a final resolution of outlooks was utterly impossible even though a technique might be evolved to enable one to thread one's way among them with fruitful results. The fact would remain, however, that Schopenhauer and Leopardi are confounded by Fourier and Dr. Pangloss, — Henry Adams by Walt Whitman !

What distinguishes a philosopher's truth from that of the ordinary man is that it is reasoned. But the reasonings are often of far less significance than the original vision and indeed may be but logical rationalizations of the fundamental perceptions. Since perception may come to any thoughtful person, James believed in encouraging young thinkers to get their thoughts into form, regardless of how pedantic scholars may treat them, to bring freshness and spontaneity in a field notable for its dryness and dullness. It was not so important, he thought, to define one's relations to Kant or Spinoza or Rousseau, or to be perturbed by being disposed of as a mere variant of one of these, as to say oneself out. The big point is to join one's thinking to human nature, and technical virtuosity was not necessary for that.

Running lightly over the field, James divided all thinkers

into two divisions, the tough-minded and the tender-minded. These distinctions have become proverbial and so limber are they that they are freely bent in directions James never intended. In his own mind the contrast worked out as follows:

The Tender-Minded	The Tough-Minded
Rationalistic (going by "principles")	Empiricist (going by "facts")
Intellectualistic	Sensationalistic
Idealistic	Materialistic
Optimistic	Pessimistic
Religious	Irreligious
Free-Willist	Fatalistic
Monistic	Pluralistic
Dogmatical	Sceptical

The most obvious thing about this contrast is that one may be predominantly one type or the other and yet rather hopelessly mix the subordinate characteristics. James recognized this confusion, as how could he not? for he himself was both tough- and tender-minded. He was empiricist, sensationalistic, pluralistic, sceptical, a free willist, optimistic and religious. Obviously what was necessary was some reconciling method which would enable one to cross freely between the two divisions. The need was to discover a "system that will combine both things, the scientific loyalty to facts and willingness to take account of them, the spirit of adaptation and accommodation, in short, but also the old confidence in human values and the resultant spontaneity. . ."

This aspect of his thought has been touched upon before with the notation that it was his fundamental aspiration to meet this demand. We have also noted that the method by which these contradictions could be reconciled, so he thought, was pragmatism, and in a moment we shall examine in some detail what he meant by pragmatism. But, following out of his own way of thinking, his pragmatism was merely his logical rationalization of his essential vision. It was a *via media* to reconcile the discrepancies in his own thinking. Since he was not strong on logic and since, also, as he grew older he became increasingly suspicious of logic, his method was weak. James's pragmatic method will appear, therefore, as an inadequate method for universal use and it is only important as illustrating how he made his mental peace. His central vision is much more interesting, and by his own confession, much more important. Since it was so decidedly basic in his thinking we have hardly progressed this far without shadowing forth its essential outlines. At this point it may be profitable to pause and review the points already made and to cast the general position in as precise terms as possible.

In William James's eyes the universe was not fixed and closed. It was free and open. A philosopher could not ask it to sit for its portrait, but his task must be to make a track of some sort through the jungle it presented to the naked eye. The factor of change, of movement, was basic. On the other hand the universe was not hostile and inimical but warm and living. It was the theatre of God's drama and the essential happenings in that drama had to do with the conquest of evil and the triumph of good. It was man's duty to collaborate with God in this task, sustained by free will and faith in his ideals. Though it was likely that evil could never be entirely eliminated short of Heaven and that it was a permanent element in the irreducibly mixed world, still the possibilities of worth while accomplishment were very great, for man was decidedly capable of imposing his wishes upon the world. Evil was in fact but one of the many elements in the world and the presence of disparate elements required one to take a pluralistic view of nature. However one strove to encompass nature in a single formula there would always be something left over. And just as the essential duty of man to strive with God's help for the triumph of good, so it was his duty to accept without complaint the fact that the goods of which he could gain knowledge were provisional. Such a good as truth was not something which existed externally and eternally, but something which grew out of life. To James *the* TRUTH was an idol of the tribe. Truth was always in the making, like the perfect society; it was made true by events; and it was a weapon in the moral battle. Like everything else, it was provisional. The essence of life to James, always recall, is its fluidity. Movement, mixture of elements, moral struggle, indetermination, chance — these were fundamental in James's world. It was a world constantly in the making.

THE ORIGINS of pragmatism are as obscure as the origins of most ideas. It seems to have been precipitated out of a mixture of sources and in the hands of Charles Peirce, the founder, it took a rather different tack from the direction it got from William James. Peirce saw germs of the idea in Socrates, Aristotle, Spinoza, Locke, Berkeley, Auguste Comte and Kant. It seems to have been chiefly suggested to him by Kant, so far as it was the product of book learning at all. For in Peirce's eyes the doctrine was largely the product of his observations of the way scientists worked in the laboratories.

James saw roots of it there also. He thought that

it owes its being to the breakdown which the last fifty years have brought about in the older notions of scientific truth. "God geometrizes," it used to be said; and it was believed that Euclid's elements literally reproduced his geometrizing. There is an eternal and unchangeable "reason"; and its voice was supposed to reverberate in *Barbara* and *Celarent*. So also of the "laws of nature," physical and chemical, so of natural history classifications — all were supposed to be exact and exclusive duplicates of pre-human archetypes buried in the structure of things, to which the spark of divinity hidden in our intellect enables us to penetrate. The anatomy of the world is logical, and its logic is that of a university professor, it was thought. . . It is to be doubted whether any theorizer today, either in mathematics, logic, physics or biology, conceives himself to be literally re-editing processes of nature or thoughts of God.

James had experienced this sort of thing under Louis Agassiz. As he looked back into history for the forerunners of pragmatism, he named Hume, Dugald Stewart, Thomas Brown, James Mill, John Mill (to whom he dedicated his book called *Pragmatism*), Bain and Shadworth Hodgson. Curiously enough he tried to rule out Kant and proposed that philosophy detour around him, for the critical tradition came from the Scotch and English thinkers. However much these men may have moved in the pragmatist direction, it was beyond question to Charles Peirce that James was indebted for the concrete suggestion. As we have seen, he first heard Peirce's exposition about 1872 and he read the printed paper, "How to Make Our Ideas Clear," in *Popular Science Monthly* for January 1878. In 1898 he took up the theory in his lecture before the Philosophical Union of the University of California and used as his illustration of its utility, the theism-materialism contrast. Eight years later still, in 1906, he formulated his most finished exposition. In the thirty-four year interval between first hearing Peirce expound it and his own extended espousal of it, James considerably modified the principle in the direction of looseness. This fact is a clear example of the deleterious effect of his feeling it necessary to break down intellectualism.

Charles Peirce's pragmatism was, writes Ralph Barton Perry, based on a scientist's and logician's insistence "upon the importance of technique." Peirce was the son of the famous Harvard mathematician, Benjamin Peirce. He was educated at Lawrence Scientific School, the class ahead of James, and spent years of his life in laboratories. Unlike most scientific workers he was acutely critical of his mental processes and took an active interest in logic and psychology. His natural bent was toward an academic career but, writes Dr. Morris Cohen, "A certain inner instability or lack of self-mastery is reflected in the outer moral or conventional waywardness which, except for a few years at Johns Hopkins, caused him to be excluded from a university career." Nevertheless his intellectual career was of high distinction. "He made," to quote Professor Cohen again, "important contributions not only in mathematical logic, but also in photometric astronomy, geodesy, and psychophysics, as well as in philology." His whole intellectual training and career was the opposite of James's. The latter was almost blind mathematically, he hated laboratory work, and he was chiefly interested in morals. Taking an idea out of Peirce's extensive repertory of undeveloped insights, he could not fail to give it a peculiar twist. Going directly to the Peirce paper to which James refers, we find Peirce writing:

And what, then, is belief? It is the demi-cadence which closes a musical phrase in the symphony of our intellectual life. We have seen that it has just three properties: First, it is something that we are aware of; second, it appeases the irritation of doubt; and, third, it involves the establishment in our nature of a rule of action, or, say for short, a *habit*. . . The *final* upshot of thinking is the exercise of volition, and of this thought no longer forms a part; but belief is only a stadium of mental action, an effect upon our nature due to thought, which will influence future thinking. The essence of belief is the establishment of a habit, and different beliefs are distinguished by the different modes of action to which they give rise. If beliefs do not differ in this respect, if they appease the same doubt by producing the same rule of action, then no mere differences in the manner of consciousness of them can make them different beliefs, any more than playing a tune in different keys is playing different tunes.

These ideas he elaborately explains, and ends his paper on this note: "It is certainly important to know how to make our ideas clear, but they may be ever so clear without being true." What, then, makes ideas true? It is in getting this part of his insight into words that Pierce radically differed from James, as we shall see in a moment. Once we have made our ideas clear it is necessary to test them to make them true. The best method of testing, Peirce contended, is the scientific method. "The opinion," he wrote, "which is fated to be ultimately agreed to by all *who investigate,* is what we mean by the truth, and the object represented in this opinion is the real." James overlooked this passage, so it seems. On the basis of it it is easy to see why John Dewey, in his exposition of Peirce's pragmatism, says that "everything ultimately turned, for Peirce, upon the trustworthiness of the procedures of inquiry. . . The appeal in Peirce is essentially to the consensus of those who have investigated, using methods which are capable of employment by all. It is the need for social agreement . . . which finally forces upon mankind the wider and wider utilization of the scientific method." James has little to say about this, as will shortly develop, for he became more and more suspicious of logic — more and more anti-intellectualistic. James advanced a "temperamental" pragmatism.

Under James's handling pragmatism was divided into two parts, first the method and second a conception of truth. It is not altogether easy to separate the two even with the aid of his subsequent expositions in his replies to critics. In *Pragmatism* (1907) his exposition of pragmatic truth was confined chiefly to one chapter. His replies to misconceptions and criticisms eventually filled a book, *The Meaning of Truth*, (1909).

What James sought to combine was "the scientific loyalty to facts and willingness to take account of them . . . (with) the old confidence in human values. . ." It hardly need be said again how loyally he served this purpose. In pragmatism *as he conceived it* he thought he saw an instrument to use in the battle. Pragmatism as method did not stand for any particular set of results. Under pragmatic treatment "Theories . . . become instruments, not answers to enigmas, in which you can rest. . . No particular results then, so far, but only an attitude of orientation, is what the pragmatic method means. The attitude of looking away from first things, principles, 'categories,' supposed necessities; and of looking towards last things, fruits, consequences, facts." How was this to be accomplished ? For the best statement of the Pragmatic Rule we must turn to *Some Problems of Philosophy* written after most of the criticisms were in:

The pragmatic rule is that the meaning of a concept may always be found, if not in some sensible particular which it directly designates, then in some particular difference in the course of human experience which its being true will make. Test every concept by the question "What sensible difference to anybody will its truth make ?" and you are in the best possible position for understanding what it means and for discussing its importance. If, questioning whether a certain concept be true or false, you can think of absolutely nothing that would practically differ in the two cases, you may assume that the alternative is meaningless and that your concept is no distinct idea. If two concepts lead you to infer the same particular consequence, then you may assume that they embody the same meaning under different names. This rule applies to concepts of every order of complexity. . .

Surely this is simple and obvious enough. So far James and Peirce seem close together. It was when James tried to extend his field to include truth that he got into trouble. It was then also that he departed from Peirce's principles !

Professedly James borrowed his conception of truth from science. But he had nothing much to say about method — he laid no emphasis there — and he did not go on to define the Peircean social ratification. In *Pragmatism* he wrote:

Pragmatism . . . asks its usual question. "Grant an idea or belief to be true," it says, "what concrete difference will its being true make in any one's actual life ? How will truth be realized ? What experiences will be different from those which would obtain if the belief were false ? What, in short, is the truth's cash-value in experimental terms ?"

The moment pragmatism asks this question it sees the answer. *True ideas are those that we can assimilate, validate, corroborate and verify.* But how ? By what method ? *False ideas are those that we can not.* That is the practical difference it makes to us to have true ideas; that, therefore, is the meaning of truth, for it is all that truth is known — as . . . The truth of an idea is not a stagnant property inherent in it. Truth *happens* to an idea. It *becomes* true, is *made* true by events. Its verity *is* in fact an event, a process; the process namely of its verifying itself, its veri-*fication*. Its validity is the process of its valid-*ation*.

THIS is a long way from the old-fashioned notion of truth from which pragmatism was a reaction. But there was a surviving element of the agreement formula, for our ideas must "'agree' with reality." In the account of Peirce's pragmatism we quoted a passage saying that what is agreed upon by all who investigate is the truth "and the object represented in this opinion is real." Peirce followed this by the statement: "That is the way I would explain reality." Reality becomes, then what science agrees upon. James wrote:

Realities mean . . . either concrete facts, or abstract kinds of things and relations perceived intuitively between them. They furthermore and thirdly mean, as things that new ideas of ours must no less take account of, the whole body of other truths already in our possession. But what now does 'agreement' with such threefold realities mean? . . . To 'agree' in the widest sense with a reality can only mean to be guided either straight up to it or into its surroundings, or to be put into such working touch with it as to handle either it or something connected with it better than if we disagreed. . . The essential thing is the process of being guided. Any idea that helps us to *deal*, whether practically or intellectually, with either the reality or its belongings, that doesn't entangle our progress in frustrations, that *fits*, in fact, and adapts our life to the reality's whole setting, will agree sufficiently to meet the requirement. It will hold true of that reality.

James pushed on as follows: "the possession of true thoughts means everywhere the possession of invaluable instruments of action. . . The possession of truth, so far from being an end in itself, is only a preliminary means toward other vital satisfactions." Truth then is not a static commodity which can be appropriated and banked until the possessor becomes rich like a miser hoarding dollars. One must always look to the "functional possibilities" to get at the "whole logical content" of a truth. Truth was important only insofar as it led us directly back into reality. Truth then is a phase of the adaptive function of the mind and nothing else. James says in another place that "If the reality assumed were cancelled from the pragmatist's universe of discourse, he would straightway give the name of falsehoods to the beliefs remaining, in spite of all their satisfactoriness." The relations to reality was, then, the crucial thing. The "satisfaction" taken in an idea was not personal satisfaction. The satisfaction was in the idea's agreement with reality. "Realities are not *true,* they *are;* and beliefs are true *of* them." So James reasoned. It would seem that his teleological bias has considerably interfered with his desire to be clear.

A few other stumbling blocks remain. There is the phrase "whether practically or intellectually." Numerous misinterpretations of James's meaning arose from the word, "practically." 'Practically,' he used to mean 'particular' — and with reference to *mental* as well as physical concerns. Ideas "work indefinitely inside of the mental world" of course.

"Not crediting us with this rudimentary insight," wrote James, "our critics treat our view as offering itself exclusively to engineers, doctors, financiers, and men of action generally, who need some sort of a rough and ready *weltanschauung,* but have no time or wit to study genuine philosophy. It is usually described as a characteristically American movement, a sort of bobtailed scheme of thought, excellently fitted for the man on the street, who naturally hates theory and wants cash returns immediately.

But even when James with unusual fierceness replied to his critics, misunderstandings remained. There were plenty like Santayana who couldn't stomach that way of looking at truth. And indeed any candid student of James's writings must find it difficult to discover how he expected understanding and agreement. He perversely left out all reference to the question of method and he apparently could not see that the discovery of truth was a social as well as an individual enterprise. His individualism, indeed, was leading him deeper and deeper into the mire of subjectivism. In his horror of "intellectualism" he was going to boggle in the swamp of the particular. His final conclusion was that the whole issue between the pragmatists and the anti-pragmatists boiled down to "concreteness *versus* abstractness." He would show the viciousness of abstractness.

James, an acute critic has observed, is distinguished by the fact that "he not only didn't know precisely what he meant but knew he didn't know, and made no attempt to state it precisely." The truth of this disconcerting observation is nowhere more excellently illustrated than in his effort to retain a direct contact with the aboriginal facts of life while at the same time giving abstractions their proper place in the intellectual scheme. With his inveterate habit of setting up a middle course between pure anarchy and pure absolutism, he tried to enunciate a sort of representative democracy as a philosophical principle. His temperamental bias carried him over to the side of the anarchists, but he was unable finally to bomb the castles of the abstractionists. It was entirely natural that a self-scrutinizing individualist should be more impressed by the diversity of the world than the unity. Man is protean to himself.

He was forced, nevertheless, to recognize that without abstractions thinking is an impossibility. They represent the funded experience of the race and if we reject them we will immediately revert to savagery. Unless we translate our percepts into concepts we are hopeless in the face of reality. Our capacity to do so is the source of superiority over brutes. Yet we must recognize that they are tools for handling experience and not things in themselves. We should use them as sources of "vision and of power." If we go on to build up a system for explaining the world with them, we must recognize that each step takes us farther and farther away from reality until in the end we must come to a completely unreal conclusion. We can never know a thing as it really is by its definition. We can never truly know reality through concepts. "Concepts are but as flowers gathered, they are only moments dipped out from the stream of time, snap-shots taken, as by a kinetoscopic camera, at a life that in its original coming is continuous." They help us to understand life backward. But we live forward and if concepts are to serve us well their principal function is immediately to guide us back into reality. Indeed the whole question turns upon one's idea of reality. To the man of James's temperament reality is essentially dramatic, perpetually changing, "a great unpent and unstayed wilderness. . ." He chooses to dwell there or very nearby for fear that if he turn his face away and follow fond fancy he will lose contact with the world and be deluded by falsehood. The abstractionist, on the other hand, is appalled by the messiness of reality, and even when he admits the essential accuracy of the Jamesian view of it, seeks to gain control of it by reducing it to order by erecting "noble, clean-cut, fixed, eternal, rational, temple-like systems of philosophy," based on concepts. But concepts are purely subjective in origin and not universally valid.

Yet in a sense the abstractionists' aspiration is to be admired, but just as temptations inevitably pursue the saint into the desert, so the abstractionist is dogged by the idea that because his system is logical and beautiful and emotionally satisfying, he has mastered the tricky reality with which we are all faced. He is inevitably tempted into announcing that he has hit upon the central, unifying principle that the enigma at last has its answer. But, says James in rebuttal, there never yet has been a monistic principle discovered that did not ignore some fact or facts and as long as one least little fact fails of inclusion the abstractionist structure is without value and void. The world is monistic just so far as connections can be established between the constituent parts. Experience has proved that we cannot get all the way in this fashion. The only way out is to admit to pluralism. The upshot is that James was willing to accept the fruits of abstractionism just so far as he found them valid and no farther. But he completed his philosophy by resorting to a pluralism which allowed him to take cognizance of the "wild" facts that escaped the abstractionist net. His philosophy was not, then, an *absolute* pluralism; he advocated no completely disconnected world; nor was it absolutely monistic; for that ignored the presence of facts that pressed daily upon the attention.   If he is notable for any one thing it is the fact that he constantly sought to raise to the level of respectability all sorts of "romantic" facts whether they were those of psychical research or eupeptic "New Thought." Like Montaigne, William James felt that the last word was hardly likely to be spoken until the last man to live had turned in his evidence.

It is easy now to understand why he felt that the problem of the *one* and the *many* was the central problem of philosophy.   From a man's position on this problem, he claimed, he could deduce his general range of opinions and certainly could assess the nature of his intelligence.   His own mulling of the problem led him to place the emphasis on the many, the natural result of a temperamental bias in favor of the loose and fluid, of "that distributed and strung-along and flowing sort of reality which we finite beings swim in."   Considering the claims for the absolute (the one) advanced by fine and admirable minds he wrote a memorable passage notable at once as a statement of his opposition and for the candid revelation of the temperamental basis of his position. Just as his conception of reality was grounded in his psychological theory of the 'stream of consciousness' which in turn was one projection of his temperamental desire to escape the materialistic monism of Spencer and the others, so his temperament once more comes to the surface very obviously in this passage from *A Pluralistic Universe* (1909).

"Probably the weightiest contribution to our feeling of the rationality of the universe which the notion of the absolute brings is the assurance that however disturbed the surface may be, at bottom all is well with the cosmos — central peace abiding at the heart of endless agitation.   This conception is rational in many ways, beautiful aesthetically, beautiful intellectually (could we follow it into detail), and beautiful morally, *if the enjoyment of security can be accounted moral.*   Practically it is less beautiful; for . . . in representing the deepest reality of the world as static and without a history, it loosens the world's hold upon our sympathies and leaves the soul of it foreign. Nevertheless it does give peace, and that kind of rationality is so paramountly demanded by men that to the end of time there will be absolutists, men who choose belief in a static eternal, rather than admit that *the finite world of change and striving,* even with a God as one of the strivers, is itself eternal. (My italics.)

It was in the interests of his world-view that he rejected the abstracting method and the absolute, saying "let the absolute bury the absolute." And finally, "Damn the absolute!"

IN FLEEING the absolute down the labyrinthine ways of the mind he came perilously near bogging himself in the swamp of anti-intellectualism. As it is, the whole trend of his thought was in that direction and he has taken his place as a contributor to the decline of respect for the intellect which is still the characteristic mood of our time. His holding out of a fraternal hand to Henri Bergson is an expression of this tendency. What he chiefly got from Bergson (and in spite of a persistent *impression* among the careless the two are not identical) was his attack on intellectualism. He found him a sustaining influence in allowing him to follow the trend of his thinking and give up logic. It helped him to get man on his belly in the midst of booming, buzzing reality! Leon Daudet has sarcastically written: "If flies had a philosophy it would undoubtedly resemble pragmatism, since it would be the product of their multi-surfaced vision."

James never pretended to understand all of Bergson's thinking and he was too generous in recording his indebtedness to him. Bergson would have meant nothing had he not confirmed trends already started. But between them they gave force to the movement to drown reason and its instrument, logic, in the fluid of reality. James's critique of intellectualism goes directly back to his idea of the stream of consciousness and his idea of the inadequacy of intellectualism to his notion of the importance of selection in mental operations. He thus stands as a principal precursor of the contemporary intellectual debacle. We have become so stiflingly self-conscious of our minds, so aware of their inadequacy, that we are unable to do more than to take refuge in a crude and disintegrating relativism. Aided and abetted by such psychological systems developed after James's time as Freudianism, and by our fascination with the "discrediting" origins of many of our "ideas," we have taken refuge in playing idle variations on the melody of chaos. That this sort of thing has arisen simultaneously with the unparalleled progress of science is one of the ironies of history.

WHEN William James began to advance his philosophical ideas he was immediately plunged into a sea of controversy and some of his later letters are tinged with a sad impatience at the general stupidity of the human race. Citing two other critics in writing to a third he wrote that "Both are vastly worse than you; and I cry to Heaven to tell me of what insane root my 'leading contemporaries' have eaten, that they are so smitten with blindness as to the meaning of printed texts." When he came to get out his "pragmatism" the discussion rose as near to fever pitch as philosophical discussions ever rise. Pragmatism was damned as an ally of callous commercialism; as contributing to the decline of intellectual precision and exactitude; as an invitation to wallow in the naturalistic flux; as a theory only fit for the masses and those concerned sentimentally with the happiness of humanity. It was surely not a true philosophy — it was not sufficiently aristocratic !

Yet the very vigor of the counter-attack indicates the profound impression James made in his day. He forced every "philosopher" in America to take a stand on pragmatism and most of the new books were measured with reference to the doctrine. For a time it seemed as though all valuable American thinking would come out of William James's norfolk jacket as all Russian fiction of the 1840's came out of Gogol's

"The Overcoat." Not only did innumerable purely imitative pragmatists set up shop, but a vigorous new school, the Chicago instrumentalists under John Dewey, seemed to take its departure from his work. In a few years another crowd, the Behaviorists, would claim him as an ancestor. James's incursion into philosophy provoked frenzied activity among men who had long been sleeping in the arms of Bishop Butler's *Analogy*. He brought American philosophers to their feet with a yell. But he did not do his own work well for he was afflicted with the American vice of improvisation and he died before he got around to building a solid body of doctrine on which men could feed indefinitely. And now, in consequence, even those he influenced strongly are gradually abandoning him point by point. Such divergent figures as John Dewey and George Santayana now point to his *Psychology* as the truly solid contribution he made, ignoring all the rest of his writing. And the figure of Charles Saunders Peirce looms menacingly behind him. Like the crop of the Nova Scotia farmer, half of the seeds he planted didn't come up and the other half has been washed out by the scholarly rain drenched down on them since their scattering, so that the final result is hardly in keeping with the "crop prediction" of his time.

Not the least remarkable of the disciples he captured was Giovanni Papini. Papini was then in his iconoclastic stage and had not yet flung himself into the arms of the Church. In his magazine *Leonardo* he was advocating a pragmatism with extraordinary passion and it was he who advanced the "corridor theory of pragmatism." "Pragmatism," according to Papini, "is thus only a collection of attitudes and methods, and its chief characteristic is its armed neutrality in the midst of doctrines. It is like a corridor in a hotel, from which a hundred doors open into a hundred chambers. In one you may see a man on his knees praying to regain his faith; in another a desk at which sits some one eager to destroy all metaphysics; in a third a laboratory with an investigator looking for new footholds by which to advance upon the future. But the corridor belongs to all, and all must pass there. Pragmatism, in short, is a great *corridor-theory.*" It is sufficiently plain from this that James did not take pragmatism to be his philosophy, but thought of it merely as a method for getting at the practical consequences of all doctrines advanced. It is rather disconcerting, however, to know that Papini, the most ardent of the Italian pragmatists, turned to the Church, unable in spite of his insight into all creeds to escape the one from which he had temporarily rebelled. That William James should have counted so heavily on him is ironic, just as it is ironic that he felt he had a new ally in G. K. Chesterton! He was luckier with John Dewey and H. G. Wells. Wells called him his "second master," the first being Thomas Henry Huxley.

In 1905 his health required that he take a long rest and he employed his time in making a trip to the Mediterranean. A visit to Athens gave him immense satisfaction, but the true high point of the expedition was his reception at a Philosophical Congress in session at Rome. He had intended merely visiting the city to see his Italian allies, but once there thought he might as well register for the sessions. "When I gave my name," he wrote his wife, "the lady who was taking them almost fainted, saying that all Italy loved me, or words to that effect. . ." The fact is that he was eagerly sought out at every meeting of philosophers. His popularity was truly immense and extended to those who could not master his name and called him "Weelyam Yams." The authorities of this Congress inveigled him into giving an address which he wrote with amazing celerity in French and delivered it in the same language with equally amazing finesse. But in spite of the linguistic triumph he was completely and unanimously misunderstood by the earnest philosophers there assembled. His great satisfaction was to talk to his lay friends, Papini and his allies. They set him up immensely and he with equal energy advised all and sundry that philosophical life was to be found in Italy rather than in moribund Germany. "Papini is a jewel! To think of that little Dago putting himself ahead of every one of us . . . at a single stride. And what a writer! and what fecundity! and what courage (careless of nicknames, for it is so easy to call him now the Cyrano de Bergerac of Philosophy)! and what humor and what truth!"

The following year he had a rarely exciting experience of a different nature. He had taken leave from Harvard to go to Stanford to lecture during the Spring term and was in the midst of his work when the San Francisco earthquake occurred. Almost the last words to him before he left Cambridge were from a Californian, Charles Bakewell who said, "I hope they'll give you a touch of earthquake while you're there, so that you may also become acquainted with *that* Californian institution." When he was awakened on the morning of April 18, 1906, he exclaimed, "By Jove, here's Bakewell's old earthquake, after all! And a jolly good one it is, too!" It was indeed and James was fortunate enough to get a first hand glimpse of it. With one of the young women instructors at Stanford who wished to get into San Francisco and try to find her parents, he caught the only train into the city on that fateful day, spent the whole day prowling around observing the damage wrought and particularly studying the conduct of the survivors, and then with equal luck caught the only train out that night. He made his mid-day meal on Zu-Zu sugar snaps and cheese! It pleased him immensely to find that such a catastrophe brought the resourcefulness of mankind to the surface and that in the midst of natural chaos, the inhabitants improvised order and resumed living with amusing celerity. He also observed that while the physical suffering came to those immediately on the ground, the mental anguish was reserved, at least during the first few weeks, for he predicted an epidemic of nervous breakdowns once the pressure was eased, for those far away who had relatives or friends on the spot.

In his own family he had a perfect illustration of this, for his brother Henry in England was highly wrought up over the fate of William and his wife and wrote letters full of deep concern and sent off excited cablegrams. The devotion of the two brothers is touching and charming. They wrote to one another fully and regularly through all the years of their separation and the only touch of asperity in the correspondence rose out of William's attempt to turn Henry from pursuing his "later manner" to its logical conclusion. To Henry, William, after the death of their father, was the head of the family and more, for from childhood he had looked with awe and wonder on his mastery of the world they lived in. The relation was, of course, partly the admiration of a passive man for an active one. It was, in addition, high brotherly affection. But it transcended that and became, on Henry's part at least, the loyalty one has to that person who beyond all others makes an earthly career endurable.

Fortunately the whole episode of the earthquake was merely an "experience" to William and its only effect on his fortunes was to bring his work at Stanford to a premature close. He went East very shortly after for it was decided that the damage at the college put further college work out of the question. He was now a bit oppressed with the fear that he would die before he got his message out. After a summer at Chocorua, he delivered his lectures on pragmatism before the Lowell Institute in November and again at Columbia University in New York in January. This last was a happy experience from which he derived an immense amount of stimulation. Once he got into the swing of New York life he enjoyed the pace and even found himself exhilarated by the speed of the subway. Furthermore he was thrown into contact with some of the typical men of the day, taking dinner one night in company with Norman Hapgood, Frank Moore Colby, Mark Twain and Peter Finley Dunne (Mr. Dooley). It was the era of the ten cent magazines and in a certain rough sense James was a part of the movement. With his emphasis of consequences he could not but sympathize with the efforts being made to bring about a contact between the common people and the reforming journalists. Knowing this Norman Hapgood once made an effort to get him to write editorials for *Collier's* but James refused on the grounds that he could not express himself in short units; he could not meet Hapgood's own conviction that an important subject was one which could be disposed of in five hundred words. Nor did James look upon certain of the ten cent tendencies with an approving eye. He had a horror of a country of ten cent minds and as a corrective to this consummation he proposed that the college bred should take their places as leaders of the masses. Without entirely disapproving of the ten cent sheets, he did look with distrust upon the fact that they were displacing the colleges from intellectual leadership. But in this case as in so many others, James was disappointed, for the intellectual leadership of the country declined from the ten cent magazines to the one cent newspapers !

His own days as a leader of the college youths were over. In February of 1907 he resigned from Harvard and hoped to be able to devote himself to "getting his message out." His health, however, plagued him. He was in very poor physical condition and reading, writing, talking and walking all became a burden to him. Yet to a superficial observer he was still an active man. He always walked with a remarkably light step and carried himself erect. His true state of health remained concealed from the casual observer long after his intimates knew that he was in a very bad way. His intellectual aspirations were as vigorous as ever. He began reading in a more or less systematic way for a work variously entitled in his mind as *The Psychology of Jingoism* and *Varieties of Military Experience*. And he managed with infinite labor to write out and deliver the Hibbert Lectures at Oxford University. These were published in 1909 as *A*

Pluralistic Universe and the substance of them has already been given. This was the last great effort of his life and the book the last he saw printed. Just as the universe appeared to him never to be finished, so his own life exemplified the principle. With William James as with the universe it was a question of "ever not quite."

In the spring of 1910 he went once again to Europe. Henry James was very ill, in fact he was stricken with an illness which plagued him the remainder of *his* life, and William wished to be near him. Equally important was the fact that he needed medical attention himself. He proceeded through England and Paris (where he overexerted himself talking to friends) to Bad Nauheim. In spite of the treatments he did not improve. His condition became so bad that he himself finally gave up hope of ever resuming work. Yet in these last desperate months he found energy enough to pay a long delayed tribute to Benjamin Paul Blood who had given mystical ratification to his own insights and to rebut with considerable vigor Henry Adams's pessimistic conclusions about the future of the universe. His cosmic optimism never deserted him, no matter how heavy his personal troubles.

As it appeared that he was not to improve under European medical attention, it was decided to take him home. Henry was too ill to part from his brother and his sister-in-law, and accompanied them. They made a calm and uneventful trip via the Canadian Pacific Route and proceeded directly from Quebec to Chocorua. As William entered his loved country house he sank into a chair and exclaimed, "It's so good to get home."

He seemed to have expended his last resources in the effort to reach home and within forty-eight hours he took a definite turn for the worse, and on August 26, 1910, he died.

"I sit heavily stricken and in darkness," wrote his brother Henry a few days later, "for from far back in dimmest childhood he had been my ideal Elder Brother, and I still, through all the years, saw in him, even as a timorous boy yet, my protector, my backer, my authority and my pride. His extinction changes the face of life for me — besides the mere missing of his inexhaustible company and personality, originality, the whole unspeakably vivid and beautiful presence of him. And his noble intellectual vitality was still but at its climax — he had two or three ardent purposes and plans. He had cast them away, however, at the end — I mean that, dreadfully suffering, he wanted only to die."

And he wrote as with a deep cry of anguish to the old family friend, Grace Norton, "Think of us, dear Grace, think of us."

Henry James was the last surviving member of his father's house.

BOOK IV

HENRY JAMES

"We don't know what people might give us that they don't — the only thing is to take them on what they do and to allow them absolutely and utterly their conditions."
— *Henry James to W. D. Howells, May 17, 1890*

I. CHILDHOOD AND YOUTH

". . . il eut, contrairement a la tradition qui veut que les debuts litteraires soient durs dans le Nouveau Monde, toutes les facilites possibles pour se devellopper dans une atmosphere d'etude et d'intelligents loisirs."
— *T. Bentzon, Revue des Deux Mondes, May 1, 1883*

THE SECOND son of Henry James was named for his father. The family practiced a severe economy in given names until sheer numbers forced originality. The new Henry James was born at 21 Washington Place in New York City, where the family had taken up residence on moving down from Albany in the previous year. The date was April 15, 1843. With the coming of Henry the complement of children whose distinction was to be of concern to the world was complete. Two more sons and a daughter were born to the family, of marked and distinctive personality in their development, but they remained private citizens to their deaths. They were Garth Wilkinson (1845–1883), Robertson (1846–1910) and Alice (1848–1892). It was upon Henry, Junior, and William that the world was to bend its critical gaze.

Henry James was to become an indefatigable gatherer of

"impressions," but he was not allowed to start his career in
New York. When hardly a year old he was carried off to
Europe. The "golden nail" of Europe was driven in so accurately that he could later recall a vision of Paris as it beat
upon the consciousness of a baby of two years. This acute
susceptibility is of the very heart of Henry James's make-up.
It was to constitute the larger part of his resources as a
writer of fiction in the years to come, and in recording in
words the elusive suggestions of things unseen by the physical
eye, unheard by the physical ear, he was to strain the English
language to the breaking point. Preternaturally sensitive
to the aura, the least vibrations of the surrounding scene, his
reminiscences of his childhood are extraordinarily vivid.
They tell us a great deal about his psychological development, but they are lacking in that factual and chronological
solidity and accuracy dear to the heart of the biographer.
Straining the 1200 pages of musings through the sieve of
critical interpretation and verification, one can bring more
clearly before the reader the significance of the story but one
cannot hope to carry over the emotion and the sense of the
impressioned and impressionable mind seeking to understand the world. Taking the facts and rearranging them
into a new and more summary pattern may assist the understanding, but it inevitably destroys the fine bloom of the
original.

What a world Henry James had to explore! The father
of the house, as we have seen, was a man whose course in the
world was anomalous. For his time and place he was remarkably divorced from the dominant currents of the life
about him. In an era when politics was a consuming concern (the Civil War was to be the issue) he had nothing to do
with politics; and in an age when business was expanding on
all sides he abandoned the calling of his father and even resigned the management of his inheritance into the hands of
his brother-in-law. He disconnected himself, so to speak,
from the religious establishments as well, standing free in

order to evolve his own interpretation of the relation of man to God. In short, he pursued a way of life designed above all else to mark himself off from the rest of men. His sons had to make contacts with the surrounding life on their own initiative and his second son found the task difficult. Yet if Henry, Junior, did not discover much by way of politics, business or ecclesiasticism at home he did find a great deal by way of culture and cultivation. The prevailing atmosphere of his father's house was one of literariness, of abounding interest in the things of the mind, of endless curiosity about the ends of life and the meaning of it. His father had found a solution. His brother was to advance another. And Henry himself was to evolve, in a more devious way than either, a high and complex vision of human felicity.

HENRY JAMES first began actually to explore his surroundings in New York City, though he was to recover a sense of the Albany episode in his life which came during his fourth and fifth years, through his visits to his grandmother. By 1848, miraculous time of the war with Mexico and the revolutions in Europe, the family had settled down in their Fourteenth Street house. It was from this residence that Henry was to venture into the world — the world of schools and books and theatres and men and women. As he so marvellously recovered it in his last years, it was chiefly a cultural progress, a gradual widening of his intellectual horizon and, through remarkably few by-paths, a progress to his resolve to become a writer.

His schooling was wonderfully irregular, even during the extended period, from his fifth to his twelfth years, when, during the winter months, he was constantly in New York City. Each term it was a new experiment and frequently oftener. The James boys never attempted anything in the way of a public school, but always private institutions of the sort patronized by young Cubans and Mexicans who during those years found in New York an educational Mecca. What, if anything, Henry learned in these schools is impossible to say, just as it is difficult to discover what he learned in any of the various European institutions he intermittently attended. His impressions were all colored by Dickensian associations, derived from dramatized versions of that author, and by feelings entirely dissociated from anything ordinarily identified with the learning process.

The world was a moving and fascinating pageant to him. As his years increased the color and romance of the theatre came to play a large part in his vision, laying the foundation for his constant and eventually disastrous concern with theatricals. Out of his storehouse of memories he drew great quantities of recollections of forgotten performers and performances. His youthful mind was fed upon a theatrical fare of incredible tawdriness, just as in its earliest phases it was fed upon fiction of a far from edifying sort. One of the earliest novels of which he had recollection was *The Lamplighter,* a tearful romance by Maria Cummins, who after Nathaniel Hawthorne was Salem's gift to American fiction. Inevitably his diet was enlivened with Mrs. Stowe's *Uncle Tom's Cabin* when it came along and with the numerous books by Peter Parley, who briefly employed Nathaniel Hawthorne at ghost writing and other tasks, purveyor of culture to the masses in a manner only slightly different from that followed to this day. He *vividly,* indeed, remembered making the acquaintance of that worthy's *Universal History* (parts of which Hawthorne wrote), "a very fat, stumpy-looking book, bound in boards covered with green paper, and having in the text very small woodcuts of the most primitive sort."

Above him there was a larger world of which he caught glimpses and into which he was to penetrate at a surprisingly early age. He remembered the reception of *The Scarlet Letter* in 1850, remembered "dimly the sensation the book produced, and the little shudder with which people alluded to it, as if a peculiar horror were mixed with its attractions." In those days, however, the works of the revered Hawthorne,

as he was to become, to which Henry addressed himself were
The Wonder-Book and *Twice-Told Tales*.   Herman Melville's *Moby Dick*, which was printed in New York in 1851,
produced no vibration in the James household.

The principal sustenance he received was from books
of English origin.   His father was a diligent follower of the
products of the English presses and the first magazine he provided for his son was an importation, frequently delayed by
the non-arrival of the unreliable trans-Atlantic boats.   In
the house, too, was *Punch* of the pages of which Henry was
later to evoke a brilliant vision, specially over-emphasized
for the occasion of course, when he wrote an essay on George
du Maurier:

Many years ago a small American child, who lived in New York
and played in Union Square, which was then inclosed by a high
railing and governed by a solitary policeman — a strange, super-
annuated, dilapidated functionary, carrying a little cane and
wearing, with a very copious and very dirty shirt-front, the cos-
tume of a man of the world — a small American child was a silent
devotee of *Punch*.   Half an hour spent today in turning over the
early numbers transports him quite as much to old New York as
to the London of the first Crystal Palace and the years that immediately followed it.   From about 1850 to 1855 he lived, in imagination, no small part of his time, in the world represented
by the pencil of Leech.   He pored over the pictures of the people
riding in the Row, of the cabmen and the costermongers, of the
little pages in buttons, of the bathing-machines at the sea-side, of
the small boys in tall hats and Eton jackets, of the gentlemen
hunting the fox, of the pretty girls in striped petticoats and
coiffures of the shape of the mushroom.   These things were the
features of a world which he longed so to behold, that the familiar woodcuts (they were not so good in those days as they
have become since) grew at last as real to him as the furniture
of his home; and when he at present looks at the *Punch* of thirty
years ago he finds in it an odd association of mediaeval New
York.   He remembers that it was in such a locality, in that city,
that he first saw such a picture; he recalls the fading light of the
winter dusk, with the red fire and the red curtains in the background, in which more than once he was bidden to put down the
last numbers of the humorous sheet and come to his tea.
Punch was England; *Punch* was London; and England and London were at that time words of a multifarious suggestion to the

small American child. He liked much more to think of the British Empire than to indulge in the sports natural to his tender age, and many of his hours were spent in making mental pictures of the society of which the recurrent woodcuts offered him specimens and revelations. He had from year to year the prospect of really beholding this society (he heard every spring, from the earliest period, that his parents would go to Europe, and then he heard that they would not), and he had measured the value of the prospect with a keenness possibly premature. He knew the names of the London streets, of the theatres, of many of the shops; the dream of his young life was to take a walk in Kensington Gardens and go to Drury Lane to see a pantomime. There was a great deal in the old *Punch* about the pantomimes, and harlequins and columbines peopled the secret visions of this perverted young New Yorker. It was a mystic satisfaction to him that he had lived in Piccadilly when he was a baby; he remembered neither the period nor the place but the name of the latter had a strange delight for him. It had been promised him that he should behold once more that romantic thoroughfare, and he did so by the time he was twelve years old. Then he found that if *Punch* had been London (as he lay on the hearth-rug inhaling the exotic fragrance of the freshly-arrived journal), London was *Punch* and something more.

The American world was, in fact, not fruitful of reading matter and the American authors, other than the prophetic, were held in small regard by the master of the house. It was hardly likely that Henry would have found much to his taste in the productions of Emerson — a familiar presence in the Fourteenth Street establishment — or any of the other transcendentalists, however much they appealed to his father. He was able, though, to sample the writings of Washington Irving (whose hand he was to shake on a Hudson River steamboat) and there was Edgar Allan Poe who could offer stories sufficiently bizarre to hold a juvenile intelligence and about whom strange stories were told by Rufus W. Griswold, a visitor to the Fourteenth Street house. Fenimore Cooper, too, was ardently studied and his inventions pleasantly peopled the up-state world from which Henry's father had come.

Although there certainly was no definite policy of exclusion on the grounds of American origin, the fact remains that the local productions had neither the fascination nor the power of evoking allegiance possessed by those of English origin.   Europe was in the air; in the talk; it was always a possibility that this year or the next Henry would once more see it.   Midway in this New York period his father wrote to Emerson: ". . . considering with much pity our four stout boys, who have no play-room within doors and import shocking bad manners from the street, we gravely ponder whether it wouldn't be better to go abroad for a few years with them, allowing them to absorb French and German and get such a sensuous education as they can't get here."   Such was the extraordinary reaction produced on Henry James, Sr., after a few years in New York where his boys came in contact with the "roughs" in Union Square, with Barnum's American Museum and Niblo's Garden. True, the "roughs" were named Hoe, Havemeyer, Stokes, Phelps, Colgage, Van Buren, Van Winkle, De Peyster, Coster, Senter, Norcom and Robinson, scions all of the English and Dutch traditions of New York gentility, but full to the brim, mayhap, with false notions and false standards!

Not the least of these false notions were those about morals and the James boys were treated, at home, to recondite remarks on the difference between morality and moralism; they heard the vulgar ideal of "success" ridiculed; and they got no sense that they were in any way expected to make a career on the narrowing basis of a profession in competition with such fellows as their schools and their play brought to their notice.   The vast outside world of "careers" was a sealed book to them.   When they tried to find out what, in contemporary terms, their father pretended to do or be, that they might satisfy inquisitive playmates whose fathers were merchants, lawyers, or brokers, they were told to "say I'm a philosopher, say I'm a seeker for truth, say I'm a lover of my kind, say I'm an author of books if you like; or, best of all, just say I'm a Student."

Over the barrier around them the great American world flourished, to Henry's sense a vast swamp full of quick-sands that invariably swallowed up or at least blighted the high and shining promise of his innumerable uncles and cousins. It was peopled by but three types of human being, "the busy, the tipsy and Daniel Webster." The busy were taken up with something called, enigmatically, business, a type of activity of which Henry was never to get more than a very vague notion and the tipsy were those very blighted ones whose fate filled him with obscure forebodings about careers in America. Daniel Webster, of course, represented politics, the violent and contentious art or science or whatever it was that in some vague and dimly apprehended way had to do with . . . well what? Yet was not one of the Albany aunts married to a son of President Van Buren and did not Henry's father once pause on the street for a few words with General Winfield Scott, the defeated Whig candidate for the Presidency?

Henry's world was not a world of things to be used, of concrete purposes and solid realities. It was a world of "impressions," of pictures in a floating world. At this amazing and continuous show he sat not as a prospective actor, but as one dedicated from a very early date to being a spectator. It was while watching a performance of an especially violent and amazingly "unreal" (but what was the comparative reality?) drama in the company of his elders that Henry first became conscious of the spectator attitude toward life, an attitude which, as he remarked when he considered the phenomenon in retrospect, was to lead him to the wholehearted acceptance of Matthew Arnold's doctrine of culture. Unconsciously, even the abstracted boy was drawing from his environment the traits which were later to mark him as the most extraordinary high priest of culture ever to wave a censor before that exacting god.

What was culture and where in this great New York wilderness was it to be found? In this wilderness that commodity was not traded in and devotion to it constituted no recognizable profession. However mistily such thoughts

may have floated in Henry's mind, there is small doubt that
in all essentials his reaction was correct.   For certainly no
one could erect any considerable culture out of the strange
and incongruous elements spread before one in New York
of the early fifties.   It was not to be discovered in *The
Tribune* which his father's friend Horace Greeley was editing so that he could tell people what to think.   Nor was it
to be sensed in the theatrical exhibitions at which Henry
was so assiduously attendant.   Nor in the current art exhibitions assembled from the studios of Tom Hicks, Paul
Duggan, C. P. Cranch, Felix Darley, Cropsey, Cole, Kensett,
Ives, Powers and Mozier — forgotten — rightly ? — produc-
ers all.   And Thorwaldsen's "Christ" could give one no
more than a glimpse of the larger brighter world that existed,
somehow and somewhere, for the delectation of the elect.

It was out of these elements, out of Maria Cummins and
Mrs. Stowe, Peter Parley and the Rollo books, *Godey's Lady's
Book* (examined in a dentist's anteroom !) and *Punch* and
the picture books with which the home was so liberally supplied that Henry was composing his world.   The American
contributions were certainly not answering his half-formed,
nebulous questions, nor satisfying his great need for rewarding surfaces upon which imaginatively to play.   Never
thrown into the great whirlpool of American life, as Mr.
Alger of a later day was to put it, to sink or swim like a
later and equally indefatigable devotee of "impressions,"
Henry sought an answer to his questions in a world, constantly mentioned as better and as soon to be seen by all the
James family.   It was the mystic world, Europe, that was to
provide a contact with rewarding reality, that shrine at
which one might unrestrainedly pay one's devotions with no
fear of being sucked down into the depths with the busy,
the tipsy and Daniel Webster !

It was in 1855 that one more tap was to be given to the
"golden nail."   The American world was to be abandoned.
These years — 1855 to 1860 — after which the Jameses

were once more to locate in America for an extended stay, were tempestuously "political." For during them the slave owning, free trade Democrats held the balance of power: the Presidency, the Supreme Court, the Senate, the House. With an exuberant blindness characteristic of the politically triumphant they tried to stamp on the states the image of their desire. Successful in coralling the votes with undistinguished Presidential candidates, Franklin Pierce and James Buchanan, they felt in a strong enough position to ignore the signs of the times: significantly distributed dissenting votes on crucial issues in the Senate and House, unpopular Supreme Court decisions, and angrily protested Presidential vetoes. The anti-slavery people were still wild agitators and their sympathizers —- Henry James, Sr., among them — an unimportant minority. Far more indicative of the true moral temper of the people was the Know Nothing party, an example of the recurrent upsurging of American ignorance and intolerance, blindly striking out against imagined influence of the Papacy, socialism, infidelity and foreigners. With such as these the Jameses had no concern. They could only face such things as the repeal of the Missouri Compromise, the Dred Scott decision and Buchanan's veto of the Homestead Bill, with blank disapproval. As to the Know Nothing party . . . !

But if this dark, angry, seething pot offered nothing to detain them, July 1855 saw the appearance of a book by a newspaper man, living and working across the river in Brooklyn, *Leaves of Grass* by Walt Whitman. When this amazing exploration of self and country and universe did find its way into Henry James's hands he pronounced it unimportant, a compliment the author was to return by calling Henry's work "feathers." What was the America anyway, out of the shifting depths of which this monster had appeared, but a culturally barren swamp for trapping shining talents? While Europe! But enigmas demand solution and there were to be those to whom the American enigma was a challenge.

Henry James, whose impressions were so special, found his task in other fields. His vision was of different felicities from those of Walt Whitman or any other democratic American man.

OTHER than deepening the penetration of the "nail" in Henry's consciousness it is difficult to say what this new experience of Europe meant.   To be sure he was now a boy of twelve, steeped in the "idea" of Europe, in stories and pictures of its more romantic aspects, but there is little evidence that he actually saw Europe in the observational sense.   He simply saw the pictures of Europe he had looked at in New York.   For this pilgrimage which lasted for three years was pretty much a matter of schools and teachers for Henry, a repetition in a different setting of his life in New York. Nor was it more productive of measurable education.   From the London days he was to recall, among other tutors and governesses, one who was also to be a teacher of his friend to be, Robert Louis Stevenson.   But the sole indicative happening in the way of learning tasks was a clever rendering of La Fontaine's *Fables* into English.   This, coupled with the fact that in the last of the New York days he was constantly working over nebulous dramatic compositions, showed the drift of his interests, though so imperceptibly that no sense of it reached his constantly hovering parents.

In fact the submerged nature of Henry James's talents is one of the most remarkable things about his childhood and youth and yet, on the other hand, remarkably few false starts in the way of a career were made, a fact attributable, no doubt, to his father's being unalterably opposed to the very idea of a profession.   Nevertheless, looking back over his childhood and youth through the data deposited in the selective memory of Henry James it is not difficult to discover the evidence for a fairly logical evolution of a writer.   Henry recalled that "what we were to do . . . was just to *be* something, something unconnected with specific doing, something free and uncommitted, something finer in short than being *that*, whatever it was, might consist of."

His imagination was not fed entirely on books and casual theatrical fare. To an almost equal extent it turned to pictures. This phase of his mental development was very little encouraged during the New York days, but now, during a Parisian interlude, it flourished most extraordinarily. In a way but imperfectly perceptible to those readers whose knowledge of James is based upon his more mature fictions, pictures were a perpetual fascination to Henry. The progression of his earliest characters through Europe was almost a progression from picture to picture, from artist to artist and even the extent of their mental development was measured by their reactions to the collected masterpieces.

In Paris as a small boy Henry wandered in the corridors of the Louvre, awestruck by the magnificence, the far flung glory, the heaped up accumulation of so many centuries of artistic endeavor.

At this time, however, the feverish pursuit of pictures was but to get underway. It was only when, as a mature man, Henry was to cross the mountains into Italy, there to revel in the great galleries, that it really flourished. Paris was simply more tutors and schools (one of them operated on Fourier's principles) and the summers at Boulogne-Sur-Mer were profitable only in the sense that they more intimately brought home the difference of Europe from America. Only two outstanding events were recovered from these days. The first was an acquaintance with the eventually eminent Co-queline, then a school boy, the son of a pastry cook, already impregnated with those extraordinary French bourgeois qualities which were always to be markedly characteristic of him. The second was a long and severe sickness.

The sickness, however, was happily weathered and became no more than a gap in Henry's memoirs. It was followed by a flying visit to America, spent in Newport. The visit was so little impressive to Henry that he preferred to ignore it in

his reminiscences and reopen the scene at Geneva the following year.   But from that year at least one picture survives,
that by Thomas Sergeant Perry, the earliest of Henry's
friends to take up the profession of letters.   Perry recalled
after Henry's death that Henry at this time was characterized
by "a certain air of remoteness"; that he was "an uninter-
ested scholar" at school, and that he was reading Leslie's
Life of Constable and *The Vicar of Wakefield* "with great
pleasure."   Furthermore he had caught from his father (and
perhaps the Paris school) the Fourier contagion (showing
more of a contact between their minds than he admitted in
later days) and was deeply under the influence of Ruskin.
Ruskin, indeed, remained with him for many years, but
Ruskin the critic of art apparently, not the critic of society.
Even so, when H. J. began to write about pictures in his
travel sketches he as often contended against Ruskin's views
as for them.

The lure of Geneva was felt by the Jameses in common
with many New York families.   The theory was that the
Swiss city was an admirable place to acquire languages and
languages were considered to be a desirable acquisition.   But
however valuable in that respect the adventure was to Henry,
it was otherwise profitless or nearly so as far as education was
concerned.   On the theory that he was reading too many
novels, he was placed in a technical school where his total
incompetence in dealing with mathematical abstractions was
made glaringly plain, so plain that he was released to gain
what he could from other sources.   He visited the lecture
rooms of all the local celebrities, but sat under them with
no consciousness of their relative importance in the larger
sense.   In this fashion he listened, with no sense of hearing
anything extraordinary, to H. F. Amiel !

His literary consciousness was, however, keenly alive.   Just
as he remembered the stir caused by *The Scarlet Letter* when
he was seven, so now at sixteen he even more vividly felt the
excitement caused by the appearance of George Eliot's *Adam*

Bede. This was the first novel by George Eliot he knew. She was destined to have a great deal to do with the formation of his literary outlook. He recalled how astonished his parents were to have some English friends to whom they gave the volume, return it with the observation that it was uninteresting because it dealt with low people. This curious happening first brought him face to face with the idea of social classes and indeed it was novels that guided his explorations of the world. One might almost say that his consciousness was circumscribed by the comprehensiveness or narrowness of the fiction he now or later read. His own explorations, once he settled upon a field for study, were never very wide and certainly not to be described as comprehensive. In the *Cornhill Magazine* he found another novelist whose productions were never especially to interest him and whom he found deficient in all the larger and more important qualities of fiction, but whose stories nevertheless introduced him to many of the solid English facts. This was the indefatigable Anthony Trollope, the most constantly industrious of all English fiction writers. He even explored an installment of Flaubert's *Madame Bovary, Mœurs de Province* as it appeared in expurgated form in *Revue de Paris* !

From this time on Henry James was acutely aware of new writers discoverable through the pages of the magazines that came to his father's house, or through the recommendations of friends. In these casual ways he was eventually to discover those that were of permanent influence upon his literary development. The direction his talent was to take was clearly determined by these unsystematic explorations and even though he wavered at the beginning of his writing career between out and out romance and realism, the issue of the conflict was never really in doubt. The summer following the Geneva winter was spent in Bonn studying German and as a rest from his supposedly assiduous application to the language, his father supplied *Once a Week* which was then printing George Meredith, Charles Read, and George

Du Maurier. The following September when the family was once more in America, at Newport, where, with fine "inconsequence" they had gone that William might study art, he became acutely conscious of the Second Empire riches to be found in the pages of the *Revue des Deux Mondes*. And he met John La Farge.

The influence of one young man on another is always an elusive matter and if we are to go on the evidence presented by John La Farge's biographer, his influence on Henry James was one of which he was always supremely unconscious. And yet the way James viewed the matter! To him La Farge was always a minor but supremely important god, a man whose most casual words were vastly meaningful and whose very being exuded qualities of supreme worth. He embodied Europe. Here in the bare American atmosphere of Newport, on the edge of the as yet unexplored New England, Henry James encountered one who seemingly contained the European essence to the brimming point, whose whole mental set-up was all that one could look for in the most admirable personality. No wonder, worshipful as he was, that La Farge's chance words became pearls of wisdom to James. No wonder the books he recommended — and even to the ever reading Henry he was an inexhaustible depository of knowledge — were to assume as high an importance in James's development as any he had yet encountered and that one of the authors was to be a permanent admiration, an example invoked from the first to prove the serious possibilities of fiction. Through La Farge James found Mérimée and above all — Balzac!

La Farge recommended, casually enough to be sure and with no sense of determining his friend's career, that Henry be a writer. He saw in him a capacity, rare in writers and unaccompanied by the slightest ability for graphic representation, the painter's eye. It was this unusual conjunction of talents that La Farge felt should find expression in writing. This was a confirming stroke to a resolve already vaguely

taken, for Henry was even then writing stories which reflected his current reading and the exuberantly romantic
strain which so briefly flourished in his public career. La
Farge, however, so far fired Henry with immediate enthusiasm — to say nothing of the eventual force of the encouragement — that he translated Mérimée's *La Venus d'Ille* and submitted it to a New York magazine. He never received even
an acknowledgment of the manuscript.

William James, as we have seen, soon exhausted his enthusiasm for art, a career to which Henry had but the very
slightest inclination and only really an imitative interest.
William was soon off on a new tack and in 1861 went up to
Cambridge to attend the new Lawrence Scientific School.
Henry was left to his own resources and quickly so far abstracted himself from the family world as to be unable to tell
his brother, when on a visit to him, what, if anything, his
brothers and parents were doing or saying or thinking. It
was during these last months in Newport that Henry read
Hawthorne in his entirety and drew from him the moral
that an artistic career was possible in America. The example
was to encourage him to attempt such a career himself in
spite of his persistent misgivings.

He even encountered the sort of character that interested
him. It was at Newport that he caught a glimpse of the type
of man his father had in mind when he sought to prepare
his boys just to *be*. In late life he was to regret that he had
not more assiduously cultivated the resources of this sort of
personality, but his career had then reached the point where
the possibility of retreat could not be considered. He made
amends for his own dedication to the labor of writing fiction
by modelling many of his characters after the lineaments of
his Newport friend, Alleyne Otis. "There positively existed . . ." he recalled forty years later, "combinations of
elements, practical mixtures and harmonies, that were not
to have been expected. That the tone of New England 'at
its best' should melt into the tradition of France at *its* best

and that the result should be something consistent and exquisite, was . . . a charming surprise — the simple recall of which may serve as our salutation. . . . Alleyne Otis, a figure, almost *the* figure, for supreme sophistication — a rudimentary shade of it — of the old Newport days . . . we owe something always, to those who, at the time of our freshness, were revelations, for us, of type, who rendered to our development the service of fitting images to names that were otherwise but as loose labels. . . He 'did' nothing — he only *was:* which, in the antediluvian America, was always a note of character, always argued some intensity. He persisted in survival, in idleness, in courtesy, in gallantry, and yet, even though gallant, persisted also, it seemed, in mystery, in independence of apparel, above all in an imputed economy that was his finishing mark and that indicated real resources."

That Henry conceived such a vast admiration for so anomalous an American character, points unmistakably to his own anomalous disposition. It was not likely that he could superimpose on his foundations the more characteristic American values. And it was altogether fitting that when he came to study character he should turn, like a compass needle to the north, to comparable figures and to an environment that profusely produced them.

That these matters could so far engross Henry James as to exclude from his ken all family interests is at once a testimony to his deep immersion in his problem and to his remarkable powers of abstraction from the surrounding medium. (Even allowing for William's humorous exaggeration, the case is remarkable.) For if the James household was an example of intelligent freedom according to the principles of the father, it was socialized by the same token. Thrown in on themselves by their frequent residences in Europe, the Jameses were forced to draw on their own resources for entertainment and stimulation. As a result they developed to an unusual degree powers for drawing the maximum of stimulation from the interplay of the various minds assembled. In these contests of wits the father assumed no larger place than any other individual and demanded no respect he did not exact from one for another of his boys. The result was not chaos, but rapier-like contests of keen and exuberant minds. To an outsider it appealed as at once unexampled in his experience and wholly admirable: ". . . the joyous chaff that filled the Jameses' house," wrote T. S. Perry years later, "There was no limit to it. There were always books to tell about and laugh over, or to admire, and there was an abundance of good talk with no shadow of pedantry or priggishness."

It was from his period of extraordinary abstraction that Henry James emerged to follow the only truly blind alley in his long and fruitful career. He left Newport in the fall of 1862 with the somewhat infirm purpose of studying law at Harvard. That the venture came to nothing was to be expected but that the gesture was ever made is cause for persistent wonder.

2. A SEARCH FOR A METHOD

WHEN Abraham Lincoln called for volunteers to defend the Northern side of the irrepressible conflict, Henry James was eighteen years old. He had just experienced a slight accident which had its issue in years of suffering from a sore back. This misfortune placed him in the position of spectator of the Civil War and gave him a place in the long role of American writers in his generation whose relation to it was slight or superficial. Both Jameses, Howells, Henry Adams, Mark Twain, T. B. Aldrich, G. Stanley Hall, the architect Richardson and so on, all in one way or another avoided the war. Only Bierce, Cable and Lanier really went through the conflict as participants. But the effects of the conflict upon the economy of the country were to mark them all pretty equally. Among them Henry James at least was acutely conscious of the fact that a new America emerged from the war — so new, indeed, that to recover the spirit of the old days required an effort of the creative imagination.

He passed most of the war years ostensibly studying law but no one who has set down even a few words about Henry James has ever traced the slightest legal leanings in his complex mind. Indeed it clearly appears that what he so gropingly sought was contact with reality. He saw his surroundings through the eyes of the author he was at the moment reading. He interpreted his Cambridge boarding house in terms of Balzac and he immersed himself in Sainte Beuve at the library. He listened to the lectures of James Russell Lowell at the College. None of these windows opened upon American reality.

No more did his anxious hovering about the edges of war give him what he sought. If the war was, as he later thought, a long ache to him, the ache seems to have penetrated with considerable difficulty and little success through the swathed folds of his abstraction. With all the attention he devoted solicitously to following the army careers of his brothers and his friends one has no sense that to Henry the whole affair was more than an extraordinary adventure into the swamp of American life, a little more perilous, no more satisfactory. The injuries were to the body, mayhap, and better physical than mental extinction, but somehow his solicitude did not carry him over, even in imagination, to any understanding of just what the war meant. If, as they said in New York literary circles, Thomas Bailey Aldrich was shot through Fitz-James O'Brien's arm, then Henry James was wounded at Fort Wagner in the person of his brother Wilky. In either case the war, as a war, had little effect upon the vicarious participant. Henry James's war stories are no more valid than those of Aldrich, though James had the good taste never to attempt a picture of the actual battlefield, confining himself to the reverberations of the conflict at home.

It was during these years of overhanging uncertainty that Henry James came of age, and as the war drew to a close he emerged into the "incredibility of print." He had gone to Harvard with the idea in his mind that what he " 'wanted to want' to be was, all intimately, just literary." By placing himself at school in Cambridge he was unconsciously setting the stage for his debut. It was from the shrinking eminence of Boston that he launched himself upon the sea of periodical publication and it was Boston publishing houses that were to bring out his early books. It was indeed while still officially a student of law that he sent out his first manuscript, unannounced, to have it drop heavily into the silence that so often engulfs first efforts. Logically enough it was an appreciation of an actress whose talents were on display at the Howard Atheneum.

In the year 1864 the James household was set up in Boston, in Ashburton Place, and it was in that house that Henry James first experienced the satisfaction of becoming a contributor to the American magazines. The great monthlies of the time were *The Atlantic* and *The North American Review*. Henry James was shortly to appear in both, as he was, most flatteringly, asked to be among the original contributors to *The Nation*. *The North American* had but lately been rescued from "a stale tradition and gasping for life" by Charles Eliot Norton and to him H. J. had addressed his first effort at criticism, a review of a work on the art of fiction. It was accepted and published in the very next number. More importantly it was the cause of an interview with Norton that was to become in later years the symbol of a "positive consecration to letters." This review was the sum total of H. J.'s periodical publication for the year, but in 1865 he printed seventeen reviews and one short story.*

* Leon Edel has since established that Henry James published a short story, unsigned, *before* any of the reviews. See Edel, *Henry James: The Untried Years* (Philadelphia 1953), pp. 215–217.

As the years passed his numerical score rapidly mounted until it declined once more when he became an established novelist. His literary progression was from reviewing to essay writing to short stories to novels, never quite relinquishing any one field even though a new one was conquered. From these early reviews and essays it is possible to rescue evidence that shows how his mind had been nourished and what ideas he brought with him to his chosen task. H. J.'s ideas were neither many nor complex; they were fairly constant throughout his life; and they were restated again and again in different forms much as his father's had been.

Naturally his ideas were, in the beginning, but infirmly stated. It is not possible to say, for instance, that he brought forth fully developed his conception of the technique of the novel, a conception which was to plague his critics in the days to come. The best that can be said is that he began his career with a cogently expressed liking for form. Again, his allegiance to the various authors who won his admiration underwent a traceable evolution, but that evolution on examination is apt to turn out to be a wavering indecision about the value of the major quality their work embodied. Henry James conducted a debate about many of the "points" of fiction which lasted from his first appearance in print to about the year 1880, a debate reflected not only in his criticism but also in his fiction. He wavered between romance and realism, between emphasizing passion and emphasizing conscience; he wavered on the relative importance of form and subject matter; and he diligently redefined what he meant by morals. His writing career for fifteen years was largely taken up with trial flights. When he finally settled the issues to his satisfaction he was ruthless in suppressing all evidence of his indecisions. Unfortunately he had committed his different conclusions to print and their absolute elimination was not possible.

The object of his search and of his criticism was a method

for writing prose fiction. Other than his passion for pictures, H. J. showed surprisingly little interest in any other form of art. With poetry he had little to do. Music meant nothing to him though for a man so indifferent he made liberal use of musical metaphors to convey the "shades" of emphasis in the condensation of his characters. The drama, a life-long devotion, was to be of small final use to him except as an adjunct to the development of a fictional method. With astonishing persistence H. J. scrutinized the resources of all the contemporary novelists who came to his notice, but both his published reviews and essays as well as his letters show that he had little interest in intellectual culture in the broader sense. His interest in painting was largely confined to the Renaissance and post-Renaissance schools and he was not enthusiastic about the more experimental moderns of his time, though he followed their work. The stage he followed with such avidity was the stage of his day and the prose fiction he so diligently studied was the contemporary production. Many critics of him have commented on the extreme contemporaneity of his knowledge. They have sometimes failed, in their astonishment, to ask where else he could have gone to satisfy the consuming interest of his life.

For while fiction as a form of entertainment is as old as written records and while every comprehensive manual on the subject traces its evolution through the centuries, fiction as a deliberate art is a modern invention. Henry James's interest was, perforce, in contemporary products. His appetite could not be satisfied elsewhere. He did, nevertheless, incidentally show that he had sufficient interest in the subject to investigate writers whose qualities were antithetical to his. What H. J. could have found, technically, in Tobias Smollett is impossible to imagine, but he read him. Nor was he blind to merits he did not at all aspire to equal. His life-long loyalty to Balzac, in his eyes the father of the modern novel, was not based upon an admiration for Balzac's technical facility but rather upon his exuberant vitality, his inexhaustible fertility of invention.

To his task H. J., then, brought a host of ideas or prejudices that slowly matured into ideas. He was intellectually self-conscious and rarely let any mere notion rest in that category. He assiduously cultivated and nourished it until it bloomed into a principle. His youthful addiction to novel reading stood him in good stead and his first writings clearly indicate that he always read to some purpose. As was natural he began by exploring the actual American scene. What he found was not to his taste, but in reporting on these astonishing fictions, he was enabled to state, however gropingly, his own ideas. It was rather toplofty, to be sure, to invoke Balzac or Mérimée in dismissing a "scribbling female" but it must have given H. J. considerable satisfaction nevertheless and, of course, "they'll none of them be missed — they'll none of 'em be missed !" It was equally satisfying to damn Anthony Trollope (only later to redefine his merits on a higher plane), to discover George Eliot and accept her with reservations, and to write down Dickens as "nothing of a philospher" though meritorious as an observer and humorist — this when merely to shake his hand was a memorable experience. H. J., however, was little infected with the negative habit of mind, an immunity he shared with his father and brother. He did not indulge in sharp depreciations for the mere pleasure of iconoclasm. He was rather moved by a desire to assist in the triumph of form, intellectual seriousness and morality in fiction.

Deeply embedded in H. J.'s nature was a seriousness of temper which prevented him from becoming "merely" literary. Even had he not heard his father caustically criticize the literary butterflies of New York, he would have avoided any such futile development. Eminently serious, he was also eminently moral, a fact which long escaped the observation of even his best critics. Fortunately for his fiction and unfortunately for his commentators, he had absorbed from his father at least a vague apprehension of the difference between morality and moralism, so that his work was singularly free from any touch of flagrant moralism. Yet from his earliest reviews he was to insist upon the importance of the moral qualities in an author of consequence. This insistence was to color his subsequent career even in its major lines of evolution. It was finally to dictate so important a matter as his shift from Paris to London as the center of his literary career.

Morality in writing H. J. conceived to be an intellectual quality, meaning that it was rooted in a man's philosophical view of the world. Writing of Swinburne in *The Nation* for July 29, 1875, H. J. said: ". . . With this extravagant development of the imagination there is no commensurate development either of the reason or of the moral sense. . . By this we do not mean that Mr. Swinburne is not didactic, nor edifying, nor devoted to the cause of virtue. We mean simply that his moral plummet does not sink at all, and that when he pretends to drop it he is simply dabbling in the relatively very shallow pool of the picturesque." Similarly with Theophile Gautier. Swinburne described *Mlle. de Maupin* as a "golden book of spirit and sense." Now even though James was influenced in a fashion difficult to measure by Gautier's manner of writing travel sketches, he was not misled about his moral quality. In advising H. J. to read Gautier, William James said that he had no more moral sense than a guinea pig. When H. J. had occasion some years later to write of Gautier he said of *Mlle. de Maupin* that "in certain lights the book is almost ludicrously innocent, and we are at a loss what to think of those critics who either hailed or denounced it as a serious profession of faith. With faith of any sort Gautier strikes us as slenderly furnished." It is clear that H. J. was not, in any conventional sense a moralist — he was not infected with moralism — but he demanded that there be a moral constituent in the artist's total makeup which would allow him to plumb the depths. In his famous effort to define the interest of Charles Baudelaire he found in him a "certain groping sense of the moral complexities of life" which was marred and distorted by a "permanent immaturity of vision," a judgment from which modern critics vigorously dissent. Yet the important point is made that to H. J. morality is not innocence of evil nor is it to be achieved by ignoring evil. The thing is to get it properly located "at its source, deep in the human consciousness" as Hawthorne, for example, had done; and if to splash and flounder in the moral complexities of life was based on an inadequate sense of life, on a flaw in the artist's intellectual development, it follows that morally acceptable art is the product of wholeness and soundness. This position, gropingly sensed in H. J.'s earliest criticism, was expressed very late in his career in this fashion: "There is, I think, no more nutritive or suggestive truth . . . than that of the perfect dependence of the 'moral' sense of a work of art on the amount of felt life concerned in producing it. The question comes back thus, obviously, to the kind and the degree of the artist's prime sensibility, which is the soil out of which his subject springs. The quality and capacity of that soil, its ability to 'grow' with due freshness and straightness any vision of life, represents strongly or weakly, the projected morality." It was a high quality of consciousness that H. J.'s experience was to cultivate and from it his work, as we shall see, was to grow.

If there was no wavering on this deep and fundamental point, nor any doubt about the desirability of form, H. J. still had very considerable problems with which to wrestle. At the very beginning of his story writing career, in 1865, he was confronted with two major difficulties. Should he write romance or realism? How was he to reconcile his desires to be analytical with his passion for form? The principal American influence upon him was Hawthorne and this turned him toward romance. In spite of the fact that he early recognized the importance of George Eliot and the triumph of conscience, he was at the same time even more deeply infatuated with George Sand and the case for passion. In his early stories both George Sand and Hawthorne are considerable influences. But they are loosely constructed — the analysis frequently obtrudes itself on the reader's attention. Nevertheless he seemed quite sure that his natural drive was toward realism and conscience, analysis and form. He was frankly merely experimenting with alternatives and wrestling with difficulties.

In 1866 he met William Dean Howells, newly imported to Boston from New York where he had been working on *The Nation,* to be sub-editor of *The Atlantic Monthly.* At that time Howells was not settled on his life-long devotion to the mild realism for which he became famous. He discerned, however, that Henry James was brimming over with talent and determined to encourage him. As early as December 1866, he was predicting a great future for Henry James but he did not have the discernment to encourage James's drive toward realism. It was from Howells that encouragement came to write romances and James continued his debate by writing romances for *The Atlantic* and realistic stories for a contemporary paper called *The Galaxy.* It was out of this complex mixture of influences and indecisions that H. J.'s first stories emerged. So unsatisfactory did they become to the mature artist that none of those produced during the first six years of his apprenticeship survived for inclusion in the scrupulously edited New York edition of his novels and tales.

They need not detain any reader very long, for while they tell plainly the struggles Henry James underwent in his efforts to achieve a satisfactory method, they are not of particular interest in themselves. One of them we may profitably pause over, "Gabrielle de Bergerac," which appeared in *The Atlantic Monthly.* In a way this tale was a success, as Howells generously reported to him, for its popularity with readers far surpassed that of any previous James production.

Yet in the light of James's subsequent development it is a curiously unrewarding performance having to do with life in pre-revolutionary France. To the critical litmus paper it shows traces of George Sand, Balzac and Mérimée, but in the harsher light of judgment it is exceedingly unimportant. It concerns the love of a well-born girl for a low-born, but well-educated young man. Their affair is looked upon with scorn by the young lady's brother and guardian who prefers that she marry a dissolute aristocrat. But passion triumphs over all prohibitions and inhibitions (for the young lady must conquer her class prejudices) and the marriage takes place. Both of the adventurers die in the revolutionary upheavals that follow soon thereafter. To gain greater intensity and reality the story is told by the lady's nephew to the supposed author of the piece. This pleasant little. story showed Henry James what he could do and achieved a fleeting popularity. He had his eye out, however, for larger game and instead of following with others in the same genre he seems to have chosen to use it to close the first period of his development. He was through with that sort of thing. He had made his decision and more assiduously than ever sought to bring his method to more rewarding fields.

In March of 1869 he went to Europe and remained a year, the first of several trips before he finally settled down to an extended residence in 1883. His objective was not England, but Italy and it was from the latter country, never till now visited, that he was to draw most of his inspiration for the stories that were to grow out of his trip. H. J.'s reaction to England was one of recognition or identification while to Italy it was one of discovery. "I really feel," he wrote to his sister from London a few days after his arrival, "as if I had lived — I don't say a lifetime — but a year in this murky metropolis. I actually believe that this feeling is owing to the singular permanence of the impressions of childhood, to which any present experience joins itself on, without a broken link in the chain of sensation." As if to confirm his immediate perception of the multitudinous impressions one could hope to experience in London, he was pleasantly entertained by Leslie Stephen and Charles Eliot Norton. It was his great pleasure to see John Ruskin whose writings on Italy he was so exhaustively to compare to their subjects later on. "He has the beauties of his defects," H. J. reported to his mother, "but to see him only confirms the impression given by his writing, that he has been scared back by the grim face of reality into the world of unreason and illusion, and that he wanders there without a compass and a guide — or any light save the fitful flashes of his beautiful genius." And he saw William Morris. It is entirely characteristic of H. J. that while he gave an account in his letters home of Morris's endeavors to reinstate hand-produced objects of art and utility, he had nothing to say of Morris's social views any more than he ever had occasion, in all of the innumerable references to Ruskin, to comment on Ruskin's views either. A man seemingly more impervious to the appeal of programmes for radically revising the social order never existed. It was given to him to feel, to receive impressions, to analyze and discriminate, but not fundamentally to criticize and above all not to destroy the age old accumulations of civilization. A conservative son of a radical father, a man who positively idealized ancient institutions and customs hardened by usage into principles of conduct, he was rather to be concerned with asserting the validity of old ideals than with the advocacy of new ones. Characteristic, too, was the fact that his enthusiasm for the strange beauty of Mrs. William Morris far exceeded his interest in Morris's manufactures: "A figure cut out of a missal — out of one of Rossetti's or Hunt's pictures — to say this gives but a faint idea of her, because when such an image puts on flesh and blood, it is an apparition of fearful and wonderful intensity. It's hard to say whether she's a grand synthesis of all the pre-Raphaelite pictures ever made — or they a 'keen analysis' of her — whether she's an original or a copy. In either case she is a wonder. Imagine a tall lean woman in a long dress of some dead purple stuff, guiltless of hoops (or of anything else, I should say) with a mass of crisp black hair helped into great wavy projections on each of the temples, a thin pale face, a pair of strange sad, deep, dark Swinburnian eyes, with great thick black oblique brows, joined in the middle and tucking themselves away under her hair, a mouth like the 'Oriana' in our illustrated Tennyson, a long neck, without any collar, and in lieu thereof some dozen strings of outlandish beads — in fine complete." Note the literary and pictorial allusions. Note also the closeness of the observation.

The total effect of this orgy of impressions was, he felt, to emphasize his essential Americanism, a reaction which he entirely forgot when he attempted to reconstruct his reaction in later years. Then he became 'the passionate pilgrim,' the man overwhelmed and in love with every minute English thing. If this were so, it is hard to understand how it came about that he did not tarry long in England, nor did he for many years yet, decide to dedicate himself to the Londonizing process. In spite of the fact that everywhere he saw traces of the England he had read about in novels, he left but one record of the visit in his fiction, the story called "The Passionate Pilgrim." There has been considerable disagreement about which of the two major characters in the story represents Henry James, the pilgrim or the narrator, but the weight of the evidence favors identifying him with the narrator. In this case, which harmonizes with his immediate rather than his retrospective reaction, he viewed the English scene with pleasure and approval but with a saving detachment. He did not feel, as was the case with the pilgrim, that he was returning to his birthright, nor did he in any sense seek to convince himself that he instinctively knew the significance of every thing and custom. The story exploits to the full his emotion of recognition and his sense of reveling in a scene both fine and grand, but it does not show him as accepting it at face value and without analysis.

It was on this very point of analysis that Henry James was permanently to differentiate himself from the Englishman to the manor born. Five years earlier he had noted that "It has long seemed to us that, as a nation, the English are singularly incapable of large, of high, of general views. They are indifferent to pure truth, to *la verite vraie*. Their views are almost exclusively practical and it is in the nature of practical views to be narrow." Now that he was on the ground he was to discover and note the presence in the English of the prime barrier to the achievement "of large, of high, of general views." "The English," he wrote to his brother William, "have such a mortal mistrust of anything like criticism or 'keen analysis' (which they seem to regard as a kind of maudlin foreign flummery) that I rarely remember to have heard on English lips any other intellectual verdict (no matter under what provocation) than this broad synthesis — 'so immensely clever.' " As one already devoted to 'maudlin foreign flummery' H. J. was to find this habit distinctly baffling. His intellectual makeup was permanently to mark him as something other than an Englishman.

It was Italy that was to overwhelm him. As one of those spirits "with a deep relish for the element of accumulation in the human picture and for the infinite superpositions of history . . . the results of an immemorial, a complex and accumulated, civilization" it could do no other. He found these things "impregnated with life." How different from his father ! Henry James, Sr., had chiefly objected to Europe because of these very accumulations, this ruck of outmoded and hampering institutions and preferred the American scene because it was less binding upon the human personality. No contrast between father and son is more remarkable than this very fundamental disagreement. Yet by some strange twist of H. J.'s imagination he was to introduce into this scene in the years to come Americans who were to typify the pure in heart and often picture them defeated by Europeans deeply impregnated by the marvelous accumulations. Did he after all agree with his father that in spite of the immense appeal of these heaped up associations, so rich in possibilities of impressions and discriminations, they were destructive of the finer essence of the human personality ? Did he agree that in America where institutions weighed less heavily, where there was greater freedom, there was, in spite of great drawbacks, more chance for fine, innocent, characters to develop ? Nevertheless, the immediate appeal of Italy was tremendous and the country was to make so deep a mark that he was drawn back again and again throughout his life.

Never elsewhere was he to take such pleasure in the galleries. In Italy he gave full play to his delight in pictures and carried his accumulated information and store of reactions into the stories he wrote in the year following. These efforts, most of which were eventually discarded as hopelessly apprenticelike, are deeply encrusted with references to the art and the descriptions of pictures and buildings are very little assimilated into the texture of the stories, thus violating one of the principles H. J. had derived from Balzac: ". . . as the soul of the novel is its action, you should only describe those things which are accessory to the action." Nothing could be a more complete violation of this dictum, lately invoked against an American lady novelist, than a tale like "Traveling Companions," a thin love story tricked out with reminiscent descriptions, lovingly done, of the pictures and buildings of Florence and Venice. Italy indeed was in the large just what he was later to describe as the effect of Rome: "no Rome of reality was concerned in our experience . . . the whole thing was a rare state of the imagination, dosed and drugged . . . by the effectual Borgia cup, for the taste of which the simplest as well as the subtlest had a palate. . . They haunted Vatican halls and Palatine gardens; they were detached and pensive on the Pincian; they were silent in strange places; the habit of St. Peter's they clung to as to a vice; the impression of the Campagna they stopped short in attempting to utter. And just as the lowly were brought up, so the mighty were brought down, there being no tribute to the matters in question that was not of the nature of sensibility."

Overwhelmingly wonderful as it all was, H. J. was home-sick. He longed for America where there was nothing like this, try as he would to discover it and try as he would to find an equally appealing substitute. His imagination was ensnared by Europe and his affections by America. It was there that his mother and father and brothers lived and it was there that he should make a career. He could not, as it turned out, for he could not get in touch with America. Yet he battled hard against his weakness for Europe, writing, "It's a complex fate, being an American, and one of the responsibilities it entails is fighting against a superstitious valuation of Europe." Certainly he had no superstitious valuation of America nor of the Americans he saw in Europe. He felt that in spite of the fact that he had "seen too few specimens and those too superficially" the English were superior to the Americans, chiefly on the grounds that the American vices were "the elements of the modern man with *culture* quite left out." But was culture quite all that mattered? For if it was how did it come about that H. J. was to draw so many admirable figures from America to place in flattering contrast with the Europeans? How did it happen that he was to picture so many Americans destroyed by a too close identification with the common social culture of Europe? The truth is that he saw both continents analytically and assessed their inadequacies, according to his lights, with marvelous precision, shadowing forth over and above both a vision of a higher and better civilization to which man could aspire.

Meanwhile it was necessary to make the effort to penetrate to the American secret. "Looking about myself," he wrote to Charles Eliot Norton a year after his return to America, "I conclude that the face of nature and civilization in this our country is to a certain point a very sufficient literary field.

But it will yield its secrets only to a really *grasping* imagination. To write well and worthily of American things one needs even more than elsewhere to be a *master*. But unfortunately one is less!" H. J. did look, but for what and where? He did not look where we now know and perhaps some few even then knew were the secret and tremendous drives in American life. The year 1870 is commonly taken as marking a transition in American life from a predominantly agricultural country to one marked out as the scene for the greatest industrial development the world has known. It was in the new factories, in the new cities, in the hustle and bustle of commerce and manufacturing and transportation that the American secret was hidden. But business was a closed field for Henry James and his interest was not there but in the leisure class, then so small in America and almost exclusively feminine. Unlike William Dean Howells he could not content himself with the writing of delicate, thin and fluffy comedies of country boarding house life. And his explorations of the fashionable resorts at Saratoga, Lake George and Newport roused his sense of irony more than anything else. Saratoga for instance. "The piazzas of these great hotels," he wrote to *The Nation*, "may very well be the biggest of all piazzas. They have no architectural beauty; but they doubtless serve their purpose — that of affording sitting-space in the open air to an immense number of persons. . . The rough brick wall of the house, illuminated by a line of flaring gas-lights, forms a natural background to the crude, impermanent, discordant tone of the assembly. In the larger of the two hotels, a series of long windows open into an immense parlour — the largest, I suppose in the world, and the most scantily furnished in proportion to its size. A few dozen rocking-chairs, an equal number of small tables, tripods to the eternal ice-pitcher, serve chiefly to emphasize the vacuous grandeur of the spot. . . I confine myself to the dense, democratic, vulgar Saratoga of the current year. You are struck, to begin with, at the hotels, by

the numerical superiority of the women; then, I think, by
their personal superiority. It is incontestably the case that
in appearance, in manner, in grace and completeness of
aspect, American women surpass their husbands and brothers
. . . I should add, after the remark I have just made, that
even in the appearance of the usual American male there
seems to me to be a certain plastic intention. It is true that
the lean, sallow, angular Yankee of tradition is dignified
mainly by a look of decision, a hint of unimpassioned volition, the air of 'smartness'. This in some degree redeems
him, but it fails to make him handsome. . . Casting your
eye over a group of your fellow-citizens . . . you will be inclined to admit that, taking the good with the bad, they are
worthy sons of the great Republic. . . They suggest the
swarming vastness — the multifarious possibilities and activities — of our young civilization. . . I seem to see in their
faces a tacit reference to the affairs of a continent. They are
obviously persons of experience — of a somewhat narrow
and monotonous experience certainly. . . They are not the
mellow fruit of a society which has walked hand-in-hand with
tradition and culture; they are hard nuts, which have grown
and ripened as they could. When they talk among themselves, I seem to hear the cracking of the shells. . . It is an
old story that in this country we have no 'leisure-class' — the
class from which the Saratogas of Europe recruit a large
number of their male frequenters. . . The surrounding
country is a charming wilderness, but the roads are so abomi-
nably bad that walking and driving are alike unprofitable
. . . you may recall certain passages of Ruskin, in which he
dwells upon the needfulness of some human association,
however remote, to make natural scenery fully impressive. . . You feel around you, with irresistible force, the
eloquent silence of undedicated nature — the absence of
serious associations. . ." In fact, Henry James did not find
such evidences of American life as he did examine to his
taste and he was barred by circumstances from examining

those — they would have been even less to his taste ! — that were pregnant with the American future. He was unable, furthermore and most importantly, to effect any contact with the "genuine culture (that) was beginning to struggle upward in the seventies."   He knew Henry Adams and John La Farge. His brother William knew Charles Peirce, N. S. Shaler, and other hopeful figures. But where were Marsh and Gibb, Ryder, Eakins, Roebling, Richardson and Sullivan ?

In the late spring of the following year (1872) he was once more in Europe, accompanied by his sister and his aunt, and was to remain a year. He arrived with a commission from *The Nation* to do travel sketches and he immediately plunged into the necessary sight-seeing. Travel sketches were of far greater importance to H. J. than is commonly understood. They required direct and in some sense original observation which was of great value in distracting him from his dangerous habit of seeing the world in terms of past reading. Under the tutelage of Theophile Gautier, whose *Travels in Spain* he regarded as a masterpiece of the form, he learned to record the surfaces of the external world with wonderful accuracy, but he did not, like Gautier, tend to stop there. As can be seen from the long passage on Saratoga, just quoted, he was distinctly capable of making reflections on the significance of what he saw.   H. J. was not, it is apparent, merely following in the American tradition of travel literature to which Irving, Cooper, Willis, Longfellow, Emerson and Hawthorne had all made their contributions. He was at once producing vendable copy and sharpening his instruments of observation.

These papers for *The Nation* make clear the nature of the struggle that was going on in his mind. Conscious though he was of the fact that great fiction could be written in America, given a "grasping imagination," he was yet baffled and disconcerted by the harshness of the surfaces, the narrowness of the characters and the incompleteness of both the

scene and the men and women. Dedicated from far back
to the analytical discussion of scene and character he could
find little material on which to operate in America. The
leisure class, which he correctly saw offered him the largest
number of acceptable objects for his attention, was something America decidedly lacked. He found little satisfaction in the slight and narrow American character developments. Or did he not see deep enough? In any case he
was repelled so far as settling down to a lifetime of study.
Yet he was to undertake the treatment of a theme which required some comprehension of American character and he
was to produce two novels with American settings, both of
which, logically enough, were rejected when the canon was
selected. And so now when Europe was once more his subject he was enthralled. After two summers spent in Saratoga
and Newport, Niagara and Lenox, how pleasant to meditate
upon the walls of Chester: "There could be no better example of that phenomenon so delightfully frequent in England, — an ancient monument or institution, lovingly re-
adopted and consecrated to some modern amenity." There
was the whole case. H. J. was interested in the spectacle of
life not in raw nature but in the deposits of civilization to
which he could address an assiduous scrutiny. In a sense
he was the perfect tourist, enthralled with any revelation of
the intimate manners of a people, especially those manners
obviously grounded in an ancient usage. Acutely aware of
the historical and literary overlay on the surface of Europe
he viewed the spectacle with a painter's eye and reported it
with a novelist's hand. The mellowed surface — the spectacle of life! Even Switzerland repelled him a bit for he
found a demanding necessity for "a human flavor in my
pleasures, and I fancy that it is a more equal intercourse
between man and man than between man and mountain."
Bending his eye upon the people, he found himself possessed of an American characteristic of immense value to
him. "The observations of the 'cultivated Americans'," he

wrote, "bear chiefly, I think, upon the great topic of national idiosyncracies. He is apt to have a keener sense of them than Europeans; it matters more to his imagination that his neighbor is English, French, or German." But is this true? Is an American so acutely aware of differences of the finer sort and only impressed with large contrasts? Was not H. J.'s discovery peculiar to himself and his fellows who had moved in the somewhat restricted circle of New York, Newport and Boston where the individuals had been somewhat assimilated to a common type? I think this is true, for even in those days great waves of immigrants were breaking over the country. It was rather that H. J. was possessed of a preturnatural sensitivity to differences. He was feeling his way — the process had begun two years before in Italy — toward a form of fiction he was to make peculiarly his own, the European-American contrast.

He had landed in England with his party in May and after a short tour to some of the more interesting monuments of antiquity, had passed over to the continent, and after visiting Germany and Switzerland, found himself in Paris in the fall. He settled down for the winter, absorbing impressions and, on one occasion guiding Emerson through the Louvre. He was to perform the same function of guide in Rome the following year. The result was not too satisfying. Emerson's "perception of the objects contained in these collections was of the most general order." Indeed the contact between H. J. and Emerson was of the slightest. Emerson was not attracted to novels and would have but dimly understood H. J.'s aspirations had he enquired into them. Had he not said that Hawthorne's novels were "not worthy of him?" "This is a judgment odd almost to fascination," wrote James, "we circle round it and turn it over and over; it contains so elusive an ambiguity." And so it must have appeared to a mind whose highest satisfaction was the solution of a problem of fictional composition.

It was Italy that had drawn him to Europe and the first

day of 1873 saw him in Rome. He revelled in it and his
observations were shortly to find expression in a novel. The
summer of 1873 was spent in Hamburg, fitfully reflected in
his fiction by a longish and unimportant story entitled "Eu-
gene Pickering," and early in the year following he was at
Florence with his brother William. They had tried Rome,
but William had come down with a fever and forced the
abandonment. Henry James was now thirty-one years old.
He had written thirty stories, innumerable book reviews and
a quantity of critical essays, as well as numerous travel
articles. He had been actively writing for nine years. It
was time to try his hand at a novel and in Florence he began
one. It was called *Roderick Hudson* and stands today as
volume one of the New York Edition, the accepted canon
of his work. It dealt with Americans in Europe, and the
Europe was Italy, not England. England was still in the
distance.

To H. J.'s later sense *Roderick Hudson* was an unsatisfactory novel. It was wrought out painfully over a period
of many months. After a Florentine beginning it was continued during a summer holiday in Germany, at home that
autumn in Cambridge and during the following winter in
East 25th Street, New York. Though it is not precisely a
novel of contrasts the action takes place in both America,
briefly, and Europe (Italy, Germany and Switzerland). The
theme is essentially a moral one and has exercised a peren-
nial fascination over the minds of successive generations. It
is the struggle of an artist to effectuate his talent, his moral
inadequacy, his disintegration and death. Roderick Hudson is a talented son of a widow accidentally located in
Northampton Massachusetts. His task is to study law; his
passion to be a sculptor, an art which many Americans of
that and an earlier generation were to attempt. There was
Greenough, Fenimore Cooper's protege, in the 1830's and
H. J.'s friend W. W. Story of a later time.

Roderick Hudson is more remarkable for his passional

development than for any exhibition of the restraints of conscience. He leaps with avidity and with little consideration of the consequences to his loved ones, when a chance visitor to the village, a typical Henry James leisure class type, senses his genuine ability and offers to carry him off to Europe for study. With novelistic precipitancy the scene is transferred to Rome where Hudson's disintegration begins. He has not the faculty of persistent application, nor has he the moral power to restrain his impulses when they tend in directions destructive to his finer sensibilities. For that reason he is inferior to the meagrely talented but industrious and conscientious artists who also have found their way to Rome. By an unfortunate accident of circumstances he becomes acquainted with Christina Light, an American girl of European education, the first of a long line of American personalities in James full of good impulses but ruined by the European virus, who fascinates Roderick both by her great beauty and her perverse conduct. Under the stimulus of his love he models a superlatively fine bust of her and plans still greater works all to be executed under the same aegis. But Christina has no sense of any obligation to him, though he powerfully appeals, and furthermore she is subjected constantly to the pressure of her mother's desire that she give her hand to Prince Casamassima and make a "good" marriage.

Hudson is conscious of the complications of the situation but perversely believes that he will win Christina's hand and meanwhile is content to let his work slip away from him. In an effort to get him once more at his proper task, his patron, who anxiously hovers over the scene and through whose eyes we watch the entire proceedings, sends him off for a vacation in Germany. But to no avail, for Husdon runs up debts in frivolous pleasures and gambling. He is apparently irretrievably damned. In a despairing gesture, his patron sends for his mother and for the girl to whom he has discovered Roderick is engaged, in the hope that they will exert a steadying influence. In a sense they do, for Roderick immediately does a splendid bust of his mother. Fundamentally they do not, for they cannot keep him at his work. His passion for Christina Light has quite destroyed his sense of duty either to his mother, his fiancée or his patron. When Christina follows the dictates of her mother and marries Prince Casamassima, Roderick is in despair and in the hope of curing him, his patron carries him, his mother and his exceedingly sensible fiancee to Switzerland. But no cure results and in the end Roderick dramatically commits suicide by jumping off a cliff.

Enough has been said to show that this novel contains elements not characteristic of the later James. For one thing, the play upon the passional nature of Roderick's fault and his almost total lack of conscience betrays that H. J. was still under the influence of George Sand. The whole performance was written, moreover, in the shadow of Balzac. Furthermore there are constructional flaws impossible to indicate in any summary. In his characteristic manner, H. J. revealed his sense of these in the preface to the final edition. The "time-scheme of the story is quite inadequate," he wrote. Now this question of time was one with which he was to wrestle all his life long and that he should have muffed the matter in his novel is not a cause for wonder. But more serious is the other matter to which he points: "My mistake on Roderick's behalf — and not in the least of conception, but of composition and expression — is that, at the rate at which he falls to pieces, he seems to place himself beyond our understanding and our sympathy." This, of course, is related to the matter of time, but it also points inexorably to the central flaw of the book. One has an uncomfortable feeling in reading that the dice are too obviously loaded against Roderick; that he is scarcely given time even to experience Rome before he begins to disintegrate; and that consequently too severe a case is made out against his moral development on the one hand and against the influence of Christina Light on the other. So over-played is Roderick's part that James's obvious idea that what one needs to confront the demands of art is diligence and discipline becomes lost in the sudden debacle of his central character. Furthermore, in his rush to carry the novel to a conclusion, H. J. availed himself of the melodramatic device of suicide without convincing us that no other issue, in the light of the facts, was possible and without giving us enough sense that sufficient time *had* elapsed for Roderick to be convinced that he was irretrievably ruined. Yet *Roderick Hudson* is not a failure. It achieves a fairly skilful balance between narrative and analysis; it is sufficiently vital to engage one's interest without a sense of strain; and it does give out the impression that it is the product of a man who is serious. When it was published in book form in 1876, to compete with the novels of Edward Eggleston, Bret Harte, Julian Hawthorne, E. P. Roe and William Dean Howells, it must indeed have appeared to be a marvelous accomplishment and a strange portent. Yet a writer in *The North American Review* found it lacking in human feeling!

The composition of *Roderick Hudson* was carried out in the midst of an extraordinary busyness. During the year 1874 H. J. turned out twenty-nine articles, reviews and stories. He did considerable traveling. And most importantly he was conducting an exasperating debate with himself. The time had come, he felt, to decide the tremendous question of America vs. Europe. Writing to Grace Norton early in 1874 he said: "What Charles says about our civilization seems to me perfectly true, but practically I don't feel as if the facts were so melancholy. The great fact for all of us there is that, relish Europe as we may, we belong much more to that than to this, and stand in a much less factitious and artificial relation to it." "It would seem," he went on, "that in our great unendowed, unfurnished, unentertained and unentertaining continent, where we all sit sniffing, as it were, the very earth of our foundations, we ought to have leisure to turn out something handsome from the very foundations, we ought to have leisure to turn out something handsome from the very heart of simple human nature."

That, however, was precisely what H. J. could not do. He was not interested in "simple human nature" but in complex and highly developed human nature. So he wisely added a saving "But after I have been at home a couple of months I will tell you what I think." His brother William was also urging him to settle on his future course, but he was reluctant to consider any action he might take in the immediate future as final. He fully intended to return to America in the fall but "I shall go with the full provision that I shall not find life at home *simpatico,* but rather painful, and, as regards literary work, obstructively the reverse, and not even with the expectation that time will make it easier; but simply on sternly practical grounds; i. e., because I can find more abundant literary occupation by being on the premises and relieve you and father of your burdensome financial interposition." It was thus reluctantly that he returned to America in the early summer of 1874. He remained one year.

The first three months, as has been said, were spent in Cambridge working over *Roderick Hudson.* A book of short stories, planned two years earlier, was also put through the press, containing but three that eventually found a place in the canon, "The Passionate Pilgrim," "The Madonna of the Future," a study of artistic futility obviously an outgrowth of the writing of the novel, and "Madame de Mauves," foreshadowing vaguely a later novel, *The Portrait of a Lady.* In December he went to New York City to stay with a friend in East 25th Street, the first extended stay in the city of his birth since 1855. Still working on *Roderick Hudson,* which he here brought to completion, he turned his hand to the writing of innumerable reviews for *The Nation.* But what became of the debate during this period we have no means of knowing, for no records of it have come to light. All we have is the decision, and it was, in spite of the abundance of literary employment, immediate and prospective, to return to Europe, which he did in the autumn of 1875. It was not to be Italy this time, for, as he confessed later, it was not conducive to literary labor and he saw too little of people stimulating to him. He set out to storm Paris. It was there, his reading told him, that he would find an answer to all the problems of fiction writing which were baffling him.

H. J.'s attitude in Paris was that of a learner and his disappointment with it that of a student who finds his professors inadequate. He had little to do by way of gaining new impressions of the externals of the city, for his very earliest recollections went straight back there. Unless association with the writers of the day could bring him satisfaction, there was nothing to be gained. They both profited and failed him, but failed him on a crucial and deciding issue. That issue was morality. "The collective sin" of the French writers, he wrote, was "against proportion" and the consequence was "in the circumstance that when they lay their hands upon the spirit of man, they cease to seem expert." This judgment runs like a *leitmotif* through all of the essays he wrote on the writers of the day, as we shall see and while he remained an appreciative friend of the French, he was not able finally to accept their literature.

His first contact was with Ivan Turgenev, and it was through him that he penetrated to the Flaubert circle. All his life he remembered Turgenev with pleasure and admiration and however much he had to qualify his views of the French writers, he never withdrew from Turgenev the slightest bit of his first enthusiasm. Before meeting him, he had in common with the whole family read such of Turgenev's novels as could be found in French and German, among them *A Nest of Noblemen,* a permanent favorite. "I never heard you speak so enthusiastically of any human being," wrote William James of Henry's description of his first visit.

It was true. He rarely was to respond so completely to any writer of a foreign nation and while he was later suspiciously to deny the worth of Tolstoy and Dostoevsky, he was never to withdraw from Turgenev. And that there was a certain measure of response on the other side we may assume. H. J. was invited to Mme. Viardot's, both to the Thursday musical parties and to the Sunday parties *en famille*. It was to Mme. Viardot that Turgenev was devoted, even declaring that he would follow her to Australia if need be. And though the Sunday parties reminded H. J. of Concord festivities he was pleased by them. He wrote his father ". . . it was both strange and sweet to see poor Turgenev acting charades of the most extravagant description, dressed out in old shawls and masks, going on all fours, etc. The charades are their usual Sunday evening occupation and the good faith with which Turgenev, at his age and with his glories, can go into them is a striking example of that spontaneity which Europeans have and we have not. Fancy Longfellow, Lowell, or Charles Norton doing the like. . ." There was one coming American author who did have that spontaneity, Mark Twain, of whom H. J. was to make nothing.

Better than these musicales and intimate parties were the talks the two were able to have in the cafes. It was there that H. J. got revealing glimpses into Turgenev's workshop, profitable glimpses too. ". . . I always left him in a state of 'intimate' excitement, with a feeling that all sorts of valuable things had been suggested to me. . ." And what were these things? It is difficult to say now that the recipient is no longer here to testify. Much that can be detected as derived from Turgenev could have been drawn from his books without personal contact. Nevertheless H. J.'s deductions were undoubtedly strengthened and corrected during these talks, and finally he was to carry away two valuable pointers.

One was the fact that plot was not too important but

that more might be done by imagining characters in a small group and letting them settle their own destiny by inter-action. The other was that there was a high moral interest in the victories to be had through failure. "I have always fondly remembered," he recalled over thirty years later, "a remark that I heard fall years ago from the lips of Ivan Turgenieff in regard to his own experience of the usual origin of the fictive picture. It began for him always with the vision of some person or persons, who hovered before him, soliciting him, as the active or passive figure, interest-ing him and appealing to him just as they were and by what they were. He saw them, in that fashion, as *disponsibles,* saw them subject to the chances, the complications of ex-istence, and saw them vividly, but then had to find for them the right relations, those that would most bring them out; to imagine, to invent and select and piece together the situa-tions most useful and favorable to the sense of the creatures themselves, the complications they would be most likely to produce and to feel. "To arrive at these things is to arrive at my 'story,'" he said, "and that's the way I look for it. The result is that I'm often accused of not having 'story' enough. I seem to myself to have as much as I need — to show my people, to exhibit their relations with each other; for that is all my measure. If I watch them long enough I see them come together, I see them *placed,* I see them en-gaged in this or that act and in this or that difficulty. How they look and move and speak and behave, always in the setting I have found for them, is my account of them — of which I dare say, alas, *que cela manque souvent d'architec-ture.* But I would rather, I think, have too little architec-ture than too much — where there's danger of its interfering with my measure of truth. The French of course like more of it than I give — having by their own genius such a hand for it; and indeed one must give all one can. As for the origin of one's wind-blown germs themselves, who shall say, as you ask, where *they* come from ? We have to go too far back, too far behind, to say. Isn't it all we can say that they come from every quarter of heaven, that they are *there* at almost any turn of the road? They accumulate, and we are always picking them over, selecting among them. They are the breath of life — by which I mean that life, in its own way, breathes them upon us. They are so, in a manner prescribed and imposed — floated into our minds by the current of life. That reduces to imbecility the vain critic's quarrel, so often, with one's subject, when he hasn't the wit to accept it. Will he point out then which other it should properly have been? — his office being, essentially *to* point out. *Il enserait bien embarrasse.* Ah, when he points out what I've done or failed to do with it, that's another matter: there he's on his ground. I give him up my 'architecture,' my distinguished friend concluded, 'as much as he will.' So this beautiful genius, and I recall with comfort the gratitude I drew from his reference to the intensity of suggestion that may reside in the stray figure, the unattached character, the image *en disponsibilite*. It gave me higher warrant than I seemed to have met for just that blest habit of one's own imagination, the trick of investing some conceived or encountered individual, some brace or group of individuals, with the germinal property and authority."

If on this point Turgenev was a stimulus and a confirmation, so was he also a light in the darkness on another matter. It was he who first gave H. J. an insight into the fact that the victories of failure are as important as the victories of success. It was a lesson he was diligently to apply and with a success as often productive of bafflement in his more forthright critics as illumination.

Turgenev took H. J. to Flaubert's, the center of French literary life and there he was disillusioned with his brave hope of making some sort of contact. It had seemed to him that the French mastery of form and style must be indicative of deeper and subtler virtues, helpful to the aspirant for fictional honors. But it was not so. Flaubert was of the school of Balzac, H. J. noted, and the Goncourts, Zola and Maupassant were of the school of Flaubert. But aside from method what had they to offer? Indeed they seemed to have nothing, for H. J. carried away only one great lesson from the master, the importance of unity of tone. And from another member of the group, Alphonse Daudet, he got light on how to reproduce the delicate shades of the actual. Otherwise his explorations turned up nothing. What, indeed, was there in this small harvest to warrant one's attaching oneself to so self-contained and self-satisfied a group, hounded with narrowing prejudices, hampered by petty aspirations? The gap between them was too wide to be closed and indeed it became wider instead of narrower the deeper the explorations went. The French cult of indifference made small appeal to his moral temper. To be sure he found "a remarkable art of expressing the life, of picturing the multitudinous, adventurous experience of the senses, "but in comparison the deeper, stranger, subtler inward life, the wonderful adventures of the soul, are so little pictured that they may almost be said not to be pictured at all." Even the great Flaubert himself could not meet the test. "I had the other day a very pleasant call upon Flaubert," he wrote his father in April, 1876, "whom I like personally more and more each time I see him. But I think I easily — more than easily — see all round him intellectually. There is something wonderfully simple, honest, kindly, and touchingly inarticulate about him."

What did H. J. see that led him to think he had seen around him — besides of course his moral inadequacy? He found ". . . the strange weakness of his mind, his puerile dread of the grocer, the bourgeois, the sentiment that in his generation and the preceding misplaced, as it were, the spirit of adventure and the sense of honor, and sterilized a whole province of French literature. That worthy citizen ought never to have kept a poet from dreaming. . . He passed his life in strange oblivion of the circumstance that, however incumbent it may be on most of us to do our duty, there is, in spite of a thousand narrow dogmatisms, nothing in the world that anyone is under the least obligation to *like* — not even (one braces one's self to risk the declaration) a particular kind of writing." Indeed the gap was wide ! There was no hope of sympathetic cooperation here, no hope of penetrating a closed corporation whose stock was purchasable only on stultifying terms.

If Flaubert failed him, so did the rest to an even greater extent. The Goncourts, Maupassant, Zola he admired for the positive virtues and rejected because of their negative qualities and their incapacitating lacks, "coarse, comprehensive, prodigious" Zola who was totally lacking in taste but for whom he had an unaccountable personal liking, and Maupassant, a "case," a brilliant and powerful writer but with no windows on the moral side of his mind, just a blank wall. He had listened to their talk and their plans. He had heard Zola say, "Well, I on my side am engaged on a book (*L'Assommoir*), a study of the *moeurs* of the people, for which I am making a collection of all the 'bad words,' the *gros mots*, of the language, those with which their familiar talk bristles." There must be no mistake about the matter. H. J. was profoundly sensitive to the positive virtues of these men. He was not narrow and blind to their merits, but they failed to meet his larger demands and they, with the shocking provinciality of the French, could not imaginatively take in what he felt necessary. They knew nothing of English literature. They knew George Sand but they did not know George Eliot.

The ineluctable necessity was to abandon the siege of Paris. Meanwhile there was the novel he had begun. It was to be called *The American* and it was to explore the reactions of a "compleat American" confronted with the beckonings and the final duplicity of Europe. The idea for the story had occurred to him one day while riding in a Cambridge horse car and as he enthusiastically elaborated it in his mind, his determination to make use of it grew. Circumstances, though, were not quite ripe and it was dropped into his subconscious, there to acquire "a firm iridescent surface and a notable increase of weight." Now, in Paris, the man in the case appeared fully armed for the fray. His name, symbolically, was Christopher Newman — Columbus and the new American dispensation all in one. A Columbus however, who was turning back on his course and backtrailing beyond the Eastern seaboard where so many successful (as well as disappointed) pioneers came to satisfied rest, to Europe. He had made his money in various ways in various parts of the country and not the least part of his fortune was gained selling washtubs in California. Here was, thought H. J., the typical American, full of a sense of American possibilities in a commercial way, canny in money matters, untutored culturally, but compounded of sensitivity and generosity. Familiar with the "tall tales" of the southwest, Newman was to experience in his own person a tale taller than any ever before imagined and he was to wrest from it a substantial reward even in defeat.

He had come to Europe to enjoy the fruits of his labor and to marry. With the assistance of the wife of an old-time friend — a representative of the American type so often to figure in H. J.'s stories who took the pleasures of Europe with complacency but got nowhere with the finer essence — he was introduced to the widowed daughter of a proud aristocratic household. Characteristically forthright in his methods, Newman won the love of this highborn lady and got so far as having their impending marriage announced. But he was too bitter a pill for the "family" to swallow. A man of fabulous antecedents, a creature of incomparable wealth, but too immediately associated with the getting of it, he failed of the test of European snobbery. With the more perceptive younger son he was a complete success. With the lady of his choice he made his impression. They discerned the quality of this reversed Columbus. But to the calculating elder brother, since the death of the father the titular head of the house, and the intriguing Duchess, he was impossible of acceptance. They led him on, beguiled by his incomparable wealth, but threw him down in the end. They rejected him for social reasons, for considerations too "highfalutin" to appear as just in Newman's eyes and his first reaction was to seek revenge and force them at the point of a pistol, so to speak, to give up his loved one. Though he did find his weapon, and a formidable one it was, he withheld the blow and acquiesced in the placing of his love in a convent. It was not in him, this American, a new man unpoisoned by Europe to strike a blow that might in the end irretrievably damage his beloved and which would give him, then, no final satisfaction. He acquiesced in his defeat. He won his victory by exhibiting finer virtues than his opponents. And though it was to them that the world awarded the victory, it was he who, morally, captured the prize.

There was a flaw in this account of the matter however and H. J. was later clearly to perceive it. This was romance. For after all Newman possessed one thing that would have caused his opponents to overlook every other flaw: money. What they would have done, had H. J. not cut the cord, all unknowingly, that held his balloon to the ground of actuality, was to "haul him and his fortune into their boat under the cover of night perhaps, in any case as quietly and with as little bumping and splashing as possible, and there accommodate him with the very safest and most convenient seat." So, thirty years later, was H. J. to see the matter, and so after but a few years was he to treat the matter, making harder than ever for the Americans he so admirably implicated, to wrestle a moral victory from the toils in which they suffered defeat.

Italy had failed, France had failed, England remained. "I have seen almost nothing of the literary fraternity, and there are fifty reasons why I should not become intimate with them," he wrote to Howells in May, 1876. "I don't like their wares, and they don't like any others; and besides, they are not *accueillants.*" But stay! There is Turgenev. "Turgenev is worth the whole heap of them. . ." And after all there is a word to be said for Gustave Flaubert. *"He* is a very fine old fellow, and the most interesting man and strongest artist of his circle." He had even tried to be instructive to the young American, reading to him in private from Gautier's verse to illustrate a point of distinctively French psychology. Yet two months later the decision was finally made. He wrote to his brother William: ". . . my last layers of resistance to a long-encroaching weariness and satiety with the French mind and its utterance has fallen from me like a garment. I have done with 'em, forever, and am turning English all over. I desire only to feed on English life and the contact of English minds. . ." He crossed to London in the latter part of 1876. He was not the sort of screamingly *American* American to be lionized as was Joaquin Miller a few years earlier; nor was he forced into the slums of the London intellect like Ambrose Bierce. He was rather to find a place among the cultivated and the socially accepted, like James Russell Lowell.

Within the next five years H. J. was to move forward with astonishing rapidity artistically. The period was to culminate in his first major work, *The Portrait of a Lady.* He was also to produce several abortive novels which can only be explained on the grounds of uncertainty and need for experiment. In addition to his extensive activity as a writer he was to submit himself to the Londonizing process. London overwhelmed him. His impression of 1869 was revived and confirmed a hundredfold. He explored in all directions and rather self-consciously set himself out to find a place in the London scene. It was the English leisure class he wanted to study and for many years he was to be a most assiduous attendant of dinners and teas and house parties, inexhaustibly curious, inexhaustibly hospitable to impressions.

Yet the English dullness was to stupefy him and he was never to be able, so persistently analytical was he, to accept as one would the wind and the weather, the facts and prejudices of English life. He sought to bring them into the consciousness of his characters and in so doing marked himself as a foreigner. It couldn't be helped. Undoubtedly H. J. at length felt that he had larger matters to be concerned about than conformance to English habits of mind, however much he admired the end product as it exhibited itself in conduct. Furthermore, he was permanently barred from a complete experience of much of English life. He was not, after all, the product of the English public schools nor of a University. Nor was he able to penetrate the English consciousness far enough to appropriate its feeling for country homes, church, politics and the professions. He was to the end an appreciative outsider and to look into his work for any complete picture of the English world is to look in vain. His only salvation was to appropriate what was of use to him as a garment for his "testimony" and to conceal in it the vision of life which was peculiarly his. Since he was never a reportorial realist, this was not a burdensome necessity, but one to which his mind turned naturally. His fiction, unlike his person, was never Anglicized.

As he walked the streets of London, by day and by night, with friends, he vocally revelled in it all. He burst forth in long excited monologues of praise and comment. This "rather dark and decidedly handsome young man of medium height, with a full beard" was destined for great things and at last he had found the place where, with preliminary fumblings even the best are guilty of, he could do them. He might in his first excitement think that "a position in society is a legitimate object of ambition" but not for long would he take society at its face value. He would soon be assidu-

ously tracking down its false standards, discriminating in
a fashion already second-nature to him between the good
and true and the bad.   He might for long years come peri-
odically to regret that America did not offer, to his vision, a
field for his talents, but in the end he accepted his destiny
and made the most of it.   He was not, until in the stress of
an unusual, an unexampled emotion, finally to sever the
cord that bound him to his homeland and even then he was
to direct that his ashes rest with those of his father and
mother and brothers.   Not even political emotion could
obliterate the claims of family piety.

He lost patience with English fifteen times a day and he
could not even think jokingly of taking an English wife,
but he kept at his task.   While his imagination played over
the facts of this world he had determined to appropriate,
his creative work was drawn in other settings.   *The American* had been finished in France and he came to London
unentangled.   His first task was to revise *Watch and Ward*
from its earlier serial version.   It was laid in America, so
one gathers, but so tenuously was it related to that country,
to Boston and New York, that a jaundiced eye might well
wonder if H. J. had ever seen the country.   Indeed the
whole performance is, as Walt Whitman found all of James's,
"feathers."   Its concern is with the adventures of a young
man of fortune and leisure (how indispensable these pre-
liminaries are to H. J.'s fiction !) who undertakes to raise a
young girl to be his wife.   This is a bit incredible and so
is the working out of it.   There is a brave effort toward
the end to raise the story to tragic heights by having the
girl reject her pseudo-guardian's hand, and there is a side
glance at a young American cousin of hers who attempts to
betray her offered confidence.   He is one of those Americans
who plagued H. J. all of his life, a young man of parts
ruined by too close contact with the disintegrating actualities of American business and he is an obvious fraud imaginatively.   Other than demonstrating that H. J. could

force his imagination through so petty a performance, the book is worth little. It is chiefly the incidental matters that interest us, like the ruined young man, and the fact that the girl is "finished" not in England but in Italy.

Nor can much more be said of the novel that succeeded it, *The Europeans.* In this little book H. J. undertook, experimentally, to reverse the situation of *The American.* Instead of an American approaching Europe, we have two Europeanized Americans approaching America. The Europeans, for so these Americans have become by virtue of birth and training abroad, are not presented invidiously for the novel moves on the plane of comedy. The contrasts are drawn firmly however and the book gave H. J. a chance to do a finely appreciative study of the New England character. There is unfortunately a strange thinness about the novel which is felt in spite of the fact that comedy is the medium and great depth would be an impertinence. Whether or not this experiment convinced James that he was not ripe for this sort of exercise or that the material could best be exploited in the reverse direction is impossible to say, but the fact is that his next study "Daisy Miller," was of the American in Europe and it scored his first great success.

"Daisy Miller" later embarrassed H. J. by its very popularity. He was not the sort of writer who felt under any obligation to follow up a success with other wares of the same character and as he went deeper into his chosen themes and his public left him, he resented their continued allegiance to "Daisy." The story had a curious history from the beginning. It was offered to *Lippincott's Magazine* in Philadelphia and rejected, probably as a friend of the editor later explained to H. J. as a libel on American girlhood. It was then submitted to James's old friend, Leslie Stephen, and printed in *Cornhill Magazine* for June-July, 1878. Its success was electrifying and it was immediately pirated by American publishers. "Harry James waked up all the women with his Daisy Miller, the intention of which they misconceived, and there has been a vast discussion in which nobody felt very deeply, and everybody talked very loudly," wrote Howells to James Russell Lowell a year later. "The thing went so far that society almost divided itself in Daisy Millerites and anti-Daisy Millerites. I was glad of it, for I hoped that in making James so thoroughly known, it would call attention in a wide degree to the beautiful work he had been doing so long for very few readers and still fewer lovers." Such a storm as beat around the frail little craft! For "Daisy Miller" is a slight fable having to do with a free, blithe, innocent American girl to whom the social conventions of Europe mean nothing. Unknowingly she transgresses the society code and is seen in the Coliseum by moonlight (the climax is in Rome) with a man and unaccompanied by any chaperon. The weight of the disapproval which follows from this innocent if unconsidered act is appalling and when, in immediate sequel, she contracts a fever, it breaks her spirit and she dies. That is all, but apparently in 1878 it was enough. We of a later day can recover the emotion only with difficulty, if at all.

It was followed by an effort to combine both methods within one story, "The International Episode." Here we have Europeans in America and Americans with the same Europeans in Europe. The result is a heartening example of virtuosity and a discriminating study in the relativity of customs, but it did not settle the issue for in 1880 H. J. tried still another method. In a thin and trivial thing (he immediately told Howells it was "poorish") called *Confidence* he tried the experiment of having a group of Americans work out their difficulties in Europe, in America and then in Europe again. The whole affair revolves around the complications of getting married (James was to return to this theme many times and eventually to produce a masterpiece on no solider basis) and is indeed "poorish" not to say trivial and unworthy. But all these preliminary experiments were necessary, for how else could he feel his way to the expression of that theme, now so dear to him and already in his mind for nine years ? He had fairly well succeeded on one occasion, in the composition of *The American*, but he could not know except by trial and error whether that was the *best* way or not. What amazes one is that so little of the soldier merits of H. J. carried over into these experimental abortions.

And now suddenly he abandoned the task and returned to a study of American life. *Washington Square*, published in 1880, was laid in his beloved New York. It is H. J.'s version, in an American setting, of Balzac's *Eugenie Grandet*. The merits of the book have been considerably overestimated by those critics who have felt that James should have stayed at home. In reality it is a pleasant, easily read little story about the daughter of a Doctor Sloper, a clever practicing physician whose absorbing passion is observing his plain and unclever child. H. J. portrays her difficult position with considerable feeling, not to say pity, but he works out his theme to the end nevertheless. Catherine Sloper is beguiled into giving her affections to an allegedly worthless young fellow who has dissipated an inherited fortune and now proposes, so Dr. Sloper thinks, to recoup his losses by marrying Catherine. She has a small fortune of her own and will inherit more money when her father dies. Dr. Sloper inexorably opposes this match and it is his pleasure to observe Catherine's efforts to define the relative place she shall give to her duty to her parent and her love for the young man. The father wins. The young man goes away. And Catherine grows old in the Washington Square house, rejecting all subsequent suitors and building about her a narrow world from which eventually she has no desire to escape. Now the impressive thing about this novel in the way of setting is that it does not require the New York scene at all. The selection is entirely adventitious and while it shows that James could, if he chose, write about New York, there is nothing to show that he was compelled to by the nature of his talent. It is rather a memento of his affection for his native city. He was well advised to abandon this field to William Dean Howells.

How well advised can be seen by considering *The Portrait of a Lady* which appeared in 1881. With that novel the great period, to last for twenty-odd fruitful years opened.

The year of the publication of *The Portrait* H. J. made a visit to America, the first since 1875. America appealed to him. It always did. ". . . after you have got the right point of view and *diapason,*" he wrote to Miss Henrietta Reubell, "it is a wonderfully entertaining and amusing country. . . I have seen multitudes of people, and no one has been disagreeable. That is different from your pretentious Old World." Yet the reverse of the picture was appalling for if the people were pleasant, politics was horrible. "Poor Henry James thinks (Washington) revolting in respect to the politics and the intrigues that surround it," wrote Henry Adams to an English friend. The pull of Europe was stronger than the appeal of America and to it he inexorably planned to return.

In February 1882 his mother died. The part played by James's mother in the family life is one we can but imperfectly realize. When H. J. came to revive his memories of the family life he could not bring himself to portray her as he did his father. When the omission was pointed out he said with emotion that her memory was too sacred for treatment. Unfortunately his feeling has deprived the world of an understanding of one whose steadying influence in a difficult household must have been pervasive and in a sense determining. Certain it is that her passing destroyed the will to live in H. J.'s father. For H. J., who returned to England in May and went immediately on a 'little tour in France,' was called home in December by his father's serious illness. His brother William was in Europe for a rest and the family arranged that his holiday not be interrupted.

Henry arrived too late. His father was buried on the day H. J.'s ship docked in New York.

He remained in America long enough to take care of certain items of business connected with the settlement of his father's estate and returned to Europe in August, 1883, to remain without a break for twenty years. Before he saw America again he was to write his greatest novels and after his visit he was to do little in the way of creative work. It was during these coming twenty years that his "testimony" was to be given. "A small, pale, noticeable man, with a short, pointed beard, and with large, piercingly observant eyes," hesitant of speech, as he had been from youth — such was the outward appearance at forty-two of the man who was to become a Master.

3. ANNOUNCING A TESTIMONY

HENRY JAMES faced toward Europe in 1883. He knew he was going to be away from America for a long time. He felt that he had now reached a point where the claims of family loyalty being all but completely severed, he could settle down in England permanently. With *The Portrait of a Lady* shining there before him, the road to glory seemed open and free. Nevertheless for the next fourteen years he pursued a devious and difficult course and it was only after sustaining a major disappointment that he suddenly settled down to the rapid production of his great and final works. He was, too, to experience recurring periods of unhappiness, mental depression and homesickness, in spite of his intimacy with such British friends as Edmund Gosse and Robert Louis Stevenson. Yes, homesickness for the America he had assessed and found inadequate, but which was to remain obscurely at the basis of his consciousness to the last, to keep him an American more subtly than any other American of his time, but an American still.

With that remarkable talent for conserving literary energy,

he proposed just to devote himself to the composition of
an American novel.   It was called *The Bostonians* and like
Washington Square must be put down as definitely one of
the lesser products of his pen.   It lacks a really fundamental
theme.   The interest it has is definitely of the secondary
order and the execution is far from being at the top of his
bent.   Taking as his theme the story of the rescuing of a
young and talented girl from the clutches of an older woman
who is attempting to suborn her friend into being the
mouthpiece of the woman suffragettes, James gives us a mildly
satirical picture of the whole female reform group in latter
day Boston.   The society he portrays is that which had
produced Brook Farm gone to seed.   Olive Chancellor who
is the *advocatus diaboli* in the story is represented as one
of the lesser lights in Beacon Hill society, who is consumed
with a passionate and quite irrational hatred for the male
sex.   She is not herself, because of unconquerable diffidence,
able to appear on the platform to expose the wrongs women
have suffered at men's hands and advocate changes in the
laws to eradicate them.   Yet she is consumed with a burning
desire to make a large contribution to the cause.   Quite by
accident, while attending a meeting at the home of Miss
Birdseye, a lady who has grown old in the service of miscellaneous reforms from abolition to homeopathic medicine, she
sees and hears Verena Tarrant.   Miss Tarrant is quite un-
educated but has a beautiful voice and manner and a gift
for words.   Her father, Selah Tarrant, a bedraggled reformer whose latest foible is mesmeric healing, alleges that
his daughter can only speak under mesmeric influence.
This is subsequently proved not to be the case, but it illustrates the curious position of Verena Tarrant when she
is taken up by Olive Chancellor.   Olive is fascinated by the
young girl and takes her into her home to educate her and
prepare her for the largest services to the great cause.

Unfortunately for her peace of mind, she has taken a
distant Mississippi cousin whose fortune was destroyed in

the war, to Miss Birdseye's with her. Basil Ransom is quite as sceptical of reform as Olive is fervent for it, and he is particularly opposed to woman's suffrage. He falls in love with Verena Tarrant but sees no immediate way of rescuing her from Olive's clutches. As he views the matter, Verena Tarrant ". . . was made for love. . . She was profoundly unconscious of it, and another ideal, crude and thin and artificial, had interposed itself. . ." The book resolves itself down to a contest between Ransom and Olive for the possession of Verena; or a contest between two people both of whom love Verena, but one who wishes her to be a public speaker for reform and the other who wishes her to be his wife. Naturally such a situation give James plenty of room for satire and he uses it to the full, but the strength of his bias against woman's suffrage is plentifully illustrated. The upshot of the novel illustrates it. For while Olive fights hard to retain Verena — with a strength that gives color to the charge that Lesbianism is a factor in her interest — Ransom, with much less direct contact, eventually wins her love and hand. In the climactic scene he breaks up a huge rally in Boston at which Verena is to make her first appearance since her "education" and which is to launch her on her career. Henry James obviously believed that woman's place is in the home! *The Bostonians* was written to illustrate his belief and to exhibit the tawdriness of those who thought otherwise.

To the end of his days, Henry James felt that this novel was not treated with justice by the public, and he felt that his omission of it from the celebrated New York Edition was the only regrettable gap in that astonishing array of productions. The case was complicated by the fact that numerous Bostonians thought they detected caricature and contempt in some of the leading figures and never quite forgave him for an injury he had never remotely intended and for which he most humbly apologized in letters to his friends. And the whole matter was even more involved by the fact that later critics found in the novel a hatred for politics and reform which was no part of his purpose. He was truly indifferent to the urgent claims of both ways of life, but not hostile to either. He was never to be sure, to have any great or penetrating understanding of the subject, but he did have stray insights which were rendered rather ridiculous to the better informed by the inadequacy of the form in which they were clothed.

Hard on the heels of *The Bostonians* he made another adventure into the field, dealing in *The Princess Casamassima* with social unrest and economic radicalism. England was in an immensely disturbed state. In the very year that *The Princess* was published the country touched the lowest depths of a lengthy trade depression. Two years earlier the Fabian Society had been founded, presaging a new attitude toward life and eventually letters toward which H. J. was to feel little social, and less aesthetic, sympathy. A few years later the Labor Party was to begin its slow march to power. It is to James's credit that he sensed the significance of the prophetic rumblings, even if but dimly. It is impossible to rise to any great heights of enthusiasm about the "truth" or insight of the novel he wrote under the stimulus of his insight, but it was important as betraying in advance a sense of the final catastrophe, postponed, happily for nearly thirty years, when he was to see his world crumble and fall about him in fragments. *The Princess Casamassima* was, in its scenic parts, the product of that inveterate habit, cultivated by day and by night, of walking in the streets of London for the sole purpose, except that it also be exercise, of absorbing impressions. And at the same time there was always deep in Henry James's mind the realization that while he did not care, as a subject for fiction, for the simple and the undeveloped, he must carefully cultivate a consciousness of the fact that they constituted a large part of the world and that their tribulations were no less real than the complications and implications of his more favored beings. Nor was he ever to achieve any more than a partial blindness to the fact of the evil and misery on which the brighter social life of his characters rested. To evil morally viewed, Henry James was anything but blind, but from the social misery which accompanied the onward pressing of Victorian civilization he customarily turned his eyes. He saw, vividly, sexual corruption and personal perversions, but he saw but dimly the conditions which engendered economic radicalism.

"The condition of (the English upper class) seems to me to be in many ways very much the same rotten and collapsible one as that of the French aristocracy before the revolution — minus cleverness and conversation," he wrote to Charles Eliot Norton just after completing *The Princess Casamassima,* "or perhaps," he went on, "it's more like the heavy, congested and depraved Roman world upon which the barbarians came down. In England the Huns and Vandals will have to come *up* — from the black depths of the (in the people) enormous misery, though I don't think the Attila is quite yet found — in the person of Mr. Hyndman. At all events, much of English life is grossly materialistic and wants blood-letting." It was in some such light that he saw the events portrayed in this huge, imperfect, disappointing novel, for however brilliant the perception, Henry James did not have the facts with which to portray the situation he was to exhibit and he was completely awry in the matter of motivations.

What a phantasmagoria *The Princess Casamassima* really is ! What an astoundingly muddled mixture of profound insight, sympathetic understanding and weird *mis*understanding. The name part in this drama was taken by that same Catherine Light who had lured Henry James's first major character to his death. She was drawn from *Roderick Hudson* of 1875. And how logically she walked into the situations the novel required ! For it was only by positing a character whose nature was perverse and unpredictable that Henry James could make the necessary connections be-

tween the highest aristocracy and the partisans of radicalism.
"The Princess," he wrote, "was an embodied passion — she
was not a system: and her behaviour, after all, was more addressed to relieving herself than to relieving others. . . To
do something for others was not only so much more human
— it was so much more amusing." Amusing to play with
ideas for destroying the class of which she was a member, to
consort with and encourage those who were plotting to upset
society in the interests of the oppressed classes from whose
deprivations were drawn those funds which supported such
as she and made possible the cultivation of every impulse —
even that which now led to alliance with the radicals from
the depths ! But such a motive is strong compared to that
which Henry James invented to guide the conduct of the
most pathetic figure in the novel, Hyacinth Robinson. This
lad, "bastard of a murderess, spawned in a gutter out of
which he had been picked by a poor sewing-girl," was also to
play a part in joining the two worlds together and by his
"psychology" to make pathetically unreal the whole nature
of the radical movement. Of him Henry James asks us to
believe that since he was the illegitimate son of an aristocratic
father and of whose condition he was in utter ignorance until
long after his views were formed, he was plagued with an
hereditary memory of the felicities of aristocratic life. His
radical impulses were not, then, inspired by any idealistic
desire to improve the condition of the class among whom
destiny had thrown him, but by a sense of deprivation of
things and ways of living of which he was a natural heir !
By the aid of the Princess he is enabled to glimpse the benef-
icences of upper class life almost simultaneously with his
selection to perform a wild deed of assassination which his
fellow conspirators feel will advance their cause. The conviction that it is senseless to do anything, no matter how
small the act, to destroy the upper classes leads to the climax
of the novel in his suicide.

It hardly needs emphasizing to bring home to the reader

that this is incredibly and hopelessly befuddled. Yet strewn through this nightmarish unreality are stray passages, chance remarks, oblique hints which show that Henry James was not entirely without an understanding of radicalism. He saw clearly that "centuries of poverty, of ill-paid toil, of bad, insufficient food and wretched housing hadn't a favorable effect on the higher faculties." He spoke blightingly, through the lips of the possessed Princess of "the selfishness, the corruption, the iniquity, the cruelty, the imbecility of the people who all over Europe had the upper hand." He could, through the testimony of Hyacinth Robinson, see the poor: "There were nights when every one he met appeared to reek with gin and filth and he found himself elbowed by figures as foul as lepers. Some of the women and girls in particular were appalling — saturated with alcohol and vice, brutal, bedraggled, obscene. 'What remedy but another deluge, what alchemy but annihilation?' he asked himself as he went his way; and he wondered what fate there could be in the great scheme of things for a planet overgrown with such vermin, what redemption but to be hurled against a ball of consuming fire. . . In these hours," and the reader should note these words, "the poverty and ignorance of the multitude seemed so vast and preponderant, and so much the law of life, that those who had managed to escape from the black gulf were only the happy few, spirits of resource as well as children of luck: they inspired in some degree the interest and sympathy that one should feel for survivors and victors, those who have come safely out of a shipwreck or a battle." Yet deep down in these depths of poverty there was unrest. Inspired idealists, of whom Paul Muniment was an example, were plotting to lead these bedraggled specimens of humanity, on whose necks the "happy few" were standing, into a happier and more beneficent world. Paul Muniment, the one revolutionist in the book approaching reality in conception and motivation "went in for the great grim restitution," a scheme which, with the wrappings of conspiracy removed

appeared as no more astounding a programme than shifting
the conditions in which these unfortunates lived and the re-
placement of oppression with "democracy with a *chance*."
Henry James got no nearer to the heart of economic radicalism, even in its contemporary expression, than that! Like
Hyacinth Robinson, he was beguiled by the "happy few"
and it was with them that he threw his lot. It was to the
leisure class that he addressed both his study and his literature. Fleetingly, he glimpsed the fact that these very classes
were "living in a fool's paradise" and that "the ground's
heaving under our feet." He could even catch sight of the
truth that the two great forces of "democracy" (as he so
weakly denominated it) and privilege would certainly soon
"come to a death grapple." He was unable to penetrate
deep enough to give his random insights any great force or
reality in fiction. He was in the position of those startled
aristocrats in William Balfour Kerr's powerful piece of pictorial propaganda whose revels are interrupted by the penetration through the floor of the dirty fist of a workman.
Henry James saw that fist and, being imaginatively alive,
saw its import. From the scanty evidence it offered he re-
constructed, like an anthropologist handling a skeleton, a
picture of the world from whence it had come and the circumstances motivating the thrust of it into the midst of the
"happy few."

HENRY JAMES was very much disturbed in these years, and
his depression about the state of English society was complemented by his personal condition. "I have entered upon
evil days — but this is for your most private ear," he wrote
to William Dean Howells. "It sounds portentous, but it
only means that I am still staggering a good deal under the
mysterious and (to me) inexplicable injury wrought — apparently — upon my situation by my two last novels, *The
Bostonians* and the *Princess,* from which I expected so much
and derived so little. They have reduced the desire, and the

demand, for my productions to zero. . ." His weariness
further overflowed to his brother William, to whom he complained about many things he never disclosed to others. The
chief burden of his cry on this occasion was that his old theme
of international contrasts seemed "idle and pedantic" and
he longed to escape it. He longed, too, to have time to
think over his condition and to recover somewhat his sense
of real life. The failure of his novels led him to turn to
short stories that he might "leave a multitude of pictures of
my time, projecting my small circular frame upon as many
different spots as possible and going in for a number as well as
quality, so that the number may constitute a total having a
certain value as observation and testimony." It was a large
aspiration which he carried out with remarkable success.
But it did not resolve his unrest, nor did it permanently
satisfy his requirements even in fiction. He was still, after
this period of dissatisfaction, to turn once again to the longer
form and produce his greatest works. Furthermore, he was
to feel himself, falsely or not is not the point, in need of
money and he turned at last to the theatre. He was indeed
in a strange case and one from which he was to be rescued
only by so signal a disaster that it would permanently have
broken the spirit of a lesser man. A glimpse of him, in a
letter of William, pictures him to us at this time as we think
of him in old age. Indeed it is difficult to put one's finger
on the period when Henry James ceased to be very young
and began to be rather portentously old. Louisa May Alcott found him solemn in 1865. Edmund Gosse found him
"mildly avuncular" in 1884. Now in 1889, William found
that he had "covered himself, like some marine crustacean,
with all sorts of material growths, rich sea-weeds and rigid
barnacles and things, and lives hidden in the midst of his
strange heavy alien manners and customs. . ." Not the
least of his "covering" was the increasingly elaborate style
in which he clothed his stories. And as he grew older, the
richness and strangeness grew and grew. It became an in-

tegral part of Henry James and without it most of the exotic
flavor of his personality would be missing.

Between 1885 and 1900 Henry James wrote the bulk of
the short stories he eventually chose to preserve and included
among them are those considered to be his masterpieces.
Reaching back into the past we find three or four not previously mentioned which it is worthwhile bringing to light
here.   In "Four Meetings" (1877) we find an example of the
use he made of the pull of Europe in the story of an elderly
woman who has saved for years in order to make the trip,
only to be deprived of her chance by the unscrupulous conduct of a Europeanized relative who "borrows" all her funds
immediately on her landing at Havre, forcing her to return
on the first boat.   Instead of seeing Europe in the concrete
she sees it vicariously for years later, on the occasion of the
narrator's fourth meeting, he finds her in her New England
home saddled with the care of a vulgar woman, supposedly
her relative's wife, who passes herself off as a countess.   So
Europe to her means exploitation and disappointment.   A
variation on this theme was played in "Europe" (1899).   The
story here is the pull of Europe once more and has to do
with the fortunes of a group of four New England ladies, the
mother and three daughters.   In this case the mother has
been to Europe in the far distant past and wishes the same
advantage for her daughters, but conveniently falls ill whenever there is the slightest chance of their going.   Finally one
does break away, only to refuse to return to her home, a second dies and the third is left with her mother and bitterly
rejects the idea of going to Europe on her mother's death
which cannot be long postponed.   In both these cases Europe
has poisoned the lives of these women without their ever
having directly seen it!   The only one who did get there
stayed, and then, it is hinted, only because of the unendurable character of her American home!   Europe in another
guise appears as the motivating force behind "A Bundle of
Letters" (1879).   In this story we see Henry James moving

toward his theme of the America-Europe contrast, in a technical exercise which shows him appreciative of national contrasts on a wider scale than that he eventually chose to illustrate. He gives us the essence of the contrast in the letters home of a young woman from Bangor, the letters of an English girl, a Frenchman and a German. This small story, then, exhibits the many facets of international differences.

In "The Pension Beaurepas" (1879) we arrive at a study of the Americans in Europe which plays a variation on the difference in the reactions of the women and the men. The mother and daughter of the tale are infatuated with Europe and take full advantage of the opportunity to acquire all the "culture" and material luxuries available, while the father unregardedly worries about his business at home, tortured by the knowledge that while they are lingering in these splendors, his affairs are going down to ruin. A different father is to be found in "The Reverberator" (1888). This tale has to do with the fortunes of an American father, blandly indifferent to Europe but agreeable to the wishes of his two daughters. His affairs at home are in the best of order and no catastrophe may be expected from that quarter. The younger daughter is in the marriage market and her vendor is her elder sister. The family is favored with the friendship of the European correspondent of *The Reverberator*, a society scandal sheet published in America. He aspires to the hand of the pretty sister, but is scorned by her mentor and rejected as not to her fancy by the girl herself. She then, by merest chance, meets the son of a thoroughly Gallicized American family of Southern origin, who promptly falls in love with her. In preparation for his marriage and after he has with difficulty encompassed the acceptance of his choice by the family, he goes to America to look into his father's affairs. During the interval the correspondent of *The Reverberator* pumps the younger sister and she unsuspectingly tells him all the scandal she had learned about her prospective husband's family. The publication of this matter releases a storm of which the victim is the son's fiancée and she takes it as axiomatic that her engagement is over.   The struggle then becomes centered on a theme endlessly interesting to Henry James.   The young man has to decide whether he will accept the judgment of his family and so forever resign his freedom, or abandon his loyalties and cleave to his wife-to-be.   After intricate debate he decides for freedom and the Americans leave Paris with him in tow.   In "The Pupil" of 1891 we once more have Americans in Europe and Americans of a peculiarly shabby sort.   It was this story to which Joseph Conrad made reference when, in writing to John Galsworthy, he sought to prove that Henry James wrote from the heart.   The pupil is the younger son of a family of Americans who live in a haphazard fashion in the better parts of France, changing their abode with the seasons.   Their income is an indefinite but exceedingly unreliable quantity and the young English tutor only stays on from pity of his charge.   The pupil is acutely aware of the low morals of his family and his subtle and cynical comments on their actions both horrify and fascinate his tutor.   How he preserves his moral integrity in such surroundings is a bit mysterious.   The story traces the rapid disintegration, break up and dispersal of this amazing family.   When the tutor with an extraordinary access of generosity offers to take his pupil away to live with him, the shock of the unparalleled concern for his welfare brings on a heart attack from which the poor child dies.

The theme of the contagion of corruption appears in "The Liar" (1888).   In this story a painter has accidentally met in a country house a lady with whom he was in love long years before.   He finds her married to a fascinating man, retired from the army after service in India, whose one weakness is a chronic inability to tell the truth.   Realizing that no more simple or straightforward person has existed than this man's wife, the painter endeavors to discover how she accepts the moral obliquity of her husband.   He is unsuccessful until he undertakes to paint the husband's portrait in such a manner as to reveal to all who care to look his moral irresponsibility. The husband encompasses the destruction of the picture and explains the matter to the painter in a characteristically lying fashion. Since the wife acquiesces and indeed sustains this grotesque bit of fiction, the painter reluctantly concludes that the girl has consciously or unconsciously been poisoned by her association. The most masterly variation on this theme of innocence in contact with evil and the probable effect, is "What Maisie Knew" (1897). In this story, one of the most famous of the whole range of Henry James's productions, we have the case of a little girl who is hurled back and forth between her divorced father and mother, alternately assured of the evil of the one by the other, and exposed further to the knowledge that not satisfied with separating themselves they have chosen to further complicate the matter by endless intrigues all of which come directly under the observation (if she does observe them) of the child. We are never made aware of the issue of this tangle, but are left perpetually with a wonderment about what Maisie knew. An extension of this theme into the realm of the ghostly, led to the production of one of the most gruesome horror stories of all time, "The Turn of the Screw" (1898). Taking his influences out of the realm of the concrete and the actual, James transferred them to the world of spirits and imagined the effect upon a boy and girl of the influence of the ghosts of a wicked and designing governess and butler. The heightening of horror reaches perilously near to the screaming point, and the suggestiveness of treatment was never surpassed.

A return to the general atmosphere of "Daisy Miller" (1879) was made in two stories, "Pandora" (1885), and "The Chaperon" (1891). It should not be thought that there is any exact correspondence, but we must consider the fact that in all of these stories we have a resolute girl facing the world. In "Daisy Miller" the issue was defeat. In "Pandora" the nearest in spirit to the greatest handling of the theme, we find an American girl of indifferent origin determined to make her way to a position in society. We observe her through the eyes of a young German, Count Vogelstein, who encounters her on shipboard while he is on his way to Washington for diplomatic duties. Learned but neither light nor humorous, he desires to intelligently observe American society. Pandora strikes him as an unusual type and he follows her with fascinated attention. On arrival in Washington his studies and duties engross him for some years, until one day Pandora suddenly reappears, heralded as one of the really fascinating young women of New York society. He is amazed at the transformation and hovers about her, half in love, in an effort to understand her view of things. With admirable restraint Henry James indicates the fascination-repulsion motif in Vogelstein's attitude, and precipitates the climax under his eyes. Pandora "gets what she's after," an appointment in the diplomatic service for the young man to whom she has become engaged since childhood. She has, at a stroke, made him fit to marry by gaining him a position which will allow her to take him without sacrificing any of her hard won gains. An equally resolute girl appears in "The Chaperon," though she is English and not American. The story tells of her efforts to rehabilitate her mother who has been disgraced and socially ostracized by a particularly odorous divorce. With intelligent "push" she accomplishes her task and incidentally makes a good marriage for herself. A third interesting example of a return to an earlier situation is "Flickerbridge" (1902) which goes back to "The Passionate Pilgrim" of 1871. In this story we have the case of a young American artist who by merest chance is introduced into the home of an elderly lady and there finds the epitome of the old, the accumulated graces of a past social situation. He savors it to the last drop and then leaves precipitately when it is apparent that his fiancée, a writer, is to join him there and, as he feels, advertise to the world and so spoil this paradise. He sacrifices marriage to his memory of something hallowed and perfect.

Before examining swiftly a large group of stories of literary origin, we may pause over six tales of rather disparate nature, but each one illustrative of the range of Henry James's curiosity. The first in order of time is "Brooksmith" (1891). This story is the only one in the whole James canon that deals with a servant. Brooksmith is the butler of a retired member of the diplomatic service, unmarried, but whose house is decidedly a place one visits. It is apparent that some unseen hand guides the gatherings there for one never meets the wrong people, nor are the wrong topics ever brought up in conversation. The house, indeed, is the perfection of the social amenities and on analysis of the situation the narrator discovers that Brooksmith is largely responsible. He not only keeps up the tone, like an artist, but he finds emotional and intellectual satisfaction in doing so. On the death of his master, who was too poor to provide liberally for him, Brooksmith is unable to make any adjustment to ordinary servant life and after various unfortunate experiments commits suicide. This curious story would seem to be an offshoot of *The Princess Casamissima* of 1886 in that it portrays the dilemma of a member of the lower classes appreciative of the life of his superiors but unable to penetrate into their circle except by accident. "The Real Thing" (1893) deals with a fascinating enigma arising out of the fact that the false is often more convincing than the true. This is revealed to an artist (the artist is du Maurier) whose subjects are of the *haut monde,* but whose models are from the shiftless representatives of the lower classes who go in for posing professionally. Offered a chance to substitute for them an impoverished Colonel and his wife, he accepts eagerly only to find that 'the real thing' is not to his purpose and that he must if he wishes to get on with his work, return to the imitative ! In "The Altar of the Dead" (1895) we come to a story about which a mild dispute has taken

place, some critics alleging it to be a perfect example of the
lack of "real" motivation in James's stories and others finding it of high serene beauty. Yet it is, so it turns out on
analysis, one of the most moral of all of James's tales (and
any reader who has not by now agreed to the conclusion that
James was a moralist is singularly recalcitrant to evidence),
for it tells of an elderly man whose life has been permanently
marked by the death just before their marriage of the one
woman with whom he has been able to fall in love. He
hits upon the idea, by accident, of erecting a shrine to her
memory and burning a candle on it for every other member
of his cluster of dead friends as well as she. His shrine with
its bank of candles attracts the attention of a lady who adopts
it as the scene of her devotions. Her case intrigues the
gentleman, but he is only slowly to penetrate to its core,
when it turns out that she is paying devotion to the memory
of a man who has terribly injured him in early life. The
shock of this revelation unnerves him, for of all "his dead"
this man is the only one to whom a candle has not been dedicated. When it is revealed to the lady what his relation to
this man has been, she refuses longer to pray before the
shrine and he is forced to struggle with the problem of forgiveness for one's enemies. It is a long and hard struggle
which he carries with him into the shadow of death but he
emerges triumphant and with a desperate wrench orders that
the final candle be placed. The next story on our list, "The
Spoils of Poynton" (1897) is conceded by all hands to be a
masterpiece and it is also of supreme interest as one of the
earliest turned out after James's encounter with the theatre.
We can see in it the first flowering of that absorbed pursuit
of the ultimate impression and relation which was to characterize all his later work and which was to dictate the endless development of allusiveness to his style. It deals with
the abnormal growth of the possessive instinct in the breast
of a widowed lady who is cursed with an insensitive son.
The "spoils" are all the fine furniture, pictures and bric-a-

brac which she has accumulated through long years chiefly dedicated to accumulation. They have been deposited at Poynton which has become in consequence a veritable museum. Her son proposes to marry a very insensitive girl, whose taste is notable only for its ordinariness, while his mother proposes that he marry Fleda Vetch, whose fondness for the fine is on a plane with his mother's. The struggle which goes on to dispose of this heritage of antiques is what makes the story, and the endless complications which arise are of point only in relation to the "spoils." The struggle ends, for all time, by the destruction of Poynton by fire, a consummation reached after it has become clear to Fleda Vetch that she will never possess the coveted objects. "In the Cage" (1898) deals with the perceptions of a telegraph clerk who, in handling the messages which pass under her hand, finds herself mentally implicated in a social situation of some complexity. The story, as James himself pointed out, is related, somewhat tenuously to the situation of Hyacinth in *The Princess Casamassima*. It is, above all, a well-nigh perfect example of James's unusual ability to pursue the most elusive relations of men and women and things to their ultimate implications. The last of our miscellaneous group is "The Beast in the Jungle" (1903), a story which is fairly sustained in mid-air, like a spider's web, by virtue of its tenuosity. It deals with the life of a man whose obsession it is that he is marked out for some signal disaster which will distinguish him from the rest of mankind. It is that which is the beast in the jungle and his life becomes little more than a series of speculations upon when the tiger will spring. His one and only confidante, through the long years, dies without revealing to him her vision of his disaster and he tries to divert himself by travel in order to escape his obsession. But eventually he returns to London, visits her grave, and there has it revealed to him that his distinction is, horribly enough, that nothing is to happen to him and that he has, in his infatuation, avoided his happiness which was plainly intended to be his marriage to her. This story has obvious relations to *The Ambassadors* of the same year. Its moral, like that drawn by Lambert Strether from his encounter with Parisian life, is that leading a life in which nothing happens is as cruel as one in which tragic "happenings" are characteristic.

Sir William Rothenstein has observed that no writer of fiction has ever been able to enter into the life of a painter with complete success and many of Henry James's stories about writers have been dismissed as inadequate in spite of the fact that he was one himself! One in particular, "The Author of Beltraffio," has been designated as hopelessly inadequate in spite of the fact that it was based on an anecdote reputedly dealing with a passage from the life of John Addington Symonds. There is considerable interest, then, in examining with reasonable thoroughness (since we are not aiming to produce a catalogue) a group of James's stories of the literary life. In "The Aspern Papers" (1888) is an episode related to the life of Byron. It seems that a young literary man has gotten wind of the fact that there still lives in Venice an old lady who in her youth was intimate with Aspern (Byron) and that she undoubtedly has in her possession a quantity of papers of untold value. The young man resolves to get them and in his pursuit insinuates himself into the confidence of the lady and her niece, gracelessly pretends to make love to the unattractive younger lady, and even verges on the edge of stealing the precious papers. In the end he does not get them, for in a fit of conscientious scruple the niece burns them one by one after her aunt's death. What we have here, it seems, is little more than a satire on the devouring passion of posterity for information about the illustrious literary dead. "The Lesson of the Master" (1888) is similarly satirical, but in a rather more devastating way. A young writer meets an older writer whom he admires to distraction and in the course of his acquaintance with him introduces his fiancée in whom he has inspired a similarly adulatory respect. He then goes off to the continent to write a novel which he hopes will be of an excellence only to be attributed to the inspiration of his fortunate contact. While he is away the lesson proceeds and is revealed to be no more than that the master has carried off and married his sweetheart!

The ironic vein is kept up in "The Death of the Lion" (1894), "The Coxon Fund" (1894) and "The Next Time" (1895), all of which appeared in the most famous periodical of the English nineties, *The Yellow Book*. Considerable moralizing has been expended upon Henry James's connection with this periodical, even extending to the allegation that he was forced to associate with the company clustered around it in the desperation aroused by his inability to find any "respectable" magazine open to him. If that explanation is true of James it must apply with equal measure to those other "respectables" who joined him in the first number, Arthur Christopher Benson, Arthur Waugh, and Edmund Gosse. The less striking but more reasonable explanation is to be found in his preface to the volume containing the three tales mentioned where he attributes his association to the editor of the magazine, Henry Harland, like himself an expatriated American, but, as James sadly observed to Edmund Gosse, confronted by "a chasm too deep to bridge . . . in the pitfall of his literary longings unaccompanied by the *faculty*," a judgment singularly kind when one considers the book for which Harland is now chiefly remembered, *The Cardinal's Snuff Box*. When Harland made his appeal for James's association in the enterprise he was accompanied by Aubrey Beardsley of whom James later recalled that while he was "touching, and extremely individual . . . I hated his productions and thought them extraordinarily base — and couldn't find (perhaps didn't try enough to find!) the formula that reconciled this baseness, aesthetically, with his being so perfect a case of the artistic spirit." The dear old moralist! Yet the claims of friendship were ever to figure largely for him and he appeared in the first number, within a cover decorated by Beardsley ! with "The Death of the Lion." This story tells us of the extraordinary last hours of a distinguished novelist who has been invited, in company with two scribblers, to a country house where they are all to be equally feted as representatives of literature. Everything goes as might be expected, except that the "lion" catches cold and dies and through the indifference and intolerable carelessness of one of the guests (it is impossible to say which) the manuscript of his last and presumably most glorious book is lost ! So much for literature ! "The Coxon Fund" deals with the case of Coleridge (with overtones perhaps, of A. Bronson Alcott) who is portrayed with no very heavy moralistic emphasis as hopelessly lacking in moral roots, a grand, luxurious tropical plant throwing off great blossoms of imperial conversation. In "The Next Time" we return again to the sad case of literature when confronted with the competition of literary articles of commerce. The man in the case tries desperately to debase his wares, always 'the next time' planning to turn out a best seller, which he is absolutely unable to do, going on to the end writing brilliantly, while the lady in the case makes a try for literature only to turn out a novel which sells better than her ordinary productions. The irony of these stories is vastly interesting because it is possible by taking them seriously to find in them confessions of Henry James's own predicament.

By changing the emphasis from irony to confession it is possible to say that "The Death of the Lion," particularly, is a confession of Henry James's own feeling with regard to his position among the class he had so assiduously cultivated. It would seem, however, that this is subtracting from his literary product a constituent which has never been sufficiently remarked, in the interests of "thesis." There is perhaps more warrant for this sort of exercise in "The Middle Years" (1893) which tells of the last hours of a writer who has striven all his life for perfection of style, only to find himself dying with the conviction that he is being deprived of the needed chance really to do "it." He is sustained, however, by the devotion of a chance acquaintance and tremendous admirer, who assures him that he has "done it" in his last book which he was amending when his final crisis came upon him. Certainly the aspirations and emotions of this tale were derived from James's own feeling and there is a large and motley group of critics who find in the last story to be mentioned here, "The Figure in the Carpet" (1896) a hint that James felt himself but inadequately understood and a further hint that at the core of his vast array of novels and stories, there was a "figure," a design, a message, or some esoteric principle which he wished, all ambiguously, to communicate to the world. Such at least is the broad hint of the author-protagonist of the story which then deals with the efforts and eventual success of a listening critic to dig it out. He dies without revealing it, even to his wife, who marries a lesser man whose interest in her is the possibility of eventually possessing the answer. He is disappointed, of course, and the "figure" remains unrevealed.

This story is perhaps the most unfortunate of all of James's productions, for it has provoked a critical reaction out of all proportion to its probable significance. It is exceedingly likely that it symbolizes nothing more than the fact that James, like many writers of unusual originality, never got, in his lifetime, anything like comprehending criticism, but that he meant to hint at any esoteric message one may presume to doubt. Nevertheless from this hint has sprung a great mass of critical exegesis of dubious importance. The critics of Henry James have not been noted for their agreement about his merits. It is not so much that a variety of intricate figures have been discerned in the carpet he wove as that there has been considerable disagreement about the kind of carpet he made and even doubt about its being a carpet at all. It has been adjudged something too fine and delicate to be trodden by the feet of democratic men; as something too bizarre and improbable to be approved by stern American moralists; as something too antiquated to be anything but a wall-hanging in a museum. His machinery for weaving his carpet has been condemned as too intricate to be of use and doomed to the same oblivion as Mark Twain's type-setting machine. It has been alleged that he operated it scientifically without emotion; that he ran it under a full head of emotion; and that he had emotion but no science; that he was fascinated with its capacity for turning out a fine product without moral substance; and that he was fundamentally a moralist running an intricate machine. Henry James has been called a devotee of culture, a man without culture, a scientist, an aesthetician, a delicate and discerning observer and reporter of life, a man divorced from life altogether, a writer who, stylistically, made a fetish of obscurity and a writer whose passion was clarity and precision. He has been praised and condemned for all the contradictory reasons any discerning and critical reader can invent or imagine as he reads through the endless line of volumes containing the work which for over forty years flowed from James's pen.

As IF as a prelude to his engagement with the theatre, Henry James published *The Tragic Muse* in 1890. This novel, which will be viewed here only from one angle, is curiously bulky, yet without the pith and savor of the great fiction from Henry James's hand. Strewn about in it are various themes and complications that do not bear any obvious relation to the on-going of the narrative, such things as the relative claims of painting and politics. So far as the reader is concerned the primary interest of the novel is in the attitude it illustrates toward the theatre and it assumes especial interest in the list of Henry James's productions because it was written *before* he went into the theatre to make money rather than after. The first point that he made is that there is a sharp distinction between the drama and the theatre. For the former he retained always the highest respect, while for the latter he had only harsh words and bitter criticism. From far back, as we have seen, Henry James was a devotee of the theatre and he knew it well in three countries, America, France and England. He was not a parvenue when he approached it in the early nineties as a possible solution of his financial and artistic difficulties.

The evidence he gives in *The Tragic Muse* of diligent study of the conditions upon which success in the theatre must be based speaks well for his insight, for very few of the remarks fail of pertinence today. "Do I think it's important?" one of the characters asks. "Is that what you mean? Important certainly to managers and stage-carpenters who want to make money, to ladies and gentlemen who want to produce themselves in public by limelight, and to other ladies and gentlemen who are bored and stupid and don't know what to do with their evening. It's a commercial and social convenience which may be infinitely worked. But important artistically, intellectually? How *can* it be — so poor, so limited a form?" In fact it was upon the conditions of the theatre that Henry James heaped his scorn. He wrote of the audiences: "the *omnium gatherum* of the population of a big commercial city at the hour of the day when their taste is at its lowest, flocking out of hideous hotels and restaurants, gorged with food, stultified with buying and selling and with all the other sordid preoccupations of the age, squeezed together in a sweltering mass, disappointed in their seats, timing the author, timing the actor, wishing to get their money back on the spot — all before eleven o'clock." "Fancy," the character goes on, "putting the exquisite before such a tribunal as that! There's not even a question of it. The dramatist wouldn't if he could, and in nine cases out of ten he couldn't if he would. He has to make the basest concessions. One of his principal canons is that he must enable his spectators to catch the suburban trains, which

stop at 11:30. What would one think of any other artist —
the painter or the novelist — whose governing forces should
be the dinner and the suburban trains? The old drama-
tists didn't defer to them — not so much at least — and
that's why they're less and less actable. If they're touched
— the large loose men — it's only to be mutilated and trivi-
alized. Besides, they had a simpler civilization to represent
— societies in which the life of man was in action, in passion, in immediate and violent expression. Those things
could be put upon the playhouse boards with comparatively
little sacrifice of their completeness and their truth. Today
we're so infinitely more reflective and complicated and dif-
fuse that it makes all the difference. What can you do with
a character, with an idea, with a feeling, between dinner and
the suburban trains? You can give a gross rough sketch of
them, but how little you touch them, how bald you leave
them! What crudity compared with what the novelist
does!"

Surely that is stating the case harshly enough, but it does
not bring to the end Henry James's objections to the
theatre. He objected, most strenuously, to the emphasis
in the dramatic criticism of the day, on the actors and
actresses. It is especially interesting, therefore, to catch a
glimpse of his view of the conditions of an actress's career.
The central character in *The Tragic Muse* is Miriam Rooth,
represented as half-Jewish and half-English, without talent
to begin with, but susceptible of training and full to the
brim with resources in the way of application. She also
shows that, to a point, she has emotional and intellectual
resources not at first apparent. A friend remarks to her
that she is "a strange girl." "Je crois bien!" she replies.
"Doesn't one have to be, to want to go and exhibit one's self
to a loathsome crowd, on a platform, with trumpets and a
big drum, for money — to parade one's body and one's
soul?" But worse than that, as it emerged as her career
progressed, the actress was hardly a personality. "It struck

him abruptly," this correct Englishman who fancied himself in love with Miriam "that a woman whose only being was to 'make believe,' to make believe she had any and every being you might like and that would serve a purpose and produce a certain effect, and whose identity resided in the continuity of her personations, so that she had no moral privacy, as he phrased it to himself, but lived in a high wind of exhibition, of figuration — such a woman was a kind of monster in whom of necessity there would be nothing to 'be fond' of, because there would be nothing to take hold of." What indeed, he later thinks, is an actress anyhow but "a female gymnast, a mountebank at higher wages? She didn't literally hang by her heels from a trapeze and hold a fat man in her teeth, but she made the same use of her tongue, of her eyes, of the imitative trick, that her muscular sister made of leg and jaw."

These are bitter words and of course not delivered in Henry James's own person. But as we shall see, his own personal reactions were but little removed from the emotionally overemphasized conclusion of his implicated character. The whole situation footed up to the conclusion that to satisfy the exigencies of the theatre and the performers the play became "a more or less idiotised version of a new French piece, a thing that had taken in Paris a third-rate theatre and was now proving itself in London good enough for houses mainly made up of ten-shilling stalls." It was into this sorry world of which if "one half's what's called brilliant the other's frankly odious" that he proposed to launch himself. What, if we waive the money question, did Henry James expect to gain from such an excursion?

He gained only a confirmation of his views about the theatre as an institution and about the drama as a form. In other words he came out the same door that he went in, but a sorer and wiser man as who would not be when buffeted and bruised even by a venture one had thoroughly evaluated before hand? His service to the "vulgarest of the muses," fortunately, threw him back even beyond his resolve to do only short stories — to the novel form where his talent flowered in a series of amazing fictions which not only allowed him intellectual freedom but for which he took the right to indulge in a luxuriance of phrase and development never before heard of. In the five years from 1889 to 1894 he wrote seven or eight plays (since he did not publish all it is difficult accurately to say) of which only two were produced. The first was a production of *The American* which flourished briefly in the provinces but failed in London and the second was *Guy Domville,* produced on January 5, 1895, in London with catastrophic results. It was the total failure of the latter that led him to abandon the effort, though the lure of the theatre never quite lost its power to beguile him.

He put the case to his brother William when he wrote that "The whole odiousness of the thing lies in the connection between the drama and the theatre. The one is admirable in its interest and difficulty, the other loathsome in its conditions." And, indeed, in prefacing the two little published collections of plays he put out he elaborated this theme, until we can realize just what he gained, technically, from his adventure. "I know not whether," he wrote, "for the effective playwright the fascination be less than for the perverted man of letters freshly trying his hand at an art of which, in opposition to his own familiar art, every rule is an infraction, every luxury a privation and every privilege a forfeiture, so that he has if possible even more to unlearn than to learn; certain it is such a desperate adventurer promptly perceives that if the job were easy it would not be worth undertaking." It was necessary to work with "the foul fiend Excision" at one's elbow, cutting here, jabbing there, until only the bones of the material remained. In fact it was the extraordinary meagreness of the form that fascinated him for his manner was the opposite of meagreness. And the controlling element was time. There was a race between the dramatist and the hands of the clock so that

nothing could be done by way of development. But if excision was the bane, selection was the task and the result was
intensity, an intensity peculiarly theatrical and perhaps the
justifying reward for so much labor. In any case, Henry
James found that the experiment was productive of "more
stores of technical experience than any other aesthetic errand." His reward then, was aesthetic, but the fruits of
his errand he was never to apply. The "foul fiend Excision" was never too constantly at his elbow and if he applied the law of selection to heighten the drama in novels,
he allowed himself so much room for development that he
did not achieve a theatrical intensity exactly. Such was the
gold he found in his purse after five years of intensive labor.

   The bitterness he quite promptly forgot. That night
when *Guy Domville* was produced was one of torture. He
did not attend the play himself, but went rather to see Oscar
Wilde's *An Ideal Husband* which he judged to be "crude
. . . bad . . . clumsy . . . feeble and vulgar," but which
gave immediate signs of a huge popular success. When it
was over he approached his own theatre with trepidation.
He was called before the curtain to answer the customary
cries for the author only "to be subjected . . . to a storm
of hoots and jeers and catcalls from the gallery, answered by
loud and sustained applause from the stalls, the whole producing the effect of hell broken loose, in the midst of which
the author, white as chalk, bowed and spread forth deprecat-
ing hands and finally vanished." The theatrical passage in
his life was, except for feebly flickering revivals, over.

   Two years later he settled at Rye where he bought "a delightful old house, in a decayed mediaeval town, oak panel-
ing, king's room, sweet garden and lawn, and all the requi-
sites for the 'long home' of a bachelor tired of the world,"
and devoted himself assiduously to the composition of his
huge, glittering novels. The spell of London was weakened
and he no longer, until late in life, felt its pull. What
broke the London spell is difficult to say. It could hardly

have been the theatre entirely, for it was an aspect of the London scene which could be easily avoided.

The fact is beyond dispute, however, that at this period Henry James's depression was heaping itself up and that it would have to issue in some radical change of scene or activity. It may not be outside the bounds of probability to guess that he went down to Rye in an effort to recover his spirits and that in that lovely village he sought peace and happiness which seemed denied him in London. It was precisely at this time that William Dean Howells saw him in London and found him "needlessly but deeply discouraged." Howells found himself "able to reassure him of his public here." And William James also sensed the troubles with which his brother was laboring and diagnosed them as the results of being "weaned for fifteen years at least" from "the vital facts of human character."

This would coincide with James's conviction that America was slipping away from him, a conviction which had been working on him since 1890. Furthermore in 1892 just when he was midway in his disastrous theatrical experiment his sister Alice who had been living in retirement in England since 1885, died and cut the only local tie that bound Henry James to his family and youth. For seven years he had been assiduously her attendant and though he concealed it from his friends that his ailing sister might not be disturbed by importunate visitors, he not only comforted her but found comfort in her. He stored up things to tell her and he found her talk better than any in London. The whole period was characterized by accidents and obsessions that contributed to the decline of his optimism, always a rather small element in his outlook, and of his spirits.

His personal difficulties did not prevent him from getting over vast quantities of work and at Rye his days were passed in an unvarying routine of labor. "I am divorced from contact With The Improper Person of Babylon," he wrote to Violet Hunt, "and the call of London in however honied

tones, simply appalls me. I am here at Rye where I in-
veterately work — and should, with all the Graces, Wits,
Beauties and Celebrities crowding my lordly hall at once
from 10.15 to 1.30." He was writing novels.

IMMEDIATELY breakfast was finished he would leave his guest
to his own devices and, in carpet slippers, go through the
garden to a "red brick summer house built at right angles
to his front door, with one big window on the street."
Here James would pace up and down, cigarette in hand,
dictating his wonderful stories to a stenographer. In speech
he was always deliberate and the habit grew on him with the
years. His words came from him in "gusts" and he searched
audibly for the correct word as he gradually built his huge,
elaborate, sentences. Yet in spite of the fact that dictation
is a constant temptation to looseness, he never succumbed
and each sentence was an architectural masterpiece. The
weakness it did allow him to cultivate was "overtreatment,"
though it can hardly be said that this habit was not apparent
long before he adopted the method of dictating to a stenographer who worked directly on the "cumbrous machinery"
of the typewriter.

His procedure was to dictate an elaborate scenario before
settling down to the actual composition of a novel. Unfortunately he destroyed his notes immediately on completing
the story or novel and but two of these fascinating documents have been printed, from which we see that they were
not only used to explore the possibilities of the theme he
had in mind but also to record all sorts of ruminative comments on his characters, his methods, even his state of mind
with regard to his work at the moment, becoming in fact
"an interminable garrulous letter addressed to (his) own
fond fancy." Nothing could be less characteristic of James
than the preparation of a diagrammatic plot outline. His
books do not have plots. They develop. They deal in
situations, relations. After analysis the novels of his ma-

turity can be discussed under eight headings: characters, theme, dramatic relations, time element and action, aspects with a glance at detachment, the mind and the development of implications, style and design.

Long before Turgenev had confirmed the rightness of his method he found himself thinking in terms of characters and imagining a story from their relations to one another. He would even think of one character and build around it the others necessary to complete the story he had in mind, no character being "copied" from life. A hint, mayhap, and then the evolution of the final product in his "moral consciousness." His characters visualized, he sought out carefully the proper names with which to designate them, never stopping short of a sense of perfection. While not Victorian in his use of symbolic names, one may perhaps detect in his choices a certain correspondence between the name and the nature of the situation of the person designated. In exploring this matter he carried his analysis to the ultimate perfection of debating whether to use a one or two syllable name so as best to bring out the quality of the person he had in mind. About the central character the others were arranged in their functional relations, carefully defined. There was never any improvisation in a James novel, though once launched upon a story the development of the narrative might lead him to make minor changes in the relations previously imagined. No major alteration seems ever to have taken place.

The characters were also arranged around a central theme which while controlling their relations did not dominate the story. His ideas were always quite clear cut and he could recall them long after he had completed a story. A few of his notes about origins have been used earlier: the fact that the idea of *Roderick Hudson* came to him during a horse car ride in Cambridge. We shall see, later on, that the whole marvellous structure of *The Ambassadors* grew out of five chance words dropped by William Dean Howells and it may be mentioned that both *The Portrait of a Lady* and *The Wings of the Dove* developed from his memories of a loved cousin. Indeed, it was the anecdote, the chance remark, a turn of phrase, a casual observation, or the elaboration of a cherished memory that set Henry James's imagination to work and after he had ruminated on the seed, had dropped it into his unconscious even, for a period, it would emerge splendidly dressed, enormously elaborated, unrecognizable even to the original teller (if that was its origin!) and fitted out with the requisite characters. A theme without characters was useless to him. His perceptive passion even led him to the ultimate rudeness of refusing to listen to the "point" of an anecdote if, before it was reached, he had seen the germ of a story. "I used to suffer, like other people," Violet Hunt recalls, "from the truncated anecdote. I used to take little mice — accounts of incidents or things I fancied would interest him — and lay them at his feet. So they did, as raw material. But while one was trying to be accurate, massing every detail painstakingly, so as to be of use, he would unerringly extract the ore from the matrix of one's recital and would hold it up — extend a finger— 'Thank you . . . thank you, I've got as much — all I want. . .' and leave you with the point of your anecdote on your hands. You consoled yourself with the reflection that he might have perhaps got another 'Turn of the Screw' out of your relation of some childish aberration or some more 'Spoils of Poynton' from your reminiscences of your old North Country aunt."

The relations of the characters were supposed to be dramatic and ideally they all had their exits and entrances just as in a stage production. In the extraordinary development to which the novels were subjected it is not entirely easy to detect the dramatic nature of the relations obtaining between the characters, for a James novel lacks that essential quality of a play, rapidity of development, obviousness of action. We may borrow a term from another art, to him unknown, and designate his stories as dramas in slow motion. If the motion of his stories is slow and "action" in the cruder sense no part of his method, he compensated for the absence of these ordinary qualities by the subtlety of the developments which seemingly unfold under the reader's astonished eyes like a picture being slowly freed from a curtain which has been hiding its perfection. Here again, the method is superficially dramatic but the result far from theatrical, for if there is a progression in the revelation, it is so *teasingly* slow that only patient readers can savor the full delicacy of the treatment. Nor is the progressive revelation designed to lead up to some striking final exposure of intent, some climaxing scene in which the pieces will fall together with a click. You can never solve the meaning of a James novel by looking at the end to see how the story comes out. The development must be followed through its gradual evolution with all patience, realizing only when the last page is turned that, at last, in the final relations of the characters, the drama has been worked out. For every James novel does work out. If they did not they would possess a fault he regarded as intolerable; they would have loose ends.

In these carefully thought out dramatizations of life, nothing could be left hanging in mid-air. Each episode was planned in functional relation to the total story, and each major episode or climax (extract from the word all suggestion of violence !) became a "joint," or connecting link between the successive parts of the story. By so relating the successive episodes, the characters, also functional in their relations, and the episodes, were placed in compositional relation to one another. At the same time that all suggestion of the loose-ends, false-starts, and blind-alleys of life were eliminated in the interests of drama, there was also a heightening of the design which was being imposed upon the material.

If, as James thought, the stage drama had become fabulously emaciated in its race with the clock, that does not mean that Henry James was unconcerned about the time element in his fiction. It was one of his most constant worries that the time scheme be exact and that there be no incongruities on this score. If, in his ruminative scenario, he detected at some late point in the imagined development a flaw in the time scheme, or if a new turn to the proposed narrative came up, he would alter the whole story to rectify his error. The problem was, of course, to create the proper illusion of time and with the innumerable difficulties of foreshortening and extension he conscientiously wrestled. Thus while his novels do not develop with the rapidity of stage dramas they do not, either, stand still like pieces of set description. They move. They have "action."

Once the characters, the revelatory scenes, the climaxes had been determined and the time scheme was settled, James had to develop the matter of successive aspects. He sought to see the development of his story from one or several (usually the latter) points of view. This matter puzzled him a good deal and his success was not at all uniform. Indeed one of his major novels is notable for the fact that this matter was handled with a marked lack of success. Nevertheless he sought so to shift the center of gravity from time to time that he could work through the consciousnesses, or from the point of view, of first one of the major characters and then another. In this way the whole story would gradually be revealed and these shifts would correspond with the development of the narrative. This does not mean that the story was by any means retold each time the shift was made. It simply means that new values, new appreciations, new imaginative apprehensions were revealed. The story continued its normal development but under the eyes of a new spectator, or evaluator. Sometimes the shift was made to place the final development in the mind of a person of greater imaginative sensitivity than the one who had been sufficient for the earlier stages of the story. And again, the change was made because the later developments of the story

passed out of the knowledge of the first character selected.
The reasons for the shift sufficiently appear in each story.
One should not carry away the idea that James took any particular delight in constantly shifting his coign of vantage.
Quite the contrary. The thing was to achieve the whole
narrative in such a fashion that it would logically be viewed
through the minds of as few characters as possible and yet
extract all the values possible. Naturally this took a good
deal of planning and while he frequently succeeded in narrowing the field down to two, he got his greatest measure of
success in *The Ambassadors* where we follow the action
through the mind of but one, Lambert Strether.

This habit of presenting the story to the reader through
the mind of a character who may not be of importance to the
action of the narrative he seemingly borrowed from Meri-
mée. The point to be made here is not, however, the origin
of the device, but the fact that it takes the author out of the
story altogether, or it places him at one remove from the
action and it is this lack of a personal authorial presence that
has led many readers to be shocked by the seeming coldness
of James's novels. He did not, of course, write his entire
range of stories without the use of the first person singular,
but it is difficult to recall a case where the first person singular has reference to Henry James in any of his mature work.
The "I" is the narrator, through whose mind we are following the development. James escaped, then, the characteristic subjectivity of the English novel. Yet there is, after
all, only a relative impersonality about James's work, for if
he does not intrude to moralize and does not *exploit* his personal feelings about the characters and the action, he never
for a moment leaves the perceptive reader in doubt as to the
values he wishes finally to aggrandize. If he did, it would
be impossible to extract from his work any "testimony" and
we would be left high and dry when we came to consider the
"meaning" of his fiction. The superstition of absolute impersonality never much beguiled him, for as has been shown,

he abandoned the French precisely because their cult of impersonal realism excluded just that factor of moral judgment. What he objected to was not "morality" but subjectivism on the author's part. That is why he was able to make large drafts on the French for technical devices while yet rejecting their tutelage in the deeper matters.

In none of James's novels is the entire matter transacted in the minds of the characters. It is the evaluation, the weighing of possibilities, the scrutinizing of emotions, the imaginative apprehension of meanings, that goes on there. It is as though the external events are enacted only that they may be threshed out in the intimacy of the mind. (The one obvious exception to this is *The Awkward Age*.) A further extension of this method of examining the implications of the action is to be found in the use of a confidante to whom the character explains the action and with whom he debates the implications. The confidante need not be at all implicated in the events, or even know the persons under discussion personally, though that is not an adamant rule and the confidante on occasion contributes some vital and illuminating information, like Maria Gostrey in *The Ambassadors*.

It is this infinite elaboration of the implications that has been a barrier to anything like general appreciation of Henry James's work. For he not only pursues the implications into their ultimate material expressions, but into their remotest and most elusive mental and imaginative configurations. He neglects no device in his pursuit, for he does not pause with probings of the mentalities of his "central" characters. He extends it to the debates a character may conduct with some foil. In every sentence of the story most scrupulous attention is paid to the subtlest overtones. The "he saids" and "she saids" of conversation became vehicles for furthering the exploitation of this interest, and indeed James's scrupulosity about never making a gross remark, a plain, flat, unadorned statement (he occasionally, rather ludicrously, labels a speech as that), makes his conversations perilously resemble games of mental ping-pong. "It could *not* but be exciting to talk, as we talked," remarks the narrator of *The Sacred Fount,* "on the basis of those suppressed processes and unavowed references which made the meaning of our meeting so different from its form." This is characteristic of his behavioristic moods as well as his more usual analytical stories. He is at his best and most characteristic, moreover, when he is exploiting to the full every device for "opening the door . . . of the subjective community" of his characters. It is then that the question of overtreatment comes up, for after long years of practice his capacity for developing the implications of a situation flowered so luxuriantly that he himself was a bit appalled by his inability to keep within reasonable bounds. When he sought compression he turned from dictation to the pen, only immediately to defeat himself by reading his pen-draft, with interpolations, to his secretary !

All these remarks should not lead the reader to suspect Henry James of flabbiness for if he could not entirely forestall his weakness for treating his material until the last drop of significance had been wrung out of it, he was dominated by an equal desire to pack each passage with significance and he rarely neglected to provide adequate "bony structure" — meaning character and theme.

Since the vehicle which had to carry the weight of all this "treatment" was his style, it follows that in proportion as his ability to realize his intent increased, his style increased in complexity as well. There has been a good deal of loose talk about his various "manners" but if one perceives that from the very first he strove for analytical comprehensiveness the manners develop out of one another quite logically. The evolution is perfectly perceptible. His critics early protested against this tendency and a chorus of protest arose when he touched up all of his novels in the light of his final development in preparing the New York edition. But as far back as the review of *Roderick Hudson* in *The North*

American Review for April, 1876, the note is struck: "The effect of this perpetual analysis is fatiguing; the book never ceases to interest, but it taxes the attention like metaphysics." The analytical tendency was basic and the style responded to it. Quite without any theory of being disregardful of criticism and cautioning, James could not fail to regard protests against his analysis and his style as products of critical obtuseness. It was just precisely against what he most wanted to do that the critics earliest showed a disposition to protest. To a generation that has experienced the efforts of the Symbolists to render the finest shades of feeling, of "difference," in words, these objections are not so very important, but there can be small doubt that it was the early appearance and tremendous development of these tendencies that contributed to the alienation of James's audience during his lifetime — this in spite of the fact that he never consciously overlooked the fact that the primary function of style is to communicate the author's vision to his readers with a minimum of "interference." He thought that by packing his style to the bursting point he was getting closer and closer to what he truly wanted to say !

James's aspiration was to compose novels and all the devices that have been discussed are simply means to that end. The word compose is used advisedly and in the pictorial sense, for it was not his habit to indulge in reporting, the way so many of our novels today get written. His dominating passion was technical perfection and he sought above all else to impose a design or pattern on the life he chose for treatment. Formlessness enraged him ("I *am* damned critical — for it's the only thing to be, and all else is damned humbug," he wrote) and led him constantly to scold that incorrigible improvisor, H. G. Wells, and to reject Tolstoi and Dostoevsky as acceptable models of the young writers. He would have nothing to do with heaps of facts flung down in a mad jumble. Selection, composition was the thing. It is just at this point that we can part company with those critics who have been excessively perturbed over the fact that his novels are not real in the sense that they do not, down to the last ignoble detail, correspond with the messiness of life. James was not reproducing life. He was composing from the materials of life great works of art full of meaning, bodying forth a vision of the world not to be duplicated elsewhere. We may profitably postpone any discussion of just what that vision was until later, noting here that it was of such a nature as to require for its adequate presentation the utilization of all the social machinery he found in Europe and which was notable by its absence in America.

Naturally novels of this character cannot be read carelessly or taken on the run. "Attention of perusal," he wrote, "I thus confess . . . is what I at every point . . . absolutely invoke and take for granted. . ." There can be no escape from this condition, no leniency is allowed to anyone, no privileged characters admitted to the circle. Yet there is such a thing as too close attention which results in mistaking the trees for the wood and it is readers whose attention has been so diverted who have insisted that it is impossible to plot the outline of the wood. Technicians have scared away ordinary readers by failing to emphasize the story which in their enthusiasm for the method they have neglected. It is impossible to find the story without some understanding of the technique, but once the story is found an understanding of the technique follows almost automatically. A *liking* for the technique must be cultivated. It is important, therefore, that just what happens in the novels be clearly established. It is therefore altogether fitting and proper that now that we have gathered together here the necessary observations on how Henry James composed his novels we should, keeping clearly in mind the fact that we are surveyors tracing outlines, devote attention to the stories in the major novels, first glancing back imaginatively to his study from which he has just emerged, half an hour earlier than is customary to join his guest. " 'An event has occurred today,' he began, exactly as if he was still dictating (the friend later recalled), 'which no doubt to you, fresh from your loud, your reverberating London, with its mosaic of multifarious movements and intensive interests, might seem justly and reasonably enough to be scarcely perceptible in all that hum and hurry and hubbub, but to me here in little Rye, tranquil and isolated little Rye, a silted up Cinqueport but now far from the sea and more readily accessible to bicyclists and pedestrians than to sea captains and smugglers; Rye, where at the present moment, so happily, so blessedly I hold you trapped in my little corner, my angulus terrae—' On and on went the rich interminable sentence, shaped and modelled under his handling and piled with picturesque phrases which I can no longer recapture; and then I suppose (not having a typist to read it over to him) he despaired of ever struggling free of the python-coils of subordinate clauses and allusive parentheses, for he broke off short and said, 'In point of fact, my dear Fred Benson, I have finished my book.'"

Portrait of a Lady (1881) is the first of the list of "great" novels produced by Henry James. It was written during 1879–1880 and serialized before publication in both England and America. The fact is indicative of his rapid rise to eminence in England and of the continued popularity he enjoyed in America. It was not, indeed, until his career was interrupted by the fashion for romance, for Anthony Hope and Stevenson and Rudyard Kipling, that he ceased to be able to print his stories where he wished. And even then he was able at the end of his life to assume the title and position of the Master. By steadfastly pursuing his course he was able to triumph over a temporary fashion in a manner only allowed to the author of classics.

The novel is remarkable in many ways but in none more so than in the fact that the action is seen through the consciousness of a woman. For this departure from the habitual orientation of novels James had the example of Hawthorne. But he took nothing else from him. *The Portrait of a Lady* is the first of James's masterpieces of psychological exploration. It concerns the fortunes of Isabel Archer who is rescued from the provinciality of Albany (the scenes are reminiscences of the family home) by an eccentric aunt who desires her to take her place in the larger world of Europe. Under the aunt's guidance she is introduced first to a small circle in England and later to a still more circumscribed circle in Italy. It is notable that all of the principal figures in both groups, with a few exceptions, are Americans — Europeanized Americans ! The Touchetts, the aunt is one of them, are incompletely Anglicized, "assimilated yet unconverted," for while the father, a banker and perhaps reminiscent of George Peabody, is unlikely ever to return to his native Vermont, he has had his son educated at Harvard. There is just enough American flavor in the son, Ralph, to distinguish him from a European and just enough European flavor to distinguish him from an American. It is he who first perceives the rich and fertile soil of Isabel Archer's imagination (imagination is essential in a Henry James character) and who, since he is by illness deprived of an opportunity to act in his own behalf, determines to make possible a career of the best sort for her. Isabel desires the highest freedom and the most shining destiny. "Altogether, with her meagre knowledge, her inflated ideals, her confidence at once innocent and dogmatic, her temper at once exacting and indulgent, her mixture of curiosity and fastidiousness, of vivacity and indifference, her desire to look very well and to be if possible even better, her determination to see, to try, to know, her combination of delicate desultory, flame-like spirit and the eager and personal creature of conditions: she would be an easy victim of scientific criticism if she were not intended to awaken on the reader's part an impulse more tender and more purely expectant." Since she wishes to take in, discriminatingly, all that Europe can offer in the

way of experience, to explore and savor lovingly the unexpected, like a good American, she has no desire to resign
herself into accepting the first desirable offer of marriage,
made by Lord Warburton, a charming liberal peer, who
meets with Ralph Touchett's strongest approval. She refuses him in spite of the fact that she recognizes his goodness, for she is conscious, not only of a desire for more experience, but also of a premonition that her destiny is to be
unhappy and with true American scrupulosity she has no
desire to escape it.

The charming directness and purity of her motives both
indicate the high value Henry James placed upon the finer
specimens of American womanhood. For he indicates no
feeling that Isabel Archer required special preparation to
meet the world as she did, nor does he attribute to her any
touch of the corrosive experience which would have allowed
her more adequately to perceive the deviousness of the experienced. "With all her love of knowledge she had a
natural shrinking from raising curtains and looking into
unlighted corners. The love of knowledge coexisted in her
mind with the finest capacity for ignorance." In conso-
nance with his vision on the piazzas of Saratoga that American women were more developed morally and imaginatively
than the men, James's conception of Isabel Archer is more
beguiling than that of her American suitor, Mr. Caspar
Goodwood, though in the name we may be permitted to see
a symbolic reference to his quality. For in spite of his
imaginative inadequacy when faced with Isabel's course of
conduct, he does perceive that the essence of her case is to
suffer defeat as the American innocent confronted with the
deviousness of Europe.

Her fate meets her in England, in the home of her aunt,
under the eyes of the intelligently observing Ralph Touchett. Her fate takes shape in the person of Madame Merle,
who "had become too flexible, too useful, was too ripe and
too final. She was in a word too perfectly the social animal

that man and woman are supposed to have been intended to be; and she had rid herself of every remnant of that tonic wildness which we may assume to have belonged even to the most amiable persons in the ages before country-house life was the fashion." This exquisite lady of mysterious origin and equally mysterious purpose, who lives, apparently, by visiting around in a fashion rather closely resembling the habit of country school teachers of the old days, undertakes to guide Isabel through the intricacies of Europe and to place her in the hands of a husband and a protector.

Though she is warned by Ralph not to trust Madame Merle too far, Isabel does allow herself to be more than needfully guided by her. With an astonishing solicitude for Isabel, animated by a desire to see her work out her problem to the end, Ralph persuades his father, who is on the point of dying, to leave half of the money set aside for him, to Isabel. "I call people rich when they're able to meet the requirements of their imagination," says Ralph. "Isabel has a great deal of imagination." So provided Isabel becomes exceedingly desirable in the eyes of Europeans. (We see that James has corrected the error of *The American !*) Under Madame Merle's skilful hand she goes swiftly to her destiny. The elder Touchett dies. Isabel and her aunt go to Italy where they are joined by Madame Merle who introduces Isabel to Gilbert Osmond. Osmond is a Europeanized American, a creature debased by the European virus until he has become an obtuse and rigid prig and who has made such a fetish of taste as to become a sterile aesthete. He has a daughter, exquisitely educated and exquisitely sensitive, a reminiscence of Pearl in *The Scarlet Letter,* who, when he is adequately "placed," he hopes to sell in the open market to the most desirable bidder. This moral obliquity which leads to the cultivation of divine innocence only to debase it into the coinage of worldly advantage, occurs again and again in Henry James's stories. It is proposed to marry Isabel Archer to this decadent person, for she has beauty and money (a utility Osmond sadly lacks) and she is morally so innocent and inexperienced that she cannot perceive the quality of Osmond. With startling precipitancy the whole matter is arranged and Isabel finds that she has at once married a man of taste and a fiend. For that is what Osmond is. Isabel has met her destiny in "Europe." It is defeat.

But stay. An escape is made possible, for her hovering friends are not blind to her predicament. Ralph Touchett, Caspar Goodwood, Lord Warburton, all see it plainly. Indeed Lord Warburton wishes to marry her stepdaughter that he may be always close to her, but he cannot in the end take the step. For this miscarriage of a desirable marriage Osmond vents all his spleen on his wife. The episode provides the excuse for the most marvelous of Henry James's peculiar "interior monologues," which can be reproduced but brokenly here:

". . . when, as the months had elapsed, she had followed him further and he had led her into the mansions of his own habitation, then, *then* she had seen where she really was. . . She could live it over again, the incredulous terror with which she had taken the measure of her dwelling. Between these four walls she had lived ever since; they were to surround her for the rest of her life. It was the house of darkness, the house of dumbness, the house of suffocation. Osmond's beautiful mind gave it neither light nor air; Osmond's beautiful mind indeed seemed to peep down from a small high window and mock at her. Of course it had not been physical suffering; for physical suffering there might have been a remedy. She could come and go; she had her liberty; her husband was perfectly polite. He took himself so seriously; it was something appalling. Under all his culture, his cleverness, his amenity, under his good nature, his facility, his knowledge of life, his egotism lay hidden like a serpent in a bank of flowers. She had taken him seriously, but she had not taken him so seriously as that. How could she — especially when she had known him better? She was to think of him as he thought of himself — as the first gentleman of Europe. So it was that she had thought of him at first, and that indeed was the reason she had married him. But when she began to see what it implied she drew back; there was more in the bond than she had meant to put her name to. It implied a sovereign contempt for every one but some three or four very exalted people whom he envied, and for everything in the world but half a dozen ideas of his own. That was very well; she would have gone with him even there a long distance; for he pointed out to her so much of the baseness and shabbiness of life, opened her eyes so wide to the stupidity, the ignorance of mankind, that she had been properly impressed with the infinite vulgarity of things and of the virtue of keeping one's self unspotted by it. But this base, ignoble world, it appeared, was after all what one was to live for; one was to keep it forever in one's eye, in order not to enlighten or convert or redeem it, but to extract from it some recognition of one's own superiority. On the one hand it was despicable, but on the other it afforded a standard. . . His ideal was a conception of high prosperity and propriety, of the aristocratic life, which she now saw that he deemed himself always, in essence at least to have led. He had never lapsed from it for an hour; he would never have recovered from the shame of doing so. That again was very well, here too she would have agreed; but they attached such different ideas, such different associations and desires, to the same formulas. Her notion of the aristocratic life was simply the union of great knowledge with great liberty; the knowledge would give one a sense of duty and the liberty a sense of enjoyment. But for Osmond it was altogether a thing of forms, a conscious, calculated attitude. . . But there were certain things she could never take in. To begin with, they were hideously unclean. She was not a daughter of the Puritans, but for all that she believed in such a thing as chastity and even as decency. It would appear that Osmond was far from doing anything of the sort; some of his traditions made her push back her skirts. Did all women have lovers? Did they all lie and even the best have their price? Were there only three or four that didn't deceive their husbands? When Isabel heard such things she felt a greater scorn for them than for the gossip of the village parlour — a scorn that kept its freshness in a very tainted air. . . Very often, however, she felt afraid, and it used to come over her, as I have intimated, that she had deceived him at the very first. They were strangely married, at all events, and it was a horrible life."

Madame Merle's interest in the affair has been so emotional — she has shown herself for the first time capable of sharp censure — that Isabel suspects her of a more than friendly interest in the child, and rightly. It is revealed by Osmond's sister, no less Europeanized but hating her brother's coldness more than she loves his cultivation, that the little girl is Madame Merle's by Osmond. It is the deepest blow of all, the clearest sight Isabel gets of the dark pit into which she has unconsciously stumbled.

With calculated malignancy, Osmond forbids Isabel to go to the bedside of Ralph Touchett when the news comes that he is dying, even threatening to take her disobedience on this point as signifying the dissolution of the marriage. The matter becomes an issue of the greatest magnitude, of freedom versus slavery, and with a deep consciousness of her indebtedness to Ralph, Isabel chooses Freedom. It is undoubtedly on this note that the reader would best like to have the novel end. It is unquestionably because it is not on this note that the novel does end that many critics, European and American, have found Isabel's creator to be without moral standards. For while he has guided this girl, so extraordinarily pure in heart, into the blackest of moral situations, and has placed freedom within her grasp, he snatches it back from her. Since this is predicated upon her own action it is alleged that the psychology is false. To think so reveals a profound ignorance of the compulsions governing the conduct of the older Americans. Isabel's own comment on the situation is perfectly logical and understandable in the light of knowledge: "I don't know whether I'm too proud. But I can't publish my mistake. I don't think that's decent. I'd much rather die." She goes to Ralph's bedside but returns to Osmond knowing that her situation will be even worse than before, perhaps somehow to gain a difficult and precarious victory out of this seemingly overwhelming defeat. Or to die.

The next great novel in the order of production, *The Awkward Age* (1899), had but one fly in the ointment of its perfection. It was too bulky. Following on the heels of James's experiments with the drama, it brought to flower the dramatic side of his talent, and realized more complexly than in any other novel he wrote his desire to exhibit the action from a series of different but mutually complementary angles.   Yet there is no confusion.   In effect *The Awkward Age* is an enormous and elaborate comedy of manners. There is no great theme underlying it, no marvelous encounter with malignant destiny, no high hopes frustrated. It reduces itself down to so simple a matter, already treated in the shorter lengths, of getting married.   In the course of this business the entire social scene is illuminated and a variety of truly various characters are dissected with skill and circumspection.   But the interior monologue is as conspicuously absent as is any other device to facilitate analysis.   The whole book moves on the plane of conversation and is, as we should say today, behavioristic.   Henry James never again manipulated his material so skilfully within the limits of his purpose as in this book.   We have yet to examine the novel, *The Ambassadors,* where he brought the analytical method to perfection.   The joke of the contemporary reception of the book is that James sought to make it all so clear that it would be transparent even to that most obtuse of audiences, the theatrical — and yet his publisher told him that of all the novels he had published, "I've never in all my experience seen one treated with more general and complete disrespect."

It is impossible to put one's critical finger directly on the cause of this reaction, but one can mildly speculate that we have here an admirable illustrative case of that bugbear of James's life, "overtreatment."   For if this huge novel, five hundred and forty-five pages in the New York edition, is to be taken as a comedy (and how else could it be taken even if we did not have Henry James's profession of intention?), it must be admitted that it is an astonishingly prolonged comedy.   It is, indeed, a comedy on a scale to which we but reluctantly grant tragedy the right to be written.   For the action takes place with but a few characters most of whom give their names to the ten scenes of the book — the ten angles from which the action is viewed.

We are introduced into the household of a miraculously clever woman, Mrs. Brookenham, who possesses to perfection those attributes of mind which James most admired: imagination, feeling and a power of expression. Surrounding her are her husband, a charming but inarticulate and unimaginative man, her daughter, a member of the younger generation demanding freedom of action and her son Harold, a potential rotter, but with a good deal of his mother's cleverness. These are of her immediate family. They form the background against which she works, but they are not so vividly present, with the exception of her daughter, as her social circle. Most immediate in this group are Vanderbank, Mr. Mitchett, Mr. Longdon, the Duchess and her step-daughter, Little Aggie (always), and to a lesser extent, though still fulfilling their function of providing a foothold for an angle of vision, Mr. Cashmore, Lady Julia and Tishy Grendon. The problems which incite these people to brilliance of imagination and exceeding cleverness of speech are marrying, marital troubles with a cleavage potential, the motives of an elderly and benignant and possible patron, lovers and such like. There is hardly a word in the whole book, as is proper with a comedy, about any of the more serious issues of life. It is Mrs. Brookenham's ambition to arrange an advantageous marriage for her daughter Nanda, who is, unfortunately, without money of her own. Nanda has placed her hopes on Vanderbank, a charming but indigent bachelor, a close friend of her mother's and a man who moves in the best circles in spite of his employment in the civil service. Her mother wants her to marry Mr. Mitchett, a wealthy man but one generation removed from the *purlieus* of "trade."

Mr. Longdon has lately returned to London after a prolonged absence in the country. He was in his youth an admirer of Mrs. Brookenham's mother and, at another period, of Vanderbank's mother also. He does not fancy Mrs. Brookenham, who strikes him as being *too* calculatingly manipulative, too concerned with advancing herself through her daughter, but he does, once he recovers from the shock of finding one who so much resembles her grandmother, so very different in outlook and speech, admire Nanda. He quickly senses that she would have Vanderbank if he would have her and he discreetly discovers that the barrier is money. He offers to close that gap by settling a goodly, though unspecified, sum on Vanderbank. Nanda's most urgent admirer is Mr. Mitchett, a character the like of which one rarely sees in James.

"Mr. Mitchett had so little intrinsic appearance that an observer would have felt indebted for help in placing him to the rare prominence of his colourless eyes and the positive attention drawn to his chin by the precipitation of its retreat from discovery. Dressed on the other hand not as gentlemen dress in London to pay their respects to the fair, he excited by the exhibition of garments that had nothing in common save the violence and the independence of their pattern a belief that in the desperation of humility he wished to render public his having thrown to the winds the effort to please. It was written all over him that he had judged once for all his personal case and that, as his character, superficially disposed to gaiety, deprived him of the resource of shyness and shade, the effect of comedy might not escape him if secured by a real plunge. There was comedy therefore in the form of his pot-hat and the colour of his spotted shirt, in the systematic disagreement, above all, of his coat, waistcoat and trousers. It was only on long acquaintance that his so many ingenious ways of showing he appreciated his commonness could present him as secretly rare."

Mr. Mitchett, then, is vulgarity with goodness (*that* is the "note" most consistently sounded), though with a certain sense of fitness and a nimbleness of mind quite equal to Mrs. Brookenham's. He stands in marked contrast with Gilbert Osmond and the judgments James implies on the two are most revelatory of his standards. Just as he is careful to bring out that Mr. Mitchett's goodness quite overrides his lack of taste, his goodnatured vulgarity, so he has equally brought out that Gilbert Osmond's fine taste is accompanied by a moral corruption which is unspeakable. We have here

proof that James did not make taste synonymous with virtue, just as we had in the case of Isabel Archer proof that
he did not identify goodness with quick insight. His alli-
ances of qualities were personal to the characters concerned
and to draw a conclusion as to his opinions from one is
quickly to find it contradicted by another.

Nanda finds Mr. Mitchett unacceptable even though she
realizes that there is small chance that Vanderbank will conquer his reluctance and ask her to marry him. Instead she
persuades Mr. Mitchett to marry Little Aggie. Little Aggie is another one of those carefully cultivated, delicate little
buds, like Osmond's daughter in *Portrait of a Lady*, who is
thoughtfully prepared for hawking in the cruelly realistic
marriage market. Nanda perceives that the Duchess, her
step-mother, is too crude a woman, even though she has assiduously cultivated "delicacy" in her charge, to hesitate
about selling her child into a gross and destructive situation. In Mr. Mitchett she thinks she has found a desirable
partner who will at once give Little Aggie marriage and
protection. Obediently, Mr. Mitchett marries her.

With his elimination Vanderbank's course is supposedly
free and we are given a large chance to speculate on his motives for hanging back. Meanwhile we glimpse the situation through the eyes of Tishy Grendon, stupid and vaguely
improper, Mr. Cashmore, grossly improper, and his wife
Lady Julia, who is on the verge, constantly, of running away
from him. In each of the books to which these several characters give their names we find that the action progresses
and have revealed to us new angles of the complicated situation. Mr. Longdon has done his best to advance the matter
to a climax by carrying Nanda off to his home for the summer and while Vanderbank is politely interested he does not
advance to action. When Mr. Mitchett has returned from
his honeymoon, which has been made somewhat trying by
his pensioner, Lord Petherton, whose face exhibited "a certain pleasant brutality !," who is also, amusingly enough, the

Duchess's lover and supposed protector of Little Aggie, he finds the whole matter in a stalemate. Vanderbank has not only failed to propose to Nanda but he has also deserted Mrs. Brookenham's drawing room. To Mr. Mitchett is delegated the delicate task of telling Mr. Longdon how matters stand, a task he undertakes out of loyalty to Nanda to whom he has rendered the extraordinary service of marrying the girl she chose for him that he might be eliminated from the field for her favors! For this service he expects nothing from Nanda beyond sympathetic understanding when it appears, vaguely, that his marriage is not a success. Mr. Longdon now proposes to bring matters to a conclusion by taking Nanda out of her mother's house and into his own, leaving Vanderbank, to whom Nanda, strangely, appeals in that sense, to Mrs. Brookenham. We are led to believe that this consummation has really been desired from the very first!

Now the comedic element in this tremendous work is easily lost sight of in the very bulk of the story. Ten long books to resolve so inclusively, but so amusingly, the problem of getting a girl married. Yet one would be a very poor reader of Henry James who could pass this book by as a mere monstrosity of overtreatment. It might, indeed, be taken as a test, along with *The Golden Bowl* of one's staying powers, of one's capacity of appreciation to which staying power is so closely allied in Henry James's case. From this novel we learn, as with a divining rod, to discover the humorous passages in the other novels. It is not generally understood that Henry James did have humor and he has been passed off more times than one cares to notice, as a man of portentous gravity whose equanimity was so profound that he was seriously infatuated with such problems as those exhibited in *The Awkward Age*. Nothing could be further from the truth. His humor is rather unobvious and almost consistently ironic. But it is there and anyone penetrating to the core of his mind will find it winking out at one in the most serious of the novels. In *The Awkward Age* it comes to the surface and while it can hardly be said to bubble, it does roll, does rise, to change the figure, in huge gusts. The nimbleness in the wit of his father was passed on to William James. But Henry James did not miss inheriting a good share of its deeper quality.

If one were to examine all of the opinions expressed of *The Sacred Fount* (1901) one would be impressed by the fact that, with a few dissenting voices, it had been judged a failure. James himself thought poorly of it. "I am melted at your reading *en famille The Sacred Fount*" he wrote to Howells, "which you will, I fear, have found chaff in the mouth and which is one of several things of mine, in these last years, that have paid the penalty of having been conceived only as the 'short story' that (alone, apparently) I could hope to work off somewhere (which I mainly failed of), and then *grew* by a rank force of its own into something of which the idea had, modestly, never been to be a book . . ." The idea, he went on to say, was indeed too tenuous to support all the treatment to which it was subjected and the total result was far from warranting the effort. Yet in the midst of this chorus of dismissal there are one or two notes of dissent which warrant a rather careful examination of the misbegotten novel. It has even been pointed out as the key to all of the work of James and its omission from the New York Edition has been justified on the grounds that perhaps James intended writing a general preface and never did. In the absence of such a preface, *The Sacred Fount* is suggested to the faithful reader.

The first point about the book is the fact that it comes to nothing in particular. Of all the novels of Henry James which have been examined and will be examined, it portrays the complete bafflement of the protagonist. Instead of tracing out the relations of the characters, the book boggles in a swamp of false clues and repudiated conclusions. Thus no pattern is imposed upon the material. It retains all the loose ends characteristic of life. Imbedded in the novel, however, are plenty of clues to an apology for James's method, and it is in the light of them that it is profitable to treat the novel here. Before considering them, however, the general idea of the fiction may be sketched.

The protagonist, on his way to a country week-end, is excited by the problem posed by the discovery that a previously dull man has become clever. He also discovers that a beautiful woman has become of very ordinary appearance, a common enough event, except that it is complemented by the fact that a previously ordinary woman has become beautiful. Similar shifts and changes come under his eye in others of the party. What he seeks to discover is what causes these changes. He wishes to put his finger on the sacred fount from which these ordinary people draw the elixir of life.

Naturally enough the only motive here is sheer curiosity and an indecent curiosity is something for which Henry James is frequently indicted. But his curiosity is never gross; it never consists of brutal detective work.

"We ought to remember . . . that success in such an inquiry may perhaps be more embarrassing than failure. To nose about for a relation that a lady has her reasons for keeping secret — "

"Is made not only quite inoffensive, I hold," — he immediately took me up — "but positively honorable, by being confined to psychologic evidence."

I wondered a little. "Honorable to whom ?"

"Why, to the investigator. Resting on the *kind* of signs that the game takes account of when fairly played — resting on psychologic signs alone, it's a high application of intelligence. What's ignoble is the detective and the keyhole."

This, then, is Henry James's method of investigation; or rather, it is Henry James's method and here he gives a direct apology and explanation of it. Furthermore, he comments on the results:

"It appeared then that the more things I fitted together the larger sense, every way, they made — a remark in which I found an extraordinary elation. It justified my indiscreet curiosity; it crowned my underhand process with beauty."

Naturally one could not expect quick results from this method of observation and it was altogether likely that no two investigators would reach the same result. One "spelled out" one's answer by the application of a discriminating imagination. It was possible to proceed on the assumption that more people were dense than were penetrable and that the "votaries of the grossly obvious" would dominate any company. Even among "the children of leisure and pleasure and privilege" the proportion of the supremely intelligent was small, and one's private psychological studies were not apt to be detected. Such intellectual adventures were their own justification and as excitement they were supreme.

We have here an implied confession of method and a defense of it. Henry James tried to puzzle out an explanatory pattern in every situation that confronted him. He did so by applying a discriminative imaginative intelligence to the psychological signs available to any observer. He recognized that the field for observation was vast and that two people could work in it without getting in each other's way. He saw, too, that such a habit of mind persistently cultivated would lead to one's being called insane. In *The Sacred Fount* we are given a glimpse of what would happen *if James's method were followed out in real life*. In this book all the various factors are allowed to crowd in on the investigator until he is drowned in a plethora of conflicting data. Furthermore his particular interlocutor is directly implicated in his investigations and his conclusions are not flattering to her. In real life, it is suggested, such a method can only result in bafflement and despair, because there is no way in which to apply the great principle of selection.

It is the principle of selection which gives the final justification to Henry James's method. Then the constituent parts fall into their places. That principle omitted, we get *The Sacred Fount* for that novel carries all the other rules to their logical conclusion in a debacle. Introduce it, and the inevitable disorderly crowding of facts, which is life, is put to rout. An arbitrary pattern is imposed and life takes on meaning. Facts in themselves have no meaning. Art, in this sense, creates life. And it was the imposition of a meaningful pattern on life that was Henry James's great aspiration.

With *The Wings of the Dove* Henry James returned to the main line of his development and in three years published three superlative novels, *The Wings* (1902), *The Ambassadors* (1903) and *The Golden Bowl* (1904). *The Wings of the Dove*, James later found to be a vastly imperfect novel, comparing the, to him, excellent execution of the first half with the awkwardness of the last. The chief cause for disapproval was the fact that he found it necessary to shift from one character to another for a reflective observer so frequently that he confused the story. There can be no doubt that this constant movement back and forth through the consciousness of so various a group of characters, is a bit disconcerting, but in his passion for technical perfection, James rather underemphasized the total worth of his story.

In it, we shall see he returned to the theme of *Portrait of a Lady* of twenty years earlier and treated it in a more adequate and mature fashion, (without implying, be it said, that the *Portrait* is inadequate and immature) with less moral ambiguity and with an ending that can mystify none but those readers to whom James's beginnings, middles and endings are equally mystifying. *The Wings of the Dove* is another story of the urge to freedom in one who is pure in heart and of defeat experienced at the hands of the morally oblique.

The central figure is Milly Theale and she is viewed

through the consciousnesses of Kate Croy, Merton Densher, Miss Stringham, Mrs. Lowder (Kate Croy's Aunt Maude) and various others. It was just precisely his inability to focus the story through the consciousness of one or at most two members of the company that led James to find the novel rather rickety in structure. The story triumphs over the difficulties. Milly Theale is envisaged as "the slim, constantly pale, delicately haggard, anomalously, agreeably angular young person, of not more than two-and-twenty summers, in spite of her marks, whose hair was somehow exceptionally red even for the real thing, which it innocently confessed to being, and whose clothes were remarkably black even for robes of mourning, which was the meaning they expressed. It was New York mourning, it was New York history . . . multitudinous, of the loss of parents, brothers, sisters, almost every human appendage . . ." Indeed, there was behind her, "moneyed New York" beyond all else, but also a record of "used-up relatives, parents, clever, eager slim brothers — these the most loved — all engaged, as well as successive and succeeding guardians, in a high extravagance of speculation and dissipation that had left this exquisite being her black dress, her white face and her vivid hair as the mere last broken link. . ." That was the image that hung before the Londoners who were to encompass her destiny. But one point was to give a bright romantic flush to her whole experiment. She was beyond question doomed to an early death. She lived in the shadow of imminent fatality and London to her was Harley Street. Yet "Milly's range was thus immense; she had to ask nobody for anything, to refer nothing to any one; her freedom, her fortune and her fancy were her law; an obsequious world surrounded her, she could sniff up at every step its fumes." A reminiscence here, beyond a doubt and freely confessed by Henry James, of his cousin Mary Temple, who was so similarly endowed and also doomed to early death. And she too sought to live.

Kate Croy and Merton Densher are engaged, secretly, to marry, but they lack money. Though Kate has a father, she lived on the freely given charity of her Aunt, Mrs. Lowder. As though to account for her later conduct Kate Croy's father is of such a character that "No relation with him could be so short or so superficial as not to be somehow to your hurt; the inconvenience — as always happens in such cases — was not that you minded what was false, but that you missed what was true." Densher, a journalist of rather an easily influenced nature, has met Milly Theale in New York. Mrs. Lowder meets her through her old school friend, Miss Stringham, Milly's companion, and Milly's introduction to Kate follows naturally. Densher is pleased to meet her again through Kate. It is in contemplating the rare combination of admittedly precarious health and great monetary resources that Kate resolves to stake her future on a very subtle game which will gain Densher Milly's money. We are thus treated to a vulgar scramble for money and through it we are to see how Milly's desire briefly but fully to live, to make the most of her freedom, is cruelly defeated. It is Kate's idea that Densher shall marry Milly who shortly dying will leave him her fortune, whereupon he can marry Kate. So far had Henry James proceeded since *The American !*

To carry out this nefarious plan it would be necessary for Kate to conceal from Milly her engagement to Densher, which is precisely what with great circumspection she proceeds to do. When Milly goes on to Venice (the pull Italy exerted over James to the end !) Densher follows. He finds Milly in precarious condition indeed, so ill in fact that her physician makes a trip out from London to treat her. She is still dominated, however, by a tremendous will to live, to know life in its highest sense. Densher had perceived in London that she liked him and that to hurt her in any way, through a revelation of his equivocal position, would be the equivalent of killing her. The perception of this fact, in abstract reasoning, was equally clear on Milly's side, though she has not suspected *actual* duplicity. Densher put the black obliquity of the matter clearly to Kate Croy when he said to her plainly, "Since she's to die I'm to marry her ?" The very blackness of it weighed upon his mind, for he was straight and honorable himself, swayed only from the straight gate, by the influence of Kate. He had perceived the beauty, the fine, high, shining quality of Milly's spirit. It was he, more than Kate, with whom the figure had originated, who perceived that Milly was a dove in spirit, one to whom peace and beauty of spirit had come unasked.

Faced with the deep, murky difficulties of his position, Densher could not act. He could not propose himself to Milly with clean hands and he realized that to do so otherwise would give him an unendurable malaise of conscience. During those Venetian days "His main support really was his original idea, which didn't leave him, of waiting for the deepest depth his predicament could sink him to. Fate would invent, if he but gave it time, some refinement of the horrible." It did, for it was from the lips of her doctor that Milly Theale learned of the quiet engagement of Merton Densher and Kate Croy. She "turned her face to the wall," her will broke down, and she quietly died.

But she must have realized from whence the blow had come — from Kate — for her will provided plenty of money for Densher. Milly Theale must have perceived in those last moments as she reviewed her pitifully short-lived career, that his hesitation, his inexplicable scruples in the face of her obvious liking for him, had come from a realization that the revelation of his duplicity would kill her. She honored him, even though he seemed a party to the fraud, for his being unable in his own person to be an agent of cruel infamy. And on his side he came more and more to cherish the memory of Milly's noble spirit. He offered to complete his bargain with Kate Croy, even more, to resign his inheritance and take her without money, but she had sufficient insight to see that he was in love with Milly Theale's memory, and she gave him up. They had both been defeated by a spirit greater than either. One who was pure in heart had confounded them, the wicked and the weak. Though death had come to Milly Theale, it had not brought victory to the survivors, and Milly had left behind her one who would cherish her memory forever.

The Ambassadors (1903) is morally less interesting, even though autobiographically more significant and technically more perfect. Choice among the five great novels is somewhat invidious, since it is possible to view them from so many different angles, but the fact remains that *The Awkward Age* and *The Ambassadors* are, in their respective ways, perfection, the former in the "behavioristic" manner and the latter in the analysis of consciousness.

There have been discovered in *The Ambassadors* many elements of autobiography and it has been taken as a reminiscent expression of just what Europe meant to Henry James. If that be so then we must take as the essence of his appreciation of Europe the chance it gave to disencumber one's self of all Puritanism and rise to the appreciation of a freer life than that granted in the stricter American environment. For the fable that carries the story along is the adventure of Lambert Strether in rescuing, or attempting to rescue, Chad Newsome from the flesh-pots of Paris. Strether, a middle-aged American, cultured and reflective and above all imaginative, has been commissioned by Chad's mother, as the price of her hand in marriage so it strangely seems, to go out to Paris and bring her son home to engage as is his "duty" in the family business at Wollett, Massachusetts. Strether has all his life lived in Massachusetts in the fading shadow of the Puritan fathers. He approaches his task with the finest resolution and with the conviction that, after all, Mrs. Newsome is quite right in her evaluation of the Parisian way of life and that, shockingly, Chad's only reason for staying on and on is that he is entangled with a woman who won't let him leave.

His response to Europe is immediate and the subtle disintegration of his resolution to act in accordance with Massachusetts conceptions of right immediately begins. He arrives in Paris to find that Chad is not in town and the absence of his quarry gives him an opportunity to savor the Parisian atmosphere. As his task progresses he finds himself not only beguiled by Paris, but by the way of life of which Chad's experience is but one expression. He has slowly revealed to him that Chad's tie to Paris is indeed a woman, but that such a blunt statement of the case, while conducive of as sharp a moral judgment, hardly does justice to the situation. It is imperceptibly borne in upon his consciousness and it is in Strether's consciousness that the psychological drama takes place — there is no such scattering of the focus as in *The Wings of the Dove* — that the beauty of Chad's entanglement is not entirely that he is in love with a charming woman, but that his way of life offers such a large chance for freedom, for appreciations and discriminations. Madame de Vionet is somewhat shadowy as she emerges under James's hand and her daughter is but another of those Hawthornesque children that flourish so freely in his fiction, but her charm is accurately conveyed. We are not allowed to view her in any other light. That is her recurrent "note." Strether falls under her dominion as completely as is possible for one acutely sensible of the fact that he is not carrying out his mission.

The splitting of his consciousness between his duty to Mrs. Newsome and his appreciation of the way of life he is so excitedly exploring, reduces his letters home to hopeless inanity; they are worthy only "of a showy journalist, some master of the great new science of beating the sense out of words." He is so far unable to make out a convincing case for his dereliction from duty that Mrs. Newsome dispatches her daughter and son-in-law to Paris to rescue both Strether and Chad from the insidious siren. But they can carry off neither one, and Strether resigns Mrs. Newsome's hand, though he returns to Wollett to end his days.

The conviction he has achieved is that he has irretrievably missed his chance for a freer, more happy life and that he cannot interfere in the realization of such a benificence by another. The whole novel was grounded in this idea and took its origin from a chance remark made by William Dean Howells. "I have it on my conscience to let you know," James wrote Howells, "that the idea of the fiction . . . had its earliest origin in a circumstance mentioned to me — years ago — in respect to no less a person than yourself. At Torquay once, our young friend Jon. Sturges came down to spend some days near me, and, lately from Paris, repeated to me five words you had said to him one day on his meeting you during a call at Whistler's. I thought the words charming — you have probably quite forgotten them; and the whole incident suggestive — so far as it was an incident; and, more than this, they presently caused me to see in them the faint vague germ, the mere point of the *start*, of a subject. I noted them, to that end, as I note everything; and years afterwards (that is three or four) the subject sprang at me, one day, out of my notebook." And we may, by way of getting farther along the path to the emotion which so obviously informs this narrative, note a remark made in a letter from James to Hugh Walpole, dated August 21, 1913: "I think I don't regret a single 'excess' of my responsive youth — I only regret, in my chilled age, certain occasions and possibilities I didn't embrace." The personal note is strong, therefore, in Strether's outburst to Little Bilham, one of Chad Newsome's intimate friends:

"It's not too late for *you*, on any side, and you don't strike me as in danger of missing the train; besides which people can be in general pretty well trusted, of course — with the clock of their freedom ticking as loud as it seems to do here

— to keep an eye on the fleeting hour. All the same don't forget that you're young — blessedly young; be glad of it on the contrary and live up to it. Live all you can; it's a mistake not to. It doesn't so much matter what you do in particular, so long as you have your life. If you haven't had that what *have* you had? This place and these impressions — mild as you may find them to wind a man up so; all my impressions of Chad and of people I've seen at *his* place — well, have had their abundant message for me, have just dropped *that* into my mind. I see it now. I haven't done so enough before — and now I'm old; too old at any rate for what I see. Oh I *do* see, at least; and more than you'd believe or I can express. It's too late. And it's as if the train had fairly waited at the station for me without my having had the gumption to know it was there. Now I hear its faint receding whistle miles and miles down the line. What one loses one loses; make no mistake about that. The affair — I mean the affair of life — couldn't, no doubt, have been different for me; for it's at the best a tin mould, either fluted and embossed, with ornamental ex- crescences, or else smooth and dreadfully plain, into which, a helpless jelly one's consciousness is poured — so that one 'takes' the form, as the great cook says, and is more or less compactly held by it: one lives in fine as one can. Still, one has the illusion of freedom; therefore don't be, like me, without the memory of that illusion. I was either, at the right time, too stupid or too intelligent to have it; I don't quite know which. Of course at present I'm a case of re- action against the mistake; and the voice of reaction should, no doubt, always be taken with an allowance. But that doesn't affect the point that the right time is now yours. The right time is *any* time that one is still so lucky as to have. You've plenty; that's the great thing; you're, as I say, damn you, so happily and hatefully young. Don't at any rate miss things out of stupidity. Of course I don't take you for a fool, or I shouldn't be addressing you thus awfully.

Do what you like so long as you don't make *my* mistake. For it was a mistake . . . Live! . . ."

The last novel in the great series should be, theoretically, the very best, but the critics of James have found considerable difficulty in following that logic. Lack of sympathy with James's final phase is patently the cause of this reluctance and that it is not entirely just requires little demonstration.

The Golden Bowl is, unlike his other great works, the story of a complete success. In it he deliberately experimented in creating an interest in victory. He had long been convinced of the greater amount of spiritual significance to be wrung from failure and that he should, at the end, have tried to portray success is in itself an indication of the extraordinary interest of the novel. On the other hand, he continues in the familiar channels when he identifies his good characters with America and his bad characters with Europe. Of course the good and bad dichotomy is arbitrary for while a James character may be completely good, bad character is never quite completely bad. It is never made necessary that they should be, for their vices are the politer vices and even the stigma of adultery is worn with an air.

The hostile critics of *The Golden Bowl* emphasize the thinness of the theme. In *The Golden Bowl,* as ever, it is not the theme so much as the situation of the characters that interests him. The characters are explored for themselves and their potentialities are brought out by their relations. For so large a novel the characters are surprisingly few. They are, above all, Maggie Verver and her father, Adam Verver, Prince Amerigo and Charlotte Stant, Mrs. Assingham and her husband. The central figures are Maggie and the Prince. They are set off and related to Adam Verver and Charlotte, while Mrs. Assingham takes the familiar role of confidante. Colonel Assingham is still further subordinate, being a foil for his wife and obviously serving only to bring out her reflections on the general situation in which the characters find themselves involved.

Adam Verver is a retired American business man, resident in Europe for the purpose of acquiring works of art with which to furnish a museum he intends giving to the city in which he earned his fortune. Late in life he has discovered in himself a surprising amount of artistic sensibility which finds expression not only in the judgment of pictures but also in the judging of life. His daughter, Maggie, is one of James's pure in heart of the same type as Isabel Archer in *Portrait of a Lady*. She is represented as being entirely unacquainted with evil and it is constantly emphasized that her discovery of it will permanently damage her fine spirit. "She wasn't born to know evil," says Mrs. Assingham. "She must never know it." Nevertheless, as a wealthy girl she is a legitimate object for an impoverished Prince to covet. At Mrs. Assingham's suggestion and with her encouragement, Prince Amerigo both covets and wins Maggie and the book opens on the eve of their marriage.

Prince Amerigo, as a complete European, finds it difficult to understand his prospective wife though he can hardly be said to undervalue her. He has an acute sense of the fact that the accumulations of tradition in his own family offer abundant excuse for conduct on his part which can hardly fail to bring the condemnation of Maggie. His moral judgments are subtly controlled by factors of which she would have no appreciation and it is present in his consciousness that his great danger is that he may unconsciously offend his wife's standards. At the same time he places no fictitious valuation on his own ways and in fact has a high appreciation of Maggie's, which makes him desire to conform to them if he can.

While Maggie is entering into the marriage with a full knowledge of the Prince's historical past and presumably with an understanding of the differences in their traditions,

she has no knowledge of his personal past and it is that ignorance which almost brings the whole affair to ruin.
Prince Amerigo has always felt the necessity of making a
wealthy marriage, and has resigned his inclinations under
that necessity. He found himself in love with a beautiful
but very poor, American girl of European education. They
both realistically faced the situation and recognized the
impossibility of a union. By a curious accident this girl is
an intimate friend of Maggie, who does not know of the
passage in her friend's history. The only person to whom
it is known is Mrs. Assingham and she has not felt the least
compunction in promoting the Prince's cause with Maggie
in spite of it.

The girl in the case is Charlotte Stant. After parting
from the Prince she has returned to America with the resolution of making her life there, but on the eve of his marriage
she suddenly returns to Europe. She wishes once more to
see and talk with the Prince before he irrevocably marries
her friend. She stays with Mrs. Assingham in London, but
she, dear lady, quietly ignores Charlotte's purpose and hopes
for the best. During their final walk and talk, the Prince
and Charlotte attempt to discover some suitable wedding
present for Charlotte to purchase. In their explorations
they turn up a remarkable crystal gold-encrusted bowl which
seems to be just the thing until it is discovered that it contains a flaw, whereupon the Prince refuses the gift, on the
grounds that he feels that the bowl is symbolic of his marriage and to encourage its presentation with knowledge of
the flaw, would be courting disaster. The gift is resigned
and Charlotte, in fact, is represented by nothing in the
flood of presents that descend upon the Prince and Maggie.

The marriage bids fair to be a complete success. The
Prince shows himself a model husband and with the birth of
a son and heir, happiness is complete. Maggie's marriage
has not broken up, either, her most precious relation, that
with her father. But it is obvious to her that by being

married she has thereby separated herself from him in subtle ways, even though not to the observing eye. She consequently advises him to marry and her choice falls upon Charlotte. Charlotte's reluctance to enter into this marriage is interpreted by both Adam Verver and his daughter as no more than the reluctance of a beautiful young woman to ally herself to an elderly man with a married daughter. The reader of course knows that her reluctance is caused by the fact that the Prince, her former lover, will become her son-in-law. It is only after obtaining the Prince's approval that she accedes to Mr. Verver's desires and with that marriage the stage is set for the final evolution of the drama.

Maggie and her father seemingly draw closer together after his marriage than they were before and Charlotte and the Prince are thrown into each other's company. "What had happened . . . was that Charlotte and he had by a single turn of the wrist of fate — 'led up' to indeed, no doubt, by steps and stages that conscious computation had missed — been placed face to face in a freedom that extraordinarily partook of ideal perfection, since the magic web had spun itself without their toil, almost without their touch." Mrs. Assingham is immensely perturbed by the turn events have taken and genuinely upset by the fact that the presence of the Prince and his mother-in-law at numerous parties as the representatives of the family, is giving rise to invidious comment. She feels a certain sense of guilt in having encouraged Maggie's marriage without making her fully aware of Amerigo's past and yet she is stopped from doing anything now. She can only count on the moral delicacy of Amerigo and Charlotte to avoid disaster. And indeed there is every reason to think that their discretion and Maggie's apparent inability to suspect evil will carry the matter off.

Yet in the end Maggie does suspect and she taxes Mrs. Assingham with her suspicions, trying all the while to con-

vince herself that she is wrong. She genuinely wishes not
to have her suspicions confirmed. Mrs. Assingham manfully lies about what she knows and suspects in her own
right and the strain continues until quite by chance, while
searching for a present for her father's birthday, Maggie
chances upon the same golden bowl and gets from the dealer
who brings the bowl to her home and sees photographs of
the Prince and Charlotte in the drawing room, the fact that
they were together before her marriage. This chance episode confirms her suspicion and she tells Mrs. Assingham
of her conclusion. As a gesture, Mrs. Assingham smashes
the tell-tale bowl on the fireplace hearth as if symbolically
to destroy the whole matter. But her gesture does not succeed. Prince Amerigo, by the merest chance, observes her
action and on her precipitate retreat gets from his wife the
knowledge that she suspects his relations with his mother-in-
law, but leaves him completely in the dark as to just what
she knows.

From that point the novel is concerned with the subtle
and unspoken ways in which Maggie maneuvers for advantage. She is willing to do anything but something gross to
gain complete possession of Amerigo. It is only by dint of
the most extraordinary manipulations, she encompasses her
object. Adam Verver and Charlotte go to America and
Maggie and the Prince stay in Europe. Maggie's triumph
is complete, a triumph obtained by sheer power of character
and by the deftest use of suggestion. In the James canon
she is unique in that she triumphed over the forces that in
the past uniformly defeated his American characters. She
has faced evil and won a rousing victory over it.

HENRY JAMES once sought out a quotation about art suitable
for inscription in a public place. After a diligent search
through his many books, he hit upon a passage from Shake-
speare which, while it was rather long for the purpose in
mind, seemed to him to state the case exactly:

. . . this is an art
Which doth mend nature — change it rather;
But the art itself is nature.

It is perfectly clear that he selected this passage because it
shadowed forth his own idea that art was not a reproduction
but a recreation, a mending, of nature. It tells us plainly
that the artist must do more than copy. He must select and
interpret. All art is selection according to some preposses-
sion in the mind of the artist. An artist's prepossessions may
never rise to the dignity of a philosophy; may never be
elaborated into a theory; but unless he be a fumbling incompetent his fiction will tell us what he thinks about life.
Whether he be a humorist, a writer of tragedy, a concocter
of sweet-meats for the feeble-hearted or feeble-headed, it is
possible to trace out by observing what he puts in or leaves
out, his own scheme of values.

Henry James had a definite point of view which he never
attempted to formulate, self-consciously, into a theory. It
was something apart from his idea of how to write a novel,
but at the same time the theory was most applicable to the
sort of society he was defending and advocating. Since he
thought that art was based on selection and that the creation of a world within a world was the artist's purpose, we
have every reason for seeking out and elaborating his own
picture of a desirable world. In tracing the outlines of his
conception we must work from both positive and negative
evidence. We must observe what he praises and what he
condemns. There are more ways to condemn than make an
impression on an untrained mind. It is as effective to condemn by irony as by emotional denunciation, by suave and
subtle methods as by finger-pointing. Henry James never
used the emotional method in his fiction. That he did not
increases the difficulty of following what he sought to picture as his vision of the world.

He was beyond all else the great exponent and defender
of the leisure class. He joins himself, therefore, to the great

aristocratic tradition in European literature.　Coming late
in the history of the leisure class, on the very edge as we
shall see of its ruin, he was lacking in many of the sharper
prejudices cultivated before the middle class revolutions of
the seventeenth and eighteenth centuries.　He accepted with
entire insouciance the fact that the class must recruit its
members from the children of newly rich business men.
Indeed, as we have seen, he often placed them on a higher
plane morally than certain of the impoverished representatives of the class who belonged to it traditionally.　Neither
was he without a certain sympathy for the proletariat, as
shown in *The Princess Casamassima,* even though his understanding of proletarian unrest was ludicrously inadequate.
Henry James was, in a word, a man of his time.　His insight
into social forces was weak.　His vision was of a static world.

The bias of his mind in favor of the leisure class was
deeply rooted.　His father had deliberately cultivated the
idea that none were so admirable as the leisured and cultured.　In Newport just before the Civil War he caught a
glimpse of what the representatives of this class might be and
when he came to examine American society after the war he
was shocked to find that even the saving remnant that had
perilously maintained its footing in Newport had disap-
peared.　The whole emphasis of American society was hostile to the immediate development of the class.　The next
step in America was to be the development of a plutocracy.
James perceived the result of the American development
very clearly since he had been trained to believe that the
leisure class represented the *ne plus ultra* in human development he was not able to forego it as a subject for his fiction.
He wrestled conscientiously with the American society that
was before his eyes, but he could make nothing of it.　He
was permanently barred from contact with the dynamic individuals in American society, the business men, a fact which
he regretted to the end of his days.　Obscurely he knew
that if he could grasp them in his understanding he would

be close to the American secret. Not being able to do so, he accepted as final wisdom a conclusion he had drawn from his study of Balzac. Late in life he wrote: "What we on our side in a thousand places gratefully feel is that (Balzac) cares for his monarchical and hierarchical and ecclesiastical society because it rounds itself for his mind into the most congruous and capacious theatre for the repertory of his innumerable comedians. It has, above all, for a painter abhorrent of the superficial, the inestimable benefit of the accumulated, of strong marks and fine shades, contrasts and complications." It was forced in on James that if he wished to deal with complex people he must search for them in a society exhibiting at least some of the paraphernalia exploited by Balzac. He found his resting place in the nearest approximation to Balzacian society available after the revolutionary upheavals that had swept the world since his day. But he also went beyond Balzac in the sense that he concentrated his attention upon the finest types in that society. With his ineluctable prejudice against "simple organisms" he could hardly do otherwise. He knew that he was doing something unique and special and the fact was confirmed during a lifetime of change. Scanning the works of his predecessors and contemporaries, Balzac, Flaubert, Zola, Maupassant, Serao, D'Annunzio, he found them all deficient in insight into superior people. None of them obtruded except in the crudest fashion upon his own selected domain and in that way if in no other he differed from his generation.

But as he pursued his quarry into its most secret places, he left behind him the seething world of naked social forces, and found it possible to deal with life and living without reference to the passions that are necessary to successful functioning in it. "In all the life that has energy enough to be interesting to me," wrote George Bernard Shaw, many years ago, "subjective volition, passion, will, make intellect the merest tool. But there is in the center of that cyclone a certain calm spot where cultivated ladies and gentlemen live on independent incomes or by pleasant artistic occupations. It is there that Mr. James's art touches life, selecting whatever is graceful, exquisite or dignified in its serenity." Henry James's people lived in sublime unconsciousness of their position, in the center of a cyclone and their creator was but dimly aware of the cyclone himself. He could only imagine that those who were excluded from it by birth and economic circumstances might be restless because they could not get to the "center." His careerists moreover, were not Julien Sorels but Mr. Mitchetts ! The idea that reasonable men might wish to destroy it altogether never entered his mind. Only unreasonable men could cherish such an idea. And if he once reflected upon the terrible basis of exploitation upon which such a society rested, he was so enamoured by the possibilities of the situation that he was able to blink away what he had glimpsed. His severest criticisms were reserved for the decay of manners and the corruption of ideals among those happy few whose hereditary or achieved resting place the "center" was.

In his search for a society which would in some vague way provide him with the materials for the construction of his ideal world, he tried first the United States, then Italy, then France. He finally settled upon England, not because it completely corresponded with his conceptions but because it offered the nearest replica in the actual word and because living there was pleasurable to him personally. In England he found the requisite social machinery for the lives of the happy few in operation and while he did not make use of it all in his stories, it provided him a background against which to paint his pictures. In the famous passage from his critical study of Hawthorne, he described the machinery he found necessary, by enumerating the items lacking in the American scene:

No sovereign, no court, no personal loyalty, no aristocracy, no church, no clergy, no army, no diplomatic service, no country gentlemen, no palaces, no castles, no manners, nor old country-houses, nor parsonages, nor thatched cottages nor ivied ruins; no cathedrals, nor abbeys, nor little Norman churches; no great Universities, nor public schools — no Oxford, nor Eton, nor Harrow; no literature, no novels, no museums, no pictures, no political society, no sporting class — no Epsom nor Ascot !

Yet if he thought that to do a completely satisfactory novel one should work with a background in which all these and more were present, he made singularly little use of them in his own fiction.   He simply felt that without them present to him in the surrounding air his people existed in a void. Their very lives were conditioned by these factors even if they were not dragged in on every possible occasion.   They formed a part of the mental furniture of his people.

He concentrated his interest on his people, in this fashion still further removing himself from questions of social forces, historical movements.   Character was James's consuming interest and character in its highest expression which he took to be under the conditions of a leisure class life.   His people are very special types, carefully trained, specially disciplined, having ideals of conduct and motives for their conduct far removed from those galvinating more ordinary mortals. They were controlled neither by social compulsions nor by unconscious psychological drives.   Indeed they were supremely self-conscious.   Never for a moment did they lose an acute awareness of the freedom of their wills and they were portrayed as acting according to the dictates of conscience controlled by taste and imagination.   While their values might be based on traditional accumulations, they never acted without thought (therein differing from Englishmen), but only after the most scrupulous examination of their motives.   Correct conduct became with them the product of taste, conscience and imagination and in consequence high, fine and above all beautiful.   James is very close to the Third Earl of Shaftesbury in his opinions.   If his people were deficient in any one of these factors, their conduct was aberrant and a fatal indictment of a James character is to say that he lacks taste and conscience. He may, though never and be one of the truly celebrated, lack imagination. But if he lacks conscience of which taste is the overt expression, he is damned. Taste may be rather strange so far as dress and manners go, as in the case of Mr. Mitchett, but in moral matters it is impeccable as in Mr. Mitchett's case also. And as conscience is the basis of taste, so taste is the correcting and controlling factor with regard to imagination. It is imagination that carries James's people to the highest pitch of mental development.

It has been persistently emphasized that James's characters were not English because they habitually indulged in analysis and criticism of their own conduct. With the three great factors active the only logical result was an almost tedious self-consciousness about action. And it is the very fact that in James's world they are active that makes his "dramatic" novels seem so nearly static. No James character remains unconscious of his predicament. In direct contrast to the deterministic novels with their emphasis upon man as the creature of socio-psychological compulsions, the James novels deal with men and women who are acutely "aware." No more illuminating contrast can be drawn as illustrating not the whole difference between James and one of his most notable American successors, Theodore Dreiser, but the difference between James's self-conscious people with their free wills, and the men and women of Dreiser's novels who are at once supremely lacking in awareness, completely victims of a determining environment and psychological compulsions. This contrast goes deeper than any mere difference in fictional method. Its roots are in the fact that Dreiser explored with as active a receptivity of impressions as James, the very American waste land that James rejected. He found his impressions crystallized and confirmed by the mechanistic evolutionary monism of Spencer and others of that time. This contrast is a measure of what in all probability James escaped as it was precisely at the time that his ideas were taking definite shape that Spencerianism was most active and impressive. Would he have been able at once to closely study American society and escape the Spencerian conclusion after the fashion of his brother William? There is every reason to doubt it, for if ever a society seemed to justify a deterministic point of view it was American society from 1870 on. It is the absence of these factors with which Dreiser is so deeply concerned from James's world that makes it seem vague and unreal to those whose taste is for the sociological novel. They cannot see any rational basis to his psychology. That it had a scientific basis the writer would be the last to argue, but he does argue that properly and sympathetically viewed it makes James's world intelligible. Furthermore it often results in the characters acting from motives which are in exact correspondence with those current in the Anglo-Saxon world at large so far as it is untouched by modern psychological findings.

Since James's chosen way of handling his material was dramatic and since he could not work without placing his characters in "predicaments" it follows that he juxtaposed his evil and good characters to bring out the drama and define the predicament. Looking back over the summaries given it will be plain that the characters he admired are the "pure in heart." It is to Isabel Archer, Milly Theale and Maggie Verver that his heart goes out. His disapproval weighs upon Gilbert Osmond, Kate Croy and Charlotte Stant. And if their cases be considered thoughtfully it will appear that the pure in heart are trying to live beautifully in freedom. They are defeated by the malignancy of the world. There is no doubt that James had a profound realization of the vileness of the world. "A prouder nature never affronted the long humiliation of life," he wrote of Fanny Kemble and that judgment might almost stand as an epigraph for his great characters. The struggle for beautiful living, for freedom, for a situation in which one can act spontaneously from the purest of motives tells us by plain implication his vision of the highest of human felicity. He thought he saw the requisite fundamentals for such a society in the leisure class of his time. He did not take the leisure class at its own evaluation, but starting from what it presented to the discerning eye he projected a vision of society higher and more noble than any he had found. In writing his fiction he was compelled to admit that his completely admirable characters could only expect to suffer defeat from the contemporary conditions. And he censured the conditions in no uncertain terms whether they were new growths or long established traditions of human obliquity.

Notice has already been taken of the fact that his pure in heart were usually Americans and this in spite of the fact that he had rejected America as a scene on which to work. It has also been suggested that he may have been influenced in this view of the American character, particularly the female character, by his father's ideas unconsciously and inadequately absorbed. Whatever the origin of the bias it is apparent that he thought that these women and men would suffer an even more complete defeat under American conditions and that if they were to gain any satisfaction from life at all, it would be in the European situation. And if, in any imaginable future, they were to flourish in complete freedom it would be in a society which was a sublimation of European leisure class life into something unimaginably higher and finer.

Yet in spite of the splendor of James's vision there is something seemingly shallow and limited about it. In his curious distaste for "simple organisms" we may find one of the important limitations of his reasoning. It led him to consider the case of complex and highly disciplined people working on narrow "class" problems and to ignore the more simple and naive types whose "implications" were more "human." In this way he narrowed the appeal of his treatment by seeming to narrow the application of truth with which he was dealing. It is only when we consider his version of the difficulties of the pure in heart in comparison with that of Herman Melville's that we see that he treated here a universal problem in a specialized manner. We find Melville dealing with the pure in heart in his last novel, *Billy Budd*. The problem worried Melville to a far greater extent than it did Henry James, but he presented his version of the difficulty on a far simpler plane than James. Billy Budd, our example, is the type of morally naive man — a man of primitive Adamic purity — victimized and brought to his death by a corrupt creature whose moral obliquy is beyond Budd's comprehension. Now Melville persistently visualized this situation and found no way of resolving it any more than James did. But — and here is the point — he saw that good and evil are permanent factors in the world whether we deal with their expression in simple or complex people and that evil will triumph over good as often as not. Higher than either is justice and the best that we can pray for is that those delegated the function of dealing out justice really meet the exacting demands of their position. James had just as firm a grasp on the problem as Melville, but with his narrower social sympathies he so specialized the problem that it is with difficulty that we realize that he is dealing with a matter of universal import. This weakens the appeal of his work even if it does not detract from its validity.

Continuing on this same line we find in this point the key to the fundamental flaw of his whole vision. In concentrating his attention upon highly complicated representatives of a highly specialized social group, he brought the interest of his stories to the narrowest possible point. And by developing a complex method with which to deal with his very special people, he still further narrowed the appeal. The fundamental problems remained the same, but his people expressed themselves, not directly with reference to native emotions, but in self-conscious and even niggling debates over points of conduct — secondary and tertiary growths. By burying the problems under a thick and luxuriant covering of manners, the careless reader is easily led to believe that manners are the whole story. But they are not! James was unquestionably right in insisting that the more complex the people and the more acutely self-conscious they became, the more interesting they became to the analyst. But in pandering to the analyst in him he hid the moralist. Indeed he almost destroyed him and his vision got almost hopelessly entangled in the enormous enveloping tropical plant of adventitious circumstances! If the critic may be so presumptuous as to put his finger on what he thinks to be James's first misstep, he may place it on that period in his life, the Newport time before the Civil War, when he got the idea that leisure class life in a complex society was the highest expression of human living. Once that vision got a firm hold over Henry James's mind it was only a question of time until he would end up by writing so baroque a fiction as *The Golden Bowl*.

Had James lived in a feudal society at the height of its glory and had at his command (an impossible conjunction of circumstances to be sure) all the resources he developed for fiction writing, he would have been one of the chief glories of that sort of society. It was his misfortune to live at the very end of an epoch in world history when even the grip of the middle class over the governments of Western Europe was weakening and the proletarian ideal was in the making. He accommodated himself very well in the world so long as no overt and dislocating catastrophe took place. He could ignore, with a certain complacency, the warning voices of such writers as H. G. Wells and Bernard Shaw. He could take a mild, scared interest in the stirrings of the proletariat without finding any more drastic remedy than "democracy with a chance" necessary to repair the tottering social structure. But he could not envisage the extinction of his world. He could not foresee a time when the leisure class

would be written down as a mere parasite on the social body,
worthy only of the drastic treatment meted out to parasites
in the physical world. In direct contrast to the world of his
brother William, he believed in the fixed and the permanent.
His world was a static world, a closed universe. His system
was bound to suffer the fate of all who ignored the factor of
change. Had his social vision been broader, and had his
sense of historical change been greater, he would never have
been led into this astonishing error. Far from being a defender of civilization against barbarism as a distinguished
and cultured critic has recently celebrated him for being, or
the proponent of cosmopolitanism against provincialism as
he frequently envisaged himself, he was the supreme representative of the leisure class advanced to the stage of selec-
tively admitting the moneyed middle class to a part in the life
on sufferance, but not to the stage of seeing that the whole
structure was in acute danger of extreme dishevelment as political liberalism and radicalism, invoking the shibboleth of
equality, pushed toward the welfare state."

WHEN Henry James established himself at Rye in 1897 he
was endeavoring, we have speculated, to resolve a devouring unrest and depression. In spite of the perfectly astonishing production of the years between 1897 and 1903, when
he completed *The Golden Bowl,* the depression continued
and overflowed into his letters. He regretted, on one occasion or another, his whole career. He regretted his expa-
triation, his following the career of a writer, his electing to
be a bachelor and end his days alone. It was a period that
comes all too frequently in the life of every man when a
conviction of the total idiocy of his way of life settles upon
him. He desperately needed a change of scene.

His thoughts wandered back to America. "It's a memory of the American time, which revives so at present —
under some touch that doesn't signify," he wrote in the first
paragraph of "Europe" (1899). The thought began to agitate his mind that he might even, once again, visit America.

He was advising his brother William in 1899, to see to it that his sons contracted "local saturations and attachments in respect to their *own* great and glorious country, to learn, and strike roots into, its infinite beauty, as I suppose, and variety," the occasion for the outburst being an excursion into the country William had reported.   Even reading about New England in the novels of William Dean Howells, "makes me," he wrote to him, "homesick for New England smells and even sounds."   Howells replied in a manner further to exasperate the already sufficiently homesick James: "I can understand your hunger for New England, in these later years.   I feel it myself in New York, even, though it is not my country [nor was it James's !]   It has a sort of strange, feminine fascination.   It is like a girl, sometimes a young girl, and sometimes an old girl, but wild and shy and womanly sweet, always, with a sort of unitarian optimism in its air."

Yet the greeting Henry James's resolution to take the great step got from his brother William would have discouraged him if he had not been firmly settled on the course. He hoped, he wrote to William, that such a trip would provide him with "exotic experience, such experience as may convert itself, through the senses, through observation, imagination and reflections now at their maturity into vivid and solid *material,* into a general renovation of one's too monotonized grab bag."   Indeed, the trip would be an adventure in romance, for in the long years since he had last seen it, or seen that little corner of it which he had traversed in his young manhood, it had become "almost as romantic to me as 'Europe,' in dreams or in my earlier time here, used to be . . ."   William, with a vision of his brother all covered with sea-weeds and barnacles, so strange to him as to make it impossible "rightly to judge" him, was not so confident that the realism of American life wouldn't defeat any touch of romance.   He descanted on the pain that it would give him to see his companions "at hotels and dining-cars having their boiled eggs brought to them, broken by a negro, two in a cup, and eaten with butter," on the "incredibly loathsome . . . vocalization of our countrymen," and numerous other major and minor irritations. When Henry insisted that he was resolved to make the trip, he countered by advising that he avoid the Eastern cities and really see America, travel south to Florida and west to California and above all to take the American on their own terms.

It was Theodore Roosevelt's America Henry James was proposing to see and if there was a man in the world he couldn't endure it was Roosevelt — "the mere monstrous embodiment of unprecedented resounding Noise." The Spanish-American War had just passed over the country and the question of imperialism was still one of consuming interest to the American people. William James was one of the group of leading Americans who were deeply opposed to imperialism, and Henry James, while recognizing that the imperialistic impulse had contributed a vast deal to the formation of the English character in the way of discipline, was dubious about the effects of a war, which Howells succinctly described to him, on the American people, "Our war for humanity," wrote Howells, "has unmasked itself as a war for coaling stations, and we are going to keep our booty to punish Spain for putting us to the trouble of using violence in robbing her." The war had thrown up Roosevelt as the supreme exemplar of the American middle class reforming spirit and he was in the very year of Henry James's American pilgrimage, 1904, to ascend to the Presidential chair in his own right. The insurance scandals were about to break. America was on the verge of muckraking. Lincoln Steffens was exposing the "shame of the cities." The country was a perfect ferment of "exposure" and the middle class conscience was functioning more openly than it ever had before or ever would again. The country could not more perfectly prepare itself to prove all of Henry James's misgivings about the fruits of a career in it, misgivings which he had, so it logically seems, poured into his story "The Jolly Corner" (c. 1900). In this tale he had imagined that a returned expatriate had confronted the ghost of his self as he would have been had he attempted a career in "business" in America, the revelation being of a face showing as terrible a corruption as that which confronted the young man in Oscar Wilde's *Portrait of Dorian Grey*. The personal connotations can easily be overstressed, but the fact that the vision was of deep emotional import to James cannot be questioned.

He approached a country whose literature must have been strangely repellent, for he could take no more interest in the popular romance than he could in the products of the serious writers. To be sure he had viewed Stephen Crane in England living in "a parody of baronial state" with fascinated delight, sending him autographed books, listening calmly to Crane's enthusiastic recommendation that he read Anatole France, and accepting his unconventional arrival for dinner with equanimity. He knew talent when he saw it but his final view of Crane must have been of a piece with his verdict on Aubrey Beardsley. And how could he confront, without the benefit of personal acquaintance as in the case of Zola, Frank Norris's *McTeague* (1899) and the world it portrayed and what would he make of the deliberately journalistic writing of *The Octopus* (1901) when he was constantly rebuking H. G. Wells for his sins against the artistry of the novel? Nor could the America which threw up such an extraordinary person as Jack London be entirely clear to him. London had visited England in 1902 and instead of viewing the coronation had plunged down into the abyss to portray the horrors of the East End. Now in 1903 he was to print his epic of primitivism *The Call of the Wild* and in 1904 he was to get out *The Sea-Wolf*. Theodore Dreiser, who was to go to the heart of the very American business world outside the door of which James stood baffled all his life, had recently published *Sister Carrie*

(1900) and entered upon his long silence. He was not en-
gulfed but engrossed in accumulating those impressions by
which James set such store. Such elementality of emotion,
such simplification of character development as these men
portrayed, could mean nothing to Henry James and yet it
was their America and that of the lighter writers like Richard
Harding Davis and O. Henry which he was about deliberately to explore.

GERMANY was alienating the European nations, driving
France and England together. Russia was striving desperately for leadership in the Balkans against her traditional
enemy, Austria-Hungary. In a few years A. P. Isvolsky
would suffer a severe rebuff and would turn from the position of Minister of Foreign Affairs for the Czar and get
himself appointed Ambassador to France, where with President Poincare he would cement the unnatural alliance of
republican France and Czaristic Russia. Nicolai Lenin was
living in London where he had lately been joined by Leon
Trotsky, just escaped from Siberian exile. Henry James
looked out on his world and, little knowing that in ten short
years these unseen, to his vision, men and the forces they
represented would indeed confirm his conception of the actual world "as a more or less mad panorama, phantasmagoria
and dime museum."

4. WITHIN THE RIM

JAMES FENIMORE COOPER, who had sufficient experience in
such matters to form an accurate judgment, wrote that
"When an American returns from an excursion into the old
world with 'I come back better satisfied than ever with my
own country,' it is an infallible sign that he did not stay
long enough abroad; and when he returns only to find fault,
it is equally proof that he has stayed too long." Henry
James returned after twenty years. It was generally be-

lieved that he had come back to record his "depressions" of America, but the readers of his *American Scene* must have been agreeably disappointed. He did not get a full report of his visit into its numerous pages, but he did get enough to make it clear that he was *impressed* by America even if he was not pleased. And, carefully considered, his report contains nothing worse than the old indictment given in the Hawthorne book of 1879. He had expressed his fundamental opinion then, and twenty-five years later, he found nothing to alter, though his elaboration of his favorite ideas was immensely studied and subtle.

He found himself heartily welcome and every opportunity for seeing was extended to him. The curiosity about him was immense and even though he retreated to his brother William's place at Chocorua immediately he had landed, a lady reporter for a New York paper pursued him to his fastness. He was offered dinners and receptions and public honors of various sorts; which he refused with elaborate circumlocutory letters; he wrote and delivered public lectures, a marked departure from his habit of personal effacement, because of the money offered, but he persistently declined to accept any status but that of private citizen. In conformance with the advice of his brother he made a sweeping tour of the country, going south into Florida and west to California. Alternately charmed by nature and disillusioned by the works of man, he put up with discomfiture with surprising equanimity and accepted boons with heartfelt gratitude.

He was of "medium height, slightly bald, his black hair turned iron gray at the temples," reported a veracious lady who went on to say that his "face is long and strong, broad of cheekbone and jaw, narrower in the high doming forehead. . . . His nose is massive and fine, mouth large and tender." He was, in fact, as many observers have made note, a rather ugly man, but one whose benignancy of manner quite obscured his deficiencies in pulchritude. His talk was a fascination. After conversing with him, the salt of ordinary conversation lost its flavor. It was the usual thing for him to phrase his unpremeditated remarks with as scrupulous care as his most polished sentences in a story. One day in a club A. C. Benson paused a moment at James's table and the latter said: "My dear Arthur, my mind is so constantly bent upon you in wonder and goodwill that any change in my attitude could be only the withdrawing of a perpetual and settled felicitation !"

Such a kind of speech implied a formality of manners remarkably out of place in American life. The deliberate ponderosity of it could find no use in a society noted for the clipped and rapid utterance of its perpetually hurried and agitated members. And indeed all of the foundations that Henry James had put down upon which to erect his way of life were lacking in America. His personal predicament was little different from his social. Yet he found it easier to make friends, to understand individuals, than to evaluate intelligently the surrounding social medium. He found that America lacked, "a visible Church, a visible State, a visible Society, a visible Past; those of the many visibilities, in short, that warmly cumber the ground in older countries." He had known this all his life. His latest exploration was only unique in being the widest he ever undertook and his report unique in being the most elaborate of all the various variations he played on the theme.

Yet if he was only illustrating anew his familiar indictment of American society there can be no question of the scrupulosity with which he examined the evidence. He refers to himself in *The American Scene* with monotonous frequency as the "restored absentee" and the "restless analyst." He was superconscious of the fact that he was back in his own country. He was in an exasperated state of analytical attention. "To be at all critically, or as we have been fond of calling it, analytically minded," he wrote, "over and beyond an inherent love of the general many-colored picture of things — is to be subject to the superstition that objects and places, coherently grouped, disposed for human use and addressed to it, must have a sense of their own, a mystic meaning to give out: to give out, that is, to the participant at once so interested and so detailed as to be moved to a report of the matter." For one who was so "analytically minded" he had surprisingly little to say about the positive values to be discovered in America and an equally surprising lot to say about what was absent. It was lucky, in a way, that he did not make his belated trip to Argentina or Australia, for then he would have labored in an even more frightening manner to make up a decently balanced account about what he had concluded by his restless analyzing. He could see on the positive side of the sheet chiefly the "particular type of dauntless power," but he by his own confession could make nothing of that for lack of a contact with the manipulators of it. He saw, too, the gregariousness of American life, and its tendency to a flat level of unoriginality in personalities. He saw the south in Menckenian terms as a Saharah of the Bozart. But he was not able to make a truly revelatory assessment of the country. Too many prejudices stood between him and his object. It was possible for him to admire the California climate, but he felt much happier in Rye. And to Rye, with happy precipitateness he returned.

His life had eleven years yet to run but his work was nearly done. For the remaining years he engaged in brushing up the results of his long and exhausting labors and only one or two newly projected tasks were carried to completion. While in America he had arranged with Charles Scribner's Sons to bring out a collected edition of his work which eventually filled twenty-four volumes. He labored over this task for two weary years, not only preparing by way of prefaces a complete treatise on the art of fiction as he had come to conceive it, but also revising the text of his numerous volumes, taking each in hand as though it were an example of an extremely corrupt text and ruthlessly rewriting it, to suit his mature taste. Had he had more room he would undoubtedly have included some of the books he rejected. *The Bostonians,* for example, but he would not have been less ruthless in his revision had the heavens fallen. It was his chief reason for preparing the edition. Various explanations have been advanced for his course in the matter, but none of them is very satisfactory. Nor is it possible to find any thread of agreement running through the numerous comments on the results of the revision. Reaction to it has been largely determined by personal taste. Yet it would seem fairly obvious that James wished merely to bring all his work to the level of excellence he thought himself to have reached after many years of effort. If he had had a greater interest in the historical evolution of his talent he would have undoubtedly foregone the pleasure, but he was notably deficient in the factual sense and felt no compunction about erasing those parts of his record which displeased him. He pursued his course over the protests of his friends with a steadfastness that illustrates a profound conviction of his rightness. Edmund Gosse tried to get him to let *Roderick Hudson* stand as written. James replied that "the only alternative would have been to put the vile thing behind the fire and have done with it." On that they went off to bed and the next morning when Gosse made the conventional remarks about hoping he had slept well, James burst out: "Slept ! was I likely to sleep when my brain was tortured with all the cruel and — to put it plainly to you — monstrous insinuations which you had brought forward against my proper, my necessary, my absolutely inevitable corrections of the disgraceful and disreputable style of 'Roderick Hudson' ?"

The revisions were, in truth, chiefly stylistic. Almost every sentence was touched up in some fashion but the order of the paragraphs was not changed nor was the general structure of the narrative altered. The whole case against the revisions rests, therefore, on the familiar objections to James's style as being too ornate, too elaborate, and altogether too bizarre for any reasonable use.　If there has been any soundness in the earlier analysis of his method it will appear to the reader that James's style was simply the inevitable result of his evolution as an artist.　It was not an excrescence but an integral part of his work.　And since it is difficult to see how he could have escaped his normal evolution it is also difficult to object to his pious effort to make his work all of a piece.　For those who are fascinated by linguistic problems the original editions still remain.　He was quite unable to destroy the records and every book an author issues, however unfortunate it later seems to him to be, is a hostage with fortune.　Enquiring minds can try the unrevised *The Bostonians,* and then the revised *The Ambassadors* and soon decide which they prefer, the embryonic or the developed Henry James.

The final expression of his talent in finished form followed hard on the heels of his labors over the collected edition.　It was a group of stories collected under the title *The Finer Grain* (1910).　With this brilliant book, the record of memorable productions is complete.　He continued to put out books from time to time and some came posthumously, but none of them is more than a fitful flame from the expiring powers of genius.　The stories in *The Finer Grain* are quite other, however.　They are beautiful parables on familiar texts.　"The Velvet Glove" is literary in its subject matter, but wider in its implications.　A recently successful literary man meets a brilliant and fascinating Princess at a party and she uses all her blandishments to get him to write a preface to her new book.　She has been composing trashy novels under a pseudonym and desires the prestige he can give her worthless efforts.　The situation agitates the young man and violates his sense of fitness, so he carries on the discussion to the very doorstep of the Princess only, as a parting word to admonish her: "You don't need to understand.

Don't attempt such base things. Leave those to us. Only
live. Only be. We'll do the rest." Only be ! That was
his father's message many long years ago ! In "Mora Mon-
travers" we have a question of *being* at the bottom of much
useless agitation. Mora seeks freedom to live and against
the opposition of her aunt takes certain drastic steps which
seem to point to her irretrievable ruin. Her uncle is more
philosophical and points out that he and his wife have no
knowledge of life, for they have lived in solitude and quies-
cence all their days: "What do we know about the scene of
life — when it breaks out with real freedom. It has never
broken out here, my dear, for long enough to leave its breath
on the window-pane." He further emphasizes and praises
the imagination as the key to his niece's desire for a wider
and freer life and tells his wife that imagination leads to "a
life exquisite, occult, dangerous and sacred." He will brook
no interference with one who so marvellously possesses it.
The last of the group to have significance worth iterating
here (for all of them are variations on old themes) is "Crapy
Cornelia." An elderly gentleman finding himself alone and
in poor circumstances is tempted to marry a rich parvenue
in New York who knows nothing about his life or his traditions. On the visit to her when he plans to present his case
he encounters an old family friend, known because of her
widow's weeds as Crapy Cornelia. He had not thought of
her for years and is fascinated by the possibility of reviewing
the past with her. He foregoes his wealthy marriage, if indeed he would have been accepted, so ignorant is the lady of
his social "value," to spend his declining years in the company of his old and indigent friend. "The high pitch of
interest, to his taste, was the pitch of history, the pitch of
acquired and earned suggestion, the pitch of association, in
a word; so that he lived by preference, incontestably, if not
in a rich gloom, which would have been beyond his means
and spirits, at least amid objects and images that confessed
to the tone of time." In such fashion did Henry James

reiterate his testimony.   His task was done and all that remained was to explore his own past.

In 1910 he completely broke down in health and suffered
severely from mental depression.   William hurried out to
join him, really the sicker of the two.   The family group,
one leaning pathetically on the other, returned to America,
William to die and Henry to struggle on alone.   His sister-
in-law, in her efforts to distract Henry's mind, suggested that
he set down in words some of the glorious evocations of the
past to which he had been treating her, and when he returned
to England in August 1911, he set himself to the task and
produced two stunning volumes, *A Small Boy and Others*
and *Notes of a Son and Brother*.   In the midst of his troubles signal public recognition had come to him in the form
of honorary degrees from both Harvard and Oxford.   But
he was miserable and unhappy still.   His health seemed
permanently broken and he reported himself "interminably
and miserably ill."   The world at large displeased him.   The
modern novel seemed to him to prove nothing so muc.: as
the bankruptcy of the form.   The geniuses the young were
hailing were not to his taste and the writers he could approve
did not strike them as warranting the accolade.   The woman's suffrage agitation left him cold.   He had disposed of
the issue thirty years before.   The militants retaliated by
slashing his portrait by Sargent as it hung in the Royal Academy !   He was convinced by the chauvinistic writers who
were exploiting the German peril and he was "eager at present only for Dreadnoughts and Aeroplanes and people to
man, not to *woman,* them !"   He was an old, sick, disillusioned man.

It took the World War finally to down his indomitable
artistic spirit.   For a time he kept on slowly and painfully
working.   He left behind him two manuscripts partly done
entitled *The Sense of the Past* and *The Ivory Tower*.   The
first was a semi-historical work in which he could partially
lose himself and shut out the excruciating reality of war

and the second was a return to America. It exploited the
old theme of *The Europeans,* in an immensely elaborated
form. But his heart was not in them.

When the war swept over Europe he was shocked and
hurt and the immediate effect was to wind him up to a
higher pitch emotionally than he had reached in all his life.
It was, in effect, the ruination of his fondest hopes. He had
managed to brush aside the reiterated warnings that a new
age was coming to birth and that if radical changes were not
made, catastrophe was ahead. He had heeded the chau-
vinists but not the liberal and radical social critics. The
younger writers who were assuring the world that Europe
was in a sorry state did not unduly disturb him as social
prophets, however much he felt it necessary to scold them for
their aesthetic sins. The war, however, seemed to wipe out
his world at a blow and to make unreal, even to him, the
vision on which he had so long labored.

He felt that there was no answer to his difficulty other
than a firm devotion to the cause of England. He had long
lived and labored there and he had many deep personal attachments. All his life he had been dissociated from politics and there was no question of his understanding the
deeper issues involved in the war. Indeed there was no
personal example, among his circle of acquaintances, of any
skepticism about the official version of what was happening.
H. G. Wells, who was to all intents and purposes a social
skeptic engaged himself in the task of sophisticating and
"liberalizing" the war propaganda. James tried, however,
to get in as intimate touch with the situation as possible.
He got a diary from Margot Asquith and wrote in returning it:

I have lived, you see, wholly out of the inner circle of political
life, and yet more or less in wondering sight, for years, of many
of its outer appearances, and in superficial contact — though
this, indeed, pretty anciently now — with various actors and
figures, standing off from them on my quite different ground and
neither able nor wanting to be of the craft of mystery (prefer-

ring, so to speak, my own poor, private ones, such as they have
been) and yet with all sorts of unsatisfied curiosities and yearn-
ings and imaginings in your general, your fearful direction.

But while Margot Asquith's notes seemed to him to give a
wonderful glance into the intricacies of political life, they
could not offer him any shrewd hints as to the actualities of
the political situation.   Nor could he learn much more by
visiting the American Embassy and adding lustre to the
court of Walter Hines Page; realities were not popular there.
He was reduced to the pathetic excitement of retailing war-
impassioned anecdotes in Mrs. Humphrey Ward's drawing
room and to contributing his bit to keeping up the morale
of the country by working in the Belgian Relief, turning his
pen to charitable uses and mystifying the readers of the London *Daily News* by informing them that:

Personally I feel so strongly on everything that the war has
brought into question for the Anglo-Saxon peoples that humorous detachment or any other thinness or tepidity of mind on the
subject affects me as vulgar impiety, not to say rank blasphemy;
our whole race question became for me a sublimely conscious
thing from the moment Germany flung at us all her explanations
of her pounce upon Belgium for massacre and ravage in the form
of the most insolent "Because I choose to damn you all" recorded
in history.   The pretension of smashing world rule by a single
people in virtue of a monopoly of every title, every gift and every
right ought perhaps to confound us more by its grotesqueness
than to alarm us by its energy; but never do cherished possessions whether of the hand or of the spirit, become so dear to us
as when overshadowed by vociferous aggression.   How can one
help seeing that such aggression, if hideously successful in Europe, would, with as little loss of time as possible, proceed to apply itself to the American side of the world, and how can one,
therefore, not feel that the Allies are fighting to the death for the
soul and the purpose of the future that are in us, for the defense
of every ideal that has most guided our growth and that most
assures our unity?   Of course, since you ask me, may many
years of exhibited attachment to the conditions of French and
of English life, with whatever fond play of reflection and reaction that may have been involved in it, makes it inevitable that
these countries should particularly appeal to me at the hour of
their peril, their need and their heroism, and I am glad to declare that though I had supposed I knew what that attachment

was, I find I have any number of things more to learn about it.
English life, wound up to the heroic pitch, is at present most
immediately before me, and I can scarcely tell you what a privilege I feel it to share the inspiration and see further revealed
the character of this decent and dauntless people.

He had one way left in which to testify to his attachment
to the English people and that was by joining himself to
them in citizenship.   It had come to him as something of a
shock that his movements were controlled by the authorities
as an alien in the early days of the war.   He, in his emotionally overwrought condition, had hoped against hope that
he could do his small part to bring the United States to the
side of England and so make unnecessary the sacrificing of
the last strong threads attaching him to his native land.
Though he may have served his part in confirming the
natural bias of many pro-Ally Americans with whom he was
in agitated correspondence during these months, the government showed no signs, to his unpolitical eye, of moving.
With infinite regret, but with a high sense of performing a
noble and unavoidable duty, he decided to apply for naturalization.   He wrote to Prime Minister Asquith:

My dear Prime Minister and Illustrious Friend, —
   I am venturing to trouble you with the mention of a fact of my
personal situation, but I shall do so as briefly and considerately as
possible.   I desire to offer myself for naturalization in this
country, that is, to change my status from that of American citizen to that of British subject.   I have assiduously and happily
spent here all but 40 years, the best years of my life, and I find
my wish to testify at this crisis to the force of my attachment and
devotion to England, and to the cause for which she is fighting,
finally and completely irresistible.   It brooks at least no inward
denial whatever.   I can only testify by laying at her feet my ex-
plicit, my material and spiritual allegiance, and throwing into
the scale of her fortune my all but imponderable weight — "a
poor thing but my own."   Hence this respectful appeal.   It is
necessary (as you may know!) that for the purpose I speak of
four honourable householders should bear witness to their kind
acquaintance with me, to my apparent respectability, and to my
speaking and writing English with an approach to propriety.
What I presume to ask of you is whether you will do me the

honour to be the pre-eminent one of that gently guaranteeing group? Edmund Gosse has benevolently consented to join it. The matter will entail on your part, as I understand, no expenditure of attention at all beyond your letting my solicitor wait upon you with a paper for your signature — the affair of a single moment; and the "going through" of my application will doubtless be proportionately expedited. You will thereby consecrate my choice and deeply touch and gratify yours all faithfully,

HENRY JAMES.

On July 26, 1915, the shift was accomplished. If he had felt able to tell Mr. Asquith that he had no reservations about the matter, he was not able to keep from his friends certain misgivings. He was above all disappointed that the step had been necessary. In September he wrote to the T. S. Perrys: "I think it quite natural you should regret my not having been able to stick to my American citizenship; you can't regret it more than I do; but that 'able' contains the whole essence of the matter. . . The comfort of having rectified that false position is, I find, unutterable — though Mr. Wilson could have rectified it long since, I mean could have relieved me, as I say, with one waggle of his little finger. With that waggle to hold on to, I should have left the matter quite lucidly alone."

One matter of very considerable import he did not change. He did not change his mind about his final resting place. A codicil of his will, dated August 25, 1915, reads: "I direct that my body shall be cremated at Golders Green (if I shall die in England) and my ashes afterwards laid near those of my parents, my elder Brother and my Sister in the cemetery of Cambridge, Massachusetts." The claims of family piety quite over-rode those of political patriotism.

The pitch of emotion that he had reached in changing his citizenship seemed to exhaust his powers. He was far from well in any case for he had never fully recovered from the illness of 1910 and on December 2, 1915 he suffered a stroke. He was in his seventy-third year and had long since drawn upon any reserves of recuperative power, but he lingered on for some weeks. When the New Year's honors for 1916 were announced it was discovered that the King had conferred the Order of Merit upon him and the formal investiture of it was made at his bedside by Lord Bryce. Mrs. William James had come from America to be with him. "Henry will have his wish for 'no partial recovery,'" she wrote a short time before the end came. "He is not suffering. Even the consciousness of his helplessness and mental confusion has translated itself into happy wandering, and pleasant foreign places, and old friends. And so he lies all day on an invalid's lounge, where he can look off over the river, and see the barges make their slow way back and forth, and watch the clouds and the sunsets. He was pleased to see Harry, but does not miss him when he goes. It is long since he has refused to have letters, messages or even names. And he has never once asked about the war. We sit with him . . . but we do not talk. Everything seems trivial in the presence of this great serenity of spirit." On the 28th of February, 1916, he died.

When Mrs. Humphrey Ward received the telegram announcing the event she was watching the Germans launch a counter-attack in the Ypres salient. Henry James died when those violent and destructive social passions of which he had taken so little account were more actively at work than they had ever been before. They were irretrievably shattering all that he held most sacred. It was well that he did not stay to see the shifts to which men were put to live among the ruins.

BOOK V

EPILOGUE

THE BEQUEST OF THE JAMESES

I T IS impossible to assess in very precise terms the bequests left to posterity by writers and thinkers. They leave behind them, to be sure, the whole body of their works, but no one in whom the world feels called upon to take an interest ever exactly reproduces the work of his master or masters. If a writer or thinker is so misguided as to appear before the world as a mere simulacrum of his master, he is immediately put down as a man of the inferior sort and dismissed from the notice of questing minds. The much more likely fate of a truly seminal figure is that parts of his work will remain for all time his private possessions, while other parts will be assimilated to the general stream of intellectual life. The latter frequently become dissociated from the initiator's name and in time the source is forgotten, and almost impossible to identify.

The Jameses are no exception to this general rule. What they did, individually and collectively, has long since become a part of the general stream of culture in the European-American world. Tendencies they initiated or gave impetus to, have been taken up and further developed and sometimes re-directed by later thinkers until it is well-nigh impossible to say that the contemporary manifestation of that tendency is properly to be listed under the heading of a James bequest.

Unlike the inventory of a great estate filed for purposes of reference with the proper legal authorities, any account of the intellectual bequest of this remarkable family must be generalized and suggestive rather than specific and arresting.

All of the Jameses were psychologists; all of them were biased toward social values; and all of them were individualists. Henry James, Sr., conceived of redemption as a social matter; he argued vehemently for the destruction of selfhood; but he remained nevertheless an individualist, for he was against the institutionalizing tendencies of mankind. In the same way, — William James definitely tried to cultivate those values which would contribute to meliorating the lot of mankind, yet he, also, remained firmly wedged in the idea of individualism and conceived of social health as the product of the action of beneficent individuals. Henry James Jr. sought diligently to erect a society which would give freest play to the greatest number of highly developed individualities. His thinking was less comprehensive than that of his father and his brother, but in general tendency he came around to the same ends.

How and in what way they were all psychologists needs very little demonstration. It is very clear that Henry James, Sr., was an introspectionist of a sort and it is plain that his religion required a very definite conception of human psychology. It was in the mind that he placed the struggle of the Divine and diabolic tendencies. William James tried to correlate scientific psychology with the moralistic principle of free will and to bring the support of scientific psychology to the religious experience. Henry James applied the family skill in psychological analysis to the infinitely delicate task of discriminating the reactions of leisure class people living a highly developed social life.

While these similarities may be set down, it is much more profitable to differentiate the three men. Henry James, Sr., was a thoroughgoing supernaturalist. His concern was to reconcile God and Man. He conceived of this reconciliation in psychological terms and of its fruits in social terms. In doing so he transvaluated all the values of his time. He was a radical libertarian. A man of powerful intellect, he chose to deal in generalizations rather than in particulars. His bias was toward affirmation on the one hand and toward analytical destruction of what he disapproved on the other. In him one finds all the tendencies which came to expression in the lives of his sons.

William James abandoned the details of his father's philosophy, but tried to conserve its essence by bringing to its support the new science of psychology. He got his psychological bias from his father. However, he did not proceed from God downward, but from the earth upward to God. Far from being entirely a naturalistic thinker, he was yet predominantly that. The overtones of his thought and its ultimate implications were *moral*. To support moral ends he was willing to abandon his naturalism and seek support from supernaturalism. This gave his mind a mixed quality which allows the thoroughgoing on both sides to find him an ally, and at the same time a traitor.

He was, like his father, concerned with the ultimate problems of man's relation to the universe and to God. His universe was moral and to work for its improvement it was necessary to *act*. Consequently he cultivated all those techniques and points of view which made it easier for man to act. God was conceived as a stimulus to action, in the first place, and in the second as a source of exceptional power to fortunate individuals. Heaven was defined as the place where the moral drama being enacted on earth would be resolved in a victory of good.

He definitely departed from the generalizing habit of mind of his father, and attempted to cultivate particulars. It was his desire to keep to the facts. In cultivating this disposition he ran himself gradually into an anti-intellectualistic frame of mind. Furthermore, he became impressed with diversity and multiplicity instead of unity and simplicity.

Instead of a tight and ordered universe, he pictured a loose
and open universe.   Instead of monism, he cultivated pluralism.   In doing so he laid himself open to his father's condemnation as one who encouraged "that dreary Socratic
ratiocination about their (things of sense) shifting superficial
appearance, which give great talkers a repute for knowledge."
In sum, he was his father's child, but not his father's replica.

Henry James, Jr., was even less his father's replica, but
still he was his father's child.   He was differentiated from
his father (and his brother) by never having experienced that
world-fear which came to the former at thirty-three and to
the latter at twenty-eight.   This enabled him mentally to narrow and specialize his interests and exclude the larger matters of man's relation to God and the universe.   He focused
his interest on man's relation to man.   He took over his
father's social interests (Fourierism and social redemption)
but removed the religious overtones and redefined the whole
matter on a lower plane.   They were both analysts, but
Henry James, Jr., operated within narrower limits.   The
younger Henry James did not try to take in all heaven and
earth.   He did not, even, try to embrace all of society.   He
concentrated upon a special point of rest in the midst of the
social whirl-wind.   His world was an indoors world and his
Nature was so impregnated by human values as to be altogether assimilated to the classification of a human habitation.
He wanted everything under the control of the regulating
hand of man.   He disliked wildness.   He disliked, indeed,
anything that was uncontrolled and uncontrollable.   But
within the limits of his world he dealt with the profoundest
problems, in which he showed himself a James.

It is not my intention to support the thesis, advanced by
Lewis Mumford, a rather destructive critic of the James
family, that William and Henry James were but fragmentary
men as compared with their father.   I cannot accept such an
opinion, for it seems to me the product of a mere willful
desire to asperse the sons and aggrandize the father without

paying too close attention to what the father was like.   In
my view all three were remarkable and distinguished men.
That in studying their works one is able schematically to
show how William and Henry split off from their father, does
not contribute to the lessening of their importance or to increasing their father's importance.   It is merely an interesting happenstance.   For everything they subtracted from their
father's intellectual outlook they added something of their
own.   In the end they were just as complexly organized as
ever he was.   They were just as completely men.

HENRY JAMES, SR., forms the intellectual background out of
which his two sons grew just as William James the First,
forms the economic background for the whole family.   When
it comes to defining the contributions of the Jameses to the
general stream of thought it is necessary to concentrate one's
attention upon the younger men.

As the years pass, two great contributions appear to be
peculiarly identified with William James, one philosophical
and one psychological, and the latter the most important.
The philosophical idea is that of the open universe which
has not, however, worked itself out in social life so much as
in science.   This does not invalidate its importance, for
while James was concerned with the social implications of it,
it was developed primarily in reaction to a very definite type
of scientificism which has passed.   Much more important,
however, is his contribution to psychology.   Dealing only
in the broadest and most suggestive terms, we may define
William James's great psychological contribution as the idea
of "the stream of consciousness."

This idea was a great contribution to the breaking up of
the notion that the human ego was a definite, fixed thing, of
hard and immutable outlines, superior to all the vicissitudes
of man's earthly career.   It was a definite contribution to
the gradual dis-integration of the psychological life of man
and it found its most complete expression in literature.

William James, therefore, takes his place as one of the fore-bearers of such writers as James Joyce, Marcel Proust, Dorothy Richardson, Aldous Huxley, Luigi Pirandello, William Faulkner, Conrad Aiken and so many others as to make any catalogue tedious. This idea has been complemented by another which appeared in embryonic form in William James's work under the title of the subliminal. He derived it from F. W. H. Myers and applied it to the explanation of all sorts of psychological phenomena like psychical happenings, split personalities, multiple personalities, sudden accesses of previously untapped energies, and the religious experience. James, however, did not anticipate the modern version of the content of the subliminal (or as it has come to be called, the unconscious). That version was supplied by Sigmund Freud. James had been impressed by the work of Charcot and Janet on personality, but he had been content to borrow the findings in the form in which the authors themselves expressed them. Freud, on the other hand, found in these same reports a suggestion for a new departure which would revolutionize psychology. He was able, by developing the suggestion to evolve the theory of psycho-analysis. Psycho-analysis has carried the disintegration of the mental life of man to a point far beyond that reached by William James. It has, furthermore, made its chief contributions in the field of abnormal psychology and has conclusively demonstrated to what a great extent supposedly normal minds are compounded of socially accepted abnormalities. William James, as we have noticed, was deeply impressed by the lack of a precise line separating the normal and the abnormal.

Gathering these matters up in summary, we find that James contributed to destroying the idea of a neatly rounded, rigidly outlined consciousness, that he accepted the idea of the subliminal without grasping its full implications and certainly without in any way anticipating its contents correctly, and finally that he was impressed by the intangibility

of the differences between "normality and abnormality."
A highly competent student of the characteristic psychology
of modern literature, Houston Peterson, has summed up that
psychology in these words:

Below the ordinary surface of consciousness is a great reservoir
of unconscious impulses, energies, interests. Those impulses
which were repressed in early years, secretly shape our later lives,
in health as well as disease. In trying to compensate for his
weaknesses, man often devotes his most intense efforts to what he
is least fitted for attaining. Reasoning is largely a matter of self-
justification after the fact, as much humor turns out to be an in-
direct expression of malice rather than a direct expression of
good will. Finally we have given up the sharp distinction between the normal and the abnormal, with the realization that
the so-called normal is only a social wish and a statistical fiction.
Perversions, complexes, mental anomalies, are scattered indis-
criminately through the populace. Most of us are out of insane
asylums simply because our little quirks are not obviously dangerous and do not prevent us from making a living.

Now this is a long way from being a summary of William
James's views but, and this is the point of the digression, it
represents the present-day formulation of *trends all of which
can be found in embryonic form in his writings*. William
James's is, consequently, a forerunner of contemporary literary psychology and as such is perhaps a greater influence
on the intellectual life of the time than through any influence
he may still exert upon the development of academic psychology.

Turning to Henry James we find a different situation.
He was, of course, a literary man and his relation to subsequent writing should naturally be closer. On examination
it does not turn out that it is closer. Psychologically, Henry
James was not a proponent of the passions (like say George
Sand) or of the will (like say Stendhal) or of the God-tortured
intellectual (like say Dostoevsky). He was the proponent of
the intellect in its most self-conscious, discriminating and
analytical development. He agreed with his brother William in positing free will. But he disagreed with him in

not disintegrating consciousness. He insisted upon making his figures think with the "tops" of their minds, so to speak. A measure of this important difference is the contrast between William's definition of the stream of consciousness and the celebrated "interior monologue" from *Portrait of a Lady,* from which passages have been quoted earlier. There are no hints in this monologue of the disintegration which was to overtake the mind only a few years later. It is, rather, a picture of the reflections of a hyperorganized mind. Yet there are in Henry James hints of later developments. In his pursuit of the ultimate implications and overtones of each and every situation in his stories, he was moving in the direction of Marcel Proust. And in his insistent development, to the point of fearing that he had "over-treated" them, of each individual moment, he was moving toward James Joyce.

There is one important way in which James differs from his great successors in the novel. He was firmly convinced of the importance of structure. Now those of his successors who took over from him his emphasis on structure and organization have been writers, pretty uniformly, of much lesser stature than he. Of them all, Edith Wharton is perhaps the only one for whom we can claim high honors. The more usual tactic has been to borrow or extend certain of his characteristics other than the structural. And, furthermore, there has been a very definite tendency, to abandon his conviction of the necessity of a moral basis for high literature. Matthew Josephson, in a discriminating study of Virginia Woolfe, noted that "much of the 'new type of fiction' written during the 1920's has sacrificed some important principle of energy. . ." He also noted that "the wide-spread moral certainties which had buoyed up the prolific realists were generally lost." Without assimilating James to the "prolific realists" it may be pointed out that he was in possession of the lacking "principle of energy" and that it was a deep moral conviction. His possession of it, like his possession of structure, makes him differ from his great successors.

If, in rebuttal, it be alleged that James Joyce's *Ulysses* has a structure and a very elaborate and difficult one, then all one can say in reply is that it is pretty well obscured. Furthermore, those who have borrowed technical devices from Joyce have uniformly failed to borrow his structural proclivities and have shown themselves much more impressed by his disintegrative tendencies. On the other hand, there is no debate about the fact that Marcel Proust's novel is organized on such different lines that if James's fiction is called structural, Proust's cannot be called that at all. Edmund Wilson writes: ". . . we perceive that *A la Recherche du Temps Perdu,* which begins in the darkened room of sleep, stands alone as a true dream-novel among works of social observation. It has its harmony, development and logic, but they are the harmony, development and logic of the unconscious."

Both Joyce and Proust read like authors who have read Henry James *and* William James *and* who have kept abreast with all the philosophic and psychological developments of the day. It is difficult to say directly and positively that there is a connection between the two Jameses and the dominating figures of recent fiction. If Joyce took over from Henry James the idea of infinitely expanding the moment, he added to his technique of exploring the moment not only William's disintegrative idea of the stream of consciousness, but the subsequent developments in the theory of the content of the unconscious ! If Proust learned from Henry James how to develop the ultimate implications of every happening, he also would seem to have borrowed precisely those elements from his philosophic master, Henri Bergson, which would lead one to think that he had also read William James ! It would seem just to say, then, that the bequests of Henry and William James have become so intricately interwoven into the pattern of contemporary literature that only an eagle and argus-eyed critic can hope to tease them out.

Whether, with the decline of the tendency under which Edmund Wilson has subsumed both Joyce and Proust, Symbolism, there will be a revival of interest in the structural side of Henry James's talent is difficult to say. It would seem logical to suppose that the passion for analysis and discrimination and logic by which those contemporary critics not effected particularly by economics are beset, should have its creative counterpart in fiction of the structural sort. The great danger is that it will be, if it comes, fiction definitely apart from life which is, today, so immediately conditioned by economic influences expressing themselves through science and technology. In the light of the social forces at work in the world I cannot help agreeing with Edmund Wilson that the next period in fiction will be characterized by the social novel, the pre-war development of which Henry James so thoroughly ignored. Whatever happens it seems correct to believe that, long after William James's ideas have been so thoroughly assimilated in the cultural stream that his name is no longer associated with them, long after Henry James, Sr., has ceased to be interesting even as an unregarded protagonist of supernaturalism, Henry James's novels will still be viewed as great and shining masterpieces of the fictional art, the perdurable legacy of this family of exceptional minds.

BIBLIOGRAPHICAL NOTES

In THIS bibliography I have not listed every item I have examined
or even every item one could profitably examine if one were to
duplicate this book. Needless to say I went on many wild-goose
chases and much that was pertinent to the formation of opinion,
is hardly a candidate for mention here. I have merely put together some notes on the more important sources with remarks
on their significance and usefulness. If any scholar wishes to
query me about specific points I shall do my best to answer him
in detail. For the general public, I think, these notes will be
more than sufficient.

WILLIAM JAMES THE FIRST

THIS is the first organized account of William James the First in
print. Some information about him is contained in the "Introduction" to *The Letters of William James* (the psychologist). A
primary source is Mrs. K. G. Hastings' article, "William James
(1771–1832) of Albany, N. Y., and "His Descendants" in *The New
York Genealogical and Biographical Record* for April, 1924.
Where it differs from the previous item it is to be followed.
H. A. Larrabee in his article in *Union Alumni Monthly,* May,
1926, supplements this slightly on the personal side. William's
son Henry writes about him in his semi-fictional autobiography
printed in *The Literary Remains of Henry James.* William
James's speeches at the Erie Canal celebration are printed in part
in Joel Munsell's *Collections on the History of Albany,* Volume II.
Scattered bits of information can also be dredged out of Munsell's *Annals of Albany,* Volume I to X. The information about
James's connection with Union College is to be found in the documents covering the transactions in the custody of H. A. Larrabee at the College. James's will is on file at the Surrogate's
Office, Albany County Court House, Albany, N. Y. Accounts of
his death are to be found in the *Albany Evening Journal,* December 17, 19 and 20, 1832; and the *Daily Albany Argus* for December 20, 1832. The celebrated item in the *New York Evening*

Post merely reprints the *Journal* account of the 19th in part.
For background in general see Beard's *Rise of American Civiliza-
tion* (as indeed all through the book) and, in particular, S. P.
Orth's *Five American Politicians.*

HENRY JAMES, SENIOR

HERE again, this sketch is the first extended study of the subject
in biographical form. There was an account of James's philosophy published in 1883: J. A. Kellogg, *The Philosophy of
Henry James: A Digest,* but I have not seen it and since William
James did not make any particular use of it in his "Introduction" to his father's *Literary Remains,* I take it that it is not
very illuminating. (It is not in the New York Public Library or
the State Library at Albany.) A tantalizingly brief autobiography in semi-fictional form is printed in the *Literary Remains.*
Henry James had a habit, too, of introducing autobiographical
interludes into his theological works and I have made extended
use of the material as the reader has noticed. There is also a
good deal of material in the editorial matter and the letters in
The Letters of William James and *The Letters of Henry James.*
Henry James, Jr., also gives a good deal of information about his
father, not all of it accurate, in *A Small Boy and Others* and
Notes of a Son and Brother. There is an inaccurate account of
Henry James in *The National Cyclopedia of American Biography.* Ralph Barton Perry has written an account for the *Dictionary of American Biography* which I have seen in typescript.
H. A. Larrabee's article previously referred to is primarily concerned with Henry James's career at Union and is very important. Something can be learned from *John James Garth Wilkinson* by Clement John Wilkinson (London: 1911). There are
scattered notes in Emerson's *Journal.* Henry James was an anec-
dotist and he survives in anecdotes in many places, autobiographical and biographical. Unfortunately he was but infre-
quently understood and some of the anecdotes are unintelligible
until one has become familiar with the general drift of his theology. Nevertheless one may refer to *Memories of a Hostess*
by M. A. De W. Howe, *Reminiscences* by Julia Ward Howe,
Henry David Thoreau by F. B. Sanborn, *Life and Letters of E.
L. Godkin* by Rollo Ogden, *Correspondence of Carlyle and Emerson, A. Bronson Alcott* by Sanborn and Harris, *Louisa May Alcott, Her Life, Letters and Journals, With Thackeray in America*
by Eyre Crowe, *Literary Friends and Acquaintance* by W. D.
Howells, and *Early Years of the Saturday Club* by Edward Waldo
Emerson. Bits can also be found in other biographies and personal records of the period, but the sum total is not very great
for Henry James, while a big enough man to be the companion

of the great and near-great, was not big enough to seem a candidate for extended mention when they sat down to write their autobiographies and certainly rarely appealed to biographers as significant. One will find but the most trivial notes in the official accounts of figures with whom he was intimate. There are a few letters from Henry James to Parke Godwin in the Manuscript Room of the New York Public Library, but nothing very weighty is in them. Other letters are being prepared for printing by Ralph Barton Perry and I was denied the use of them for that reason. It is highly unlikely that they will modify the basic outlines of my account. Gilbert Seldes's *The Stammering Century* gives sufficient information on the cults that flourished in Henry James's time. For the general intellectual background see V. L. Parrington's volumes. For the various matters touched upon not strictly American origin, see any encyclopedia. By universal consent Henry James's most important books are *Substance and Shadow* (1863), *The Secret of Swedenborg* (1869), *Society the Redeemed Form of Man* (1879), and *The Literary Remains* (1885). The last contains a bibliography which, while not complete, is sufficient. The other books James wrote are referred to with their dates in the text. As has been indicated, James hated the sight of a book once it was in print. What he thought of his journalism can only be imagined !

WILLIAM JAMES

THE WORKS of William James are all in print. The publishers are Longmans, Green & Company (the bulk of them), Henry Holt and Company and Houghton Mifflin Company. His letters have been edited by his son Henry, *The Letters of William James* (Little Brown & Co.). The last is by far the most attractive and revealing volume for the general reader and is a classic of the epistolary art as practised in America. There are also some interesting letters in Elizabeth Glendower Evans's article, "William James and His Wife" in *The Atlantic Monthly,* September 1929 and in "A Packet of Wendell-James Letters" by M. A. De W. Howe in *Scribner's Magazine,* December, 1928. One should also study the letters of his brother Henry for sidelights. Ralph Barton Perry has prepared a bibliography of James's writings, published by Longmans, Green & Company.

The best book about James seems to me to be *William James* by Emile Boutroux. It is much superior to Theodore Flournoy's *The Philosophy of William James*. Other books on James are *William James and Henri Bergson* by Horace Kallen and *Religion in the Philosophy of William James* by J. S. Bixley. John Dewey has written some important essays on James, now collected in *Characters and Events*. George Santayana's studies are printed in *Winds of Doctrine* and *Character and Opinion in the United States* and they are of the first importance. George Heibert Palmer mentions James in many places, most lately in his *Autobiography*. Some of his incidental observations are extremely revealing. Royce's chief essay on his friend is in a book of essays called *William James*. Woodbridge Riley deals with Pragmatism in Chapter X of *American Thought*. Paul Elmer More's verdict given in *Shelburne Essays: Seventh Series* is surprisingly sympathetic but finally adverse. Irving Babbitt is against James's general tendency, as one might suppose, but in particulars agrees with him, as shown in *Rousseau and Romanticism* and *Masters of Modern French Criticism*. Lewis Mumford is hostile to him on different grounds in *The Golden Day*. There are numerous essays of various value in books and magazines and reminiscences of him in the autobiographies of his friends, professional and lay, and lately he has begun to appear in the autobiographies of his students.

Henry James

HENRY JAMES made a selection of those novels and stories he wished to preserve in the *New York Edition* published by Charles Scribner's Sons. Two volumes, both incomplete novels, were added after his death. The stories and novels he published during his lifetime but did not select for preservation, have mostly gone out of print but can be found in any good library that was in existence during his lifetime. Some of his early stories have been collected and published but the general reader need hardly bother with them. Indeed, the general reader need go beyond the *New York Edition* for novels, but for *The Bostonians* and *Washington Square,* if at all. He must certainly, however, read the *Finer Grain,* a late book of short stories. James's three volumes of autobiography are also out of print: *A Small Boy and Others, Notes of a Son and Brother* and the posthumously published and very brief fragment, *The Middle Years*. The same news must be given of the various books of literary criticism, travel and biography. James was an important critic but not a great one; his travel stories are out of date; and his biography was devoted to a forgotten man, W. W. Story. The ordinary reader will find it most profitable, in reading James's criticism, to look down the title pages of the various volumes and read the essays on figures that interest him. No one volume can be recommended in its entirety. James's letters have been admirably edited by Percy Lubbock, *The Letters of Henry James* (Scribners). Several small collections of letters have been published in book form, but none of them is of overwhelming importance. Others have appeared here and there in magazines and in biographies of James's acquaintances. Once in a while there is a revealing paragraph, but not often. Lubbock took the cream and put it in his two volumes. The following are the most important books about James: *Henry James: Man and Author* by Pelham Edgar, *Henry James* by Rebecca West, *The Pilgrimage of Henry James* by Van Wyck Brooks, *The Method of Henry James* by J. W. Beach and Ford Maddox Ford's peculiarly inane and inexplicably influential *Henry James*. The most important essays are perhaps those of Stuart Sherman in *On Contemporary Literature*, W. C. Brownell in *American Prose Masters*, Theodora Bosanquet in *Hogarth Essays*, Herbert Read in *The Sense of Glory*, Ezra Pound in *Instigations*, Edmund Gosse in *The London Mercury*, Volume I and Edmund Wilson in *The New Republic*, May 6, 1925. Many other critics have commented on his work, sometimes with insight on particular aspects or particular books. There is a vast mass of incidental reminiscence in various memoirs, etc. The latest bibliography of Henry James is that by Le Roy Phillips and it should be consulted by all interested in the details.

Epilogue

An ADEQUATE bibliography of this section would include references to the literature of Europe and America since the flowering of the talents of William and Henry James. I merely cite a few interesting recent titles: Edmund Wilson's *Axel's Castle* (by far the best book in its field), Houston Peterson's *Melody of Chaos*, and "The Novel from James to Joyce" by J. W. Beach, *The Nation*, June 10, 1931. Almost any essay on a modern writer who is in the general stream of tendency in psychology offers hints for defining the relation of the Jameses to that tendency.

ADDENDUM, 1962

AS HAS been made clear, *The Three Jameses* was a pioneer effort to deal with the Jameses as a family of minds. It appeared late in 1932 just as the banks closed under the impact of depression developments in finance when public interest in the Jameses was not very lively and the reputation of the novelist was at a rather low ebb in literary circles. The book was in effect, and especially with regard to the novelist, counter-cyclical in its evaluations. A few years after, there was a great and enduring revival of the novelist which to some extent also increased interest in the other members of the family. (Was the famous Henry James number of *Hound & Horn*, April-June 1934, the trumpet-blast to announce the change?) However, as the writer of *The Three*

Jameses had a stance as critic to which those who engineered the James revival were unsympathetic, it was not allowed too openly to appear that the book was of much significance in the reversal of the cycle of evaluation. Nevertheless the book promptly entered upon an underground career of considerable and, to its author, fascinating and heartening dimensions. The pleasure the author gets from its formal revival after thirty years is considerably increased by his memories of the recognition granted it during the three decades when it was only uncommonly available for purchase and only uncertainly to be chosen for reading from the few libraries which possessed it. He wishes, therefore, here warmly to thank those who extended recognition to it while it was underground, whether in print, by letter, or *viva voce*.

Since 1932 a very great deal of material about the Jameses has been printed, more about the novelist than any of the others, but since it is relatively easy to find bibliographies of this material it is not proposed to enter all the details here with the implication, which would be false, that the compiler had read and made his peace with every last item. Rather it is proposed to deal with the matter in the spirit of the *Bibliographical Notes* of 1932 and cite mostly publications which the writer would feel it obligatory to study were he writing such a book as this today, or which are collections of vital material not easily available thirty years ago. This will lead him to neglect much of the critical writing, particularly with regard to the work of the novelist. I find myself greatly impressed by what I did not have while working on this book so long ago and I think the reader will be too.

THE JAMES FAMILY

THE ONLY book about the family to be published since mine is the late F. O. Matthiessen's *The James Family* (New York 1947). The subtitle of the book, "A Group Biography, Together with Selections from the Writings of Henry James, Senior, William, Henry, and Alice James" clearly indicates that Mr. Matthiessen skilfully salted his biographical mine with significant writings by his subjects. The mention of the name "Alice James" recalls to mind that our first opportunity to gain an understanding of that member of the family was on the occasion of the publication of *Alice James: Her Brothers, Her Journal*, edited by Anna Robeson Burr (New York 1934).

WILLIAM JAMES THE FIRST

SMALL BITS of additional information about the first William James are to be found in the post-1932 books cited in this Addendum dealing with the family or one of the grandsons.

HENRY JAMES, SENIOR

Two BOOKS about Henry James, Sr., have been published since 1932, Austin Warren's *The Elder Henry James* (New York 1934) and Frederic Harold Young's *The Philosophy of Henry James, Sr.* (New York 1951). Dr. Young's monograph includes the best bibliography of Henry James, Sr.'s writings of which I have knowledge. It is important in placing James in relation to the contemporaneous Swedenborgian Church (or New Church or Church of the New Jerusalem) to read Marguerite Block's *The New Church in the New World* (New York 1932). Some of his writings are now prescribed for reading at the New Church Theological School, Cambridge, Massachusetts. (Incidentally, my connection with Swedenborgianism neither began nor ended with my work on Henry James, Sr. . . .) Matthiessen, as cited above, prints some hitherto elusive writings of James, and some letters, while Ralph Barton Perry in his compilation ostensibly devoted to William James (cited in full below) prints a good many letters, probably the letters to which I was denied access at the time I was working on this book. It may also be noted that one of James's "social" essays, first printed in 1861 as a pamphlet, is included in Joseph L. Blau, editor, *American Philosophical Addresses 1700–1900* (New York 1946). The James-Emerson relationship figures extensively in Ralph L. Rusk's *The Letters of Ralph Waldo Emerson,* 6 vols. (New York 1939). However, it is my observation that the books and pamphlets by Henry James, Sr., are just as elusive now as they were thirty years ago. I know of no *complete* collection in any library or in the hands of any private person. Over the years I have acquired six of his hard-cover books, as follows: *Lectures and Miscellanies* (New York 1852), *The Nature of Evil* (New York 1855), *Substance and Shadow* (Boston 1863), *The Secret of Swedenborg* (Boston 1869), *Society the Redeemed Form of Man* (Boston 1879) and, edited with an Introduction by William James, *The Literary Remains of the Late Henry James* (Boston 1884). There is a discussion of the thought of James in Herbert W. Schneider, *A History of American Philosophy* (New York 1946).

WILLIAM JAMES

On WILLIAM JAMES the most important single book published since 1932 is unquestionably Ralph Barton Perry's *The Thought and Character of William James, As Revealed in unpublished correspondence and notes, together with his published writings,* 2 vols. (Boston 1935, reprinted New York 1961). As noted above, this compendious work includes much material on William's father; it also contains much about his brother. In future nobody can possibly write about the Jameses without studying these volumes.   Recalling that I said above that in 1932 all of William's books were in print (which could not then be said of his brother's or his father's), they subsequently largely went out of print, but they have now begun to reappear, lately in paperback editions, and in a selective fashion that is, I think, a curious commentary on them.   The two I have noted as in the paperbacks are *Principles of Psychology* and *The Varieties of Religious Experience.*   For some years, however, there have been single-volume selections of William's writings available.   There is a discussion of William James's thought in Herbert W. Schneider's *A History of American Philosophy* (New York 1946) and the bibliography lists studies of his thought published since 1932. Further on how historians now see him, Merle Curti, *The Growth of American Thought* (New York, 2nd ed. 1951) and Henry Steele Commager, *The American Mind* (New Haven, Conn., 1950).

HENRY JAMES

ONE OF the extraordinary developments in James studies in recent years has been the vast multiplication of critical studies of Henry James's works.   Even after I had ceased to be a producer of James criticism, I remained a consumer of it.   However as it swelled in volume I felt no moral, and had no professional, obligation to read all of it and therefore exactly what proportion of this literature I have read I do not know.   I have no exact knowledge of its ultimate dimensions, though I believe them to be terrifying.   I can but say that as year succeeded year I thought I was reading "a lot of" it.   I dipped into the rushing stream and once in a while came up with a refreshing draught, while at other times I got exceedingly roiled critical water.   Much that I read was in periodicals.   I shall give no notes on this material here, but see Dupee and Cargill below.   Some of the critics later reprinted their periodical essays in books, often along with essays on other subjects.   I shall not attempt a complete guide to these printings either, but content myself with referring to Edmund Wilson's *The Triple Thinkers* (New York 1948) and the terrible-tempered F. R. Leavis's *The Great Tradition* (London 1948, Anchor paperback 1954) in which James figures as one of the five novelists of Leavis's tradition in spite of the fact that he thinks James "went wrong" in his later development and therefore has based his case on *The Portrait of a Lady.*   As to doctoral theses, I should like to call attention to one I inexplicably did not mention in 1932 but which I had closely read, Cornelia P. Kelley's *The Early Development of Henry James* (University of Illinois, 1930) and to one of some years later, a useful product of hard labor in dusty files, R. N. Foley's *Criticism in American Periodicals of the Works of Henry James from 1866 to 1916* (Catholic University, 1944). I should strongly recommend as intelligent sampling of the critical essays from 1879 to *circa* 1945, from Thomas Wentworth Higginson to Philip Rahv, F. W. Dupee's *The Question of Henry James* (New York 1945). This book includes a reprint of Lyon N. Richardson's bibliography of biographical and critical studies to *c.* 1940 in which my long essay is marked "indispensable." I should like also heartily to recommend Oscar Cargill's *The Novels of Henry James* (New York 1961) which is at once a survey of James criticism and a record of sturdy critical independence. Mr. Dupee is author of *Henry James* in the new American Men of Letters Series (New York 1951), a satisfactory example of the later James criticism, though I do not follow his psychiatric speculations. Having attended the university which in America first gave recognition to Sigmund Freud, I was never tempted to take seriously any variety of *literary* freudianism. F. O. Matthiessen's *Henry James: The Major Phase* (New York 1944) is also a good book. Quentin Anderson's *The American Henry James* (New Brunswick, N.J., 1957) is, on the other hand, an example of badly roiled critical water. I find I have not read several books available on "aspects" of Henry James. There is, for example, a book on James's comic sense by Richard Poirer. See my discussion of this quality, pp. 314–315. On the factual side, I take it that Leon Edel is currently the premier authority. His *Henry James: The Untried Years. 1843–1870* (Philadelphia 1953) appears to be the first volume of a multi-volume "life." A book meriting the closest study is *The Notebooks of Henry James,* edited by F. O. Matthiessen and K. B. Murdock (New York 1947). The famous James-Wells relationship is illuminated in *Henry James and H. G. Wells,* edited by Leon Edel and Gordon Ray (Urbana, Ill., 1958). Henry James's own writings are much more freely available than they were thirty years ago. A number of his books have been made available in hardcover reprints over the years, and lately some of them have appeared in paperback editions. Yet it was only in 1961 that Scribners began to reprint the New York Edition book by book. R. P. Blackmur, however, abstracted the "Prefaces" from the New York edition and made a book of them, *The Art of the Novel* (New York 1934). Probably the most highly regarded rescue of old stories from the obscurity in periodicals in which James left them has been, since 1932, Edna Kenton's *Eight Uncollected Tales of Henry James* (New Brunswick, N.J., 1950), but others were brought back to the light of day in collections of tales edited by Matthiessen, Edel, and Mordell (see Miss Kenton's "Introduction"). Henry James's autobiographical volumes came back into print in 1956 (New

York) in a single volume entitled *Autobiography,* edited by F. W. Dupee.   In paperback form (Vintage Books) Leon Edel made accessible two ranges of James's literary criticism, *The Future of the Novel* (New York 1956) and *The American Essays* (New York 1956).   Mr. Edel also edited *Selected Letters of Henry James* (New York 1955) and in "A Note" in the volume stated that of the letters one-half appeared for the first time.   A collection of James's writings on acting, the theater, and the drama was made by Allan Wade, *The Scenic Art* (New Brunswick, N.J., 1948) and James's plays, early and late, were collected in *The Complete Plays of Henry James* (Philadelphia 1949), edited with admirably factual notes by Leon Edel.   A copious sampling of James's travel pieces was made by Morton Dauwen Zabel in *The Art of Travel* (Garden City, N.Y., 1958), his *The American Scene* plus some material from another book was brought back into print under the editorship of W. H. Auden (New York 1946), G. A. Finch revived *Portraits of Places* (New York 1948), and Leon Edel and Ilse Lind recovered and edited some of his contributions to the New York *Tribune* newspaper (for which his father had written earlier) in *Parisian Sketches 1875–1876* (New York 1957).   The most exhaustive bibliography of Henry James, and wonderfully detailed it is, is *A Bibliography of Henry James* by Leon Edel and Dan H. Lawrence (London 1957).

INDEX

OF PRINCIPAL NAMES MENTIONED

DATE DUE

MAY 2 '63			
MAY 5 '64			
FEB 14 '67			
MAR 31 '71			
GAYLORD			PRINTED IN U.S.A.